Media, Ritual and Identity

Media, Ritual and Identity examines the role of the media in society, its complex influence on democratic processes and its participation in the construction and affirmation of different social identities.

Inspired by the work of Elihu Katz, one of the founding fathers of communications research, *Media, Ritual and Identity* draws extensively upon cultural anthropology, combining a commanding overview of contemporary media debates with a series of fascinating case studies ranging from political ritual on television to broadcasting in the "Third World."

The opening group of articles considers the impact of televised "media events" – such as the Watergate hearings or the beating of Rodney King – on viewing communities, and their potential both for affirming community identities and inciting violent factionalism. Other contributors address the ways in which minority groups forge a collective identity for themselves by resisting or transforming their media representation through reinterpretations such as "queering the straight text." A final section turns to the fragmentation of public broadcasting as a forum for popular debate and the growth of media reform movements aiming to restore journalism's function as an aid to democratic thought.

With contributions from: Jeffrey Alexander, Ronald Jacobs, James Carey, Tamar Liebes, Larry Gross, Daniel Dayan, Tamar Katriel, Yoram Bilu, Daniel Hallin, Todd Gitlin, James Curran, Theodore Glasser, Stephanie Craft, Gadi Wolfsfeld, Sonia Livingstone.

Tamar Liebes is Director of the Smart Institute of Communication at The Hebrew University of Jerusalem. **James Curran** is Professor of Communications at Goldsmiths College, London.

Media Studies/Communication Studies

Communication and Society
General Editor: James Curran

Media, Ritual and Identity

Edited by
Tamar Liebes and James Curran

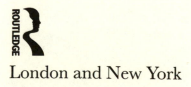

London and New York

First published 1998 by Routledge
11 New Fetter Lane, London EC4P 4EE

Simultaneously published in the USA and Canada
by Routledge
29 West 35th Street, New York, NY 10001

In editorial matter and selection © 1998 Tamar Liebes and James Curran,
in individual contributions, © 1998 the contributors

Typeset in Baskerville by Keystroke, Jacaranda Lodge, Wolverhampton
Printed and bound in Great Britain by TJ International, Padstow, Cornwall

British Library Cataloguing in Publication Data
A catalogue record for this book is available from the British Library

Library of Congress Cataloguing in Publication Data
Media, ritual, and identity / [edited by] Tamar Liebes and James
Curran.
    p.   cm.
A tribute to Elihu Katz.
Includes bibliographical references.
1. Katz, Elihu, 1926– . 2. Television broadcasting of news.
3. Mass media–social aspects. I. Liebes, Tamar. II. Curran,
James. III. Katz, Elihu, 1926– . IV. Series: Communication and
society (Routledge (Firm))
PN4784.T4M38   1998
070.1'95–dc21   97–45502
                    CIP

ISBN 0–415–15991–1 (hbk)
ISBN 0–415–15992–X (pbk)

To Elihu Katz

Contents

Part III Media, public space and democracy

Part IV Audience research: past and future

Contributors

Jeffrey C. Alexander, Professor of Sociology, University of California, Los Angeles

Yoram Bilu, Professor of Anthropology, Hebrew University of Jerusalem

James W. Carey, Professor of Journalism, Columbia University

Stephanie Craft, Teaching Assistant in Journalism, Stanford University

James Curran, Professor of Communications, Goldsmiths College, University of London

Daniel Dayan, Research Associate, Centre National de la Recherche Scientifique, Paris, and Visiting Professor, University of Oslo

Todd Gitlin, Professor, Departments of Culture and Communication, Journalism, and Sociology, University of New York

Theodore L. Glasser, Professor of Journalism, Stanford University

Larry Gross, Professor, Annenberg School of Communication, University of Pennsylvania

Daniel C. Hallin, Professor of Communications, University of California, San Diego

Ronald N. Jacobs, Department of Sociology, State University of New York

Tamar Katriel, Associate Professor, Departments of Communication and Education, Haifa University

Tamar Liebes, Director of the Smart Institute of Communication, Hebrew University of Jerusalem

Sonia Livingstone, Senior Lecturer in Social Psychology, London School of Economics and Politics, University of London

Gadi Wolfsfeld, Associate Professor of Communications, Hebrew University of Jerusalem

Introduction

1 The intellectual legacy of Elihu Katz

James Curran and Tamar Liebes

In 1955, Elihu Katz published with Paul Lazarsfeld *Personal Influence: The Part Played by People in the Flow of Mass Communications*, a historic book that is still being cited more than forty years later. In 1992, Katz published with Daniel Dayan another landmark volume, *Media Events*. Between these two Himalayan heights were ten further authored or edited books, and over one hundred essays and papers.[1] And still the flow continues, with a key article published last year intimating the gestation of another major study, this time concerned with the fragmentation of public space (Katz 1996a).

Outside Israel, Elihu Katz is known as one of the founding fathers of mass communications research. Yet in Israel itself, he is perhaps better known as the founding Director General of Israel Television, the man who helped to stamp a clear public service imprint on Israeli television during its formative early days.

Katz crossed and later recrossed the frontier between media theory and practice. Indeed, the facility with which he has traversed boundaries of all sorts is a key characteristic of his life's work. He drew upon the sociology of small groups to transform perceptions of media influence, and later imported insights from cultural anthropology to change our understanding of the ritual role of television. He took inspiration from academic research in shaping the template of Israeli television. Yet, this modified in turn his academic outlook, changing him from a social psychologist back to being a sociologist. It is because of his many facets that Katz has refracted light and illumination in different directions.

In editing this book, it was tempting therefore to seek to chronicle and analyze Katz's remarkable career, and to capture the elusive essence of this witty, lovable man through a series of affectionate anecdotes.

There is a basic *festschrift* formula that we could have followed: a reverent portrait, followed by a miscellany of papers from colleagues and friends on whatever subject they elected to write about. The result is usually a high-priced and forgettable book, with a limited sale to university libraries.

Somehow, this did not seem appropriate for Elihu Katz. A book of restricted interest would not have done justice to his central importance as a pioneer researcher. An exclusive volume aimed only at other academics would not have been consistent with the time Katz has always lavished on his students and the strays who have arrived at his door.[2] Above all, a reverential work would have been totally out of keeping with Katz's own love of argument. He is a man who has never brooked agreement.

For this reason, we hit upon a different kind of tribute: a book that seeks to be useful to students as well as interesting to academics; a text that stakes out particular areas of debate rather than being a conventional miscellany of essays; and above all something that would engage in an argumentative and critical way with the intellectual legacy of some of Katz's most important research. Whether it succeeds, partially or wholly, in any of this remains to be seen. But this book most definitely is not a conventional coterie work of fealty.

MEDIA AND RITUAL

The first part is concerned with the ritual role of the media. This is one of the most interesting themes to have developed in media studies during the last fifteen years, and is powerfully expressed and developed in Dayan and Katz's (1992) *Media Events*. They argue that special media events tend to fall into one of three broad categories: "contests" in sport or politics (such as the Olympic games or Senate Watergate hearings), "conquests" (such as Pope John Paul II's triumphant return to Poland) or "coronations" (the rites of passage of the great). What gives them a generic character is that they are usually transmitted simultaneously or extensively by different TV channels. They are generally reported uncritically by broadcasters. And they reach a mass audience who interrupt their normal routines or attach a special significance to what is being broadcast. Media events are thus monopoly communications, uncritically reproduced, that function as collective rites of communion.

Dayan and Katz's account emphasizes the role of media events in integrating society, affirming its common values, legitimating its institutions, and reconciling different sectional elements. Many of the special events they anatomize, such as Sadat's peace mission to Israel or the marriage of Prince Charles and Lady Diana Spencer, evoked a liminal sense of togetherness, the quickening of hope, the celebration of a shared sense of purpose or common values. Yet, these events were also scripted and choreographed in a pre-planned process that can be viewed as manipulative. In what way, then, are they different from the manufactured spectacles of authoritarian or totalitarian regimes? Dayan and Katz's response is that in liberal democracies broadcasters are free to say "no" to proposers of media events, or to report these events critically. Central to the success of these events is the complicity of television viewers who are free, in liberal democracies, to withhold approval or express dissent. Furthermore, media events come in different forms and are not necessarily supportive of the status quo. On the contrary, they can affirm "what ought to be" in implicit contrast to what "is," awaken suspended hopes or release submerged social forces in ways that act as catalysts for change. Also implicit in their answer, although not stated as such, is the belief that elites and public institutions have greater legitimacy in liberal democracies than in other political systems, and that therefore the values they extol and the collective identity that they celebrate are more likely to be authentic and widely shared by other members of society. The implication of Katz's later work (1996a) is also that by promoting social cohesion, media events have a positive influence in counteracting the pressures for atomization, privatization and heedless individualism.

Dayan and Katz's ritual view of television is celebrated in the opening essay by Alexander and Jacobs as a way of revitalizing liberal theory. There is a long tradition within liberal thought which stresses the need for the separation of powers, the legal entrenchment of human rights, and the multiplication of voluntary associations in civil society, as a way of preventing state and factional oppression. Within a traditional version of this model, "independent" media provide allegedly an unpolluted source of information that enables citizens to exercise properly informed control over the state. A radical version of this model, advanced by Habermas, views the media as distorted by money and corporate power, and seeks a way of restoring communicative rationality. However, common to both versions of this tradition, according to Alexander and Jacobs, is a limited understanding of the public sphere as a domain of public power, deliberation and decision-making. What this tradition fails to appreciate, and what Dayan and Katz's work helps to illuminate, is the way in which the public sphere is, in part, also a *cultural space* in which collective identities and solidarities essential for the functioning of differentiated societies are forged. Underpinning the working of civil society are shared beliefs, a feeling of mutuality and a common cultural framework that the ritual role of television helps to sustain.

However, Alexander and Jacobs also go on to argue that media events should not be understood simply as rituals through which the values and codes of society are expressed and reaffirmed. Meanings are forged through a process of inter-action, not least through competition between groups and individuals in the symbolic public form of the media. Media events, they insist, embody a particular way of "narrating the social" that signifies and makes sense of society in a form that draws selectively from the available stock of explanatory frameworks and narratives. They represent a triumph of a particular definition, and one that may potentially support change rather than stasis. In particular, media events may invoke the ideals of society in a way that mobilizes protest against their violation.

Alexander and Jacobs give as one example the 1972 break-in into the Watergate headquarters of the Democratic party by employees of the Republican party. Initially, this was widely seen as another example of dirty "politics as usual." It only took on a new significance as revealing corruption at the heart of govern-ment when it was cast in these terms by a media event, the televised Senate Watergate hearings in 1973. Similarly, the 1991 Rodney King beating by three white policemen, caught on amateur videotape and repeatedly transmitted on television, also acted, according to Alexander and Jacobs, as a ritualized spur to reform in that it came to be narrated as an example of arbitrary police violence and racial division. Both media events were in fact catalysts for change: President Nixon was forced to resign, as was the Los Angeles police chief Daryl Gates.

The authors are thus seeking to avoid an over-simple reading of media events as a ritual means by which members of society are connected to its sacred codes, and integrated into its core values. By stressing normative competition, Alexander and Jacobs are refining the argument of *Media Events*. However, this still leaves unresolved questions about how media events are devised, with what consequences. Lang and Lang (1983), for example, argue that it was mainly "political insiders" who set the terms of reference of the Watergate hearings. Their narrow juridical definition limited the effectiveness of the reforms that followed in their wake. Because the Watergate media event was scripted from within the political establishment, it led to symbolic purification rather than real systemic change.

A different argument is advanced by Hallin and Mancini, though from a similar reference point (Hallin and Mancini 1991; Hallin 1994). They argue that the Reagan–Gorbachev summit meetings were a ritual event that fostered harmony based on a global sense of community. But this evocation of mutual warmth and sense of togetherness was only temporary. It did not melt the structures of power polarized by the cold war, or dislodge the patterns of thought that informed this conflict. In other words, the focus on media ritual as a means of transcending social boundaries, and of reconciling differences, unrealistically downplays the persistence and importance of structures which divide and set people against each other.

Thus one criticism is that media events come from the heart of establishment, with the implication that they serve the interests of the establishment more than that of ordinary members of society.[3] Another reservation is that even when media events are harnessed to progressive change, they can be confined or curtailed by the prevailing structure of power. James Carey carries this reappraisal one stage further by emphasizing that media events do not necessarily unify and integrate. There is, he argues, a whole genre of media events that are rituals of excommunication and status degradation. They do not bring people together and reconcile differences, but divide and reinforce antagonism. They are about distinguishing between good and bad, marking the boundaries of what is permissible, and punishing those who step outside.

This type of media event is typified by the televised Senate confirmation hearings of Robert Bork, nominated by President Reagan to a seat on the United States Supreme Court in 1987. Carey shows that the hearings turned on the issue of whether Bork was outside the "mainstream of constitutional jurisprudence," whether in effect he stood outside acceptable limits of thought and should be counted (in a reverse of the ritualized McCarthyite investigations of the 1940s and 1950s) as being so right-wing as to be UnAmerican. Underlying this media event was an ideological struggle between the organized forces of the left and right about what should constitute the "American way." Yet while the left notionally won, and Bork was rejected, this was not the prelude to consolidating a progressive coalition, promoting a radical agenda or winning the presidential election (which the Democrats lost in 1988). The left's "victory" was shortlived and secured, in Carey's view, at too high a price. An honorable and distinguished lawyer, with a record of public service, was pilloried and destroyed in an unacceptable way.

The theme that media events can be ugly rather than the generally healing, uplifting and unifying experiences extolled by Dayan and Katz is developed in another way by Tamar Liebes. She argues that "disaster marathons" in Israel (and elsewhere) broadly conform to Dayan and Katz's definition of media events, yet promote a lynch mentality. She gives as an example the broadcast coverage of a series of bus bombings in Israel in February–March 1996. Normal schedules were interrupted to provide extended, "live" coverage of events that were viewed by a mass audience. But coverage of these events was governed by a show business logic of winning and keeping audience attention in an intensely competitive and increasingly commercialized industry. Broadcasters extracted the full melodrama of these events by dwelling on their random mayhem, filling in slack moments with a reiteration of their horror, and turning to marginalized extremists and the grieving families of victims to generate emotionally charged demands for vengeance and retribution. This had the effect of fueling anger and hatred, blocking out the past, and short-circuiting rational debate. It also undermined confidence in public authority, weakened the peace process and propelled the government into adopting a more belligerent stance than it wanted. In essence, an entertainment-oriented form of reporting elicited a populist political response.

In short the first part of this book challenges, refines or elaborates upon the central arguments advanced by Katz and Dayan. In the process, it highlights the richness of the seam they first mined.

MEDIA AND IDENTITY

The second part of this book arises from Elihu Katz's research into cultural identity. The existence of this research may come as a surprise to people who have never associated Katz with "cultural studies." The reason for this surprise may have something to do with the fact that most of Katz's work in this area has been concerned with Israelis rather than Americans or Europeans. Within the prevailing paradigm, it belongs therefore to the slipstream rather than mainstream of human experience. Its place is, by implication, not in cultural studies but in that distancing category of "area studies."

Yet, Katz's cultural work is more than of merely local interest. It began in the 1960s with an examination of the role of socializing agencies in the absorption of new immigrants in Israel. Katz looked at the culture of immigrants partly through their rule-breaking behavior, as when for example they tried to bargain with the bus driver over the fare, or haggle with the customs officer over the payment of import duties (Katz and Danet 1973). In the latter case, they found that appeals were made to reciprocity ("I was a Zionist abroad"), altruism ("You are powerful, I am weak") and accepted norms ("You should be a good and discriminating bureaucrat"). This led to an irreverent, general analysis of appeals to authority including those to God (Katz *et al.* 1969).

This early work grew into an important and ambitious study of culture and leisure in Israel (Katz and Gurevitch 1976). Among other things, Katz and Gurevitch asked themselves why Jews had been able to survive as a nation for 2,000 years without a country of their own. Their answer was that for "the people of the Book," the "Bible" (i.e. the Pentateuch) was a substitute for a homeland in that it provided a language, a common collective memory, a shared cultural framework and weekly ritual meetings for folk history to be read aloud and listened to. "Here is the key," write Katz and Gurevitch (1976: 193), "to the feeling of collective national identity which permeated the dispersed Jewish communities and which connected the present with the generations of the past." They went on to provide an absorbing account of how normative Judaism was modified and changed in the secularizing context of the early Israeli state. Twenty years later, Katz updated the study, pointing to the continued growth in Israel of individualism and hedonism, and the corresponding decline of collectivism and asceticism, but exempted television from primary responsibility for the change (Katzt *et al.*, in press).

Yet if Katz and Gurevitch's original study broke new ground, it was also characteristic of its time in that it incorporated a uses and gratifications approach to media consumption. This model was later abandoned by Katz in favor of a model of reception (a less static model of studying the process of negotiating with medium and text). In the *Export of Meaning*, Liebes and Katz (1990) showed that responses to the American TV series *Dallas* were powerfully influenced by the divergent cultural frameworks and social experiences of different groups of viewers. For example, when asked to retell a particular episode, recent Israeli settlers from the Soviet Union concentrated on ideological themes and leitmotifs. Kibbutzniks responded, by contrast, primarily in psycho-analytical terms, emphasizing personality and motivation. Moroccan Jews and Arab Israelis were different again, tending to recount a linear narrative involving the overcoming of social obstacles, interpreted in a sociological way.

Differences of interpretation were constrained by the actual content of the program. *Dallas* may also have exerted a cognitive influence on some viewers, particularly those who thought that it was offering a window on the real world. Some respondents also viewed the characters in the soap opera as bearers of high status, as representing America, or the approaching modern or western world. But overall, audiences were revealed to exercise a high degree of control over the meanings that they derived from TV viewing. According to Liebes and Katz, this contradicted an oversimplistic and extreme view that TV gobalization is inducing global uniformity and American cultural domination. However, they were also at pains to point out that their study was only of one point in the process of diffusion of American culture, and that it did not exclude the possibility of the cumulative erosion of cultural specificity.

Thus, what emerges from the body of this work – taken as a whole – is a relatively optimistic understanding of cultural dynamics. In particular, Katz's first study of the secularization of leisure in Israel offers a positive view of the ability of social groups to sustain through mediated tradition a strong sense of collective identity, and to adapt and change, while retaining a strong, stabilizing sense of the past. And his later study of audience responses to *Dallas* focuses attention on the ability of social groups to call upon collective resources in order to resist cultural colonization through television.

This central theme of cultural resilience is explored further in the first two essays of this part of the book. Thus, the opening essay by Larry Gross considers the case of sexual minorities who differ from disadvantaged ethnic minorities in that they are not born into defensive social networks and do not acquire from early socialization strategies for dealing with social prejudice. This increases, according to Gross, their need for a publicly formed and visible community with whom they can identify, and from whom they can derive a greater sense of self-worth. This desire for positive group images is further reinforced by negative representations of sexual minorities in the mass media. However, these have been modified over time from near-erasure and invisibility, through to negative stereotyping as weak/silly or evil/corrupting, and finally to the less bleakly hostile and more heterogeneous pattern of representation that prevails today (see also Gross 1989). In this context, some gays and lesbians have fought back by developing their own specialist media, "queering the straight text" (selectively understanding mass mediated meanings), influencing portrayals of themselves in majority media, and engaging in a long running battle with opponents in relation to issues of censorship and morality.

Gross's article is organized around an elegant schema for classifying majority/minority representations advanced by Katz. It fastens upon the issue of how minorities resist acceptance of negative perceptions of themselves in the majority culture which leads to self-hatred. Daniel Dayan also invokes the same Katz schema but his concern is the more fundamental one of what sustains minority communities and the sometimes fragile attachments on which they are based. His widescreen account takes note of the global and national contexts in which threatened communities are situated; the complex mechanisms by which a sense of collective membership is sustained; the ways in which these inevitably involve choosing between "identity proposals"; and the consequences of these subjective decisions, not least in terms of the minority community's relationship to the majority.

Dayan's essay is like an archeologist's excavation, in which the secondary literature is carefully raked over for evidence of clues. Informing it is a questioning orientation which sees national communities as being no less "imagined" than that of other communities, merely better supported by social institutions. One key way in which national communities are imagined is through the organization of collective memory. This is the central theme of the following chapter by Tamar Katriel which considers the case of the Hashomer Hatza'ir settlements in pre-Israeli Palestine. She begins by evoking the experience of connectedness as mostly middle class, left-wing emigrants from Europe bared their souls in a half-lit communal room after a hard day's labor in the fields. As one contemporary diarist records:

> Some of us were blessed with the power of expression; others stuttered. Many kept silent . . . and in moments of silence – utter silence – it seemed to me that a ray of light springs out of every heart and the rays merge up high into one big flame that reaches into the heart of the sky. . . . I loved those nights more than any other night, our nights of sharing.

Institutionalized "soul talks" such as these constitute collective ritual events which encapsulate key attributes of Katz's media events. They are liminal meetings, powerful enough to cause individuals to immerse their private lives in the collective. They are a means of integrating the community into what Katz calls a "subjunctive" mood. Unlike his understanding of events, however, the emotional unity created by these "soul talks" did not preclude critical discussion and oppositional decodings.

According to Katriel, these pioneer experiences are also part of the "foundation mythology" of the state of Israel. They memorialize an idealistic tradition in which the individual is fused with the collective through the sharing of work, space and inner thought. Their significance was celebrated through the publication of diaries, memoirs and novels, and renewed through the prominence given to more contemporary manifestations of "soul-talk" collectivism. However, the communal intimacy of these utopian communities was experienced by some people at the time as a collectivist nightmare. It was also criticized by another pioneer tradition which argued that solidarity was best forged not through self-disclosure but more pragmatically through communal labor and political alliance. The "sacred" tradition of pioneer utopian socialism thus represents a powerful cultural symbol that is both resonant and controversial, one that represents to some a sense of loss in the context of a market-based, increasingly individualistic society and to others a misguided and impractical episode in the pre-history of Israel. It is through such engagements in what Raphael Samuel (1994) calls "theatres of memory" that a complex relationship to an imagined national community is formed.

The next chapter more pointedly underscores the constructed nature of collective memory by chronicling the fabrication of tradition. It revolves around the sanctification of Rabbi Ya'acov Wazana, a relatively obscure holy man living in a remote part of Morocco who died in 1952. He featured in Yoram Bilu's anthropological research because he was a maverick who embraced Muslim practices, and due to this research he acquired fleeting prominence in Israel's media. This seems to have triggered a series of dreams by Yoseph, in which he was called upon to establish a holy shrine in the Rabbi's memory. The rest of the essay describes entertainingly how the author was used and then discarded by Yoseph in his successful attempt to establish Wazana as a conventional Moroccan Jewish saint, stripped of the deviancy that had made him an interesting subject of research in the first place.

These two chapters complement each other in a number of ways. They are similar in that they both reveal how memory of the past is "made" or at least edited rather than given. But they are different in that they chronicle images of the past that sustain different kinds of collective identity. The memory of pioneer settlements is about the "rebirth of a nation," sustaining a national identification with the state of Israel. The beatification of Rabbi Wazana is a positive Diaspora memory that underwrites a sectional identity of Jewish Moroccan Israelis as a group bound by tradition, with close links to a time when things were simpler and even in certain respects better. The two sets of memories also carry different political loads. The memorializing of socialist pioneers stands as an emotional monument to a specifically collectivist and utopian definition of Israeli society. By contrast the sanctification of Rabbi Wazana, sanitized and stripped of ethnic impurity, is emblematic of a more conservative, religious political tradition in Israel.[4]

MEDIA AND CONNEXITY

One portion of Katz's work has been concerned with the ritual role of mass communication in binding society together (Part 1). Another portion has focused on how social groups have sustained a sense of their own identity (Part 2). A third portion of Katz's work has concentrated on the problematic ways in which society and its constituent elements connect to each other through the media. This last concern sets the agenda of the third part of this book.

A recent interesting essay by Peter Simonson (1996) hails Katz's first and last books as landmark volumes in a progressive tradition of thought, beginning with Cooley and Dewey, which has struggled to think through the relationship of community, communication and democracy. *Personal Influence* portrays society as a honeycomb of small groups able to resist through the power of interpersonal communication elite domination and media control. *Media Events* characterizes society as a community with shared values but pluralistic differences brought together in harmony through televised rites of communion. While both make important contributions to thought, they are based according to Simonson on a limited understanding of civil society. Thus, the pluralism celebrated in *Personal Influence* is largely conceived in terms of a multiplicity of lifestyle enclaves whose involvement in the democratic process is limited to holding opinions, mostly about consumption, and not in terms of a dense network of local neighbourhood groups, voluntary associations and coherent social groups. Equally limiting, according to Simonson, is the world conjured up by *Media Events* where collective involvement largely takes the form of viewing the same TV programmes. Missing from both are notions of activity, participation, group representation and collective negotiation. Informing this, although Simonson does not say this, is a significant absence of class conflict in Katz's conception of community. This leads in turn to the relatively unproblematic understanding of social unity and the articulation of difference in Katz's work.

This said, Simonson's criticisms are both stimulating and unfair. In effect, he is taking Katz to task for failing to fulfill something that Katz did not set out to do – namely, to theorize the role of the media in the democratic system. Katz is criticized for not offering a comprehensive account when all he sought to do – and brilliantly succeeded – was to analyse two specific things: the social mediation of communications, and a particular genre of program. Simonson is also strangely silent about those publications where Katz does address more broadly the question of how a democratic society and its constituent parts should connect through the media. These have centered on two issues: globalization and the fragmentation of the public.

Katz's initial concern was that the spread of subtitled films, exported TV programs, and translated books might undermine the ability of national communities to express their own cultural traditions, concerns and collective identities. This fear featured prominently in two of his books published during the 1970s (Katz and Gurevitch 1976; Katz and Wedell 1977), and was only later partly allayed, as we have seen, by evidence of viewers' intransigence (Liebes and Katz 1990).

Katz revisited the issue of connexity (to use an ugly but useful word) in a new way during the 1990s. The central problem, he concluded, was not national cultural independence but how groups relate to each other within national societies. The combination of new technology, globalization and market values is undermining communication between social groups, and weakening integration into national political systems (Katz 1996a). Television no longer constitutes, according to Katz, the common meeting-place of society owing to the multiplication of TV channels. The eclipse of public service television, with its commitment to inform, is leading to a contraction of political communication in favor of entertainment. Furthermore, the mutual identification that underwrites civil society is being undermined by a growing disjunction between the communication system and the nation state. Viewers increasingly select on the basis of individual taste from global sources of supply rather than watch the same nationally determined schedule of programs. Where once they had talked to each other through a public service monopoly, national TV system and been integrated into a national political dialogue and democratic system, now they are sub-groups of a fragmented public viewing a plethora of entertainment channels linked to a global TV economy.

The opening essay by Daniel Hallin criticizes Katz's first "take" on the subject. He argues that Katz and Wedell's pioneer research (1977) on communications in the third world, like most work of that period, took a relatively unproblematic view of the nation as an entity for defining collective interests. This led Katz and Wedell to focus on the role of the media in promoting the national integration, economic development and cultural self-determination of third world countries without considering adequately how the media related to their structures of power. This blind spot, according to Hallin, led them to play down the way in which nation-building was used to stifle dissent in the media, and stunt the development of civil society.

This criticism in fact plugs into some of the themes of Katz's more recent work, and to this extent it is knocking against an open door. Katz said as much in a generous response to Hallin's analysis (Katz 1996b). One suspects, however, that there is still continuing grounds of disagreement between the two, rooted in their largely implicit but still significantly different attitudes towards the nation state.[5] Informing these are seemingly different conceptions of how the nation state fits into the international order.

The next two essays can be read as a commentary on Katz's more recent thesis on the decline of communication. That by Todd Gitlin implicitly endorses Katz's misgivings, though in a qualified form. Gitlin begins his survey by summarizing the classic democratic and republican conceptions of the public sphere as a forum of popular control and disinterested public deliberation. Critics, Gitlin notes, argue that the public sphere (in both senses) is in trouble because political participation is declining, public standards are falling, and the media are being debased by tabloidization. Others point optimistically to the proliferation of distinct communities of interest and participation, the growth in the number of sources of information, and the development of an international system of communication that may bring into being an international civil society. However the key point in this debate, according to Gitlin, is that the public sphere is subdividing into sphericules owing to the proliferation of media outlets, and the splintering of the mass audience. This is facilitating social secession and exclusion. It is idle to suppose, warns Gitlin, that the pluralization of the public produces a mosaic that reflects adequately the balance of social interests, or that public sphericules interconnect adequately with one another to constitute a properly functioning public sphere based on genuine dialogue. The social foundation of the democratic system is changing – for the worst.

This pessimism derives largely from observations based on the United States. James Curran, writing from a British perspective, argues in effect that the comparative picture is more complex than Katz's broad brush strokes (and, by implication, Gitlin's) allow. In Britain, for example, the multiplication of TV channels has not significantly fragmented the mass audience; the content of television continues to be mainly national rather than global; and broadcasting is still dominated by a public service system committed to inform as well as to entertain. While public service broadcasting is under attack and has been weakened, it can still be reinvigorated in Britain and elsewhere through reform. Katz's requiem for a passing communications order invokes, according to Curran, a mythical view of the past: what is needed is practical measures for realizing his idyll in the future.

These include legislation to redefine broadcasting's democratic purpose. In effect, the state is being invited to repair the public sphere – a position that appears oxymoronic to those liberals who hold that the public sphere must remain wholly separate if it is effectively to oversee the state. This principled position, well entrenched in the United States, has fuelled a voluntaristic tradition of media reform based on professionalization and persuasion. Theodore Glasser and Stephanie Craft chart the latest upsurge of this tradition in the United States, prompted by the growing culture clash between the ideals of professionalism and the reality of increased media marketization. The public or civic journalism movement's most palpable hit has been its influential attack on conventional news reporting of elections as a horse race in which the stress is on strategy rather than substance, on who is going to win rather than on what society needs. Yet, this critique is only one item in the movement's agenda for reform which includes enriching a public discourse in decline, developing a "journalism of conversation," making a greater use of non-elite sources, and striking a proper balance between dialogue and deliberation. Some of these objectives are not without problems, as the authors note in their critical survey, not least of which are the difficulties involved in persuading private media enterprises to give greater attention to their public purpose.

The last essay in this section reverses the conventional vantage point of media analysis. Instead of asking what kind of reporting makes for good journalism, it asks instead what kinds of reporting make for good government. Even to pose this question is anathema in some quarters where it is assumed that journalism and government are separate activities, never to be considered in the same breath without loss of media independence and ministerial statesmanship. But Gadi Wolfsfeld points to certain problems highlighted by media reporting of the Oslo peace process: the media's love of conflict, its stress on events rather than process, its need for melodrama, and the pressures for short-termism generated by the media spotlight. He also considers briefly how politicians have responded, and should respond, to these problems. This chapter thus continues the discussion raised by Tamar Liebes' attack on "disaster marathons" in the first part.

KATZ AND AUDIENCE RESEARCH

Several references have been made already to Elihu Katz's audience research, and many more are distributed in the main body of the book. Originally, we had hoped to include a whole section on audience research arising from this work, but were prevented from doing so owing to limitations of space. This especially extended segment of our introduction, and Sonia Livingstone's overview chapter at the end of this book, stand in its place.

Livingstone's central argument is that audience research has come to be viewed in terms of a small number of canonical texts in a way that fails to do justice to the diversity of audience work. This discourages new developments that could spring from an understanding of the diversity of past research. It is also forcing audience research into a rut, endlessly repeating the same insights into divergent readings, resistant voices and contextually embedded viewers in opposition to "straw men" traditions of naive ideologists, administrative positivists and crass psychologists. The way forward, she suggests, is to develop a fuller sense of the existing range of audience research, to confront a number of still unanswered questions, to build up generalizations on the basis of systematic analysis and above all to engage in comparative (including historical) research.

Since Katz is sometimes assigned to the "straw men" traditions to which reception analysis[6] stands opposed, or is simply written out of its accounts of the development of audience research, it is important to register here his originality. Katz is a pioneer of some of the insights to which reception studies later laid claim. In particular, Katz has argued for over forty years that media audiences are active and critical; that they respond to communications in divergent ways; and that audience autonomy is rooted in people's prior beliefs and attitudes supported by the social networks to which they belong. From this, Katz concluded as early as the mid-1950s that the critical tradition had overstated the power of the media (Katz and Lazarsfeld 1955) just as analysts in the reception tradition were to do some thirty years later.

Perhaps the simplest way to log Katz's central contribution to audience research is first to summarize the main conclusions of his work and then to highlight the extraordinarily indefatigable, ingenious and flexible ways in which he has sought an answer to an intellectual puzzle that has perplexed him for forty years. His first audience study (Katz and Lazarsfeld 1955) synthesized extensive research which showed that most people were members of small groups – families, friends and work colleagues – that influenced their beliefs, behavior and responses to the media. This general argument was exemplified by a series of case studies which indicated that media influence was regulated by interpersonal processes. In so far as the media influence people, suggested Katz and Lazarsfeld, it is through a two-step flow in which influentials, distributed across the social spectrum, absorb and pass on media influence to others. While this argument has since been refined and complexified, its core insight into the socially mediated nature of communication remains central.

This insight led Katz away from media-centered research to the study of the spread of innovation, in what was to become the second phase of his audience work. The best known study of this phase examined the adoption of a "miracle drug" (Katz 1961; Coleman *et al.* 1966). It showed that salesmen and promotional literature were sources of information rather than of persuasion. What crucially influenced the first group of doctors to prescribe this drug was peer opinion, resulting in what was almost a group decision to share moral responsibility if things went wrong. These pioneers were especially well integrated into the wider medical profession through active reading of medical journals and attendance of meetings, as well as being active in their local professional networks, and influenced in turn other doctors to prescribe the drug.

The implication of this research was that the media should be seen as merely one of a number of inputs (and not necessarily a very important one) in a patterned flow of influence. Katz also synthesized other peoples' research which indicated that audiences were highly selective in what they derived from the media. This skepticism was deployed with considerable finesse in a re-analysis of numerous studies into the 1960 televised Nixon–Kennedy debates (Katz and Feldman 1962). This showed that Republicans had been deeply impressed by Nixon, while Democrats had been greatly impressed by Kennedy. The TV debates "accelerated" electoral support in line with prior political inclination but otherwise changed very little.

From this conception of the wileful audience emerged the third phase of Katz's audience research, concerned with media uses and gratifications. The thinking behind this was that, since audiences seemed to dominate the media rather than the other way round, it was time that researchers found out more about the nature of the audience experience. The media, Katz concluded in effect, offer a cafeteria service of uses and pleasures that audiences select on the basis of motivation and need (Katz *et al.* 1974). In 1970s Israel, for example, some people read books to know themselves, watched television to feel connected to their families, and took in newspapers to feel pride in their country and its leadership (Katz and Gurevitch 1976).

However, by the early 1980s, Katz became unhappy with the limitations of uses and gratifications research. In a key collective essay (Blumler *et al.* 1985), he and close associates argued that this approach often paid too little attention to the actual content of the media, which tended to be viewed merely as a blank on which audiences' needs were projected. "Perhaps the *New York Times* can be read as pornography," they wrote acidly, "but it is unlikely to be its statistically dominant use" (Blumler *et al.* 1985: 260). Second, it encouraged "audience imperialism" in which evidence of audience activity was mistakenly equated with audience control. Third, this approach was set within an inadequate framework that paid too little regard to the way in which individual choices and roles were circumscribed, and too little attention to the wider context of media production and power.

This watershed essay marked the beginning of the latest phase of Katz's audience research. First, Katz incorporated semiology to obtain a better understanding of the way in which meanings are created through the interaction of viewers and programs (Liebes and Katz 1990). In this perspective, television no longer transmitted "messages" that were accepted or rejected, but structured symbols that were potentially accessible to plural interpretations.

This was followed by the study of media events (Dayan and Katz 1992) which again offered a semiological analysis of media content. The study was supported by detailed references to effects literature but not by a specific audience study. It also analyzed the media within a significantly different framework of analysis than in Katz's earlier audience work. Since this is the latest major destination of Katz's life-long odyssey, it is worth stopping to consider analytically where the journey began and where it has so far ended.

NEGOTIATING A TRADITION

Katz has been pursuing the elusive grail of understanding the nature of media power for over forty years. His first tactic was to formulate and reformulate with ever greater ingenuity questions about the nature of media effects. He began with the obvious question: do the media influence what people think and do (Katz and Lazarsfeld 1955)? This shifted, in his diffusion of innovation research, to the question of do the media influence *when* people think (Katz 1961)? It then took in, in overviews of research, the question of whether the media influence what people think *about* or what people know (Katz and Feldman 1962; Katz 1980). The pivotal concern remained what the media do to people, until Katz simply reversed this – in uses and gratifications research – by asking what people do to the media.

Yet behind this apparent reversal lay in fact a continuing concern with media influence, now reconceived as a "consequence." Thus social integration was seen as the wider societal outcome of the media satisfying the desire of large numbers of people to feel "connected" to society through the media (Katz and Gurevitch 1976). Slipped inside this functionalist argument were new effects questions: in particular, do the media effect *whom* we identify with, and *where* we feel we belong?

The revival of uses and gratifications in the 1970s represented a crisis in the effects tradition. Katz responded to this crisis by eventually abandoning the framework of analysis in which effects research had been conventionally conducted. This revolved – and, indeed, still revolves – around a transportation model of influence in which the media are the starting point, and the audience is the terminus. This model is rooted in a conception of the media as an independent institution that is central to the liberal tradition. From this is derived a view of the media as an autonomous source of influence transmitted to the audience that can be identified, tracked and measured.

The uses and gratifications approach stayed uncomfortably within this analytical framework, but modified it. The linear link between media and audience was given two tracks rather than one, and the spotlight was shone on freight moving from the audience to the media rather than, as before, the other way. The other change was that freight was also viewed as moving from audience to society, which became the last "station" on the line. The argument was made, as noted earlier, that the sum of individual audience gratifications could be equated with the media's functioning for society as a whole.

In fact, Katz had always been a less than fully paid up subscriber to the transportation model (like other thoughtful colleagues in the effects tradition). He had always argued that audiences are not just aggregations of individuals, and that this point is central to any intelligent understanding of the role of the media. Audiences are members of interpersonal networks which influence responses to the media (Katz and Lazarsfeld 1955). The media's influence is merely one tributary joining a complex confluence of influences within these social networks (Katz 1961; Coleman *et al.* 1966). What uses and pleasures people derive from the media are also patterned by social roles (Katz *et al.* 1974). People are situated within subcultures that shape their understandings of TV programs (Liebes and Katz 1990). In short, the terminus of media influence – the audience – has always been visualized by Katz in terms of a formative social context.

Katz finally burst out of the "media effects" straitjacket in the late 1980s by contextualizing *both* the media and the audience. His study with Liebes of *Dallas* was not simply about the interaction between audience and program as a self-contained study of audience reception (Liebes and Katz 1990). It was situated within a framework of unequal economic and cultural power within the global community, and the implication of audience responses was discussed in relation to this. Katz's next major collaborative project, concerned with media events, went even further in filling out a wider understanding of society (Dayan and Katz 1992). In particular, attention was given to the political and cultural context of program making, while some attention (though less than in the preceding study) was given also to the context of reception.

This wide-frame approach involved a change of perspective. Instead of asking what the media do to audiences and vice versa, Dayan and Katz asked in what ways the media act as channels of connection between different parts of society. Their answer was that the media articulate (in the sense of "join together") and mediate elites and the mass audience, center and periphery, antagonistic groups, the past and present, the ideals and pragmatic practices of society, and much else besides in a complex series of conjunctures. This led them in turn to think of the media more as a vehicle than as a source of influence, a means by which effects occur rather than as an originator of those effects. This conceptual leap was summed up in their argument that the connection between audience and media is "not simply a linear relationship but one that is circular and systemic" (Dayan and Katz 1992: 225). In other words, analysis of the media–audience nexus needs to be grounded in an understanding of the wider society of which both media and audience are a part.

Katz has wandered a long way from his first analysis of communication flows in Decatur (Katz and Lazarsfeld 1955) to take a grandstand view of the ritual role of television in the West (Dayan and Katz 1992). In the process, he has shifted his attention from audience responses to media messages, to the role of the media as channels of communication and mediation between different structures, organizations, groups and cultures in society. This has led to a transformation of his understanding of "media power." Where once he portrayed the media as a relatively marginal influence swallowed up in the maw of local interpersonal relationships, now he sees the media as central to the organization and functioning of society. Indeed, he now writes expansively – even a little unguardedly – about the long-term impact of mass communication in fostering or weakening national identities, promoting or undermining integration into political systems, supplanting or supporting intermediary agencies, reviving or revising collective memory, and supporting or retarding social change (Dayan and Katz 1992; Katz 1996a).

In short, Katz has moved away from the limiting framework of conventional effects research with which he is still sometimes identified. His intellectual journey offers lessons for all people engaged in audience research, including his critics in reception analysis. Foremost among these is the need to conceptualize the media–audience relationship in a wider understanding of society.

NOTES

1   For a list and description of Katz's key publications, see Livingstone (1997). She also offers an intriguing "take" on his work, rather different from our own.
2   James Curran first met Elihu Katz when, without any forewarning, he knocked on Katz's door at the Hebrew University of Jerusalem and declared that he was a Cambridge research student on a long holiday, who was interested in Katz's books and wanted to talk about them. Katz courteously offered coffee, chatted, invited him to a memorable seminar, and introduced him to Michael Gurevitch with whom Curran was later to edit three books. Tamar Liebes is a former student of Elihu Katz, and later colleague and co-author.
3   See Nairn (1988) for a forceful presentation of this argument.
4   This conservative element is brought out more fully in a fascinating account of the sanctification of another Moroccan Jewish Rabbi, in Bilu and Ben-Ari (1992).
5   Though this may be inferring too much, it would seem that for Katz the nation state is the place where democracy is mainly practiced, where reciprocity between human beings is cultivated, and where the forces for global uniformity and exploitation can be

resisted through democratic means, whereas for Hallin the nation is the cradle of nationalism and belligerence, where manipulative elites are often dominant, offering an imperfect refuge in a global economy.

6 This is not to detract from the achievements of reception analysis. For a short guide to reception studies, now perhaps the ascendant tradition in audience research save in the US, see Corner (1996). For reviews of effects research, see McLeod *et al.* (1991) and Livingstone (1996).

REFERENCES

Bilu, Y. and Ben-Ari, E. (1992) "The making of modern saints: manufactured charisma and the Abu-Hatseiras of Israel," *American Ethnologist* 19 (4).

Blumler, J. G. and Katz, E. (eds.) (1974) *The Uses of Mass Communications*, Beverly Hills, CA: Sage.

Blumler, J. G., Gurevitch, M. and Katz, E. (1985) "Reaching out: a future for gratifications research," in K. E. Rosengren, L. A. Wenner and P. Palmgreen (eds.) *Media Gratifications Research: Current Perspectives*, Beverly Hills, CA: Sage.

Coleman, J., Katz, E. and Menzel, H. (1966) *Medical Innovation*, Indianapolis: Bobbs-Merrill.

Corner, J. (1996) "Reappraising reception: aims, concepts and methods," in J. Curran and M. Gurevitch (eds.) *Mass Media and Society* (2nd edn), London: Arnold.

Dayan, D. and Katz, E. (1992) *Media Events: The Live Broadcasting of History*, Cambridge, MA: Harvard University Press.

Gross, L. (1989) "Out of the mainstream: sexual minorities and the mass media," in E. Seiter, H. Borchers, G. Kreutzner and E. Warth (eds.) *Remote Control: Television Audiences and Cultural Power*, London: Routledge.

Hallin, D. C. (1994) *We Keep America on Top of the World*, London: Routledge.

Hallin, D. C. and Mancini, P. (1991) "Summits and the constitution of an international public sphere: the Reagan–Gorbachev meetings as televised events," *Communications* 12.

Katz, E. (1961) "The social itinerary of technical change: two studies on the diffusion of innovation," *Human Organisation* 20 (2). Reprinted in W. Schramm and D. Roberts (eds.) (1971) *The Process and Effects of Mass Communication* (revised edn), Urbana, IL: University of Illinois Press.

Katz, E. (1980) "On conceptualizing media effects," in T. McCormack (ed.) *Studies in Communication*, vol. 1, Greenwich, CT: JAI Press.

Katz, E. (1996a) "And deliver us from segmentation," *Annals of the American Academy of Political and Social Science* 546.

Katz, E (1996b) "Where we stand," unpublished paper to *The Media and the Public: Rethinking the Part Played by People in the Flow of Mass Communications*, International Symposium in honor of Elihu Katz, May, Van Leer Institute, Jerusalem.

Katz, E. and Danet, B. (eds.) (1973) *Bureaucracy and the Public*, New York: Basic Books.

Katz, E. and Feldman, S. (1962) "The debates in the light of research: a survey of surveys," in S. Krause (ed.) *The Great Debates: Background, Perspective, Effects*, Bloomington, IN: Indiana University Press.

Katz, E. and Gurevitch, M. (1976) *The Secularization of Leisure*, London: Faber & Faber.

Katz, E. and Lazarsfeld, P. (1955) *Personal Influence: The Part Played by People in the Flow of Mass Communications*, New York: Free Press.

Katz, E. and Wedell, E. (1977) *Broadcasting in the Third World: Promise and Performance*, London: Macmillan.

Katz, E., Blumler, J. G. and Gurevitch, M. (1974) "Utilization of mass communication by the individual," in J. G. Blumler and E. Katz (eds.) *The Uses of Mass Communications*, Beverly Hills, CA: Sage.

Katz, E. and Haas, H. (1997) "Twenty years of television in Israel: are there long-run effects on values, social connectedness and cultural practices?," *Journal of Communication* 47: 3–20.

Katz, E., Gurevitch, M., Danet, B. and Peled, T. (1969) "Petitions and prayers: a method for the content analysis of persuasive appeals," *Social Forces* 47 (4).

Lang, G. and Lang, K. (1983) *The Battle for Public Opinion*, New York: Columbia University Press.

Liebes, T. and Katz, E. (1990) *The Export of Meaning: Cross-Cultural Readings of "Dallas"*, New York: Oxford University Press. Reprinted by Polity Press, Cambridge (1994).

Livingstone, S. (1996) "On the continuing problem of media effects," in J. Curran and M. Gurevitch (eds.) *Mass Media and Society* (2nd edn), London: Arnold.

Livingstone, S. (1997) "The work of Elihu Katz: conceptualising media effects in context," in J. Corner, P. Schlesinger and R. Silverstone (eds.) *The International Handbook of Media Research*, London: Routledge.

McLeod, J., Kosicki, G. and Pan, Z. (1991) "On understanding and misunderstanding media effects," in J. Curran and M. Gurevitch (eds.) *Mass Media and Society* (1st edn), London: Arnold.

Nairn, T. (1988) *Enchanted Glass*, London: Century Hutchinson.

Samuel, R. (1994) *Theatres of Memory*, London: Verso.

Simonson, P. (1996) "Dreams of democratic togetherness: communication hope from Cooley to Katz," *Critical Studies in Mass Communication* 13 (December).

Part I
Media and ritual

2 Mass communication, ritual and civil society

Jeffrey C. Alexander and Ronald N. Jacobs

In political theory and empirical social science alike, there is a growing recognition that a fully-differentiated civil society is necessary for the development of an inclusive, solidaristic, and democratic society. While the precise meaning of civil society is far from settled, one thing is certain: the mass media has an extraordinary impact on its forms and functions. While organizational structures are essential, the "currency" of civil society is influence and commitment, in the form of a symbolically powerful public opinion. Because most theories of civil society focus primarily on its boundary relations – its autonomy from the state and economy, and the powerful regulative institutions, such as law, which draw these boundaries in a sanctioned way – they fail to consider how civil society works as a communicative space for the imaginative construction and reconstruction of more diffuse, but equally important, collective identities and solidarities.

We will show what is at stake in this debate by reconsidering Elihu Katz's contributions to an understanding of media communication. Katz's micro-oriented work – encompassing his research on personal influence, the two-step flow model of media reception, and cross-cultural media reception (with Tamar Liebes) – exposes the errors of passive–actor models of media reception and mass culture versions of ideology critique. His later, more macro and anthropological research on media events (with Daniel Dayan) shows what is wrong with a model of mass communication predicated on rationalist and cognitivist grounds. We will argue that, when this body of work is considered as an interrelated whole, it underlines the need for re-centering civil society theory around a more empirically viable model of media communication. In the latter part of this essay, we will outline such an approach to civil society, one in which the media is involved in the construction of common identities and universalistic solidarities, in multiple publics and multiple sites of reception. While a common code and common narrative structure allows for intersubjectivity and cross-communication between different publics, the narrative elaboration of events and crises – understood as social dramas – is crucial for providing a sense of historical continuity in the crisis bound, episodic constructions of universalistic solidarity that continually form and reform civil society. We will illustrate this theoretical argument by examining some of our own ongoing empirical research into the cultural dynamics of civil society, in particular our research on the Watergate (Alexander 1988a, 1988b) and Rodney King (Jacobs 1996a) crises.

CIVIL SOCIETY, SOLIDARITY, INSTITUTIONS

It is our contention that civil society does not, in the first instance, have to do with the autonomy of organizations *per se*, but rather with the differentiation of a particular kind of social relationship, one that embodies universalistic solidarity. What this means is that civil society must be conceived not only as a world of voluntary associations, elections, or even legal rights, but also, and very signifi- cantly, as a realm of symbolic communication. Those who are or would be included in civil society engage in cooperative and conflictual symbolic "conver- sations" about who deserves membership and just how far into non-civil realms the obligations of membership extend. Civil society membership is defined in terms of certain "timeless" qualities of personal motivation, social relationship, and group organization. While specific institutions and procedures are necessary for the creation and re-creation of a viable civil sphere, it is such symbolic communications that allow for the construction of common identities and soli- darities. The incorporation of previously excluded groups cannot take place, we suggest, simply through a restructuring of power relationships or an extension of legal rights. These steps will be ineffective unless the previously excluded group is redefined in terms of the "timeless qualities" which citizens in good standing putatatively possess. Furthermore, incorporation will not be a successful motivating goal unless it is defined as a struggle that involves far more than procedural participation and more equal material rewards. It must be dramati- cally narrated as a heroic triumph over the challenge to the utopian ideals of universalistic solidarity, in relation to which the failure of inclusion is viewed as the tragic triumph of particularism.

We will provide a more detailed and sustained outline of our own position on civil society later in the chapter. As a prologomena to our initial discussion of Katz's work, however, we would like to discuss the "dominant paradigm" of civil society theory in terms of its assumptions regarding the media. By dominant paradigm we have in mind those theories which focus exclusively on the formal political arrangements, legal procedures, and narrowly defined institutional structures that are necessary for differentiating power away from the state and toward the civil sphere of voluntary action. This conception of civil society derives from the post-Hobbesian, liberal tradition of political thought. An early example of this can be found in the writings of Locke, who developed a theory about an independent sphere of fellowship, a "commonwealth" that emerges in the state of nature and is extended, via the social contract, to a civil law regulating social life.[1] Similar ideas about a differentiated sphere of voluntary action can be found in Ferguson's (1980 [1768]) argument for self control and "subtlety"; Adam Smith's (1761) emphasis on moral sentiments; Kant's discussions (1949 [1784]) of the relation between criticism, autonomy, and universal reason; and even Tocqueville's (1945 [1835]) argument that the sphere of voluntary political life is anchored in the collectively binding, extra-political world of law and the collective regulation of religion.

Even when liberal illusions concerning equality of interests and formal conditions began to erode in the nineteenth century, the central assumptions of the dominant paradigm – that the good society could be achieved through an egalitarian distribution of power and the procedural guarantee of liberty – were left intact. All that had changed was the confidence in liberal society itself. Increasingly, it was seen as an empty sphere of atomized mass subjects, helpless against the onslaught of capitalism and public relations. From the perspective of this vision, the triumph of liberal–capitalist society was the tragedy of civil society. As Marx wrote, "none of the so-called rights of man goes beyond egoistic man, man as he is in civil society, namely an individual withdrawn behind his private interests and whims and separated from the community."[2] This argument, one of the earliest and most forceful articulations of what later came to be called the mass society thesis, could envision only an institutional solution to the tragedy of civil society. The assumption was that only the state could protect the atomized mass subjects against the impersonal and coercive social control of industrial capitalism. A similar argument has been made more recently by John Keane (1989, 1992), who has pointed to the need for institutional differentiation and the multiplication of voluntary associations to safeguard society from becoming dominated by a particular faction. Claude Lefort (1988) argues for a differentiation of law, power and knowledge, so that the centralizing potential of the state can be held in check by civil society. While he has replaced the centralizing power of capitalism with that of the state, and is, therefore, much more concerned with political democracy than with socialism, Lefort's reformist efforts still largely assume the same anonymous, passive mass subject.

For thinkers from Walter Lippman and John Dewey to C. Wright Mills, Hannah Arendt and Jurgen Habermas, the disappearance of public life became axiomatic for any consideration of twentieth-century life. Their solution to the dilemma of mass society lay not so much in the statist reforms of Marxism and neo-Marxism but rather in a formalist proceduralism that emphasized civil society's regulative institutions, not its communicative ones. John Dewey (1927: 126–7) argued that the "machine age" had invaded and disintegrated the older communities without generating new ones. For him, the "problem of the public" was "to achieve such recognition of itself as will give it weight in the selection of official representatives and in the definition of their responsibilities and rights" (Dewey 1927: 77). This could be achieved by improving the methods and conditions of discussion and debate in the public sphere (Dewey 1927: 208). There is a striking similarity between this pragmatist argument and the more recent neo-Kantian one of Jurgen Habermas (1987, 1989, 1996), who argues that a proceduralist discourse ethics and an independent legal order can institutionalize and protect a sphere of public communication from the instrumental steering media of money and power, thereby maintaining a tattered tie between civil society and the lifeworld. Dewey and Habermas both assume the empirical existence of mass society, and both turn to a more rational ordering of public discussion as a necessary procedure for recovering civil society.

The problem with all of these approaches is that they can only conceive civil society as a sphere of power and decision-making.[3] But civil society is not merely about the protection of a sphere of voluntaristic action from a centralizing source of power, whether it be the state or the capitalist economy. Parsons (1971) recognized that civil society is a sphere of influence and commitment, mediated through public opinion. For this reason, the media is critically important, not as a forum for public information but, rather, for public influence, identity, and solidarity. Because the "dominant paradigm" of civil society theory ignores this fact – its concerns are primarily differentiating the media as a truth-telling medium from the instrumental and distorting spheres of economy and state – its advocates are prevented from a real consideration of how the media actually works in civil society. Implicit in their exclusive focus on differentiation is a passive–actor, single–public, rationalistic model of media communication.

This brief critical discussion of the dominant civil society paradigm and its assumptions about mass communication provides a framework for considering some important implications of Katz's very different approach to mass media. We wish to argue that Katz's research on media effects and media events shows that the assumptions of the dominant civil society paradigm are wrong. From this demonstration, we will suggest that there is a general need to rethink the relationship between civil society, communication and the media.

TOWARD A VOLUNTARISTIC AND CULTURAL VIEW OF THE MEDIA

What unites all of Katz's projects of media research is a common focus on agency and a rejection of the notion that the media text has a monolithic meaning for an atomized, passive audience. His early research concerned itself with the measurement of the media's power to change individual opinions. The findings directly contradicted the assumptions of mass society theory, suggesting that the media had very limited effects and that the latter typically were filtered through the personal influence of opinion leaders (Katz and Lazarsfeld 1955; Katz 1957). Initiated by what have come to be regarded as classical research studies, *The People's Choice* and *Personal Influence*, this research served as a definitive rejection of the "hypodermic needle" model which permeated all different types of media theory and research. Before the limited effects paradigm, media researchers had begun from the assumption that individual beliefs and personalities – not to mention "civilized culture" – were helpless against the onslaught of mass culture. The best-remembered version of mass society theory came from the Frankfurt School approach, whose practitioners argued that the "culture industry" functioned to sedate the masses and to remove those types of contradictions which make art and culture potentially liberating and revolutionary (see Adorno 1967; Horkheimer and Adorno 1972; Marcuse 1968). The same assumptions about individual effects held, however, in the conservative efforts to protect "Culture" from mass society (e.g. Leavis 1932; Leavis and Thompson 1932; Ortega y Gasset 1960 [1936]), and also in the vast corpus of research on propaganda (e.g. Lasswell 1927; Doob 1935; Jackall 1995).

What the limited effects paradigm accomplished was to recover agency and community as important components of mass-mediated communication. Community was recovered through the finding that the effects of the media in any individual "cannot be accounted for without reference to his social environment and to the character of his interpersonal relationships" (Katz and Lazarsfeld 1955: 25). The result of this finding was the "two-step flow" theory of media effects. Agency was recovered through the focus on how the media served to reinforce identity, through the diversity of ways it was used and the functions of gratification it provided. In other words, the meaning and impact of the media message varies according to how it is used: whether as information, personal identity, social integration or entertainment (McQuail 1983). And despite Gitlin's (1978) claim that limited effects arguments were no longer valid after the era of television, a host of studies have shown that agency does operate for television reception (see, for example, Morley 1980, 1986; Press 1991; Liebes and Katz 1990).

One of the striking things about Katz's research is its refusal to be dogmatically positioned on either side of the antinomy between structure and agency. It is clear that Katz rejects the passive–actor model of mass society theory, but this does not mean that he rejects all structural effects in a false celebration of unbounded agency. *Personal Influence*, for example, was never intended as a comprehensive paradigm of media research, nor did it refuse the existence of long-term effects (Katz 1987: S35). Limited effects does not mean, for Katz, an *absence* of effects. In fact, Katz (1987: S38) has criticized those gratification studies which are "too captivated by the infinite diversity of audience uses to pay much attention to the constraints of the text." The point is that media texts provide a certain flow of cultural material from producers to audiences, who in turn use them in their lifeworld settings to construct a meaningful world and to maintain a common cultural framework through which intersubjectivity becomes possible, even among those who may never come into contact with one another. While media texts themselves may be understood as potentially infinite spaces (hence Eco's [1984] theory of unlimited semiosis), in practice they are used to create and re-create certain delimited cultural forms, as Liebes and Katz showed so well in *The Export of Meaning* (1990). In other words, the media allows for the transformation of a limitless and unbounded space into a symbolically fixed place, a process necessary to the durability of civil society.[4]

While the limited effects paradigm demonstrated the importance of agency, community, and culture on the micro-interactional level, Katz's later work with Daniel Dayan on media events argued for a similar relevance of these factors at the macro-societal level. Media events – such as the Middle East peace accords, British Royal weddings, American Presidential inaugurations and debates, and the Olympics – are live events (organized outside the media itself) that break the normal routines of media broadcasting, are covered by all broadcasters, and create a cultural situation where viewing is a virtually mandatory ritual of citizenship.[5] Media events, which attract larger audiences than any other form of communication media, have tremendous potentials in terms of media power, because they erase the divide between private and public, and also because they dramatize the symbols, narratives, and cultural codes of a particular society.

Media events serve the legitimation needs for societies (not necessarily states) whose members cannot gather together in a direct way. They provide common rituals and common symbols, which citizens can experience contemporaneously with everyone and interpersonally with those around them. They provide the cultural grounds for attachment to the "imagined communities" described by Anderson (1983), and they update the "invented traditions" studied by Hobsbawm (1983). In other words, media events are centrally involved in the construction of common identities and solidarities, and for this reason they are part and parcel to the workings of civil society.

Media events cannot be understood from a cognitivist framework, but require a cultural one. As Dayan and Katz note (following Turner 1977), media events produce a shift from the "indicative" to the subjunctive mode of culture; that is, from reality as it is to reality as it ought to be (see Dayan and Katz 1992: 20, 104, 119). This corresponds well with our notion of the media as the communicative institution of civil society, where a dialogue is maintained between "real civil society" – in which universalism is compromised by stratification and functional differentiation – and normative civil society, which maintains the idealized, utopian forms. Celebratory media events of the type discussed by Dayan and Katz tend to narrow the distance between the indicative and the subjunctive, thereby legitimating the powers and authorities outside the civil sphere. Mediatized public crises, on the other hand, tend to increase the distance between the indicative and the subjunctive, thereby giving to civil society its greatest power for social change. In these situations, the media create public narratives that emphasize not only the tragic distance between is and ought but the possibility of heroically overcoming it. Such narratives prescribe struggles to make "real" institutional relationships more consistent with the normative standards of the utopian civil society discourse.

RECONCEPTUALIZING CIVIL SOCIETY AND THE MEDIA

What Katz's research suggests is how important the media is for actively constructing common identities and common solidarities. At the micro-level, this means that the media is filtered through multiple communities, multiple webs of interpersonal relations, and multiple identities. At the macro-level, it suggests that the media is concerned not only with the diffusion of information to a mass public, but also – and this is particularly true for media events – with the dramatization of civil society and the creation of a common cultural framework for building common identities. Elaborated through the most compelling narratives of civil society (see Smith 1994), media events provide the cultural grounds for attachment to the social imaginary of civil society, and they provide plot points for updating the ongoing public narratives of civil society and nation. As a communicative institution of civil society, the media produces an output which is not authoritative control but influence. By its very definition, moreover, influence is not a unidirectional phenomenon, flowing from source to receiver, but multidirectional. Because the media gains influence by placing specific statements against the background of more generalized community beliefs and commitments, it is filtered through the diverse publics and networks that make up civil society itself.

We argue that the model of the media derived from Katz's research has a strong affinity to some of the most significant current departures from the dominant paradigm of civil society theory. These challenges suggest a multiplicity of public spheres, communities, and associations nested within one another, and also within a putative larger "national sphere" of civil society (Taylor 1995: 207–15). They also suggest that, while the Habermasian (1989) notion of the public sphere has been important for recognizing the centrality of discourse, it errs by hypostatizing a notion of communication as being involved singularly with rational processes of reaching consensus (see Alexander 1989; Lash 1985; Schudson 1992). In other words, there has been a turn away from the exclusive understanding of civil society as an institutional or informational space, in which mass subjects passively receive information about public affairs so that they might be better informed, more powerful voting citizens. The new understanding sees civil society as a cultural space in which different individuals and groups jockey to "narrate the social" (cf. Sherwood 1994) and where citizens actively construct their own understandings of real and ideal civil society by filtering overarching discourse and narratives through multiple public spheres and communities.

This turn to culture and agency in civil society theory does not imply a complete absence of structures and limits. Here, we should recall Katz's warning to reception researchers who are too captivated by the infinite diversity of audience uses to look for the structuring properties of the text. There are a limited number of publics available to serve as interpretive communities for narrating the social. There is also a history of public discourse which serves to limit how events can be narrated into ongoing stories about civil society. More generally, there are structural limits to the ways in which an individual, group or community can produce publicly plausible explanations of events. In our own work we have focused on these limits, by mapping the semiotic and narrative structures of the "discourse of civil society."

The media plays a central role in our understanding of civil society, not only as a space where information is circulated so that citizens can be well-informed voters (though that is certainly important), but rather as a cultural space where actors and events become typified into more general codes (e.g. sacred/profane, pure/impure, democratic/antidemocratic, citizen/enemy) and more generic story forms which resonate with the society's culture. Expressive media – such as novels or movies – are fictional symbolic forms that weave the binary codes of civil society into broad narratives and popular genres. They constrain action by constituting a teleology for future events even as they seem to be telling stories about people and life in an ahistorical way. The fictional world thus impinges upon the "real" in a fundamental manner, even among those chroniclers who see themselves simply as objective historians *tout court* (cf. White 1973, 1978). News media, while also drawing on many of these fictional tropes, plays a more immediate role, acting as a symbolic public forum for different individuals and groups, all battling for interpretive authority over a particular event. The role of binary oppositions is critical here; contrasts between purifying and polluting motives, relations, and institutions permeate news accounts, linking the presuppositions of civil society to the ongoing rush of social events.

The mass media, then, provides the cultural environment from which common identities and solidarities can be constructed. This common cultural environment, the "discourse of civil society," consists of two structural levels. In terms of "deep structure," there is a common semiotic system through which public actors speak and through which public readers interpret what is being communicated. Alongside this deep semiotic structure there exists a "temporal structure," a set of common narrative frameworks through which public actors chart the movement of themselves, and others, in real historical time. These two cultural environments simultaneously constrain and enable public actions in civil society.

The "deep structure," or semiotic system of civil society, supplies the structured categories of pure and impure into which every member, or potential member, is made to fit. Just as there is no developed religion that does not divide the world into the saved and the damned, there is no civil discourse that does not conceptualize the world into those who deserve inclusion and those who do not (Alexander 1992). For this reason the discourse of civil society, just like the discourse of religion, constitutes a language system that can be understood semiotically, that is, as sets of homologies and antipathies, which create likenesses and differences between various terms of social description and prescription. This semiotic structure develops not so much through the agency of individual *speech*, but rather through the incremental changes inherent in the historicity of *language* (Saussure 1964 [1916]). In other words, while the semiotic code is always in a process of incremental flux, it appears to a language community as immutable.

Through this historical and cultural process of semiosis, civil society becomes organized around a bifurcating discourse of citizen and enemy, defining the characteristics of worthy, democratic citizens and also of unworthy, counter-democratic enemies. This "common code" not only allows for a degree of intersubjectivity among public speakers, but also provides a relatively stable system for evaluating events and persons. Code-like in form, it is based on binary relations of similarity and difference along the dimensions of *motives, relationships* and *institutions*. For each dimension of the code, there is a system of sacred signs and a system of profane signs. The sacred signs exist in relations of similarity to one another, and in relations of opposition to the profane signs (which themselves are understood as similar). It is this distinction between the sacred and the profane, what Durkheim (1965: 52) called society's most basic classification, that adds an important evaluative dimension to public discourse, helping to communicate information in a forceful and evocative way. Actors, as members of civil society, believe in the sacred side of the code, and thus maintain a modicum of moral reassurance; at the very least, they make their actions and representations accountable in terms of the sacred (Alexander and Smith 1993: 164–5). For the case of American civil society, the semiotic code is organized around the sacred signs of rational and controlled motivations, open and trusting relationships and impersonal, rule-regulated institutions.[6] Each of these sacred signs is made meaningful in relation to its binary opposite, and in its relation to other binary pairs added in the process of code-making.[7]

While the semiotic system of civil society provides the "deep structure" of civil society – appearing as immutable to a language community – its narrative structure allows for the construction of common identities, expectations and solidarities. Narratives help individuals, groups and communities to "understand their progress through time in terms of stories, plots which have beginnings, middles, and ends, heroes and antiheroes, epiphanies and denouements, dramatic, comic, and tragic forms" (Alexander and Smith 1993: 156). In this way, narrative transforms the static dualities of structure into patterns that can account for the chronological ordering of lived experience (Ricoeur 1984; Entrikin 1991). As studies of class formation (Somers 1992; Steinmetz 1992), collective mobilization (Hart 1992; Kane 1994) and mass communication (Darnton 1975; Jacobs 1996b: Schudson 1982) have demonstrated, social actions, movements (cf. Alexander 1996) and identities are guided by narrative understandings. Furthermore, by connecting their self-narratives to collective narratives, individuals can identify with such "imagined communities" as class, gender, race, ethnicity and nation. As Steinmetz (1992: 505) has noted, these collective narratives can be extremely important for how individuals evaluate their lives, even if they did not participate in the key historical events of the collective narrative.

The narrative structure of civil society consists of a plot, a set of characters, and a genre. *Plot* refers to the selection, ordering, evaluation and attribution of differential status to events (Steinmetz 1992: 497–9). A narrative's plot is fluid and complex in its relationship to events; as Eco (1994) has shown, it can "linger" on a particular event, flash-back to past events or flash-forward to future events. The basic plot of civil society is the story of integration and participation via citizenship.[8] In this plot, the *characters* are organized around the opposition between heroes, who fight for the extension of citizenship and rights, and the antiheroes who would restrict citizenship and threaten rights. The evaluational valences of the characters in civil society narratives are elaborated by the semiotic code, so that heroes occupy the sacred side and the villains the profane side of the code. Finally, the narrative of civil society is structured by a particular *genre*, which provides a temporal and spatial link between the characters and events of the narrative and also influences the relationship between the characters, narrator and readers. The narrative of civil society is structured predominantly by the genre of romance, which provides for a "theme of ascent" and which is the reason why civil society discourse has typically been a utopian one. In romance, as Frye (1957) has described, the hero has great powers, the enemy is clearly defined and often has great powers as well, and the movement takes the form of an adventure with the ultimate triumph of hero over enemy. Romantic genres are viewed by the audience from a perspective of wish-fulfillment, where heroes represent ideals and villains represent threats.

From the structured and generalized categories of civil society discourse to the cathartic typifications of expressive media, to the diffuse but more historically and socially directed phenomenon of public opinion and to the institutions of news production, there stretches a continuum from the synchronic to the diachronic, from structure to process, from inflexible to flexible and from general to specific. These discursive constructions create reactions in civil society itself. They can trigger violent actions, dislodge powerful people and motivate the formation of social movements. This is particularly true of the cognitively oriented news media, and even more so for media events and civil crises. In the section to follow, we will illustrate this communicative power within civil society by focusing on two important American events: the Watergate crisis of 1972 and the Rodney King beating of 1991.[9]

Watergate

In June 1972, employees of the Republican Party made an illegal entry into the Democratic Party headquarters in the Watergate Hotel in Washington, DC. While this event ultimately led to the resignation of President Richard Nixon, the incident initially received relatively little attention. Despite the efforts of some Democrats and a few journalists, the news media largely played down the story after a short time, treating it as a relatively unimportant event. During the presidential election of that year, only 15 of 433 reporters were assigned to the Watergate story, and only one television journalist. Even after the national election of that year, 80 per cent of the American public found it hard to believe that there was a "Watergate crisis," 75 per cent felt that the Watergate event was "just politics," and 84 per cent felt that what they had heard about Watergate had not influenced their voting decision (Alexander 1988b).[10] Yet two years later, this same event had provoked the most serious peacetime political crisis in American history. How and why did this perception of Watergate change? The answer, we argue, is that it became a different event, one which was narrated as a core threat to the ideals of civil society. In this new narrative, "Watergate" mobilized a different side of the discourse of civil society, and President Nixon became associated with the profane code of motives, relations and institutions.

Even though it would take until May 1973 for the "Watergate crisis" to reach Richard Nixon, the identification of Watergate as itself a sign of pollution was already well under way by the summer of 1972. It was during this four-month period in 1972 that "Watergate" began to refer to a set of related events touched off by the break-in, including charges of political corruption, legal suits and arrests. The idea of corruption resonated with the profane side of the discourse of institutions; the legal suits and arrests reinforced the discursive pollution occurring in civil society by mobilizing the regulative institution of the law as a symbol of condemnation of the "event" of Watergate. Still, while the event of Watergate had already come to be narrated as a drama of moral evil by August 1972, it had not yet been attached definitively to a set of characters. There were not as yet any heroes to this narrative, or indeed any villains. Certainly, President Nixon had not yet been symbolically polluted by Watergate (Alexander 1988b: 197).

The crucial event in transforming the meaning of Watergate was the Senate Select Committee's televised hearings, which began in May 1973 and continued through August of that same year. The Senate hearings were not simply the functional outgrowth of the discursive logic of civil society. They were caused also by forces in the non-civil spheres, most importantly by ongoing conflicts between institutional and political elites. These conflicts did, however, increase the dramatic impact of the incipient Watergate crisis, centering the ambiguity around precisely who were the heroic characters and who were the antiheroic ones. With this increase in social drama came a corresponding increase in public awareness of Watergate: from 52 per cent in September 1972 to 96 per cent in May 1973 (Lang and Lang 1983). This increased awareness encouraged the television media to broadcast the hearings live. With the live coverage, Watergate became a media event, and entered squarely into the theater of civil society. The televised hearings constituted a kind of civic ritual, counterposing the utopian aspirations of civil society (embodied in the notions of office and duty) against the "real" institutional relationships which were now required to be consonant with the ideal vision.

Within this ritualized context, the characters of the hearing were narrated in terms of the opposition between heroes and antiheroes, and evaluated in terms of the binary structure of American civil discourse. This new understanding of the Watergate "event" provided the cultural environment constraining the strategies of political elites. For Nixon and his political supporters, the goal was to deflate the ritual and to redefine the event of Watergate in terms of the everyday world of mundane politics. But in the cultural context of the media event, reinforced by the "hushed tones" of the announcers and the break in ordinary broadcast routines, such a strategy encountered much resistance. The symbolic value of Watergate was already quite generalized, and the ritual form of the hearing was already in place (and reproduced by every broadcast). The ritual context of the hearings was reflected in public opinion data; while only 31 per cent believed that Watergate was a "serious" event before the hearings, by early July 50 per cent did, and this figure remained constant until the end of the crisis (Alexander 1988b: 205).

A final event compounded the developing narrative of Watergate and served to cement Nixon's symbolic status as an evil figure and a threat to civil society. This was the "Saturday Night Massacre" of October 1973, in which Nixon fired special prosecutor Archibald Cox. The firing of Cox – who occupied a symbolic position of rule-regulated procedure – made Nixon look like a deceitful figure who used the institutional office of the presidency to satisfy his arbitrary and egoistic personal needs. By the time of the impeachment hearings in 1974, Nixon had been narrated as a selfish and fractious person who was interested in his own wealth and power at the expense of civil society (see Alexander and Smith 1993: 184). As a *New York Times* editorial noted, the Nixon presidency resembled more of a dictatorship than a democracy.

> One coherent picture emerges from this evidence. . . . It is the picture of a White House entirely on its own, operating on the assumption that it was

accountable to no higher authority than the wishes of and the steady accretion of power of a Presidency growing steadily more sure that it was above and beyond the reaches of the law.[11]

Still, impeachment was a different "event" than was Watergate. As the impeachment proceedings became added to the ongoing narrative, there was a new round of cultural constestation in civil society. Nixon's supporters argued that, while the President had made serious errors in judgment, on balance he had moved closer to a global civil society, through his major contributions to international peace, his foreign policy initiatives with the Soviets and the Chinese, and his termination of the Vietnam War (Alexander and Smith 1993: 186–7). In other words, the gulf between the indicative and the subjunctive was not as great, according to these supporters, as the public had been led to believe through the statements and actions of public figures in civil society. They argued that Nixon could not be impeached by the will of civil society, that is, through public opinion, but only through the regulative institution of the law, and that this required evidence which the pro-impeachment forces had not yet produced. With this turn in the narrative, supporters of Nixon began to pollute the motives of his critics as greedy and their relationships as manipulative (Alexander and Smith 1993: 187). Indeed, Nixon could not have been impeached by the communicative institution of civil society, but only by the regulative institution of law. Eventually, the House Impeachment Committee did decide that sufficient evidence existed to merit a legal trial in the Senate, but Nixon's immediately subsequent resignation meant that the ultimate empirical status of his actions in relation to the regulating normative structure of American civil society was never decided. It was, in fact, the mass-mediated mobilization of influence and public opinion, not the regulative institutions of civil society, that forced Nixon to resign.

Rodney King

On March 3, 1991, an African–American motorist, Rodney King, was pulled over for speeding. After a brief chase, King was met by twenty-one police officers, including members of the California Highway Patrol and the Los Angeles Police Department. In full view of all who were present, King was severely beaten by three white LAPD officers, in the presence of a sergeant and the remaining seventeen officers. Unknown to the police officers, the event was videotaped by an amateur cameraman, George Holliday, and sold to a local television station. Despite the fact that the city of Los Angeles had paid more than $20 million between 1986 and 1990 in judgments, settlements and jury verdicts against Los Angeles police officers in over 300 lawsuits dealing with the excessive use of force, it was the Rodney King case that came to be seen as the defining event of racial crisis in Los Angeles. Understanding the cultural impact of the Rodney King beating will take us a long way toward understanding the way in which the media works in civil society.

While the Watergate case began slowly, with the ritualized and televised Senate hearing coming only a full year after the initial event, in the case of Rodney King it was the spontaneously recorded and nearly contemporaneous televised event itself which provoked the crisis. This does not mean that the event captured in the videotape *determined* the subsequent narration of the crisis. There was no necessary reason why Rodney King could not have been described as out of control and irrational, as, for example, television ideologue Rush Limbaugh was to do some time later (see Fiske 1994: 131). But the videotape, which was broadcast thousands of times, did result in a focusing of public attention on precisely how this "objective" event would be narrated. As such, it focused public attention on the competing narrations offered for the event, and quickly shifted public discourse in civil society toward the "subjunctive mode of culture" that Dayan and Katz claim is central to the power of media events.

Once the Rodney King beating became a media event, a process of cultural construction occurred concerning its meaning. The event of the beating was narrated in many different public spheres throughout the nation. From March until September of 1991, for example, hundreds of articles were written about the Rodney King crisis in the newspapers of New York, Los Angeles and Chicago. Most newspapers represented the beating as a wild deviation and a "shocking" event. Descriptions of the incident cast the officers as being irrational and excitable in their work, and as having used their powers illegitimately. Accounts from witnesses reported that the officers were "laughing and chuckling [after the beating], like they had just had a party."[12] These descriptions resonated with the profane discourse of motives and relationships in civil society, depicting violations of fairness, openness and justice. The event of the beating, when linked to the videotape, was understood as a way to expose the evil that existed in the police department. An editorial in the *Los Angeles Times* proclaimed that "this time, the police witnesses, knowing about the videotape, will probably not compound their offense by lying about what really happened."[13]

Still, if it had merely been a problem of a few individuals in need of administrative control, crisis need not have ensued. But the dramatic tension surrounding the Rodney King crisis increased through the construction of another important villain character: Los Angeles Police Chief Daryl F. Gates. Gates was repeatedly described as being unaccountable, racist, and ego-driven. Editorial opinion in the press became concentrated against Gates, offering a point of symbolic concentration and a direction for possible redressive action.

> The people of Los Angeles have been unable to hold their chief of police accountable for anything – not his racial slurs or racial stereotyping; not his openly-expressed contempt for the public, juries and the Constitution he is sworn to uphold; not his spying on political enemies or cover-up of that espionage.[14]

> Chief Gates is responsible for inflammatory comments, for the actions of his officers and for the $8 million in taxpayer money paid out last year to satisfy complaints against the department. But because of rigid civil service

protections, the police chief is not accountable to the mayor, the City Council or to the city's voters.[15]

What this climate of media opinion created was a dramatic test of the ability of political elites to control the repressive apparatus of the state, to keep it from threatening the freedom of citizens in civil society. While the redressive actions called for were directed toward political elites, the source of the call was clearly the public opinion of civil society. An article in the *New York Times*, for example, reported that "public outrage" was causing the Justice Department to review every police brutality complaint made to the Federal government over the previous six years.[16] But there was also a question about whether this was a sincere effort or a "finely calculated strategy."[17] The reason for this question had to do with the increasing salience of the normative discourse of civil society, as it was now placed in a dialogue with "real civil society." Within this "subjunctive mode of culture," there was real concern that reaction to the beating was being interpreted through a narrative of class, racial and ethnic segregation rather than public unity. As an editorial in the *Los Angeles Times* lamented, "It is profoundly revealing that while middle-class viewers recoiled in horror at the brutal footage, the victim, like many others familiar with police behavior in poor and minority neighborhoods, considered himself lucky that the police did not kill him."[18]

Thus, the social drama of the Rodney King crisis was set as a "contest," at least in the mainstream media. Would political elites be able to resolve the crisis through appropriate redressive action, or would the danger of liminality (inherent to the subjunctive mode) overwhelm their legitimacy and demand massive institutional changes? The answer to this question was far from determined; it depended, instead, on the dynamics of influence and commitment as they were constructed and transformed in civil society. Several of the attempts at redressive action – such as the grand jury investigation, the FBI probe, and the attempt by Mayor Tom Bradley to force Gates out of office – failed to produce any symbolic reintegration. Had all of the redressive actions failed, civil society would have been transposed from a romantic and utopian genre to a more tragic one, where the "reality" of irreconcilable schisms prevents full incorporation of all members of civil society. This deflation of the civil society narrative would have been a tragedy in the aporetic sense of resigned acceptance, a tragedy pointing to an evil "already there and already evil" (Ricoeur 1967: 313).

One redressive action was successful, however. That was the formation of the Christopher Commission, and the release of its report about the Los Angeles Police Department in July 1991. The Christopher Commission was comprised of representatives from all institutional branches of "elite" civil society. It was co-chaired by John Arguelles, a retired State Supreme Court judge, and by Warren Christopher, a former Deputy Attorney General and Deputy Secretary of State. Also included in the commission were two university professors, a college president, three accomplished lawyers, the president of the Los Angeles County Bar and a corporate executive. The decisive move toward symbolic resolution of the crisis came with the merging of the two previously separate commissions

– one headed by Arguelles, the other by Christopher – into an expanded "Christopher Commission." As an event, the merging of the two commissions presented an opportunity for new narrations of the crisis to be made. Both Arguelles and Christopher made numerous public statements representing the merged commission as an independent, cooperative and objective body, whose orientation was directed toward the good of the public. They represented their merged commission as a movement away from the tragedy of factionalism and back toward the romance of local government. As the following excerpts demonstrate, their efforts were reflected in the media:

> The heads of the panels . . . said they were seeking to distance themselves from the clash as the Police Commission forced Gates to take a leave.[19]

> "I think it would be good for everybody if we could come up with some kind of coordinated effort," said retired State Supreme Court Justice John Arguelles, the head of Gates' five-member civilian panel. "There are [now] two committees that might be perceived as having independent agendas that they might want to advance."[20]

> "In order to maximize the commission's contribution to the community," Christopher and Arguelles said in a joint statement, "we must concentrate on making an objective and thorough study of the long-term issues without being drawn into the controversy over the tenure of Chief Gates."[21]

In the developing narrative of the Rodney King crisis, the Christopher Commission came to be identified with the sacred discourse of civil institutions. When its report was released on July 9, it became a turning point for all of the narrative understandings of the Rodney King crisis. The *Los Angeles Times*, for example, began to interpret the release of the Christopher Commission report as a symbolic completion of the crisis begun by the videotape. If the videotape provided the beginning of the narrative, the report enabled its closure, thus resembling a cultural situation that Turner (1969) has called "reaggregation." While authority figures had previously been represented as divided and politically motivated, they were now represented as being open and cooperative, unified in their support of the Christopher Commission report and motivated by the duty of office and concern for the public. Attention also shifted back to police chief Gates, who was represented as increasingly ego-driven and out of touch with the public. Former political adversaries, such as the Police Commission and the City Council, were now calling on one another to help in a common cause. Business and labor leaders, who had previously not been significant players in the social drama, were reported to be joining the unified effort. When Gates finally announced his resignation, the police department became purged of the figure around whom much of the symbolic pollution had concentrated. Public focus began to turn to the upcoming trial of the four officers indicted, the conviction of whom would signal redemption for the political leaders of Los Angeles, legitimacy for its institutions and moral uplifting for its citizens. Rather than treating the trial as a separate event, the media and its public understood it as the final chapter of the narrative, clearly expecting the result to be the conviction of the officers.[22]

Thus, what we see with the case of the Rodney King beating is a media event that developed into a social drama. In other words, the media event produced by the beating was narrated as the first plot point of a crisis narrative about police brutality, factionalism and political divisiveness. In the African–American press, however, the media event was linked to a long, continuous, ongoing narrative about police brutality, white insincerity and the need for African–American empowerment. In this more epic form of the romantic genre, the African–American community itself was identified as the hero and was endowed with the sacred characteristics of motives (active, reasonable, realistic), relationships (open, truthful, unified) and institutions (rule-regulated, lawful, inclusive). For the African–American community, even though the understanding of the event was filtered through the shared semiotic code of civil society, the emplotment of characters and events was affected by the epic romance of African–American deliverance (i.e. an Exodus narrative with continuous roots going back to the time of slavery). This is similar to what Dayan and Katz (1992: 141–5) discuss as "alternative and oppositional readings" of the event. Clearly, though, the alternative readings were motivated in large part by the subjunctive mode of culture, by the power of the utopian vision of civil society and by the semiotic and narrative structures through which the utopian vision becomes elaborated.

NOTES

1 Locke *Second Treatise on Government* (Bk II, sect. 6).
2 Karl Marx, "On the Jewish Question," in *Karl Marx: Selected Writings*, ed. D. McClellan (Oxford University Press, 1977), p. 54.
3 This is also true of many other approaches which we have not mentioned in our discussion, such as Bobbio (1987), who argues that the principle of democratic decision-making should be extended beyond the political sphere of voting into the voluntary sphere of civil society.
4 For a good discussion of the cultural distinction between space and place, see Chaney (1994).
5 Dayan and Katz also argue that media events are preplanned, although Scannell (1995) and Jacobs (1996b) have pointed to the fact that unplanned events such as crises, if they become "mediatized public processes" and incorporate the other characteristics of media events, should be viewed as part of the same class of events.
6 For a more detailed semiotic "map" of the discourse of civil society, see Alexander (1992), Alexander and Smith (1993), and Smith (1996).
7 The analytical process of code-making is described in great detail by Eco (1979).
8 Others have discussed this in far greater detail than we have space for here. See, for example, Cohen and Arato (1992: 415–20, 440–63), Marshall (1964), and Parsons (1971).
9 For a more detailed discussion of Watergate, see Alexander (1988a, 1988b,1995); Alexander and Smith (1993); Lang and Lang (1983). For a more extended analysis of the Rodney King beating of 1991, see Jacobs (1996a).
10 In fact, according to Lang and Lang (1983), only 1 per cent of those surveyed after the election listed Watergate as an important part of their choice.

11 *New York Times,* July 31, 1974; quoted in Alexander and Smith (1993: 185).
12 *Los Angeles Times,* March 6, 1991: A22.
13 *Los Angeles Times,* March 9, 1991: B7.
14 *Los Angeles Times,* March 12, 1991: B7.
15 *Los Angeles Times,* March 13, 1991: B6.
16 *New York Times,* March 15, 1991: A1.
17 Ibid.
18 *Los Angeles Times,* March 14, 1991: B5.
19 *Los Angeles Times,* April 5, 1991: A23.
20 *Los Angeles Times,* April 2, 1991: A1.
21 *Los Angeles Times,* April 5, 1991: A23.
22 Indeed, when the not-guilty verdicts were read in April 1992, the *Los Angeles Times* reported that "Outrage and indignation swept the city Wednesday as citizens rich and poor, black and white, struggled to reconcile the acquittals of four Los Angeles Police Department officers with the alarming, violent images captured on a late-night video-tape" (*Los Angeles Times,* April 30, 1992: A1).

REFERENCES

Adorno, T. W. (1967) *Prisms,* Cambridge, MA: MIT Press.
Alexander, J. C. (1988a) "Three modes of culture and society relations: toward an analysis of Watergate," in *Action and its Environments,* New York: Columbia University Press, pp. 153–74.
Alexander, J. C. (1988b) "Culture and political crisis: 'Watergate' and Durkheimian sociology," in J. C. Alexander (ed.) *Durkheimian Sociology: Cultural Studies,* New York: Cambridge University Press, pp. 187–224.
Alexander, J. C. (1989) "Habermas and critical theory: beyond the Marxian dilemma?" in J. C. Alexander (ed.) *Structure and Meaning: Relinking Classical Sociology.* New York: Columbia University Press, pp. 217–49.
Alexander, J. C. (1992) "Citizen and enemy as symbolic classification: on the polarizing discourse of civil society", in M. Fouruier and M. Lamont (eds.) *Where Culture Talks: Exclusion and the Making of Society,* Chicago, IL: University of Chicago Press, pp. 289–308.
Alexander, J. C. (1995) "Watergate," in S.M. Lipset (ed.) *The Encyclopedia of Democracy,* vol. 1, London: Routledge, pp. 1367–9.
Alexander, J. C. (1996) "Collective action, culture and civil society: secularizing, updating, inverting, revising and displacing the classical model of social movements," in M. Diani and J. Clarke (eds.) *Essays in Honour of Alain Touraine,* London: Falmer Press, pp. 205–34.
Alexander, J. C. and Smith, P. (1993) "The discourse of American civil society: a new proposal for cultural studies", *Theory and Society* 22: 151–207.
Anderson, B. (1983) *Imagined Communities: Reflections on the Origin and Spread of Nationalism.* London: Verso.
Bobbio, N. (1987) *The Future of Democracy* (trans. R. Griffin), Minneapolis, MN: University of Minnesota Press.
Chaney, D. (1994) *The Cultural Turn: Scene-Setting Essays on Contemporary Cultural History,* London and New York: Routledge.
Cohen, J. and Arato, A. (1992) *Civil Society and Political Theory,* Cambridge, MA: MIT Press.
Darnton, R. (1975) "Writing news and telling stories", *Daedalus* 104 (2): 175–93.
Dayan, D. and Katz, E. (1992) *Media Events: The Live Broadcasting of History,* Cambridge, MA: Harvard University Press.
Dewey, J. (1927) *The Public and its Problems,* Chicago: Gateway Books.
Doob, L. (1935) *Propaganda: Its Psychology and Technique,* Westport, CT: Greenwood Press.
Durkheim, E. (1965) *The Elementary Forms of the Religious Life.* New York: Free Press.
Eco, U. (1979) *A Theory of Semiotics,* Bloomington, IN: Indiana University Press.

Eco, U. (1984) *Semiotics and the Philosophy of Language*, Bloomington, IN: Indiana University Press.

Eco, U. (1994) *Six Walks in the Fictional Woods*, Cambridge, MA: Harvard University Press.

Entrikin, J.N. (1991) *The Betweenness of Place: Towards a Geography of Modernity*. Baltimore, MD: Johns Hopkins University Press.

Ferguson, A. (1980 [1768]) *An Essay on the History of Civil Society*, Brunswick, NJ: Transaction Books.

Fiske, J. (1994) *Media Matters: Everyday Culture and Political Change*. Minneapolis, MN: University of Minnesota Press.

Frye, N. (1957) *Anatomy of Criticism*. Princeton, NJ: Princeton University Press.

Gitlin, T. (1978) "Media sociology: the dominant paradigm," *Theory and Society* 6: 205–53.

Habermas, J. (1987) *The Theory of Communicative Action* (trans. T. McCarthy), vol. 2., Boston, MA: Beacon Press.

Habermas, J. (1989 [1962]) *The Structural Transformation of the Public Sphere* (trans. Thomas Burger), Cambridge, MA: MIT Press.

Habermas, J. (1996) *Between Facts and Norms: Contributions to a Discourse Theory of Law and Democracy*, Cambridge: Polity Press.

Hart, J. (1992) "Cracking the code: narrative and political mobilization in the Greek resistance," *Social Science History* 16 (4): 631–68.

Hobsbawm, E. and Ranger, T. (eds.) (1983) *The Invention of Tradition*, Cambridge: Cambridge University Press.

Horkheimer, M. and Adorno, T.W. (1972) *The Dialectic of Enlightenment*, New York: Herder and Herder.

Jacobs, R. N. (1996a) "Civil society and crisis: culture, discourse, and the Rodney King beating," *American Journal of Sociology* 101 (5): 1238–72.

Jacobs, R. N. (1996b) "Producing the news, producing the crisis: narrativity, television, and news work," *Media, Culture and Society* 18 (3): 373–97.

Jackall, R. (ed.) (1995) *Propaganda* New York: New York University Press.

Kane, A. (1994) "Culture and social change: symbolic construction, ideology and political alliance during the Irish land war, 1879–1881," unpublished doctoral dissertation.

Kant, I. (1949 [1784]) "What is enlightenment?" in C. J. Friederich (ed.) *The Philosophy of Kant: Immanuel Kant's Moral and Political Writings*, New York: Modern Library, pp. 132–9.

Katz, E. (1957) "The two-step flow of communication: an up-to-date report on an hypothesis," *Public Opinion Quarterly* 21: 61–78.

Katz, E. and Lazarsfeld, P. (1955) *Personal Influence: The Part Played by People in the Flow of Mass Communications*, New York: Free Press.

Keane, J. (1989) *Democracy and Civil Society*. Cambridge: Polity Press.

Keane, J. (1992) *The Media and Democracy*. Cambridge: Polity Press.

Lang, G. and Lang, K. (1983) *The Battle for Public Opinion*, New York: Columbia University Press.

Lash, S. (1985) "Postmodernity and desire", *Theory and Society* 14 (1): 1–34.

Lasswell, H. (1927) *Propaganda Techniques in the World War*, London: K. Paul, Trench, Trubner & Co.

Lazarsfeld, P., Berelson, B. and Gaudet, H. (1948) *The People's Choice: How the Voter Makes Up His Mind in a Presidential Campaign*, NY: Columbia University Press.

Leavis, F.R. and Thompson, D. (1932) *Culture and Environment*. London: Chatto & Windus.

Leavis, Q.D. (1932) *Fiction and the Reading Public*. London: Chatto & Windus.

Lefort, C. (1988) *Democracy and Political Theory*, Minneapolis, MN: University of Minnesota Press.

Liebes, T. and Katz, E. (1990) *The Export of Meaning: Cross-Cultural Readings of "Dallas"*, New York: Oxford University Press.

McQuail, D. (1983) *Mass Communication Theory*, Newbury Park, CA: Sage.

Marcuse, H. (1968) *Negations: Essays in Critical Theory*. London: Allen Lane.

Marshall, T. H. (1964) *Class, Citizenship, and Social Development*, Garden City, NY: Doubleday.

Morley, D. (1980) *The Nationwide Audience*, London: British Film Institute.

Morley, D. (1986) *Family Television: Cultural Power and Domestic Leisure*. London: Comedia.

Ortega y Gasset, J. (1957 [1932]) *The Revolt of the Masses*, NY: Norton.

Parsons, T. (1971) *The System of Modern Societies*, Englewood Cliffs, NJ: Prentice-Hall.

Press, A. (1991) *Women Watching Television: Gender, Class and Generation in the American Television Experience*, Philadelphia, PA: University of Pennsylvania Press.

Ricoeur, P. (1967) *The Symbolism of Evil*, Boston, MA: Beacon Press.

Ricoeur, P. (1984) *Time and Narrative*, Chicago: University of Chicago Press.

Saussure, F. (1964 [1916]) *Course in General Linguistics*, NY: McGraw-Hill.

Scannell, P. (1995) "Media Events," *Media, Culture and Society* 17: 151–7.

Schudson, M. (1982) "The politics of narrative form: the emergence of news conventions in print and television," *Daedalus*, 3 (1): pp. 97–112.

Schudson, M. (1992) "Was there ever a public sphere? If so, when? Reflections on the American case", in C. Calhoun (ed.) *Habermas and the Public Sphere*, Cambridge, MA: MIT Press, 143–63.

Sherwood, S. (1994) "Narrating the Social," *Journal of Narratives and Life Histories* 4 (1–2): 69–98.

Smith, A. (1761) *The Theory of Moral Sentiments*.

Smith, P. (1994) "The semiotics of media narratives," in *Journal of Narratives and Life Histories* 4 (1–2): 89–120.

Smith, P. (1996) "Communism, fascism and democracy: barbarism and civility as variations on a common theme," in J.C. Alexander (ed.) *Real Civil Societies: The Dilemmas of Institutionalization*, Newbury Park, CA: Sage, forthcoming.

Somers, M. (1992) "Narrativity, narrative identity and social action: rethinking English working-class formation," *Social Science History* 16 (4): 591–630.

Steinmetz, G. (1992) "Reflections on the role of social narratives in working-class formation: narrative theories in the social sciences," *Social Science History* 16 (3): 489–516.

Taylor, C. (1995) "Liberal politics and the public sphere," in A. Etzioni (ed.) *New Communitarian Thinking: Persons, Virtues, Institutions, and Communities*, Chalottesville, VA: University Press of Virginia, pp. 183–217.

de Tocqueville, A. (1945 [1835]) *Democracy in America*, 2 vols, New York: Vintage Books.

Turner, V. (1969) *The Ritual Process*, Chicago, IL: Aldine.

Turner, V. (1977) "Process, systems and symbol," *Daedalus* 106: 61–80.

White, H. (1973) *Metahistory*, Baltimore, MD: Johns Hopkins University Press.

White, H. (1978) *Tropics of Discourse*, Baltimore, MD: Johns Hopkins University Press.

3 Political ritual on television
Episodes in the history of shame, degradation and excommunication

James W. Carey

Treachery, disloyalty, cruelty, tyranny are our ordinary vices.

Montaigne, "Of Cannibals"

Out of the quarrel with others we make rhetoric; out of the quarrel with ourselves we make poetry.

Yeats

Rituals of shame, degradation and excommunication are official and sanctioned ceremonies in all societies from the simple to complex. But they are also customs of daily life: ordinary vices as Montaigne tells us, moments of both official and casual cruelty, found, Kai Erickson (1966) argues, everywhere except in societies that are completely demoralized and anomic. These episodes can be as informal as shunning, ostracism and deliberate exclusion; they can be slightly more prescribed, such as enforced public penance or the placing of insignia of exclusion on clothing or bodily markings or identifications placed on doors and mail boxes. They can also be highly stylized and elaborate formal rites: the tearing off of epaulets and breaking of swords, a drumming from the corps, religious rites of excommunication or ceremonies of deportation.

Such ritual acts are designed to bring on a psychological state of shame and a personal sense of unworthiness, though they do not always manage to induce the attitudes they seek. Socially, they mark an irrefutable demotion in status from a higher to a lower rank: from the respected to the disrespected, the esteemed to the disdained, the sacred to the profane, the normal to the abnormal. They often are occasions when persons are sent into exile: internal exile, a kind of invisible existence, when the privileges normally accruing to citizens are stripped away and they are excluded from sacred places and anathematized; or external exile when persons are physically expelled, sent packing into transportation or quarantined. These are dangerous moments, particularly in the life of democracies committed to the avoidance of cruelty, for they are episodes of high, systematic and sanctioned misanthropy when the power of the state, public opinion or both is inscribed on the body. In testimony to a still fertile historical metaphor, we often call the search for victims to collectively subject to these rituals a "witch hunt." As Kai Erickson's *Wayward Puritans* (1966) demonstrates, the episodes in colonial

Salem, Massachusetts can stand as a model for the means by which such acts of cruelty can promote, however distastefully, states of social integration.

Erickson also notes that rituals of degradation generally ceased to be public occurrences, staged in the village square, once newspapers were available to frame and publicize the liturgy of separation. When the scale and complexity of social life transcended the village, a scale and complexity to which newspapers stood as both cause and effect, rituals of shame and degradation, rituals of passage from a scared to a profane status, could be conducted, literally, *in medias res*.

Curiously, rituals of degradation have not engaged the explicit attention of Elihu Katz and Daniel Dayan in the powerful and instructive analysis contained in *Media Events: The Live Broadcasting of History* (1992). The purpose of this essay is to begin to redress that imbalance, to isolate a class of ceremonies whose import eludes the categories through which they classify out media events. However, that analysis requires a brief excursion into the nation and nationalism, the site and ideology within which media events function.

Media events are episodes in the history of the nation state, and in the age of television, the relations between states, nations and peoples. They are among the most important forms which create, in Benedict Anderson's now well entrenched phrase, "the imaginary community of the nation." Nations consist of peoples who in the main never meet, never know one another in any ordinary sense, but who none the less identify with one another, assume they possess outlooks in common and whose lives flow, by and large, in steady harmony and uncoordinated coordination. As Anderson puts it:

> An American will never meet, or even know the names of more than a handful of his 240,000,000-odd fellow Americans. He has no idea of what they are up to at any one time. But he has complete confidence in their steady, anonymous, simultaneous activity.
>
> Anderson (1983: 31)

This is the psychology of the nation as a sociological organism that moves calendrically through homogenous time: a solid community, invisible and anonymous, united by a shared reality existing under the date of a newspaper or the dailyness of television broadcasts. And that psychology is the product of or, better, made possible by certain mass ceremonies, usually performed in silent privacy, "in the lair of the skull," or in the relative isolation of the private domicile.

> Yet each communicant is well aware that the ceremony he performs is being replicated simultaneously by thousands (or millions) of others of whose existence he is confident, yet of whose identity he has not the slightest notion. Furthermore, this ceremony is incessantly repeated at daily or half-daily intervals throughout the calendar. What more vivid figure for the secular, historically clocked, imagined community can be envisioned? At the same time, the newspaper reader, observing exact replicas of his own paper being consumed by his subway, barbershop or residential neighbors, is

> continually reassured that the imagined world [the world imagined in the
> newspapers] is visibly rooted in everyday life . . . creating the remarkable
> confidence of *community in anonymity* which is the hallmark of modern nations.
>   (Anderson 1983: 39–40; emphasis and bracketed material added)

Benedict Anderson is interested in the historical formation of nation states
at the dawn of modernity: their creation via the printing press, vernacular
languages and a shared imagination of historical time. The media events that have
engaged Elihu Katz, Daniel Dayan and their colleagues come from a later stage
in the history of the nation state or in the life of new states, born after World
War II, such as Israel, or reborn, such as post-communist Poland, in the age of
television. Television permits a level of national integration in both large and
small states that was difficult to achieve, except on a reduced scale, in the age of
the printing press. The "high holy days of television," as Dayan and Katz term
televised media events, had their more ephemeral and transitory counterparts
in the "extras" of newspapers, and the moments when the natural priorities of the
telegraph were suspended in order to achieve a relatively simultaneous focus of
attention among widely dispersed readers, or in extraordinary public gatherings
where news was read or repeated to the entire community. In the age of television,
media events burst localized confines and take on a national and even international character because of the migratory habits of television signals, the global
makeup of international relations under the reign of satellites and the emphasis
this gives to the relations of peoples rather than merely states.

Nations live not only in historical time but also in media time. The remarkable
confidence in the "community of anonymity" of which Anderson speaks refers
to the ordinary, daily habits through which the world is confirmed in communication. He notes Hegel's line that newspapers serve modern man as a substitute
for morning prayers, implying that the line dividing the modern from the
premodern was drawn when people began their day attending to their state and
nation rather than to their God. He points to a moment when media time, as
opposed to liturgical time, began to provide the temporal architecture of daily life;
when the rhythms of the media displaced the rhythms of church and synagogue
and were overlaid on the "natural" rhythms – seasonal, calendrical – of daily life.
When newspapers broke through into the Sabbath, when reading the Sunday
paper became as common as attending religious services, a new qualitatively
different rhythm was imposed on the week. In short, each medium imposes its
own distinctive temporal order on its audience; it confirms the steady stream of
ongoing reality – the existence of an external world that is in order within a shared
community of awareness – within a particular organization of time: by the month,
by the week, by the day, by the hour, by the minute. As one widely used broadcast
slogan has it, "You give us twenty minutes and we'll give you the World." Media
events, on the other hand, are eruptions within both media and natural routines.
Media events declare holidays, a time out from the everyday character of both
media time and natural time, the time of communication and the time of history.
Media events reconfigure attention by disrupting the predictable regularity of the

real, the habitual flow of routines of reading and viewing. They are deviations from the norms of media and the ongoing certainty of history and of the nation itself.

Nations live within not only history but also geography. They exist not only in media time but also in media space. Nations are sociological organisms, but unlike crowds, gatherings, classes and status groups, they are boundary maintaining ones. Moreover, the boundaries that nations maintain are both geographic and symbolic. Geographic boundaries are the most common and the clearest: the customs and immigration points at which one passes into and out of the physical space of the nation. At such boundaries identities are confirmed and implanted: citizen, migrant, guest worker, alien, green card holder, and, on rarer occasions, enemy. In political terms and from the standpoint of the nation, these are points of passage between sacred and profane space – space where one is "known" and protected or unknown and unprotected.

Nations are also symbolic space – spaces of meanings, values and identities. Geographic and symbolic space come together in the immigration office on the national frontier. But symbolic space, while bounded, is inherently vaguer than geographical space because it refers to the points at which people pass out from under the sacred canopy of the nation: the system of meanings, values and identities which legitimate membership. There are places (and occasions) where people are marked, or mark themselves, as apostates, heretics, outsiders, interlopers, subversives, traitors or, simply, UnAmerican. These points are highly contestable because they are inherently vague and indeterminate – boundaries as often stumbled across as deliberately breached. We can all tell tales of the student who tried so hard to be a good student – to identify with the sacred values of the academy – that he blundered into cheating and found himself expelled. Indeed, the line between honest academic effort and plagiarism, let us say, is often obscure and sometimes shifts without advanced notice. So too with nations. Conduct or identities or values which seemed not only legitimate but honored all of a sudden become marks of treachery, deceit, disloyalty and shame. More than one person has faced a moment on the gallows, and not solely in *The Crucible*, saying "What did I do wrong?" or "I was only doing what everyone does."

The symbolic space of the nation is primarily represented within the media and accounts for the often ferocious struggles among groups over the portrayal of identities, conduct and values in news and entertainment. But this daily and largely invisible struggle, one that goes on behind the screen and the front page and in the silent "lair of the skull," sometimes erupts through ordinary media time and space to become a distinct ceremony: a marked rite of explicit passage when bodies are stigmatized, reputations destroyed and citizens expelled into a guild of the guilty. It is to these explicit rituals of degradation and excommunication that we now turn.

TYPES OF MEDIA EVENTS

Dayan and Katz distinguish among three kinds of media events: contests, conquests and coronations. They admit to the fuzziness of these categories and acknowledge that given events pass through all three stages: from contests to conquests to coronations such that any one type of event is latent in the other two. Contests they think of as the most democratic of media events: the events that should be the hallmark of democratic societies. Contests are encounters between equals who "play by the rules" and resolve differences by tests of strength and skill. They are events in which the winners are gracious and the losers sporting. In fact, athletic events such as the Olympics or the SuperBowl are primary examples of contests which serve as media events. In politics, the best examples are political conventions and elections in which the audience casts its lot and loyalty, the vanquished concede defeat and pledge cooperation with the victor and reaffirm the legitimacy of the political tradition. While contests are organized around explicit conflicts, they are rational legal ones, governed by rules of authority, shared commitments and standards of fairness.

However, in the course of outlining media events Dayan and Katz point to some of the more troubling episodes in American political history in the age of television: the Army–McCarthy hearings, the Kefavuer hearings, the Iran–Contra hearings, the Watergate hearings, and, perhaps most importantly, the hearings of the House UnAmerican Affairs Committee. These episodes do not easily fit within the category of contests, nor are they, except secondarily, conquests or coronations. In fact, these quasi-judicial hearings, which are certainly among the most important media events in the history of American television, have received relatively little attention in the media events literature.

It seems perverse to call these episodes "contests" even though a form of jousting is the televised centerpiece. They are not of the same order as political conventions or sporting events. Often they do not follow a regular or expected democratic script. They are chaotic and ungoverned and, in their own way, quite frightening. What they share in common is a peculiar bitterness and intensity that time does not easily wash away. Such events generate protracted conflict with long-term political consequences that are acridly partisan. Moreover, they represent susceptibilities of both the left and the right. These ceremonies sometimes are enacted by the right in determined search of left-wing enemies; sometimes by the left in search of right-wing enemies.

All of these quasi-judicial ceremonies attempted to send a person or persons into internal exile. But the individuals were relatively unimportant compared to the discovery process of the hearings themselves. The hearings did not attempt to heal a breach in the society, but to discover and implant a fissure or, at the least, to increase the vexious precision with which major segments of the society alienated one another. Such events did not promote reconciliation around core values before, during or after the ceremony but generated and intensified struggles over the very definition of those values. As media events often create rather than merely reveal consensus, so the hearings in question created rather than merely revealed conflict. The intensity of the struggle over the question "What is an American?" is complicated by a peculiar feature of the United States, namely that no one ascriptively represents or possesses the sacred center of the political society. Everyone has to prove their worth and loyalty to the sacral values in the act of discovering them. The social dramas of excommunication not only create and reveal the basic values of the society but also reveal and create the social structure and its fundamental and often irreconcilable cleavages.

This class of media events stretches from the investigations of UnAmerican activity in the late 1940s through a new form of political theater that emerged in the last decade: the bitter, protracted and televised struggles over nominations to seats on the United States Supreme Court. The first was over the nomination and eventual rejection of Robert Bork; the second was the even more bitter and controversial struggle over the nomination and eventual confirmation of Clarence Thomas. These media events fit the general pattern of a contest but they are also quasi-judicial investigations that assumed the form of a rite of excommunication inscribing the boundaries of political action and discourse onto the bodies of the nominees who came before the Senate Judiciary Committee for official scrutiny. Rather than treating the entire class of excommunication rites, I want to focus on the confirmation or discomfirmation hearings of Robert Bork. The Clarence Thomas hearings present some special problems because of the way in which they engage questions of race and gender, and passions surrounding those hearings still run quite high. However, the Bork hearings set the stage and can represent the general type. Ten years beyond the Bork hearings, the political passions which surrounded them have cooled, though they have not been completely extinguished. The episode is discussable, perhaps, with less emotion and partisanship. Or so I hope. In framing the discussion I want to tack back and forth between the specifics of this one case and the general theoretical framework proposed by Katz and Dayan.

STRUGGLES OVER SUPREME COURT NOMINATIONS

There is a long history of nomination struggles over appointments to the Supreme Court (Carter 1994). However, for the first 150 years nominees did not appear before the Senate to testify and the struggles were confined to the parties, the Senate and the President. Throughout the nineteenth century about one in four of Supreme Court nominees was rejected by the Senate. The most acrimonious fight in the history of the court – until Bork – was over Louis D. Brandeis in 1916. He was accused by six former presidents of the American Bar Association, along with senators, of being radical, anti-establishment and anti-big business and there was more than a little anti-semitism thrown in as well. However, the first nominee to testify before the Senate Judiciary Committee was Harlan Fiske Stone in 1925. Thereafter nominees appeared intermittently. William O. Douglas, for example, did not; Felix Frankfurter did, though he initially refused. The practice of testifying became standard in 1955, the year after Brown v. Board of Education, because Southern senators wanted to inquire as to nominees' views on integration – surely a sign of trouble ahead. In recent decades two presidents have lost on significant nominations: Lyndon Johnson lost in his attempt to elevate Abe Fortas to Chief Justice (ethics); Richard Nixon lost on Clement Haynsworth (ethics) and Harrold Carswell (competence). There have been disreputable struggles as well. Both Brandeis, as I said, and William Brennan were attacked on grounds of religion (Jewish and Catholic respectively); religion surfaced in the Bork nomination, though in his case it was his non-religion. A low point in the debate occurred when Senator Howell Heflin of Alabama announced that he could not vote for Bork because Bork did not believe in God. Thurgood Marshall's confirmation evoked a familiar racism, though he was thought to be too liberal and judicially activist as well (a reversed premonition of the Bork fight).

Struggle and conflict over Supreme Court nominations are likely to intensify in the future, partly as a legacy of the Bork and Thomas hearings themselves and the bitterness that they left in the Congress and the polity. But a more substantial political reason for the growing controversy around Supreme Court nominations is that the Constitution and constitutional law is, with the federalization of the law, no longer aloof and remote from the daily lives of citizens. These decisions increasingly penetrate to the deepest concerns of people and to the most intimate spheres of life and often challenge the authority of institutions, such as families, that generally have been beyond the reach of the law. But controversy is not what is at issue here. Rather, the controversies are now played out on television as media events: dramas encased in particular symbolic forms, proceeding along a scripted path and played before an audience sutured in like a Greek chorus.

The Bork hearings occurred before the Judiciary Committee of the United States Senate, chaired by Senator Joseph Biden (D–Del.), in September 1987. They were the most important political and, perforce, journalistic event of that political season which led up to the presidential nominating primaries. The event shaped, often silently, the primaries and the 1988 presidential campaign and election which occurred just a year later. And they remain shaping events in American politics, contributing to the ideological bitterness of party politics and forming the background and sub-text of all subsequent appointments to the Supreme Court.[1] They contributed a new phrase to the American language: "to be borked." The entire episode gives concrete meaning, in case it needed reinforcement, to Alasdair MacIntyre's comment that "modern politics cannot be a matter of moral consensus; it is a civil war carried on by other means."

The initiating moment occurred on June 26, 1987 with the surprise resignation of Justice Lewis Powell. Powell had been appointed by President Nixon to replace a legendary liberal justice, Hugo Black. While Black was a conservative southerner (he had at one time been a member of the Klu Klux Klan), he became the staunchest legal defender of civil liberties, particularly the First Amendment, for an entire generation of the court. Powell's nomination was not gleefully received by the liberal community because he had the reputation of a conservative and was denounced by the National Lawyers' Guild as a judge "who does not twist or bend the Constitution, rather he totally ignores it" (Bronner 1989: 22).

The first surprise following Powell's resignation, and no one was more startled than Lewis Powell himself, was his transformation into a liberal and a hero of the liberal community. However conservative, Powell looked rather more moderate than anyone President Ronald Reagan was rumored to have under consideration as his replacement. Whomever Reagan chose was likely to upset the delicate balance of the court and push it in a more conservative direction. Powell's transformation into a liberal was, however, an anticipation of the nomination of Robert Bork, even though that nomination was hardly assured. Bork did not believe he would receive a long sought after call to the highest judicial tribunal. He had been passed over earlier in favor of Sandra Day O'Connor and Antonin Scalia after making the White House short list of potential nominees. Indeed, he had been slated for a position on the court as far back as 1975 when John Paul Stevens assumed the seat of William O. Douglas.

Despite Bork's doubts, President Reagan nominated him and forwarded his name to the Senate to "advise and consent" on July 1, 1987, six days following Powell's resignation. His candidacy came to a sour end four months later, on October 23, 1987, when the Senate voted against confirmation 58–42, the largest margin of defeat (and the largest number of votes cast) of a Supreme Court nomination in the history of United States politics.

The entire affair then trailed off from tragedy to farce in the aborted nomination of Douglas Ginsburg for the seat and the subsequent withdrawal of Ginsburg's name when it was discovered that he had used marijuana while a professor at the Harvard Law School.[2] Another conservative jurist, Anthony Kennedy, was then nominated and confirmed in a more or less perfunctory fashion.

I described the trajectory of events as moving from tragedy to farce not because I think that Bork's defeat was a personal tragedy of melodramatic magnitude but for three disproportions contained in the incident. First, there was the disproportion between Bork's standing in the legal community, particularly the academic legal community, the magnitude and ignominiousness of his defeat and the intensity of the bitterness engendered by his nomination on both sides of the Senate as well as the deep ideological division that it left behind as a permanent scar on American politics. Bruce Ackerman, the Sterling Professor of Law and Political Science at Yale, where Bork had been a member of the faculty, is a man of genuinely liberal sentiments and he did not support Bork's nomination. None the less, he commented at the conclusion of the Bork hearings:

> I begin where [Former] Chief Justice Burger (in his comments on Bork's qualifications) ended: when judged by normal personal and professional criteria, Robert Bork is among the best qualified candidates for the Supreme Court of this or any other era. Few nominees in our history compare with him in the range of their professional accomplishments – as public servant, private practitioner, appellate judge, legal scholar. Few compare in the seriousness of their lifelong engagement with the fundamental questions of constitutional law. Of course, Bork's answers to these questions are controversial. But who can be

surprised by that? Even those like myself who disagree with Bork both can and should admire the way he has woven theory and practice, reason and passion, into a pattern that expresses so eloquently our deepest hopes for a life in the law. The Republic needs more people like Robert Bork. It is a tragedy that the Republic should repay him for his decades of service by publicly humiliating him.

(Ackerman 1988: 1164)

There was, in short, a tragic disproportion between Bork's standing in both the legal and social communities at the beginning of the hearings and his degraded status at their conclusion. He journeyed in four months from being at the top of the social and legal register to being a virtual outcast wearing the public stigmata of a racist, sexist, sterilizer of women and invader of the bedroom.

The second disproportion was that Bork had been unanimously confirmed by the same Senate Judiciary Committee and by the full Senate, peopled by most of the same senators, on two earlier occasions: first, when he was appointed Solicitor General of the United States (the government's chief lawyer) in 1973 and later as a judge on the United States Court of Appeals for the District of Columbia Circuit in 1982. In neither case did any controversy emerge concerning his legal writings. No disgrace had occurred in the meantime. He was criticized by some for firing Archibald Cox, the special prosecutor in the Watergate investigation, during the so-called Saturday Night Massacre, but he had done so on the recommendation of the sitting Attorney General (Elliott Richardson) who urged Bork to stay on the job and carry out President Nixon's order.[3] None of the cases in which he had voted with the majority as an appellate judge had been overturned by the Supreme Court. In the vast majority of the cases decided during his tenure, Bork had voted with liberals on the court and was in the majority in 95 per cent of the cases. Even the most liberal judge in the DC Circuit, Abner Mikva, had spoken well of Bork's legal competence.

The third disproportion which suggests the narrative of tragedy was that the principals – the Senate, Judge Bork, President Reagan – were led inexorably to the denouement: once the fat was in the fire events careered almost out of control. The Senate, in general, seeks to avoid these types of nakedly ideological confrontations at all costs. That body dislikes taking on a strong, popular president, let alone a lame duck in his waning days as was Reagan in 1987. But, even more, the Senate is a club and does not welcome confirmation battles. They are bruising and time-consuming; they cleave the Senate ideologically and are politically risky. Unlike legislative battles, confirmation struggles are not at all abstract. The Senate has to look a nominee in the eye after he has personally visited every key member of the body; they must reject a person – a person whom they know, indeed, who is a Washington insider – rather than an abstract issue.

If the Senate must get into a nomination struggle, senators try to avoid political issues and ideology and stay on the plane of personal ethics and legal competence, even if competence and ethics serve only as a surrogate for issues and ideology. Ethics fights can be resolved in terms of values – dishonesty, corruption – that cut across ideologies and interest groups. Similarly, an issue such as legal competence offers a handy mode of struggle, since judicial competence preserves the useful fiction that when a case is badly decided or misdecided it is a result of legal incompetence not ideology.

Fighting on general grounds of ethics and judicial competence has another advantage over contests framed by narrow legal issues. While senators are largely lawyers by training, they do not know much about constitutional law. Thus, when nominations start to turn on fine points of law, senators risk the appearance of being puppets on the string of their staffs – a problem of private face – or on the strings of lobbyists and interests groups – a problem of public face. Many senatorial staffs, particularly those of members of the Judiciary Committee, include graduates of Harvard, Yale, Columbia, Michigan and other distinguished law schools who have earlier clerked for Supreme Court justices. Interest groups and lobbyists can employ attorneys to build cases against nominees which are based on fine points and issues in the law. To paraphrase Michael Pertschuk, a lawyer, law professor and former head of the Federal Trade Commission who has reflected on the Bork case, the trick is for staff and lobbyists to make senators act like puppets without them knowing it (Pertschuk and Schaetzel 1989: Ch. 5).

So, while confirmation battles are hard on senators, they offer real opportunities for senatorial staffs along with lobbyists and interest groups, none of whom has to stand for re-election. A real live nominee allows abstract issues to be confronted in the form of an actual body. Vague feelings can be collected, crystallized and incarnated in one person who then can be canonized or demonized: made to embody the deepest hopes and expectations or fears and hatreds of the body politic.[4]

It was difficult to oppose the Bork nomination on the normal basis of ethics and competence. Bork's conduct embodied no important issues of legal ethics. Indeed, the one controversial episode discovered in his past served only to sustain his reputation, since he had once threatened a public resignation from a Chicago law firm over an issue of anti-semitism. Even after exhaustive investigation, including the revelation of the list of movies that he rented from video stores,[5] his personal life appeared beyond reproach. Early rumors of excessive drink, about the conduct of his wife, and hints of tax evasion did not pan out. And his legal competence was beyond question. There was, however, the aforementioned Archibald Cox firing which remained an issue in Washington however much Watergate had faded from memory in the rest of the country.

So, despite senatorial reluctance to enter a confirmation battle, this particular drama moved to its conclusion largely out of the hands of the principal performers. The Senate Judiciary Committee and the Senate had to vote. Reagan, as was his way, refused to withdraw the nomination, even after it was in deep trouble, unless Robert Bork requested him to do so and Bork would make no such request. If he was to go down to defeat and to have a life in the law ended (and it did end), he wanted his enemies and denouncers to have to do it publicly, on the record.

Thus, the episode was brought to a conclusion by Robert Byrd, the Senate majority leader. Byrd threatened to suspend debate for an indefinite period, which meant not only leaving the Supreme Court a justice short as its new term, with a full docket, opened but also imperiling Reagan's ability to appoint a replacement for Lewis Powell before he himself left office. Byrd informed Reagan of his decision, Reagan informed Bork, and a motion to end debate on the floor of the Senate was entered. At that moment the name of Robert Bork was brought to the Senate for consent and, as mentioned earlier, he was soundly rejected.

SENATE HEARINGS AS MEDIA EVENTS

If the disconfirmation of Robert Bork was something other than a personal tragedy, how do we frame it? The simplest formulation through which to view the confirmation struggle is simply as another episode in the perennial struggle of the left and the right in American politics. And, of course, it was precisely that. To be more partisan about it, one can adopt the outlook of the left and celebrate the event as an auspicious moment when an inert people rose up in the name of a democratic culture to smote a reactionary judge and an ideologically driven president. (Pertschuk and Schaetzel 1989). Or one can adopt the outlook of the right and see it as another meretricious attack on conservatives by left-wing media and journalists and the callow radical organizations they represent: organizations, individuals and groups who seek to win on television and the courts what they cannot otherwise win in the ballot box and the legislature (McGuigan and Weyrich 1990). There is argument and evidence to support both these views. It is certainly the case that one could justify rejection of Bork on virtually neutral grounds of judicial temperament. He was seeking confirmation to a body that depends on high levels of cooperation, whatever disagreements might exist among the justices, and Bork displayed in his writings and speeches an almost congenital willingness to pick a fight. Senators could have also rejected him solely on the basis of disagreements on judicial interpretation without framing this as a matter of consonance with American values.

There are, however, reasons for rejecting, or at least going beyond, all of these outlooks. Treating the form and script of the hearings merely as another political incident fails to capture and record the richness, complexity and enduring consequence of the process. To treat the conflict as an ideological struggle ignores the fact that the bloody and extended nomination and hearing process did not significantly alter the ideological outcome of the result. The nation still ended up with a conservative justice on the court, though in the person of the somewhat colorless Anthony Kennedy. Indeed, Alan Dershowitz, no friend of the right, described Anthony Kennedy, Bork's ultimate replacement, as someone who "thinks like Bork and writes like Powell": a back-handed compliment expressing reservations about how much of a victory Bork's opponents actually won (McGuigan and Weyrich 1990: xv).[6]

While I realize many will contend that the course of the Bork hearings was determined by ideology and politics and would have run their foreordained course without television, I want to argue that the fact that it was a televised media event was organic rather than ancillary to both the process and the outcome.[7] If we assume, at least for sake of argument, that the hearings were more than politics as usual, what kind of a parenthesis should we draw around this moment in history? How do we move beyond a thin, instrumental notion of politics so that we might recover the inherent drama and symbolic efficacy of the proceedings where the very fate of the nation seemed to be at stake? Were the hearings, then, a media event, one of the high holy days of American television?

The hearings do satisfy many of the ground conditions that Elihu Katz and his colleagues have elaborated as the criteria defining the type. First, the hearings were broadcast live and we were transported to the place where the event was taking place. The hearings were carried in their entirety on Cable News Network, the Public Broadcasting Service and C-Span and were repeated in both prime-time and late night slots. In some ways it was the first media event for cable television, since it took advantage of the expanded bandwidth of cable and the need of that expanded system for programming. However, its presence on cable meant that the networks did not have to televise the hearings and could content themselves with long excerpts on the nightly newscast along with features on magazine and late night programming.

Second, the hearings were not initiated by the media but by the advise and consent clause of the Constitution, the rules of the Senate and the Democratic majority on the Senate Judiciary Committee. While the hearings were organized with media coverage in mind, in ways we shall see, they would have occurred even if television failed to show up in the hearing room.

Third, the hearings possessed elements of high drama and were emotion and symbol laden. A conclusion to the drama was foreordained, though its exact nature remained a matter of suspense and uncertainty throughout. The outcome was rife with consequences for all of the participants: the senators conducting the hearing (Joseph Biden in particular), Robert Bork, President Reagan, the respective political parties, the journalists, lobbyists and interest groups that gathered within the hearing room and the corridors outside, and for the nation that assembled as an imagined and imaginary community.

Fourth, the event was preplanned and carefully so. In fact, the hearing was delayed from July 1 to September 15 – the longest delay in the modern history of such hearings – to allow sufficient time for the planning. Time was needed for groups working behind the scenes to put plans in place to oppose Bork but, just as much, for the press and the political system to bring the event into focus, to allow for promotion to work, for tension to build and for expectations to surface. Pre-event efforts largely centered on the Senate in a campaign to forestall senators from reaching a public decision on Bork's qualifications thereby focusing attention and uncertainty on the deliberative process of the hearing itself.

Fifth, the event was framed in time and space in such a way as to sustain and hold interest. It was sufficiently circumscribed in time for a coherent event. The effective dates were from September 15 when the hearings opened through October 6 when the committee voted 9–5 against Bork and forwarded their recommendation to the full Senate. However, the hearings in which Robert Bork appeared on stage, the core of the drama, occurred over five days from September

15 though 19. The event was spatially framed as well, not only by its enclosure within the Senate caucus room but also, as we shall see, by limitations placed on the number of television cameras that could be used to record the event thereby ensuring that only a small portion of the space was visible to the television audience.

Sixth, the event was dominated by a limited number of personalities. The dramatic structure of media events demand an antagonist and protagonist or two teams squared off against one another. All such elements were present here. The centerpiece of the hearings was Robert Bork himself, the hero, and it was his failure to live up to his heroic status on which the matter turned. Better yet, the event was dominated by a protagonist (Bork) and an antagonist (Edward Kennedy), representing, depending on one's disposition, the forces of light and darkness, and around whom flowed the dramatic action. Senator Joseph Biden was cast in the role of referee, there to ensure fairness, and the senators themselves played minor, supporting roles as members of Republican and Democratic teams.

Seventh, and finally, the televised hearings were not backed by the force of a social norm; they were not required viewing and thus fail to satisfy fully one of the criteria put forward for media events. Viewing was not obligatory at least compared to many other events in the catalogue of episodes that Katz and others have collected. There was no communal insistence that one abandon one's other roles and commitments in favor of viewing television. While we have no measures, I doubt that there was much communal and neighborly viewing beyond pubs, dormitories and other such places where people normally gather to watch television in groups. Still, the hearings attracted a large if uncounted audience in their multiple showings. I shall return to this somewhat irregular quality of this particular media event subsequently.[8]

We can turn the Bork hearings around and look at them in terms of the pragmatics, syntactics and semantics of the event. Pragmatically the Bork hearings constituted a sustained invasion of public life into private space. People may not have dressed up to watch them or invited in friends to share in viewing, though some of that undoubtedly went on among the politically committed, but the response to the event by phone, letter and contributions was quite exceptional. And this is a critical point: the hearings produced high levels of political mobilization and involvement. Paradoxically enough, the hearings may have produced more involvement than the presidential elections which followed a year later. In other words, the audience had a particular space reserved at the event: it was sutured in, not merely as spectator, but as judge. The involvement took the form of a plebiscite and was so monitored by the Congress.

Syntactically, the event was an interruption in the flow of daily life, though hardly as dramatic as, say, the Kennedy funeral, at least in so far as it disrupted the normal flow of television viewing and what we might call the off cycle flow of politics.

It is the semantics of the event that seems most problematic. The Bork hearings do not fit easily, as I earlier argued, within the three categories that Katz uses to classify media events. The hearings constituted neither contest nor conquest nor coronation. More ambiguously, the hearings were all of these things simultaneously.[9] To some degree it was a contest, though one played without agreed rules, one that magnified conflict rather than miniaturized it and obeyed no fixed cyclical pattern. To some degree it was a conquest with an indeterminate conquistador, where the hero and anti-hero remained ambiguous and from which no great man emerged. And to some degree, it was a coronation (or anticoronation) which reminded society of its basic values by representing their negation in the form of Robert Bork, an event that renewed the social contract by deliberately constructing a political center that had no room for the likes of Robert Bork.

THE STRUCTURE OF THE BORK HEARINGS

Here is the hypothesis in play: I would like to consider the details of the confirmation hearings of Robert Bork as an archetype of a hitherto unclassified group of media events: ceremonies at the social level of excommunication defining the permissible range of social discourse; and, at the individual level, of status degradation marking out the consequences for transgressing this range. With that in mind, let us look at the details of the nomination and the hearings.

The dramatic center of the struggle over the nomination of Robert Bork to the Supreme Court was the hearings which opened in the Senate caucus room some seventy-seven days after his name was sent to the upper chamber by Ronald Reagan. Those intent on defeating the appointment early on adopted the strategy of turning the hearings into a plebiscite in which his confirmation would be determined by public opinion more than by the independent judgment of members of the Senate Judiciary Committee, and this, beyond the entertainment value of the proceedings, explains the presence of television.[10]

Conducting a plebiscite however requires time and that was provided by the chairman of the committee, Joseph Biden. Biden, who was also an announced candidate for the presidential nomination of the Democratic party, postponed hearings on the appointment until after the summer recess in early September. There were contingencies in this case as with all media events, and any alteration in the contingencies would have led to a different outcome: if Republicans had controlled the Senate and the Committee, if Biden had not been a presidential candidate,[11] and if it had occurred at a time other than the summer because that is when a large number of unpaid, free summer interns are available to do the enormous amount of detailed work necessary for interest groups to mount a formal campaign of opposition.[12]

The summer hiatus was used, in the words of the opposition, to freeze the Senate; each senator was spoken to and asked to pledge to avoid public commitment for or against the nomination until the conclusion of the hearings. In fact, on the day of the announcement of the nomination 1,700 model editorials were mailed to newspapers nationwide arguing for the virtues of senatorial discretion and silence until all of the evidence was in on Robert Bork.[13]

The summer granted the time necessary to create what was called the "book of Bork," a painstaking and detailed compilation of court decisions, speeches, lectures and journal articles delivered by Bork over his long career along with video and audio tapes of conferences, proceedings and question and answer sessions in which he had participated. The "book of Bork" in turn provided a steady stream of press releases and news conferences, in all forms and media, detailing Bork's "position" on a wide variety of legal and social issues and providing forums for attacks, declarations, and announcements of one group after another that was opposed to his elevation to the Supreme Court.

Finally, the summer recess, a down-time for Washington news, permitted stories to be developed focusing on the anticipated drama of the hearings and kept the story of the nomination alive at a time when it would have fallen out of the news. All in all, the summer created a time and space for mounting a political campaign on the model of a presidential campaign; in effect, an election to the Supreme Court that, by certain measures, created greater public engagement than the presidential election a year later. Not only did the Bork disconfirmation have the intensity of a short political campaign, it showed us what such a campaign might look like.

The Bork nomination was extensively covered by the media as perhaps goes without saying. The story, in one form or another, was the lead news items for much of four months and dominated the evening news during the hearings themselves. As I said earlier, the hearings were carried live on C-Span, PBS and CNN and replayed on taped delay in the evening and during the late night virtually without editing.

For all the news and hype, the entire process allowed for few degrees of freedom. It came down to a question of who would win, Bork or Kennedy, the main combatants, and behind them the Republicans or Democrats, the President or Majority Leader. Within this overarching framework various sub-plots or duels developed between Bork and Senator Arlen Specter, between Senator Orrin Hatch and Senator Kennedy, Senator Thurmond and Senator Biden. Finally, for part of the hearings, Senator Biden's quest for the nomination provided not only a continuing story but also a critical framework for reviewing the play.

The hearings themselves were so meticulously staged that the only natural part of them – in Oscar Wilde's sense of being natural – was Robert Bork (as I hope to show) and being natural proved to be Bork's undoing. In order to set out the meticulousness of the staging let me make some simple distinctions, guided by Erving Goffman (1959: 112ff), concerning stages and framing devices. A stage may be defined as any place that is bounded to some degree by barriers to perception and is a site of continuing action. Thus, when a performance is given it is on a stage erected so as to bind perception in various ways and to place a boundary around time as well. For any given performance, front stage refers to the place where the performance is given and action in this region is subject to control by certain standards of politeness, decorum and performance. Because the Democrats controlled the stage and, to a lesser degree, the standards of performance, they were in a better position to enforce controls over the stage and the performances thereon. Back stage may be defined as a place relative to a given performance where the impression fostered by the performance is knowingly contradicted. Here the capacity of a performance to express something beyond itself may be painstakingly fabricated and illusions and impressions are openly constructed. For example, whatever the seeming naturalness of Senators Kennedy and Biden, and presumably other senators, they had been carefully rehearsed backstage with the Harvard law professor Lawrence Tribe. Rehearsals covered not only the appropriate questions to ask but also matters of demeanor and legal bearing.[14] An Assistant Attorney General similarly was assigned to give stage directions to Bork, though his attempts were a failure as Bork preferred to rely on a demeanor that can only be called that of the law professor at a seminar. In any case the audience must be kept out of the back stage because here the impression regularly fostered in the main performance will be undermined as a matter of course.

It is in the nature of the case with televised media events that the camera is kept stable and motionless and that the stage is kept in meticulous order. Likewise, the back stage is kept isolated and out of view of the audience. The camera maintains barriers between front and back stage and the directions are designed to minimize or prevent leakage between the two regions.

The front stage of the hearing was that portion of the Senate caucus room that could be or, better, was allowed to be taken in by the camera. That consisted of the table at which Robert Bork and subsequent witnesses sat; the curved, empaneled, and continuous desk or dias at which fourteen senators sat; and the bay which separated them. The only leakage into the stage were glimpses of the audience, usually Bork's family, seated immediately behind the witness and, behind the senators, their aides listening to the proceedings, moving about, whispering into the ear of their chief or passing documents to the dias. The rest of the back region, consisting almost exclusively of journalists and lobbyists and the buzz of activity and movement surrounding them, was kept from view. At solemn movements the area behind the senators was cleared to minimize distraction and to heighten the dignity of the proceedings; for example, Senator Biden's opening speech, which was also the opening address of his presidential campaign, was kept clear of temporal and spatial intrusions. The stage itself was kept free of any action that might contradict the image of rectitude, control and jurisprudential dignity, that might contradict the impression being fostered.

The front stage was not only contrived but re-contrived. The last major event in the chamber was the Iran–Contra hearings featuring Oliver North. The senatorial lessons learned during those hearings led to new arrangements for the day when the Bork hearings opened. During the Iran–Contra hearings the senators sat at an elevated dias, in effect looking down at Oliver North in a witness chair below them. Moreover, still and television cameras were allowed into the bay between North and the senators so that the Marine Colonel could be "shot" from the front. On the one hand, this lent an inquisitorial air to the proceedings as stern senators looked down upon North who had to elevate his head in order to engage their gaze. Moreover, the presence of cameras in the bay allowed North to be photographed from below, particularly when he was standing to take the oath, and that, along with his inappropriate but necessary military uniform and decorations, gave him a heroic air and the status of the persecuted being called to account before the persecutors.

To prevent a reoccurrence of the dramatic detail of the Iran–Contra hearings, the caucus room was rearranged: the dias was lowered so that Bork and the senators had direct eye contact and a relationship of equality was established; the bay was collapsed to bring the senators and witness closer together at a more conversational distance; and frontal head shots were prevented by keeping the bay clear and allowing only two stationary cameras, one for left profiles of the witness, one for full frontal shots of the senators. The senators, particularly though not exclusively on the Democratic side of the dias, asked relatively few questions (except, and this is a special case, for Biden) and instead tended to give speeches concerning the majesty of the law and the transgressions of the nominee. In the latter hearings, flag waving reverted to the senators and Bork was left to explain the technical details of the law. As space was reconfigured, so too was time. There were relatively few breaks in the proceedings, even for vote calls on the floor of the Senate, and interruptions were pretty much geared to the deadlines of reporters, though some were inserted out of courtesy to Bork who was a heavy smoker. In any event, these profanities which regulated the structure and flow of the event were not allowed to intrude onto the front stage.

In addition to staging the hearings and framing them as an inquiry into the qualifications of Robert Bork to sit on the high court, the event was "enframed" as well and this, for me, is the critical part of the process.

In July Ronald Reagan introduced Bork to the nation at the press conference at which he announced the nomination. Following the conference, as Bork walked to the west wing of the White House, he passed an office with a television set tuned to C-Span. Senator Kennedy was already addressing the nation and announcing his opposition to Bork's nomination in the following words:

> Robert Bork's America is a land in which women would be forced into back alley abortions, blacks would sit at segregated lunch counters, rogue police could break down citizens' doors in midnight raids, school children could not be taught about evolution, writers and artists could be censored at the whim of government, and the doors of the federal courts would be shut on the fingers of millions of citizens for whom the judiciary is – and often is the only – protector of the individual rights that are the heart of our democracy.
>
> America is a better and freer nation than Robert Bork thinks. Yet in the current delicate balance of the Supreme Court, his rigid ideology would tip the scales of justice against the kind of country America is and ought to be.
>
> The damage that President Reagan will do through this nomination, if it is not rejected by the Senate, could live on far beyond the end of his presidential term. President Reagan is still our president. But he should not be able to reach out from the muck of Irangate, reach into the muck of Watergate, and impose

his reactionary vision of the Constitution on the Supreme Court and on the next generation of Americans. No justice would be better than this injustice.

(Bronner 1989: 98–9)

Bork immediately dismissed Kennedy's speech as the ranting of a maniac at best, standard political hyperbole at its worst. He underestimated the power of Kennedy and the mood of the political season. Even more he failed to notice the real argument in Kennedy's accusations. Kennedy was not repeating standard political charges that Bork was too far to the right or too much of a conservative. Left and right, Democratic and Republican, radical and conservative do not appear in his address. He was laying down two themes of the hearings, one major and effective, one minor and ineffective. The minor case was that Bork would tip the delicate balance of the court. But the major theme, the theme that was Bork's undoing, was the charge, here stated implicitly, that Bork was outside of the "mainstream of constitutional jurisprudence." In effect, Bork stood accused of being UnAmerican, of having drifted outside of the sacred values of the country, of leaving the canopy under which his fellow citizens dwelt in harmony and agreement. As Fred Wertheimer of Common Cause, one of the interest groups that led the fight against Bork later asserted:

From the beginning the administration was trying to make this a partisan battle and a liberal–conservative contest. They wanted it in its most political terms. Our approach was to say "No, no, no. By anyone's standards – liberal, moderate conservative – this man is outside."

(Pertschuk and Schaetzel 1989: 117)

But, outside of what? As the hearings developed the answer would be clear: outside of the American way of life and thought.

Following Kennedy's speech, the fat was in the fire. The immense prestige of the Kennedy name was now in play, prestige that was much larger then than now. And so, as the hearings opened, Robert Bork was more on trial for his beliefs than merely a nominee to the court. Bork had allowed himself to be nominated and, he thought, considered on the basis of his ethics and competence and on these grounds he had no concern. While he was to the right ideologically, most of his views were commonplace among large segments of the legal community, including the academic legal community, and, he felt, certainly within the boundaries of permissible opinion – an elastic but none the less identifiable category. Now, quite unexpectedly, and personally unprepared, he found himself part of a moral drama to be played out during thirty-two hours of testimony over five days.

Let me reiterate: the purpose of the hearings before the Senate Judiciary Committee was, at one level, to confirm or disconfirm the nomination of Robert Bork to a seat on the Supreme Court. But, as staged on television, as a media event, it became a recurring episode in the dramatic effort to define the boundaries – spiritual, attitudinal, moral – of American life, here innocently named the "mainstream." But, again, where is the mainstream? What are the symbolic parentheses that mark the inside and outside of American life? That such parentheses exist no one doubts, but they are, like all symbolic boundaries, vague, without precise definition and location and are subject to change with alarming suddenness. The attempt to place Bork outside the mainstream of constitutional jurisprudence, outside the sacred canopy of the constitution, to deny him the status of one of "We, the people," was from his standpoint an act of political and symbolic vandalism. Looked at from another angle, however, it was an event as periodically necessary, if uncyclical, as a state funeral, coronation or presidential inaugural: one of the forms in which the social order is marked and enclosed in space and time: in which the contours of society are engraved into the bodies of its citizens.[15]

In America, Lewis Hartz says in his great book *The Liberal Tradition in America*, law feeds on the corpse of philosophy (1955: 208–9). Better, in America, law feeds on the corpse of culture. He was referring to not only the inordinate role that lawyers and courts play in American life but the degree to which philosophy and culture are instantiated through the legal or quasi-legal apparatus: how the courts or, in this case the Senate gathered as a court, are the dramatic center in American life occupying a place elsewhere occupied by castles and cathedrals.

The hearings thus became a particular kind of media event: an act of excommunication from the sacred center as well as a status degradation ceremony, the functional equivalent of the military ceremony of the tearing off of epaulets and the breaking of a sword. This, however, is a form of excommunication that does not have a ritualized ceremony of readmission.[16] Put differently, the moral contours of American society were inscribed, however imperfectly, on the body of Robert Bork. This necessary social process is made the more imperative by the fact that the country (the United States) is something other than the culture (America) and because it is not a birthright society: membership in the former does not automatically guarantee membership in the latter. American culture is, though I do not know how to make this a precise comparison, thin and elusive, vague and indeterminate; it lacks, to quote oft made comments, an institutional anchor, is all sail and no ballast or is like a bonfire on an ice-floe.

RITUAL SACRIFICE

As the hearings proceeded, the question Robert Bork asked himself was "Why, oh why, me?" It was a question that he was to answer, though not very convincingly, in a jeremiad written after the hearings with the suggestively Calvinist title, *The Tempting of America: The Political Seduction of the Law* (1990).[17] Some answers come easily enough. The hearings took their bitterly ritualistic form because of the positions that he had taken on legal issues, the role that he had played in important cases before the appellate court, his generally conservative writing and, perhaps, most importantly, his support for cutting down the role of the courts in America life. But none of these answers satisfactorily accounts for the media event that his hearings became and the dramatic form that they took. The hearings of Sandra Day O'Connor and Antonin Scalia were not televised, subject to dramatic framing or the source of bitter discord. Why not? Why did the nomination of Anthony Kennedy not raise the same dramatic tension? At one level the answer is easy.

During his 1980 campaign, Ronald Reagan promised that "one of the first Supreme Court vacancies in my administration will be filled by the most qualified woman I can find." He delivered on his promise in the same way that President Eisenhower, trying to symbolize his identity with working-class Catholics in northern industrial states before the 1956 election, delivered with the appointment of William O. Brennan. Women's groups did not much take to a conservative jurist such as O'Connor but it was difficult to fight against her as the first woman nominated to the court. Similarly, Scalia was a well-known and liked figure in Washington: a famed wit, urbane, a lover of opera and a figure on the social scene, an Italian Catholic with ten children. As a jurist, and by conventional measures, he was well to the right of both O'Connor and Bork. He had voted with Bork on many of the cases that were at the center of Bork's confirmation fight, particularly the American Cyanamid case, though such cases did not become issues at Scalia's confirmation hearings. Both Bork and Scalia were favorites of the Reagan administration among jurists and Scalia's earlier elevation to the high court was, or so it was rumored, dictated by the fact that he was younger, did not smoke or drink, was not overweight (to list some of Bork's liabilities), and offered the prospect of a longer tenure on the court. Surely some of Bork's opponents felt that the intellectual combination of Scalia and Bork would be much more formidable than Scalia and Chief Justice William Rhenquist. But the lack of a contest surrounding the Scalia nomination resulted from the importance of the Italian vote – as a group Italians were among the primary enlistees in the corps of Reagan Democrats – in the important swing states of New York, New Jersey and Connecticut.

The question "Why Bork," comes down, therefore, to extrapolitical factors that feed into the dramatic structure of this type of media event. Bruce Ackerman admits that "we will never know" the answer but then adds the following:

> What we *can* say is that Bork's remarkable virtues crystallized the question. . . . Here was a man who transparently did not owe his nomination to his sex, race, religion, national origin or regional roots. He owed it to the power of his mind, the vigor of his ideas, and his demonstrated capacity to act on his convictions in moments of crisis.
>
> (Ackerman 1988: 1170)

My argument is exactly the opposite of Ackerman's. Bork was available to a confirmation hearing conducted as a status degradation ritual, a ritual to define the American way, to shape the contours of the social body, precisely because he was not a palimpsest. His personal body was uninscribed by the categorical structure of the culture so it was available to inscribe the moral and attitudinal boundaries of the social body. He was generically American and, as such, his defeat would not alienate any important social group *en bloc*. More importantly, Bork could be used to inscribe parentheses around permissible attitudes on a wide range of controversial social questions – abortion, women's rights, minority rights, etc. – because he was, socially speaking, a blank slate, unprotected by a predetermined cultural landscape that could insulate him from the most extreme and sometimes improbable charges. For example, had Orrin Hatch been offered the nomination, as it was rumored he had (both before and after Bork's defeat), many of the issues on which Bork was defeated could not have been raised without calling into question the citizenship of members of the Church of Latter Day Saints, which for reasons both political and constitutional no one was likely to do.

There is no doubt that the Bork nomination offered a Democrat controlled Senate an opportunity to get at Reagan through Bork (much as Republicans got at Lyndon Johnson through Abe Fortas). Unlike the Iran–Contra investigation, the Bork hearings offered an opportunity to strike a blow at Reagan without endangering the continuity of the presidency or the republic. And for all the partisanship of the hearings, there were strict limits beyond which the Senate would not go in attacking Reagan. Kennedy spoke for more than one senator when he said of Reagan:

> He's absolutely professional. When the sun goes down, the battles of the day are really gone. He gave the Robert Kennedy Medal which President Carter refused to do. He received my mother. . . . He's very sure of himself, and I think people sense that he's comfortable with himself, so why shouldn't I be comfortable with him? My family always had a healthy respect for him. . . . He's got a philosophy and he's fought for it. There's a consistency and continuity at a time when many others are flopping back and forth. And that's an important instructive lesson for politicians, that people admire that.
>
> (Bronner 1989: 104)

Caught in this vise, Robert Bork was interrogated and patronized and, on the Republican side, exalted and applauded during thirty-two hours of testimony. The "book of Bork" gave Democratic senators a ready supply of opinions, quips, off-hand comments as well as judicial opinions made up to twenty-five years earlier that he was asked to defend. Many of the questions concerned issues that were and remain matters of legitimate and important difference among legal scholars.[18] The purpose of the hearings was to demonstrate whether Bork was inside or outside the mainstream and the dramatic symmetries of the event demanded a protracted demonstration. Following the hearings Bork thought himself the victim of a high-tech lynching, though the phrase would not come into play until Clarence Thomas used it. In any event, it was not a line that was likely to have been much help to Robert Bork. Bork was no victim. He desperately wanted the seat on the court and systematically prepared himself for it. And there were good and sufficient reasons for the Senate to turn him down. The questions that remain concern the moral appropriateness of using confirmation hearings for a media event that is also a ritual of excommunication and status degradation, particularly when the person who is the object of the ritual action is allowed no redressive action or any similarly ritualized path of readmission. Bork's life in the law was ended. Within weeks he resigned from the United States Circuit Court of Appeals and embarked on a book and lecture tour aimed at seeking vengeance; he put on the social persona of a victim. He now appears occasionally on Court TV and otherwise shows up on talk television, but less as a lawyer and more as a social critic and all-around grouch.[19]

Where was Ronald Reagan in the midst of the Bork hearings? While he was a notoriously loyal president, Reagan disappeared during the hearings on a vacation to California and his administration pretty much let Bork hang. Spokesmen for the President said that it was unnecessary to mount a campaign on Bork's behalf because his sheer academic and legal brilliance would eventually carry the day. Indeed, both supporters and opponents of Bork made much of his vaunted legal and professorial abilities. Reagan and his administration emphasized his talents either because they believed in him or as a cover for their inactivity. There is, of course, the possibility that Reagan was testing the boundaries of the social with the Bork nomination. Reagan too was on the hunt for social parentheses and he sacrificed Bork rather than push against those margins once they had been discovered. That too presents a ritual symmetry: the principle in terms of which Robert Bork was legally executed was the principle in terms of which the Reagan administration was to live. Bork was a sacrifice to the social contract.

Bork's opponents also played up his talents because they felt that this would defeat him. That is, by building him up to heights that no one could maintain over thirty-two hours under the television lights, they prepared him for the fall. Both supporters and opponents peddled the line that his probity, wit and intelligence would carry the day. But intelligence and legal scholarship have nothing to do with a performance on television in the midst of a plebiscite. Bork was no Ollie North. To overcome his opposition he had to make viewers form an emotional bond with him. That Bork could not do, was incapable of doing, as long as he presented himself as a judge and legal scholar.

The official denouement of the Bork nomination was a 99-page report of the Senate Judiciary Committee to the full Senate advocating rejection. The first six pages of the report concern Bork's character as evidenced in the firing of Archibald Cox. The balance, 93 pages, is devoted to demonstrating that Bork was "outside the mainstream" of American life on issues such as civil rights, privacy, judicial restraint and executive powers. And thus the storm of the hearings ended with a whimper more than a bang.

INTEREST GROUPS AND MEDIA EVENTS

The Robert Bork hearings are a rich episode in the history of American politics. The coalition that formed to defeat Bork was the most successful such effort in the recent history of politics. Two hundred groups representing virtually every part of society were welded together in a concerted campaign and they held together, particularly at the critical point in the hearings. The groups that opposed Bork did not appear on camera and were missing from the front stage of the hearings. Such groups normally seek a place in the spotlight because of the opportunities such visibility offers for recruitment and fund raising and to represent the position and prestige of the organization within the political structure. In a coalition of 200 groups if one group broke ranks and insisted on appearing at the hearings, then all would demand a place, if only for competitive reasons.

But there was a deeper reason to keep the interest groups off television and out of the hearing room. If such groups appeared, they would be questioned by pro-Bork senators as follows: What is your membership? Whom do you represent? What are your policies? Where do you get your money? How much have you raised in the anti-Bork campaign? What are your views on religion, abortion, crime control, etc? If such questions were raised it would be much harder to maintain the line that Bork was out of the mainstream because the mainstream itself would have to be reconceived. If those questions were raised, the anti-Bork campaign would itself become an issue and the relations of the back stage of partisan politics would have leaked into the front stage of judicial examination. Thus, the anti-Bork coalition submerged the normal rhetoric of interest groups, stayed away from the front stage of the hearings (confining themselves to what was called the "War Room") and addressed themselves only to broad consensual values such as privacy rather than narrow divisive ones such as abortion.

The hearings also represented the application of the mechanics of presidential elections to the realm of presidential appointments and the cast of participants that work such elections – pollsters, media consultants, campaign organizers, lobbyists and interest groups – were reunited and absorbed into the process of governing beyond the election cycle. They brought with them devices that had become standard in campaigning such as the use of automated video and audio press releases and actualities and a relatively heavy reliance on advertising. The mechanics of presidential elections were being normalized and extended to more ordinary processes. We saw that again when such tactics were applied in the first year of the Clinton administration to the so-called debate on the health care bill. No wonder that the campaign against Bork was used as a model for study in the Stanford School of Business (Bronner 1989: 155).

I have argued that the form and script of the Bork hearings fit the model of a media event but are closer to the morally ambiguous genre of degradation ceremonies than are contests of national unity and reconciliation. Paradoxically, the defeat of Bork turned into a pyrrhic victory for his opponents. Perhaps it could only have been successful in political terms if it had carried through to either of two actions. First, if the same ardor had been exercised against Anthony Kennedy and his appointment stalled, there might have been an opportunity to fight successfully for the presidency in 1988 and to control that and other appointments to the court. The second option was, by conducting a less theatrical campaign against Bork and therefore running the risk of his elevation to the court, to use the platform of his nomination to establish, as Ralph Nader argued, a new progressive agenda: to turn the occasion into a fissionable reactor and an opportunity to build a permanent presidential coalition.

Neither of these routes was taken and it was perhaps inherent in the dramatic form of a degradation ceremony to foreclose those possibilities. Bork's opponents might have lost the 1988 election anyway but it could have been the beginning of a progressive movement even in defeat. The lesson that should have been learned is that the only way to control the courts is to win the presidency. At the time of Bork's nomination Justices Marshall and Brennan were in ill health and the next president was going to appoint two justices to replace them. George Bush did that and despite the blood on the floor of the Clarence Thomas hearings, he appointed conservative jurists, although by the standards of the current court David Souter looks rather liberal. The techniques used by Bork's opponents at the hearings were turned back on Democrats during the Dukakis presidential run as vengeance that was, in terms of an Irish adage, best eaten cold. Paradoxically the defeat of Robert Bork may have made the country more rather than less conservative but that too would be consistent with the outlook presented here on media events.

EPILOGUE: THE MEANING OF MEDIA EVENTS

I do not wish to obscure or downplay the many assumptions regarding media events that I share in common with Katz and Dayan and with the intellectual background – Durkheim, Van Gannep, Victor Turner – on which they draw. The Bork hearings could be analyzed simply in terms of the transgression of social boundaries by an individual and the mechanisms of social control brought into play when such transgressive acts occur, mechanisms which serve both to correct the transgression and to celebrate sacred values. Similarly, the hearings could have been treated as a rite of passage for Robert Bork through which we vicariously lived and, therefore, as a form of social learning: teaching how not to conduct oneself if possessed of the ambition to be a Supreme Court Justice. As rites of transition, media events are performative ceremonies moving an individual between two standardized social roles. In the transitional stage lays an openness and a lack of secured definition. As betwixt and between, the transitional person carries a dangerous risk and the power of pollution and contagion that potentially disorders all social structure. For that reason Robert Bork was more dangerous *en passage* than he was as a judge, would ever be again as a citizen or even would have been on the Supreme Court.

Katz and Dayan treat media events as collective social rites, an anthropology of celebration that draws upon central sacral codes of the social order in which the elementary process underlying the dramatic forms is the rite of passage. Media events integrate a diverse set of expectations into a narrative genre. The media event is an exceptional public performance where society through the medium of television partakes in a ceremony celebrating its core, sacred values or memories of its collective history. As a dramaturgical display of society to itself the ritual occurs in a "fictional register," as opposed to the discourse typical of the daily news. The rituals, contrived and fictitious, speak to the desires of the audience in a subjunctive key; rites which display what a society most essentially is, what society should be or what society desires to be – its sacred ideals as compared with its mundane pragmatic realities.

Such rites involve moments of *communitas*, since they display the collective society as an undivided group outside of the privatized roles and differentiated statuses of individuals. They speak in the neo-Durkheimian spirit that holds that "mechanical solidarity" – a sense of membership, similarity, equality, familiarity – is at the foundation of the organic solidarity of differentiated, to say nothing of postmodern, politics. Here they point to Durkheim's special role for rituals, not just as social integration, but in the creative construction of the social categories underlying the social order.

Media events are partly distinguished from other news stories by the peculiar role of the audience; the audience's participation is central to the narrative of the rite. Such fundamental social rituals require public witness from those who represent the primordial power of society before it is organized by institutions, regulated by rules and delegated to legitimate authority. The rite of transition both invokes the primordial power of the populace as the basis of the democratic order and suggests that the transitional rites and powers have been properly delegated by the citizens to its legitimate officers.

The key aspect of media events as analyzed by Katz and Dayan is a reconciliation and reunification, a reintegration of society in its commitment to shared values and goals:

> The message is one of reconciliation, in which participants and audiences are invited to unite in the overcoming of conflict. . . . Almost all of these events have heroic figures around whose initiatives the reintegration of society is proposed. Even when these programs address conflict – as they do – they celebrate not conflict but reconciliation.
>
> (Dayan and Katz 1992: 12, 8)

Again, let me emphasize, Katz and Dayan highlight conflict and give it a prominent place in the analysis:

> We should not be so blinded by the integrative function of media events as to overlook their relation to conflict. Many of these events . . . speak directly to acute conflicts. Some speak to long-lasting crises or to deep rifts within societies. Each of these forms of events speaks to conflict in a different way. Thus the live broadcasting of Contests – the Olympic games for example – is in effect a symbolic transposition of political conflict. As has been suggested televised Contests frame conflicts and miniaturize them. Coronations demand that conflicts defer to shared symbols of tradition and unity.
>
> (Dayan and Katz 1992: 39)

In all of these matters they follow the emphasis of Victor Turner in considering social dramas as a progressive sequence that moves from conflict back to reconciliation. Conflict is a stage that is surmounted in the drama or ritual. The dominant motif, in short, is not social division, or reflexivity and enhanced public discussion. Furthermore, the congruence of accounts provided by government, media and social institutions and the ingestion of the population in the central dramatic spectacle means that rites are not especially polysemic or multivocal. Lastly the focus on integration and reconciliation means that little attention is paid to ceremonies that end in consolidating divisions, excluding groups and polarizing opposition. The thesis that media events are an expression of society's central values, combined with the notion that central social institutions must necessarily agree to the production of the ceremonies, means that all media events are characterized as largely integrative.

The Bork hearings and the larger family of events of which they are a part do not meet a model, I believe, of the celebration of consensus. They touch on core, sacred values but are episodes in the production of dissensus, episodes in the recreation, indeed redefinition, of the civil religion by social demarcation and exclusion. Rather than uniting the audience and the polity either in expectation or fact, they divide it ever more deeply. Their central element is not merely conflict but bitter discord and struggle. The event produces neither catharsis nor relief but ever widening and expanding ripples of civil disquiet. It is precisely the fact that these events are deeply ceremonial but unusually intense, laden with high stakes, with real losses and real losers, that allows them to escape to an important degree the horizons of media events as we have heretofore understood the category. In short, the existing analysis of media events is less able to handle drama without rest or resolution, drama without catharsis or consensus, drama which divides people more sharply and intensifies the perception of social difference, drama which separates rather than unites: drama involving confrontation which spills outside its ritual frame to contaminate and reconfigure social relations. As exercises in social cruelty, events such as the Bork hearings teeter on the edge of legitimacy and bear dangers beyond purely ritual ones. They threaten civil society because they suture us, the audience, into systematic cruelties and form us in their image. If Judith Skhlar (1984) is right that a liberal is somebody who believes that cruelty is the worst thing we do, they undermine a liberal and progressive politics often while pretending to defend it.

NOTES

1 The opening statements by senators in each subsequent round of hearings frequently refer to the Bork hearings; Allan Simpson's long plea at the opening of Clarence Thomas' hearings, imploring the committee to avoid a duplication of the "Bork affair," is an example. The Bork hearings have also influenced appointment struggles for lower level judicial posts and appointments to the executive branch. The opposition to and eventual withdrawal of Lani Guinier's candidacy to head the Civil Rights Division of the Justice Department was on grounds almost identical, though on the opposite side of the political divide to those used to deny Bork. As they now say, Guinier was "borked." See Stephen Carter's "Foreword" to Guinier (1994).

2 Ginsburg's withdrawal was a bizarre footnote to the Bork affair. Ginsburg was accused of what we might call the "crimes of the sixties": he had used marijuana in the presence of not only faculty but also, alas, students, and his second wife had not only kept her family's name but also performed abortions as part of her medical training in Boston.

3   This is a tortured episode, widely known as the "Saturday Night Massacre," that Bork was unable to live down. The facts seem to be these. Archibald Cox, whom Nixon had appointed as special prosecutor in the Watergate investigation, asked the President to hand over the tapes from the Oval Office. Nixon refused and Cox indicated that he would seek a contempt citation against Nixon. Nixon ordered Attorney General Elliott Richardson to fire Cox. Richardson refused and quit. Nixon then asked William Ruckelshaus, Deputy Attorney General, who also said "no" and quit. Bork was next in line of succession. Bork already had doubts about the appointment of special prosecutors (widely shared then and now) but it was clear that Nixon had the right to fire Cox. Rather than quit, Bork agreed to become acting Attorney General and gave Cox his notice. Both Richardson and Ruckelshaus said that they urged Bork to carry out the President's orders and praised his action, since both believed that the Justice Department would be crippled if Bork resigned. They said that they had given Congress their word that they would not not interfere with the special prosecutor but Bork had not made (or was asked to give) any such commitment and was free to act. No one doubted the legality of what Bork had done; the sole question was whether or not he should have resigned. Of the many accounts of this matter see Bronner (1989: 81ff).

4   By describing this as an "opportunity," I cast the issue too much in the mold of interest group politics rather than as matters of excommunication and status degradation. Media events fall more into the second category for all of the participants, even though they appear to follow an instrumental model. The energies and anxieties evoked testify to the fact that such events are not politics as usual.

5   He showed an unusual fondness, as I remember it, for Jimmy Stewart and Gary Cooper films. His wife, it was alleged, did not believe that the Holocaust happened.

6   Now, after a decade on the court, Kennedy has emerged as a more moderate and conciliatory justice and, therefore, relatively speaking, a friend of those who opposed Bork. To some this is a vindication of the tactics employed in defeating Bork. However, this is a justification by hindsight. The behavior of nominees once elevated to the court is notoriously hard to predict. Think again of Justice Hugo Black. No one knew how Bork would behave any more than they could have predicted Kennedy's judicial actions because those actions are part of both the dynamic of history and the court itself. They are not exclusively or perhaps largely determined by judicial ideology. Kennedy just happened to turn out the way that he did; no one could have predicted it with confidence in advance.

7   For example, it has been reported that there is a study, though I have as yet been unable to locate it, demonstrating that those who watched the hearings were much more likely to oppose the Bork nomination than those who saw only news stories. This would not settle by itself the direction of causality.

8   It was estimated that 60 per cent of the nation watched some portion of the live or delayed broadcast of the hearings.

9   To some degree the hearings were a hi-jacked event: stolen by interest groups from the principals – the Senate, the President and the political parties – to whom they rightly belonged.

10 The campaign against Bork began with a public opinion poll and subsequently focus group interviews, which were designed to discover the themes and issues on which Bork was vulnerable. Opponents first seized on the notion that his appointment would upset the "delicate balance of the court" and move it to the right. One of the questions in the original poll was "Do you think Robert Bork will upset the ideological balance of the court?" Surprisingly, this turned out to be a non-starter; it was not an issue with those polled who were pretty satisfied with the court and felt that Reagan, having won the election, earned the right to appoint whomever he wanted without regard to "balance." The general response seemed to echo the theme: we are not

entitled to a court of our ideological liking. However, the poll and focus groups did discover the pervasiveness of the issue of privacy, particularly among conservatives and Reagan supporters. They discovered considerable anti-government sentiment, a commitment to *laissez-faire* politics and a general sentiment that "the government should be kept off our backs." The attempt to defeat Bork then became a left–liberal cause, won paradoxically by a conservative means. It was decided to use Reagan against Reagan. So, the Bork appointment was recast as an episode in state intrusion into the lives of individuals, a violation of privacy and the spread of government control and regulation. This was a left position that was deeply anti-state and anti-communal and one that the left would later have cause to regret.

11 Biden was forced to withdraw his candidacy within a few weeks of the opening of the hearings when he was accused of having plagiarized a speech, indeed something of an autobiographical speech, from the head of the British Labor Party, Neil Kinnock.

12 One of the minor lessons learned in the Bork case, though a lesson promptly ignored with Clarence Thomas' nomination, was the following: do not nominate someone to the court during the summer when the district is filled with college students willing to work for glory and experience rather than money.

13 The campaign was successful; only three senators announced support for Bork over the summer hiatus.

14 Kennedy and Biden later remarked that Tribe was better at playing Bork than Bork was at being himself.

15 The connection of interests and symbols in the demonization of Bork was partly, of course, dictated by the constraints of the political situation. The question was how Bork could be depicted such that a senator might stand against him and not sacrifice significant political support in the process.

16 Michael Rogin (1987) connects American liberal individualism to demonological rites as follows. Somehow the atomized, isolated, insecure life of a mobile liberal society creates desires for rites of community. These rites, however, are forged in attacks on a demonological other, who, it is fantasized, violates the ideals of American political culture – the disciplined, self-sufficient liberal individual – and, therefore, must be excluded and annihilated. Jeffrey Alexander (1988) follows portions of this analysis, I believe, in his examination of excommunication rites, for example Watergate.

17 Hostile reviewers of the book took it as evidence that they had been right on Bork all along; that he was out of the mainstream as his critics portrayed him. Interestingly, this view requires that one ignore the ritual form of the hearings altogether, to pretend that the point of the hearings was not to force a redefinition of self on everyone: the nation, the Congress and Robert Bork himself. Why should we assume that someone who has been subject to such an intense, degrading, and emotional ceremony will emerge as the same person that went into the ritual, when the point of the entire exercise is to produce a transformation of self, that is, to create an "outsider?"

18 Thus, for example, Ruth Bader Ginsburg, later to be elevated to the court, agreed with Bork that the discovery of a right of privacy in and the use of Griswold v. Connecticut as a precedent for Roe v. Wade was based on mysterious and shaky legal reasoning.

17 This is a critical point but one on which I lack necessary evidence. We do know that Bork resigned from the Circuit Court of Appeals in early January 1988. Just why, if there were considerations other than to write a book and take to the lecture circuit, is unclear.

REFERENCES

Alexander, J. C. (1988) "Culture and political crisis: 'Watergate' and Durkheimian sociology" in J. C. Alexander (ed.) *Durkheimian Sociology: Cultural Studies*, Cambridge: Cambridge University Press.

Ackerman, B. (1988) "Transformative appointments," *Harvard Law Review* 101: 1164–84.

Anderson, B. (1983) *Imagined Communities: Reflections on the Origin and Spread of Nationalism*, London: Verso.

Bork, R. H. (1990) *The Tempting of America: The Political Seduction of the Law*. New York: Free Press.

Bronner, E. (1989) *Battle for Justice: How the Bork Nomination Shook America*, New York: W. W. Norton.

Carter, S. L. (1994) *The Confirmation Mess*, New York: Basic Books.

Dayan, D. and Katz, E. (1992) *Media Events: The Live Broadcasting of History*, Cambridge, MA: Harvard University Press.

Erickson, K. (1966) *Wayward Puritans*, New York: Macmillan.

Goffman, E. (1959) *The Presentation of Self in Everyday Life*, New York: Doubleday Anchor Books.

Guinier, L. (1994) *The Tyranny of the Majority*, New York: Free Press.

Hartz, L. (1955) *The Liberal Tradition in America*, New York: Harcourt Brace & World.

McGuigan, P. B. and Weyrich, D. M. (1990) *Ninth Justice: The Fight for Bork*, Washington DC: Free Congress Research and Educational Foundation.

Pertschuk, M. and Schaetzel, W. (1989) *The People Rising: The Campaign Against the Bork Nomination*, New York: Thunder's Mouth Press.

Rogin, M. P. (1987) *Ronald Reagan, the Movie and Other Episodes in Political Demonolgy*, Berkeley, CA: University of California Press.

Skhlar, J. N. (1984) *Ordinary Vices*, Cambridge, MA: Harvard University Press.

4 Television's disaster marathons

A danger for democratic processes?

Tamar Liebes

In March 1996, in the wake of a series of terrorist bus bombings, the performance of the Israeli media was the subject of a heated debate. Within eight days, three buses had exploded, in the heart of Jerusalem and Tel Aviv. The suicide attackers were Palestinians, who belonged to Hamas, a Muslim fundamentalist faction opposed to the Oslo peace process. Following the bombings, Israeli television cancelled all scheduled programs and for seventy-two hours switched into a live broadcast of an increasingly familiar kind – what I propose to call a "disaster marathon."

What we saw for three days' running was a recycling of the horrors visually and as recounted by victims and witnesses; the aggressive, sometimes whiny, interviewing of officials who were reprimanded for the catastrophe, called to admit to the failure of their policies and/or take immediate action and/or resign; the reporters' standing vigil at the decision-makers' doorstep to get word and/or speculate on "the most radical" solution, presumably cooking inside. And, in between, we listened to the studio inmates, selected for their talent of constantly inflating the drama.

The non-stop, open-ended broadcasting mode chosen by Israel radio and television became the object of heavy criticism (and was later considered a major reason for the loss suffered by the government in the May 1996 elections). The two television channels were accused of inciting hysteria, of losing all proportion in reporting and repeating the attacks, of competing among themselves over the degree of aggressiveness against government representatives. In reply to criticism, they claimed their obligation to represent the public's outrage. Editors of the popular press – whose front pages screamed "return to hell," "hell on Purim" and "a nation in fear" – were similarly accused of making the wrong assumption about what people wanted from broadcasting at that moment. One distinguished political scientist charged television's senior news anchor (Israel's "Walter Cronkite") with acting as an agent of the Hamas.

In spite of the hyperbole, there can be no question that television assumed a dominant role in the wake of the bus bombings, as it had done only four months earlier, in the days following Prime Minister Yitzhak Rabin's assassination. But this time, unlike the last, television did not know how to go about it or how to get out of it. The directors of television were pushed into open-ended live coverage of a disaster without benefit of a "script." The fact is that they had no previous experience of such coverage, and no handy genre or rules. The scope of the disaster coincided with major changes in the organization and technology of television. The ecology of media in Israel has drastically changed in recent years – with the monopoly of public broadcasting giving way to a multiplicity of fiercely competing channels, and the technological revolution facilitating live transmission from a multiplicity of points. All the old rules of reporting were now in flux. So perhaps were audience expectations of a further leap into "action news."

What follows is in three parts. The first proposes that this case of regurgitating disaster may be an Israeli contribution to an emergent mode of live broadcasting that should be considered, at least ostensibly, as a kin to Dayan and Katz's (1992) "media events." It speculates about the characteristics of "disaster marathons," and invites the analysis of similar events in these terms. The second part attempts to show how these characteristics were inferred from the specific case study which triggered these speculations. The third considers the political implications of this kind of television treatment of catastrophe.

A GENRE IN THE MAKING

Can such instant, unplanned, live broadcasts, which interrupt scheduled programmes, gathering the anxious society around the television set, be considered a new sub-genre of media events, or are its characteristics so different that we are witness to a new genre? While Dayan and Katz called our attention to a new television genre of "media events" (1992), they certainly did not relate to this kind of live broadcasting of violent disruptions in their scheme. This chapter argues that we are indeed looking at a new type of broadcasting. Building on the comparison between the social functions of media events and such disaster marathons, it goes on to propose the characteristics of this genre, and the reasons why media policy makers should pay attention to the risks it entails from the perspective of the workings of democratic societies.

Disaster marathons versus media events

Live broadcasting of "the day after" a tragic event shares a number of characteristics with media events. As in the days of the Pope's visit to Poland, or of Egypt's President Sadat's visit to Jerusalem, this is when television moves from its position of wallpaper to centre stage in the home and in the society, when private and public become one. Ordinary routines of work and play come to a halt, and people gather in front of the screen, seeking for ways of staying in touch with the collectivity, at a highly charged moment. For their part, the media interrupt their own planned schedules to devote all available air time to the event.

Dayan and Katz define media events as carefully staged occasions in which press and broadcast media cooperate with government in relating to the event as a genuine celebration, voluntarily relinquishing their tough, independent, cynical stance of critics to guide audiences toward such high moments of integration as the Prince Charles–Lady Di kiss on the royal balcony, or (*mutatis mutandis*) the Rabin–Arafat embrace on the White House lawn, and providing the fitting signs and symbols to enhance the emotional moments. Aware that journalists' taking on the role of official laudators comes very close to taking on the role of journalists in non-democratic states, Dayan and Katz emphasize that in democratic societies the electronic press and the public have the freedom to refuse.

The "celebration" of disaster differs, however, from the genre of televised ceremonies on the crucial issue of pre-planning, which correlates with its dia-metrically opposite relationship with the political establishment. To put it bluntly one might say that during media events the political establishment takes over the media (and the public) whereas during a disaster – such as urban rioting, terrorist attacks, army accidents causing major loss of life, sometimes even natural disasters – oppositional forces (internal to the society or external to it) take over the media (and the public). In both cases the media may resist but the professional norms of electronic journalists, their perception of their role in democracy, and the economic pressures on the networks (Bennet 1996) all work in the direction of acting in the service of the establishment in the first case, and against it in the second.

Glimpses of the potential of violent opposition taking a free ride on the live media's celebration of the establishment, and taking over the event and the media, appear even in the Dayan and Katz corpus. Examples of media events getting out of hand are the massacre of the Israeli sports team in the Munich Olympics, Prime Minister Rabin's assassination upon leaving a mass rally for peace in Tel-Aviv, and the assassination of President Sadat, Rabin's counterpart, during a public ceremony in Cairo (Liebes and Katz 1997). But these cases are treated by Dayan and Katz not as threatening to the genre but as discordant notes which put these particular events into a category of "hijacked" or aborted events, which do not quite qualify for the media events genre. In hindsight, however, they should be considered as an opportunity for recontextualizing media events within a new broader typology of live broadcasts.

Moreover, the genre of media events is "sanitized" in Dayan and Katz by extracting the ceremony out of its broader broadcasting context. Their definition does not take account of the possibility that in cases where the ceremony (such as a state funeral) is meant to redress a traumatic news event (such as the Rabin or Kennedy assassination), from the viewers' perspective the live broadcast may be one continuous flow. Dayan and Katz focus on the ceremonial resolution of these crises, overlooking the time that elapses between the disruption and the ceremony.[1] Television's role in such crises, whether or not redressed by a ceremonial media event (immediately or in time), merits a closer scrutiny.

Disaster marathons: the illusion that journalists have taken charge

On the whole, Dayan and Katz fail to notice that in traumatic events such as the assassination of leaders, television takes charge with live marathonic broadcasting from the moment when the disaster strikes (or immediately after) until the redressive ceremonial closure, which mobilizes the political establishment of the country or the world. Other kinds of public disasters, such as earthquakes, mass air-accidents, or mass murders by lunatics or terrorists, are also left to the medium of television, which finds itself charged with the decision of whether or not to switch to a marathon mode, what to show, and when and how to return to the normal schedule. The latter type of disasters, which have no role in the Dayan and Katz model, may be symbolically less shattering than the death of a head of state but even more traumatic for the public. The reason is that society has long prepared known constitutional ways of transferring power, accompanied by the fitting symbolic gestures and images, which are intended to preserve societal stability. These are activated at the time of the assassination of a leader. In such a classic situation, television has only to position itself as narrator and interpreter of the ceremony so that everyone can join in. Large-scale disasters, sometimes considered as indications of more to come, have no ascribed symbolic closures and, at the same time, no immediate (or long term) solutions. As such, they have the power to directly threaten people's personal safety. And live broadcasting makes their impact greater than ever.

From the media's point of view, stories of disaster invite a hermeneutic search for the culprit, someone to whom to assign the blame. The less possible it is to point to the actual villain, the less the chance of satisfactory resolution, and the more powerful the role of television in providing the framing. Thus, when the leader's assassin is caught and the murder is declared as the act of one "mad" individual, journalism can relax into the "priestly" mode. When two Israeli army helicopters crash, killing seventy-two soldiers, the question of responsibility may remain unsolved, and the live broadcast may be responsible for creating a climate in which public spirit will turn into rage (against the air force, the army or policy makers sending soldiers to Lebanon) or tamely go into collective mourning. In the case of terrorist attacks, the extent of blaming the leadership depends on the extent to which these attacks were perceived as inevitable. Thus, in Israel in the 1950s and 1960s, when the society was more collectivistic and the state of "cold war" with the Arabs was seen as permanent, the inevitable terrorist attacks contributed mostly to national solidarity (Nossek 1994). In the 1990s, by contrast, when there is vocal opposition to the Israeli–Palestinian peace process, a far more individualistic society, as well as the drama of electronic media replacing the printed press, the leadership is often held responsible. Following the 1996 bombings, the government seemed temporarily incapacitated, its credibility so badly damaged that it momentarily lost legitimacy with the people. Television anchors found themselves on live broadcasts conducting a "field trial" of the government.

Clearly, whether they be scandals or accidents (Molotch and Lester 1974), disasters signify that things have gone out of control. They are publicized against the government's will, making politicians vulnerable and supplying journalists with a crack through which to peep behind the the usual official facade. It seems that in such situations journalists are at their most powerful and can go to work as watchdogs.

But, paradoxically, in the new electronic era this investigative moment may be undermined. Television journalists are indeed allocated more power but under conditions which may make responsible journalism all but impossible. The decision to go to live coverage means scrapping all of the accepted norms. There is no time for investigative reporting, which entails a lengthy process of interviewing sources, checking reliability, searching data, editing, and so on (Katz 1992). The extreme public salience and the risks inherent in the disaster marathons genre derive from its attributes of instant, electronic, time-out journalism, which, having cleared the screen of everything else, zeroes in, live, on one traumatic event, in which all journalistic work is done in full public view.[2]

Just as traditional journalistic practices are out of synch with the breathlessness of open-studio crisis, so are the mechanisms of parliamentary democracy. Constitutional democracies have specified ways of insuring the survival of government in times of crisis such as the death of leaders, or of declaring a state of emergency when disaster strikes, but in an era marked by the omnipresence and immediacy of live TV, these proceedings seem slow, cumbersome and far behind. The new television, always there and thriving on catastrophes, ends up deciding for itself when a disaster may be defined as "national emergency."

Moreover, these are the moments in which the public spontaneously turns to the electronic media, endowing editors, producers and anchors, willy-nilly, with the opportunity to run the show (and the country) in their own way. Whether or not the political institutions share this definition, they may discover that television has already taken over and *de facto* declared a state of emergency. Through calling the shots, by imposing its own framing of the event and thereby constraining the process of political and strategic decision making, television, it seems, has acquired the power to "disintermediate" (Katz 1988) parliamentary democracy.

But the seeming independence of the media when taking charge of disasters is also something of a mirage. When the government is positioned as the bad guy, the vacuum is filled by the political opposition (Carey, this volume), which, in the case of terrorist acts, may be exactly what the perpetrators intended. Thus, journalists are inclined to fall prey to the initiators of the event, just as they do in the case of media events. But, unlike the case of pre-planned ceremonies, there is no time for broadcasters to make up their minds about whether, and to what extent, to go along with the perpetrators' framing. The force of the event leaves journalists practically no choice.

In contradiction to media events, the shared collective space created by disaster time-out, zooming in on victims and their families, is the basis not for dignity and restraint but for the chaotic exploitation of the pain of participants on screen, and for the opportunistic fanning of establishment mismanagement, neglect, corruption, and so on. Whereas the principle of broadcast ceremony is to high-light emotions and solidarity and to bracket analysis, a disaster marathon constitutes a communal public forum where tragedy is the emotional motor which sizzles with conflict, emphasizing anxiety, argument and disagreement.

DECONSTRUCTING THE CASE STUDY

In order to examine the format more closely we analyze the way in which television took charge during the series of bus bombings in February–March 1996, in Israel, to show how the elements of the case led me to generalize about the overall characteristics of the proposed genre.

Time-out for disaster

Following the 1996 bus bombings, an administrative decision was taken at the level of the Director General of Israel television. Disaster mode went into gear. All scheduled programs were cancelled and commercials abolished, in order to clear the air entirely for the flow of disaster. Viewers were told that broadcasts would continue throughout the night and into the next day "when the funerals take place."

The rationale for a disaster marathon, as presented by the directors of television after the fact, was twofold: the need to provide a shared space for mourning, and the need to update the public on current developments in the aftermath of the tragedy. Putting aside the question of whether there is a need for an open space for news in a country with radio news bulletins every hour on the hour and an update on the half-hour, the crucial question is, does television's disaster marathon provide either?

The Director General of the national Public Broadcasting system argues that "the people would not have agreed to us going back to routine broadcasting; it is a time in which normal programs are not acceptable," ending with the categorical statement, "the public would stone the television building if we continued routine broadcasting."

This admission raises a number of serious questions. Should the Director General alone have the authority to decide that the country is in a period of national mourning? If he is the one to embark on live "mourning" mode, on what should his decision be based? On the number of dead (over 10? over 20?)? On the nature of the incident and/or the identity of the attackers (carrying on as usual following, say major car accidents but switching to disaster mode following terrorist bombings)? And, most important, what are the genres that befit mourning on television?

As the traditional division of news versus entertainment has been all but abolished by the new electronic journalism, the production of disaster time-out was allocated to the department which carries most weight. The public channel (Channel One, which traditionally prioritises the news department to the exclusion of all else) put the news department in charge, incorporating its talk show stars in the time-out. Entertainment-oriented Channel Two, quicker to acknowledge that disaster time is mostly entertainment, put its major money-making talk show host in charge of the time-out (moving over, periodically, to news updates). But both did the same things anyway.

What was out, what was on?

Clearing the space for disaster created enormous pressure for repetition, anticipating developments, creating news. "Celebration" of the bus bombings ran in a number of mutually reinforcing strands. In an open-ended, live talk show, based in the studio as war-room, anchors were technically and substantively in charge of the controls maneuvred between various interviewees within the studio and short ventures into the dangerous world outside (Ellis 1982) in order to "relive," or re-enact the disaster, to monitor the cuaterizing of injuries and to update from the arenas where "action" is expected. On ordinary days the state of soldiers injured in Lebanon would be reported in a minute or two, on the regular evening news. In this case it lasted the whole night. Reporters covered the hospitals where the injured were being treated and the sites of the bombing where the damage was being repaired, they went on the trail of police officers to hear what was being done about catching the terrorists, and they stood in the lobby of the Ministry of Defense to get word of the policy that the government was going to adopt. While disaster beats are no different from those of routine news, the pressure of the frequency of "visits" and the intensity of reporters demanding to hear what went wrong, how bad the suffering was, how quick and violent the "answer" would be, was of a different order.

The competition – which has socialized viewers to expect dramatic entertainment on all TV genres, the constraints of the medium – with its demand for visual, personalized stories, and the live-studio genre – with its demand to keep the story going, all combined to confuse analytic discourse with emotional experience. Thus the program catered to the voyeuristic, even pornographic, aspects of viewing and, at the same time, called for the discrediting of the social institutions "at fault." But the discussion at such a time was neccessarily based on confounding the personal tragedy of the victims with a catastrophe for the whole of society, and so pushed the government, the military, and the other institutions in charge of security to react in accordance with the magnitude of disaster displayed on the screen (and, presumably, in the public mind) and within the time confines of the show.

Recycling blood, tears and vengeance

All during the time-out, daily commercials and promos were replaced with the recycling of bloody pictures and sounds, tightened to retain only the juiciest lines. Showing the same wounded child, another horrified witness or a bereaved parent on the way to identify a daughter's body worked to arouse anxiety and, at the same time, to provide the visceral pleasures of all soft-core pornographic genres (Fiedler 1982).

The marathon was punctuated by a carefully edited "logo," featuring the total chaos of the city square, moments after the bombing: covered bodies, broken bus parts, masses of police officers, ambulances, the fire brigade; a big blonde woman crying, looking for her son; a young man who saw people without arms, without legs, without faces; a young girl who saw the head of a woman on the pavement, her body on the street; a religious soldier of the coroners' corps collecting scattered pieces of skin and bone from the trees. At the assigned time of the major evening news, a special "official" motto replaced the daily news-logo, to symbolize that all order had been destroyed. Not by chance, this logo was a direct contradiction to the daily ritual of "we are here as always, at the usual time, with the usual logo," which is supposed to signify that the world goes on and that "we" are in control.

Thus, the periodic repetition of a tightly edited sequence of images and words created an emotionally powerful framing to the disaster-show, fixating its meaning as totally chaotic, as both uncontrolled and uncontrollable horror. As in music, sculpture or architecture, repetition carries a dynamic of its own, intensifying the images and the sounds while decontexualizing them.

Answering the criticism following after the fact, television's news directors generally defended their performance, mostly in the name of the public's right to know. They did, however, provide clues to their own loss of control and confusion, in terms of traditional professional standards, by blaming new technologies and the pressures of live transmission, which valorize the mobility of the equipment, abolish editing and curtail the capacity to supervise.[3] They did not admit their need to fill "disaster" space or worse, their servile eye to the ratings, that is, to the economic dictates which undermine the capacity of journalists, even in the public service, to act as professionals.

The churning of horror sights and stories cannot be defended in terms of journalistic duties. It is possible to argue that the press should show all, regardless of the consequences for the government, even for the country, and that Wright's (1960) definition of the role of the press – to maximize the information needed for lowering the level of anxiety – is too conservative and pro-status quo. However, these arguments would certainly justify the first showing, and repetitions in the subsequent news bulletins if appropriate, but not the visual orgy.

Waiting for "action" (and pushing it along)

Images of what had passed were not enough. There had to be something to wait for. The question that permeated the show was – what next? This type of tension was supplied by expecting, and pushing for willy-nilly, immediate retaliation. Thus, for example, the broadcast was transferred time and again to the reporter at the door of the cabinet meeting, in order to listen to the hearsay of anybody who was willing to talk or to speculate on various extreme measures that were presumably being discussed, such as the postponement of the elections or the establishment of an emergency cabinet devoted only to fighting terrorism. Opposition leaders, in the studio and elsewhere, were heard to suggest attacking Hamas bases in Gaza and thereby destroying the Oslo process. In between, running out of ideas, the reporter, awaiting word from the government, turned his attention to the anti-Peres demonstration of militants on the other side of the street. On cue, the demonstrators enthusiastically raised their signs saying "the government of the Final Solution" (at once blaming the government directly for the bombings and comparing the suicide attack to the extermination of the Jews by the Nazis), while chanting, in a rhythmic paraphrasing of Palestinian mass rallies, "in blood and fire we will throw Peres out." The longer the cabinet meeting continue, the more coverage the protesting group received and so, to improve on their entertainment value, they burned tires each time that the camera came near.

The extensive coverage of incitement to violence against the government and its premier (from inside the Jewish camp) may have been justified by the public's need to know about such marginal groups, especially in light of the allegation following Rabin's assassination that "the writing was on the wall" and that the public ignored it. But investigative, in-depth journalism would have been much more effective at interpreting the threat, and such a demonstration would have received no more than sixty seconds of air-time on a normal news day.

Expectations of "radical action" were raised so high that any decision reached by the government was bound to be disappointing and had to be headlined with acceptable rhetoric, pushing Peres to pronounce that "we are in a state of war," and Ezer Weizman, the President, to outdo him by declaring that "we in Israel have never experienced more difficult days."

Who was given voice and for what purpose?

Experts and scapegoats

In the studio, television set up and ran its self-made mixture of parliamentary debate (on what political lessons should be drawn), investigation committee (on whose fault it was), kibitzer advisers (on military operations, espionage), undercover specialists, experts (on personal security) and scholars of fanatic and fundamentalist religions and ideologies. Not surprisingly, at a moment's notice, television summoned opposition leaders (who needed only to look dignified and hide their relief about being out of power), government ministers (who, as the guilty, could not afford to put the disaster in proportion), security professionals, academic experts and ordinary people, and demanded immediate accountability in the name of the public.

Disaster is a good day for opposition party leaders and for ex-generals, or for security experts who may talk all that they want even if they have previously been found wanting on far more severe charges of negligence and perjury.[4] The Prime Minister and the Chief-of-Staff, on the other hand, are dragged in for a degradation ceremony, to be asked questions which can be answered only with a "yes" or a "no." Following reporters' long vigil at the cabinet door, one minister, sent to convey the government's decisions, was reprimanded by the open-studio host: "Is this all you have come up with? What about action, immediate action?"

Victims as public opinion representatives

Which voices of the public gain access to disaster-time? The frame of "disaster" calls for people who scream the most, either in agony or in rage – the louder, the less controlled, the better. We saw people who "miraculously" escaped, we saw victims in hospital beds and we saw families waiting outside the operating theater.

Of course, not all potentially "good" story tellers fulfill their promise. One such interviewee was a child, the son of new immigrants from Russia, who had just lost both of his parents in the bombing. The child insisted on not losing his cool on television and, in spite of all of the interviewer's efforts to have him collapse, said that he thought that life would go on. But others, caught in what might well have been the worst moment of their lives, were not only asked about their personal tragedy (where were they going? when did they find out?) but also allocated the privileged status of expressing their political opinions (what policy did they think that the government should adopt now?), having been chosen by fate as representatives of the public.

The use of victims as policy experts on terror has become an accepted news convention in the process of defining news as melodrama. This convention alone seems responsible for the worst sample of public opinion that one can have at the precise moment, as victims are too involved in their own predicament to provide a considered opinion. Can a person in extreme agony be expected to supply a policy statement? And if there is wisdom in Habermas's (1989) argument that disinterested opinion should be as separate as possible from individual concerns and directed only toward the collective good, then victims are about the worst people to interview. But they do answer television's need for emotional gimmicks. We know that television may not be concerned with the construction of a public sphere, even on ordinary days. In times of disaster, emotions, conflict and melodrama are the name of the game.

POTENTIAL IMPLICATIONS FOR DEMOCRATIC PROCESSES

I should like to conclude by attempting to point out the potentially dangerous consequences of television's disaster routine for the decison-making process of democratically elected governments.

Television's unique responsibility

Disaster marathons share with media events a departure from routine but, far from a preplanned ceremonial holiday, they communicate only its sudden breakdown. Media events are the excitement of looking forward to being securely guided toward an emotional uplift or resolution, with the near certainty of knowing what to expect every step of the way; when disaster strikes it brings the anxiety of being left out on a limb, with nothing sure to hold on to. People turn to television when they have lost their sense of personal safety for themselves and their families, and when they feel that it is still unresolved condition, that is, that terror may strike again. Thus, when people are on time-out, mostly viewing television, with no routine to support them and having lost confidence in the government's capacity to protect them, television's anchor becomes the only anchor, and television takes on responsibility under unique circumstances.

Demands for instant solutions

Disaster time-out operates according to the rules of melodrama. Dramatic tension is the outcome of witnessing an ongoing race between good and evil, in which the end is still unknown. As Disaster has called the shots, it has thereby supplied the framing of television's time-out. Disaster, as a simple, "neat" violent act (almost broadcast live), demands a comparably simple, neat, "bloody" answer – some sort of a revenge and a resolution – or else a happy ending, preferably within the time limits of the broadcast. Ideally the story should progress by allocating blame, by catching and punishing the villains, and by making certain that there are no more villains hiding in the bushes.

The need for immediate, clearcut, brutal action is exacerbated by television's visualization, recycling and magnifying the disaster. A visual tragedy demands an equally visual answer (such as lynching) and the discrepancy between showing the vivid picture of the tragedy and the complex, much postponed, and ambiguous ways in which it may be addressed makes the leadership seem inadequate by definition, as political and diplomatic processes are emotionally unacceptable and cannot be incorporated in the narrative.

In line with these requirements, time-out television is both looking for immediate and decisive action and creating some of it. While taking the opportunity, each time the studio conversation slackens, to recall how horrible the setting looked the moment after the event and to check on (and thereby egg on) the violent demonstrations, media anchors push opposition leaders to propose immediate political solutions (a government of "national unity" is the standard ritual), press more or less failed security experts to produce immediate military solutions, and feel free themselves to viciously attack government representatives as the culprits. Pressure on politicians to react, within the emotional bubble of a disaster marathon, causes tough politicians such as Minister Fouad Ben-Eliezer to exclaim that "personal security has sunk to zero," a statement which was to feature prominently a month later, as part of the Likud opposition's election campaign.

The blurring of the past

True to the logic of operating within a disaster bubble and taking for granted that the killings constitute proof of the failure of government policy, interviewers limit themselves only to the issue of personal safety, which of course cannot be separated from the complex context of trying to achieve a long term peace which will prevent more wars.

As time goes by, standing watch at the door of the government meeting takes center stage, with viewers nervously waiting for the expected "radical" decision. Worse, as the public's messenger, television is literally breathing down the ministers' necks. "We were a step from marching into Gaza, and incorporating the National Religious party in the government," said Merez Minister Yossi Sarid a week later.

Wallowing in the reality of the moment, making it fill the whole of the screen and the whole of the collective consciousness, operates to blur the memory of past events, historical contexts and long term processes, connecting the present only to other disasters, equally torn from their contexts. Forgotten are past sufferings and long-term alternatives. Washed out are the years of intifada, with soldiers stoned and attacked in the West Bank and Gaza, the Oslo agreement with the PLO, which led most Palestinians to oppose terrorism against Israel, and the gradual opening of the Arab world to Israel. All of these belong to the past and are not relevant.

Transmitting a message of failure

By its melodramatic, uncompromising, all-engulfing nature, the disaster marathon of the bus bombings transmitted a message of the complete failure of the peace process, just as mourning over Rabin transmitted the complete victory of the process, with Rabin as its eternal hero. This message has in fact generated a grave, perhaps lethal, blow to the peace process. As the critics of the treatment of disaster have pointed out, television has served the aim of Hamas of putting a stop to the peace process, that is, by building up anxiety, panic and hysteria. Public reaction may well have brought to power the Likud government which advocates a tougher policy. At the very least, television provided Hamas terrorism with a stage – "handing out a diploma for the Hamas suicider" in the words of Ron BenYishai, editor of *Davar Rishon*, while recalling the story of a terror-prone young Palestinian in Rammalla, who, viewing the hysterics of disaster time-out, said to his friends, "you'll see me on TV this evening," before driving to Jerusalem to run over people waiting at a bus stop later in the day.

The issue of working in the service of Hamas raises the question of how protective – some would say "responsible," others – "hegemonic" – the press should be (Liebes 1997). Any attempt to answer should first take into account the definition of the situation – the frame of "war" or "emergency" merits a more "responsible" approach and, having framed disaster as a time-out crisis, should point in the direction of restraint. But the disaster marathon plays by different rules.

By taking over immediately and comprehensively, and by inflating an admittedly terrible disaster into an all-engulfing national catastrophe, television is heading on a dangerous course, in which it may be in a position to put pressure on government to take immediate, perhaps irreversible, action. Democratic institutions need time and careful consideration to weigh alternatives, to plan and to act. And difficult situations sometimes demand risky decisions. They may be vulnerable enough to take hasty steps in a moment of crisis in order to cater to what they feel is the will of the public masses, as expressed on live television. This time Prime Minister Peres was moved only to declare "we are in war," but not to change course; next time his successor may be moved to take action.

The crucial question which concerns the future of television journalism as well as of participatory democracies is how to define the line between inviting participation and inciting collective hysteria in moments of crisis. On the face of it, what can be more democratic than an instant open forum set up by television in the wake of crisis, accessible to all people, which allows viewers to follow the event from a better position than they would if they had gone to the site to see for themselves? The public is party to the debate over the meaning of the disaster and its possible implications, and to the various considerations for and against particular policy measures; ordinary people may even be asked to express their own opinions. Can one argue that these are the days when television gets closest to facilitating a truly open, democratic, public forum, which, even though triggered as it were by ideological terror, touches on the society's most painful, existential issues?

Whereas theoretically television does possess this potential, disaster time is least suitable for exercising it, as man-made disasters build on and maximize the weaknesses of the electronic press, of political institutions, and of the public in our postmodern era. I should like to suggest that the "open-studio" disaster marathon, which has become the *après*-disaster television convention, maximizes the structural flaws of the dominant new electronic press, plays into the hands of ruthless violators of democratic decision making and gives voice to the least "considered opinion" of distraught representatives of the public. I argue that disaster time draws on, and exploits to the full, a number of developments which converged to transform the definition of the journalistic profession and to create a new virtual reality into which the press as we know it is disappearing.

New technologies of live broadcasting from multiple sites into the homes of viewers, "virtual" split-screen debates and instant electronic opinion polls, which are on a multiplicity of competing channels, feverishly fighting over viewers, are worked overtime in disaster and have developed too fast for journalists and scholars to deliberate on their consequences.

Close examination of disaster marathon practices – being there in real time, claiming to represent the voice of "the people" – indicates that these new characteristics of the electronic press (and the printed press, in its wake), like the demagogy of populist political rhetorics, work to generate mass hysteria of the kind that incites to lynching. While viewers watch from home, they constitute a mass much greater than any which could assemble outside in the streets.

NOTES

1 Perhaps owing to their avowedly establishment orientations (noted, among others, by Yossi Bailin, "Sefarim," *ha'aretz* 1996).
2 Before the days of live marathons, this type of news story – Tuchman's "Oh what a story" (1973) – would be revisited on the next news show, the next evening, the next day, or the next week to report that victims were buried, that the culprits were shot or arrested, or that the black box had been discovered.
3 David Gilboa, Channel One's Director of News at the time, admitted that "broadcasting live from five broadcast points and eight satellites" makes editorial control unrealistic; "If I could have prevented it I would." The more complacent Shalom Kital, head of Channel Two News, also admitted to the inability to vet the reporting from the field: "In 70 hours of live broadcast things get out of control."
4 Such as Carmi Gillon, ex-*shabak* head who was forced to resign following the Rabin assassination, or Ariel Sharon, who was found unfit to serve as Minister of Security following the Yom Kippur war.

REFERENCES

Bennet, L. (1996) "An introduction to journalism norms representation of politics," *Political Communication* 13 (4): 373–84.

Dayan, D. and Katz, E. (1992) *Media Events: The Live Broadcasting of History*, Cambridge, MA: Harvard University Press.

Edelman, M. (1988) *Constructing the Political Spectacle*, Chicago, IL: University of Chicago Press.

Ellis, J. (1982) *Visible Fictions*, London: Routledge.

Fiedler, L. (1982) *What Was Literature? Mass Culture and Mass Society*, New York: Simon & Schuster.

Habermas, J. (1989) *The Structural Transformation of the Public Sphere* (trans. Thomas Burger), Cambridge, MA: MIT Press.

Katz, E. (1988) "Cutting out the middle man," *Inter Media* 16: 30–31.

Katz, E. (1992) "The end of journalism? Notes on watching the war," *Journal of Communication* 42 (3): 5–13.

Liebes, T. (1997) *Reporting the Arab Israeli conflict: How hegemony works*, London: Routledge.

Liebes, T. and Katz, E. (1997) "Staging peace: televised ceremonies of reconciliation," *The Communication Review* 2 (2): 235–57.

Molotch, H. and Lester, M. (1974) "News as purposive behavior," *American Sociological Review* 39: 101–12.

Nossek, H. (1994) "The narrative role of the holocaust and the state of Israel in the coverage of terrorist events in the Israeli press," *Journal of Narratives and Life Histories* 4 (1–2): 119–35.

Tuchman, G. (1973) "Making news by doing work: routinizing the unexpected," *American Journal of Sociology* 79: 110–31.

Wright, C. R. (1960) "Functional analysis and mass communication," *Public Opinion Quarterly* 23: 605–20.

Part II
Media and identity

5 Minorities, majorities and the media

Larry Gross

BACK TO THE FUTURE: TALES FROM THE 1950s

At the end of a book called *Personal Influence: The Part Played By People in the Flow of Mass Communication* (1955), Elihu Katz and Paul Lazarsfeld attached "A Substantive Addendum: On Gregariousness, Anxiety and the Consumption of Popular Fiction," in which they created an index of "popular fiction" (admittedly, of limited scope, as it combined exposure to "true story" magazines, movie magazines and radio soap operas), and found that "the less gregarious women were more likely to be popular fiction fans" (1955: 378). Because this relationship could not be explained by education level or social status, the authors saw it as lending support "to the obvious interpretation that the popular fiction media serve to some extent as a substitute for socializing activity. 'Escapist' is the label that the popular culture theorist has given them" (p. 378).

Further analysis revealed a positive relationship between "self image as an anxious person and exposure to popular fiction" (p. 379), plus negative relationships with social status and gregariousness. The authors concluded: "In short, the media content which we have labeled popular fiction seems to serve needs and interests which are associated with the sub-culture of lower status groups; with lower levels of social activity; and with anxiety elements in personality" (p. 380).

A few years after *Personal Influence* was published – and long before I had heard of it – I embarked on a voyage of personal exploration that comes vividly back to memory whenever I read Appendix D:3; a voyage that began in the stacks of the Hebrew University library. As a teenager well aware of my homosexuality and equally aware that it was something unspoken, even unspeakable, I was unknowingly following the pattern laid out in that final addendum.

No, escapism was not exactly my goal, as I perused the card catalogue (making sure no one saw which cards I was examining) and then the shelves, looking for anything that might answer my questions and flesh out my fantasies. I was, however, beginning to identify as a member of a "sub-culture of lower status"; I was relatively isolated socially from a peer group increasingly focused on opposite-sex pairing and, as a consequence, I was experiencing a certain amount of anxiety.[1]

One afternoon in those quiet stacks I found a book that changed my life: Donald Webster Cory's *The Homosexual in America*. Subtitled "A Subjective

Approach," it forcefully argued that homosexuals constitute a minority within society:

> Our minority status is similar, in a variety of respects, to that of national, religious and other ethnic groups: in the denial of civil liberties; in the legal, extra-legal and quasi-legal discrimination; in the assignment of an inferior social position; in the exclusion from the mainstream of life and culture.
>
> (Cory 1951: 13–14)

Years later I learned that Cory's powerfully written, openly subjective description and analysis of the conditions of gay male life in mid-century America had served as a stimulus to the emerging homosexual self-consciousness, and that Cory had been an inspirational leader of the nascent homophile movement. While there is much in the book to make a post-Stonewall gay liberationist (let alone a radical queer) squirm, at the time it was extraordinary in its freedom from apology.

The chapter, "The Search for a Hero," noted the characteristic "of any minority having an inferior social status that it seeks at all times to identify people of outstanding achievement with the group" (p. 157), and continued by comparing gays with Jews and Blacks, all minorities "needful of finding heroes who command universal respect." In the appendix "On a Five-Foot Bookshelf" I found a lode of cultural paydirt that I mined for many years: an annotated "check list of novels and dramas" from Sherwood Anderson to Arnold Zweig, in whose work "homosexuality is the basic theme, or in which it plays an important though minor role." This list became my Virgil, guiding me through the circles of library and bookstore shelves, as I searched for images and inspiration, affirmation and arousal.

Being gay did not make me a reader, but it powerfully directed my reading choices and shaped my tastes. Years later, in 1980, when I first taught a "gay studies" course at the University of Pennsylvania, I was surprised to discover that my experience was not shared by the students in my class. How surprised should I have been? By 1980, I had logged more than a decade of mass media research, collaborating with George Gerbner on the Cultural Indicators project (Gerbner *et al.* 1994), so I should have remembered that my students were part of the television generation. Like most undergraduates today, unfortunately, even at an Ivy League university, they were not readers. But they did watch. Movies and television, along with magazines such as *Time* and *Newsweek*, formed a major part of their store of images and knowledge about a subject that touched on the core of their identities.

MEDIA, MAJORITIES AND MINORITIES

Most of the images that we encounter in the media reflect the experiences and interests of the majority groups in our society – those who make up the large common denominator audiences whom producers wish to sell to advertisers.[2] As has happened so often – to me and, I know, to many others – Elihu Katz provided an elegant scheme for representing the mediated images *of*, *by* and *for* majorities and minorities.

The term "minority" has been applied to ethnically and racially defined people as well as to women (in terms of their relative powerlessness despite their numerical superiority) and it is now commonly applied to lesbian women and gay men. All of these are categories that are defined by their deviation from a norm that is white, male, heterosexual and (in most western societies) Christian, and these deviations are reflected in the mirrors that the media hold up before our eyes. In brief, minorities share a common media fate of relative invisibility and demeaning stereotypes. But there are differences as well as similarities in the ways in which various minorities are treated by the mass media. And, because there are important differences in the conditions that they face in our society, the effects of their media images are different for members of the various minority groups (Gross 1989, 1994).

Figure 5.1 shows the patterns of media images of majority and minority groups: the solid line represents the vast preponderance of programming that depicts majority images, produced by and for majority groups; the broken line represents a much smaller proportion of programming that includes or focuses on minorities, but it too is produced by and largely for majority group members. The dotted line represents the smallest portion of media content, that which is of, by and for minorities.

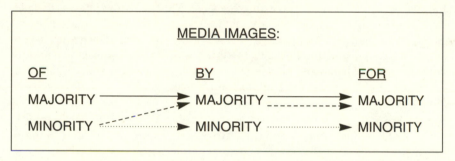

Figure 5.1 Patterns of media images of majority and minority groups

If we think of women as a minority we can readily see in Figure 5.1 the mediated experience illuminated in Laura Mulvey's influential analysis of the "male gaze" (1975). One need not subscribe to Mulvey's particular brand of Freudian/Lacanian analysis, or to her suspicion of "pleasure" as a mark of the minority "subject's complicity with an oppressive sexual regime" (Bergstrom and Doane 1989: 8), in order to appreciate the impact of her contribution. The issue that Mulvey put on the theoretical agenda, even for many who did not share her psychoanalytic perspective, was the necessity of differentiating the audience that is faced with images produced by and for the (in her case, male) majority. Other scholars pointed to the dangers of ignoring race and class differences while concentrating on gender.[3]

Unlike women, who might be viewed as minority spectators of images produced by and for male audiences, more "conventional" minorities have difficulty even finding their images reflected on the big and small screens of our mainstream media. The heterosexual male might be the center of everyone's (certainly of his) dramatic universe, but he will also be provided with appropriate female companionship (the spoils of the victor, one might say). Conversely, there is no demand for – and much resistance to – the frequent appearance of figures marked by their difference from the white, upper/middle class, Christian, heterosexual norm. Minority audiences facing their living room "window on the world" have had to make do with sparse fare. As African–American scholar Patricia Turner put it,

> In 1992 I appeared as a commentator in *Color Adjustment*, a documentary about the images of African Americans in prime-time television. Reflecting back on my childhood in the 1950s and 1960s, I said semifacetiously that while my mother loathed making long distance calls, even when there was a death in the family, she would call long distance to share news that a "Negro" was scheduled to appear on a television program. African Americans who have seen *Color Adjustment* are forever saying to me that my comments corroborate their personal recollections of the first decade of television. Our images were few and far between, and we hungered for more of them.
>
> (Turner 1994: xiii–xiv)

In a similar vein, Chinese American actor B. D. Wong, commenting on his role (as a Korean American) on the TV sitcom, *All American Girl*, starring Korean American comedienne Margaret Cho, said "When we were growing up, when an Asian person came on TV, somebody would say: 'Come quick! Come into the living room. There's an Asian person on TV.' And everybody would run and go, with this bizarre fascination: 'Oh wow, look at that. That's amazing'" (Southgate 1994: 53–4).

I would venture to suggest, however, that neither B. D. Wong nor Margaret Cho would have been called into the living room to witness one of the even more rare appearances of a lesbian or gay character on television. Despite the fact that both Wong and Cho would have had particular reason to be interested in such appearances (to engage in a bit of outing), it is highly unlikely that their families would have been aware of this interest, or that they would have indulged it had they suspected. Lesbian and gay people do not share the sort of fond recollections recounted by Turner or Wong.[4]

SEXUAL MINORITIES AND THE MEDIA

All minorities share a common media fate of relative invisibility and demeaning stereotypes. But sexual minorities differ from the "traditional" racial and ethnic minorities; in many ways we are more like "fringe" political or religious groups. We are rarely born into minority communities in which parents or siblings share our minority status. Rather, lesbians and gay men are a self-identified minority, and generally only recognize or announce our status at adolescence, or later. Also, by their very existence sexual and political minorities constitute a presumed threat to the "natural" (sexual and/or political) order of things, and thus we are always seen as controversial by the mass media. Being defined as controversial invariably limits the ways in which lesbians and gay men are depicted on the rare occasions that they appear, thereby shaping the effects of such depictions on the images held by society at large and by members of these minority groups.

Close to the heart of our cultural and political system is the pattern of roles associated with our conceptions of masculinity and femininity, of the "normal," "natural" and "moral" attributes and responsibilities of men and women that children learn – and adults are discouraged from toppling – as expectations and beliefs about what is possible and proper for men and for women.

The gender system is supported, in turn, by the mass media's treatment of sexual minorities. Lesbians and gay men are usually ignored; but when we *do* appear, it is in narrowly, negatively stereotyped roles that *support* the "natural" order. One could say the same for most media images of minorities, but our general invisibility makes us especially vulnerable.

We are among the least permitted to speak for ourselves in public life, including in the mass media. No major network television program yet has a lesbian or gay lead character. Openly lesbian and gay reporters are absent from news programs. While we are certainly present in story conferences and newsrooms, it is generally with our identities hidden, from the audience if not our colleagues.

We are also the group whose enemies are generally least inhibited by the consensus of "good taste" that protects other minorities from the more public displays of bigotry. It is unthinkable in the 1990s that any racial or ethnic minority would be subjected to the rhetorical attacks routinely aimed at lesbian and gay people by public figures, who do not encounter widespread condemnation for their bigotry.

Our vulnerability to media stereotyping and political attack lies in large part in our isolation and pervasive invisibility. Identity formation for lesbian and gay people requires the strength and determination to swim against the cultural stream that one is immersed in at birth. Those of us who are not white, male, middle class, Christian and heterosexual come to a sense of identity and self-worth in a society that focuses on attributes which we do not and mostly cannot possess by observing those around us and those we encounter through the lens of the media. Women are surrounded by other women, Blacks by other Blacks, and so forth, and can observe the variety of choices and fates facing those who are like them. Mass media may offer a narrow range of roles and images for women and minorities but their stereotypes are also balanced by the audiences' own experiences.

In contrast, lesbians and gay men are a self-identifying minority. We are presumed to be straight, and are treated as such, until we recognize that we are not what we have been told. But how are we to understand and deal with that difference? We only have limited direct experience with those who are sufficiently close to the accepted stereotypes to be labeled publicly as queers, faggots, dykes and so on and we all – gay or straight – have little choice but to accept media stereotypes which we imagine to be typical of all lesbians and gay men.

The rules of the mass media game have a double impact on gay people: they mostly show us as weak and silly, or evil and corrupt, but they also exclude and deny the existence of normal, unexceptional "plain gay folks" as well as exceptional lesbians and gay men. The stereotypic depiction of lesbians and gay men as abnormal and the suppression of positive or even "unexceptional" portrayals have served to maintain and police the boundaries of the moral order, encouraging the majority to stay on their gender-defined reservation and keeping the minority quietly hidden out of sight. The visible presence of healthy, non-stereotypic lesbians and gay men does pose a serious threat: it undermines the unquestioned normalcy of the status quo, and opens up the possibility of making choices that people might never have otherwise considered could be made.

MEDIA ARCHEOLOGY: HIDDEN IN PLAIN SIGHT

Given their centrality it is not surprising that lesbian and gay movements have focused on the role of the media in our oppression and in our liberation.

In 1919, the first gay film appeared in Germany. *Anders als die Andern* (Different from the Others) was intended to evoke support for the homosexual rights movement and included an appearance by homosexual rights pioneer Dr Magnus Hirschfeld, giving an unabashed plea for the abolition of laws criminalizing male homosexual acts. The film attracted a lot of attention when it opened in Berlin, and became news when banned in Vienna, Munich and Stuttgart. A year after it opened it was banned in Berlin, despite its commercial and critical success. Movie screens of the period were not sites where gay people could see their reflections. Thus, Richard Dyer's comprehensive account of lesbian and gay film, *Now You See It* (1990), moves from Weimar to the post World War II underground, where gay-themed "art films" began to explore territories avoided by mainstream movie-makers. Still, if we wish to understand the role of the media in the lives of gay people, we must turn to the darkened caves and the silver screens of the cinema.

Much of the early work of gay activist–scholars – and the term is appropriate, as no one unengaged by the gay movement was pursuing these matters publicly – focused on the delineation and analysis of the stereotypic portrayals of gay people in the media. In 1977, when the British Film Institute published *Gays and Film*, two of the three articles included (Sheldon and Dyer) focused on stereotyping: "relatively little explored in any systematic way and full of contradictions and confusions. Yet it remains an important area, for it is from representations of social groups that people get their 'knowledge' about those groups – and that goes for members of those groups themselves" (Dyer 1977: 2). In the two decades since, books and articles on gay people in/and the media have filled several feet of shelf space, but the issue of stereotyping remains a constant concern and is still full of contradictions and confusions. "What is wrong with these stereotypes is not that they are inaccurate," despite this being the most common line of attack, because "one of the things the stereotypes are onto is the fact that gay people do cross the gender barriers . . . [but that through stereotypes,] . . . heterosexual society [attempts] to define us for ourselves, in terms that inevitably fall short of the 'ideal' of heterosexuality" (Dyer 1977: 31).[5]

ONE-WAY CROSSOVER TRAFFIC

The experience of minorities in mass society will always include a diet of images created for the majorities whose experiences and interests they reflect. Minorities will invariably be culturally bi-lingual; members of the majority will have no such burden.[6] In fact, media images consumed by majority audiences may well have been produced by minority group members, as long as tell-tale labels are safely removed or hidden from sight. There is indeed traffic that moves from the minority to the majority, but this crossover commerce requires careful and often deceptive packaging if its cargo is to be palatable to the majority.

In an analysis of ways that "gay men have been creating culture which in turn has been assimilated into the mainstream" Michael Bronski characterizes the contributions of "this culture and sensibility, in addition to being one of the most important forces shaping Western culture," as also "one of the most progressive, liberating, and visionary" (1991: 8). And, just as Stuart Hall (1992), among many, has noted the powerful influence of Blacks on mainstream culture, through style and the physical, sexualized body (in music, fashion or sports), so Bronski notes a similar influence of gays.

> The association of homosexuality with the sexual and the cry of "sex obsession" have been used to attack homosexuals but it is precisely this quality, this "obsession with sex" which is at the basis of the liberation offered by the gay sensibility. Gay artists have constantly argued in favor of an open imagination, sought to present images of beauty to a culture which has demanded only the most utilitarian necessities, and portrayed alternative worlds as a release from an oppressive reality. Freeing sexuality and eroticism is an impulse everyone feels on some level, no matter how much they consciously support the existing system. And this has always been the potent threat of the gay sensibility. A threat which the mainstream culture constantly attempts to coopt and defuse by assimilation.
>
> (Bronski 1991: 8)[7]

In a highly influential article on "camp," Susan Sontag opened a critical Pandora's box by claiming that "Jews and homosexuals are the outstanding creative minorities in contemporary urban culture. Creative, that is, in the truest sense: they are creators of sensibilities" (1969: 290). Years later George Steiner echoed Sontag: "Judaism and homosexuality (most intensely where they overlap, as in a Proust or a Wittgenstein) . . . have been the two main generators of the entire fabric and savor of urban modernity in the West" (1980: 180). But, as with the soundtracks of the nostalgic films that Turner cites, the contributions of gays have almost always been enjoyed without acknowledgment of their creators. In this context lesbians and gays might again be closer to Jews than to Blacks. David Van Leer discusses the relations of minority cultural contributions to visibility, noting that, while the distinction between visible and invisible groups is never absolute, the routes by which less visible minorities approach power can differ from those open to the visible. . . . Ralph Ellison locates a black man's invisibility in the refusal of white culture to look at him; gay invisibility seems an effect not only of straight culture's inability to see, but also of homosexuals' unwillingness to make themselves visible through "coming out."

(Van Leer 1995: 4)

Thus, not surprisingly, the emergence of the homosexual subcultural identity proclaimed by Cory in 1951 – "a minority that cannot accept the outlook, customs, and laws of the dominant group" (p. 4) – owed much to the efforts of lesbians and gay men to pierce the veils of secrecy, to ask and to tell each other's secrets, at least within the security of the ghettos of gay bars.

"Rumor and gossip constitute the unrecorded history of the gay subculture" (Weiss 1992: 30). Writing about the emergence of lesbian identities in the 1930s, Andrea Weiss cites Patricia Spacks' analysis of gossip as an alternative discourse through which "those who are otherwise powerless can assign meanings and assume the power of representation . . . reinterpreting . . . materials from the dominant culture into shared private meanings" (p. 30). The gossip that Weiss is concerned with, however, is not the exchange of stories about one's friends and acquaintances, but the circulation of rumor and speculation about movie stars and other celebrities. Media scholars have demonstrated the central importance of stars in gay ghetto culture and the special relationship that gays have had to film (see Dyer 1977; 1979; LaValley 1985), finding escape and affirmation in the darkness of the theater and the luminance of the screen.

The crystallizing of lesbian and gay identities is somewhat akin to the re-discovery of their "ethnic roots" by third generation Americans whose parents had successfully assimilated into the mainstream. However, for gay people there were no grandparents to visit and the stars and stories of popular culture often took the place of the "old country." "In *Queen Christina*, Garbo tells Gilbert . . . 'It is possible to feel nostalgia for a place one has never seen.' Similarly, the film *Queen Christina* created in gay people a nostalgia for something they had never seen" (Russo 1987: 65). "For a people who were striving toward self-knowledge," Weiss writes of 1930s lesbian women, "Hollywood stars became important models in the formulation of gay identity" (1992: 36).

Despite the explosion of lesbian and gay visibility since the late 1960s the near total absence of openly gay celebrities insures the continuing importance of gossip in the crafting of gay subcultural identity. The denial and erasure of lesbians and gay men from the formal curricula of our schools and from the informal but even more influential curriculum of our mass media leads to the understandable desire to discover and celebrate the contributions of lesbian and gay figures. Sometimes this takes the form of "outing" – publicly revealing the homosexuality of a public figure who has hidden this fact (Gross 1993).

QUEERING THE "STRAIGHT" TEXT

If gossip and outing are exercises in unmasking the minority authors responsible for images seemingly produced *by* as well as *of* and *for* the majority, there are also reading strategies that deliberately read "against the grain" even when neither text nor author is necessarily a candidate for outing. In instances of what de Certeau (1984) called cultural "poaching," minority audiences "appropriate" majority images and read them "as if" they had been intended for the minority.[8] Alexander Doty advances an extended argument for such "queer readings," going far beyond the familiar terrain of gossip to claim a much wider cultural territory for oppositional and resistant readings:

> within cultural production and reception, queer erotics are already part of culture's erotic center, both as a necessary construct by which to define the heterosexual and the straight (as "not queer"), and as a position that can be and is occupied in various ways by otherwise heterosexual and straight-identifying people.
>
> (Doty 1993: 3–4)

Doty's map of queer readings takes us through a veritable Cook's Tour of television history, placing such classic pairings as Lucy and Ethel, Jack Benny and Rochester, Laverne and Shirley, in the company of more transparently gay figures such as Pee Wee Herman (who, nevertheless, was accepted as a popular kid's show host until he, as it were, exposed himself as a queer). In a less imperialistic mode, Mimi White cites the frequent televisual premise of *homosocial* groupings as an opening to oppositionally *homoerotic* readings (White 1987).

One of the most extensive opportunities for queer reading of a televisual text was provided by the CBS police series *Cagney and Lacey*. This long running (1982–1988), award winning series about two women police detectives garnered a large and loyal following of lesbians who were able to read the women as lesbian despite the characters' explicit heterosexuality (D'Acci 1994). Jane Feuer (1989) wrote about such queer readings, describing the *Dynasty* Nights at many gay bars on Wednesday evenings, which drew an audience of gay men who were interested in the fate of (sometimes) gay Steven Carrington as well as the dramatic excesses (and costumes) of Alexis Carrington. In a 1995 study Tanya Hands visited a lesbian bar in Philadelphia for the Wednesday night screenings of the current ABC hit, *Ellen*, starring Ellen DeGeneres. Ms DeGeneres' lesbianism has long been a staple of gay gossip, and had even begun to emerge into mainstream print. Hands' respondents were quite familiar with the gossip and claimed that much of their enjoyment derived from reading Ellen as a lesbian: "*We* know her character is gay. I just wish it was apparent to other people" (p. 62). Their wish was answered in September 1996, when *TV Guide* revealed that the character Ellen (not the performer) would come out as a lesbian that season, thus becoming the first openly gay lead character on a TV series.

ALONE IN THE FAMILY ROOM

Liebes and Katz returned from their travels accompanying *Dallas* into living rooms around the world and reminded us that "the nature of involvement varies with the cultural background one brings to the viewing" (1990: 21). They also returned to the hint dropped at the end of *Personal Influence*: "viewing escapist programs is not as escapist as it seems. In fact, viewers typically use television fiction as a forum for discussing their own lives" (p. 154). But, when Liebes and Katz go on to argue that, therefore, "The best place to begin [cultivating critical ability] is at home with familiar television programs" (p. 155) they fail to connect with the experience of those whose families might not welcome the opportunity to discuss, or even acknowledge, their lives. Particularly for lesbian and gay adolescents, home is not necessarily a haven in a heartless world.

In the summer of 1992 the US daytime serial *One Life To Live* (OLTL) began what was to be the longest and most complex television narrative ever to deal with a lesbian or gay character (since then, another daytime serial, *All My Children*, initiated a complex plot thread involving a gay high school teacher). Billy Douglas is a high school student who had recently moved to Llanview (the fictional small town outside Philadelplia where OLTL takes place) and become a star athlete and class president. When Billy confides, first to his best friends and then to his minister, that he is gay, he sets off a series of plot twists that differ from the usual soap opera complications in that they expose homophobia and AIDS-phobia among the residents of Llanview and thus offer the characters – and the audience – an opportunity to address topics that daytime serials, along with the rest of US mass media, have generally preferred to ignore.[9]

The plotline featuring Billy Douglas was the dominant thread of OLTL from July through early September 1992. Billy Douglas was played by actor Ryan Phillippe, in his first professional role, and he received an unusually large amount of mail even for a good-looking young soap opera actor. Even more unusual, many letters came from young men, most of whom identified themselves as gay – in one interview Phillippe reported getting 2,000 letters, adding "a good 45 per cent . . . from homosexual teenagers" (Mallinger 1993: 14).

Many wrote that they were particularly moved by and grateful for Ryan's sensitive portrayal of an experience much like their own, being isolated and vulnerable in a society that would prefer not to know that they existed. While it is not difficult to imagine that an African–American, Asian American or Latino actor would get letters from teenagers who identify with and appreciate their representation of an under-represented group on the public media stage, it is inconceivable that they would receive letters such as the following:

August 31, 1992

Dear Ryan,

First of all, I want to thank you for the courage you have shown playing the part of a homosexual teenager. Especially in this day and age when discrimination and violence against gays is on the rise.

As you act on *One Life to Live* as a gay teenager, I also act. I act as a straight, normal twenty-one year old. It has become routine to act like the perfect son or brother. *You are the first person I have ever told and may be the last, that I am gay. I don't think I will ever be able to tell anyone the truth.* Had not your portrayal and this storyline of a gay teen hit me so deeply, I probably would not be telling you. Your character is so realistic and you do such a great job portraying how gay teens really feel.

Recently, I saw phone numbers for gay youth in *Soap Opera Weekly* magazine. For those who are troubled about their sexuality. I honestly don't feel I have enough courage to call any of these places. For some reason, I think somehow, someone will find out. If my family or friends find out, I'm afraid they wouldn't look at me the same or would never love me as much as they do now.

I feel that way because of things I hear my family say about homosexuals. Until recently, I would laugh at jokes about gays or would pretend to dislike the way they were. I cannot and will not do that anymore. Now I just stay silent and try to ignore things that are said about gays and even AIDS itself. I overheard my father say that faggots started AIDS and normal people like Magic Johnson have to suffer for what gays have done. Well, do you think I could ever tell him that I am one of those who he thinks have caused normal people to suffer and die from AIDS? It's something I could never foresee.

I know this is just your job and I'm sorry for throwing all of my problems at you like this. I certainly don't expect you to solve any of them but it feels good just to tell someone. . . . Thank you for your time.

(Gross 1994; emphasis added)

How should we think about and try to understand the nature of the relationships that these writers feel that they have with Ryan Phillippe, an actor whom they have seen in a single role and, possibly, in TV and magazine interviews; or is their relationship with Billy Douglas, the troubled but courageous gay teenager, who reminds them of themselves?

Some writers confused the fictional character with the actor, addressing letters to Billy or, even while writing to Ryan, appeared to treat Billy and his family as real people.[10] But most seem well aware that Ryan Phillippe is an actor and Billy Douglas is a character. Why do these writers, both isolated and fearful gay teens and adults haunted by memories of unhappy childhoods, feel that a young actor (known to be straight), portraying a confused and troubled youth, is an appropriate target for their confessions, their overtures and their pleas for help?

Back in the 1950s, Horton and Wohl first addressed "para-social interaction," within a psychiatric framework, and defined such responses to media figures as pathological only when they are a "substitute for autonomous social participation, when [they proceed] in absolute defiance of objective reality" (1956: 200). Joli Jensen summarized their view:

These extreme forms of fandom . . . are mostly characteristic of the socially isolated, the socially inept, the aged and invalid, the timid and rejected. For these and similarly deprived groups, para-social interaction is an attempt by the socially excluded (and thus psychologically needy) to compensate for the absence of "authentic" relationships in their lives.

(Jensen: 17)

Apparently in the 1990s many teenagers and even adults confronting the choice between the stifling agony of the closet and the possibility – even certainty – of familial and societal rejection are living in *pathological circumstances* and do not have the option of authentic relationships with anyone who can help them to deal with their emotional crises. Thus an inexperienced but sincere young heterosexual actor can find himself playing not only role model but also confessor and phantom friend to people in great pain and need.

In recent years new options have emerged that offer isolated members of a minority the opportunity to reach and communicate with like-minded fellows: scattered cable-TV and radio programs that are available to those lucky enough to live within their range,[11] and for those with access to cyberspace, the Internet and the World Wide Web. Currently there are on-line forums, bulletin boards, home-page sites, and on-line "zines" addressed to lesbian and gay readers. These include, to give two relevant examples, a weekly listing of television programs with lesbian/gay-related content, and the *Oasis*, a web-site dedicated to providing information and contacts for lesbian and gay teenagers (Silberman 1994; Walsh 1994). These technological innovations permit the construction of virtual public spaces that can be life – or at least, sanity – saving refuges for many who have reason to feel that they are living in enemy territory.

SILENCE = DEATH

Looking back on my experience as a fifteen-year old combing the library stacks for information and validation, I readily appreciate the transformation that has occurred in the past four decades. The changes that have taken place since I first went searching for images in which I could see my reflection should not be underestimated. No teenager today faces the degree of denial and erasure that was common in those days. Today's young people are growing up in a world in which the words lesbian and gay are spoken and written in the media. Lesbians and gay men appear in the news, and within the fictional precincts of sitcoms and cop shows, prime-time drama and soap operas; and often enough these characters are (slightly) more than one-dimensional foils for the primary characters. Compared to the symbolic annihilation of my youth this is progress. But revolutionary changes have brought on a counter-revolution that can not be underestimated.

Marlon Riggs said that his controversial film *Tongues Untied* was motivated by a singular imperative: to shatter America's brutalizing silence around matters of sexual and racial difference (Riggs 1991). That silence has shown itself to be remarkably resilient: its enforcers are to be found in school boards; in the pulpits of churches, synagogues and mosques; in the editorial boards and newsrooms of the mass media; in the story conferences of Hollywood; in the halls of Congress and the Houses of Parliament.

The forces of counter-revolution are bent on closing the avenues to self-expression that have been won at great cost by a movement that has insisted on its right to speak for itself to a world that would rather not know that it exists. They see an edifice of authority crumbling under the onslaught of women and minorities demanding an equality that threatens to displace them from the center of the universe.

The mass media that tell most of the stories to most of the people more of the time are slowly shifting the terms of our public conversation towards a greater inclusiveness and acceptance of diversity. The battlefield of American popular culture will be hotly contested for the foreseeable future, as the forces of conservatism continue their attempts to push us back to the mythical past of "traditional family values" and the mainstream media, in their search for large and demographically lucrative audiences, inch cautiously towards a more accurate reflection of contemporary realities. In this seesawing progress the lesbian and gay community finds itself simultaneously sought out by adventuresome marketers and scapegoated by opportunistic preachers. And we are increasingly insisting on speaking for ourselves, both behind the scenes and on the media stages. Gay advocates and our enemies agree on one thing: the media are more than "mere" entertainment. They can be a matter of life and death.

NOTES

1 As I was writing this, the San Francisco Public Library announced the opening of a Gay and Lesbian Center in its new building. "The co-chairman of the gay and lesbian fund-raising campaign in San Francisco, Charles Forester, traces his indebtedness to the San Francisco Public Library to the early 1970s, when he was a young city planner. Like many other homosexuals coming to terms with themselves, he began his search for identity in a library, where countless books could be read with no one else the wiser (Dunlop 1996).

2 While this is a familiar conclusion from Cultural Indicators project studies, others have provided more recent confirmation. A group of Los Angeles based researchers examined 56 sitcoms and drama shows aired on ABC, CBS, NBC and FOX between October 28 and November 3, 1991 and concluded that, "characters on prime-time dramas and situation comedies are mostly male, white, single, heterosexual, in their 30s or 40s, and work in professional, managerial, or semi-professional, middle to high income jobs" (Nardi 1992: 1).

3 For example, Marsha Kinder notes, "I also think it's essential to explore spectator positioning, not only in terms of gender, but also in terms of racial, ethnic, generational and class differences" (1989: 204); and Jacqueline Bobo, speaking of her study of Black women audiences of *The Color Purple*, pointed out, "Unfortunately, when the female spectator is usually spoken of and spoken for, the female in question is white and middle class" (1989: 102).

4 Take, for example, the experience of an 18-year old Cuban American college student: "My mother made us listen to this thing on the radio, and she made a big deal about it to the whole family. It was an interview with these homosexuals . . . [my mother said] 'Look, how disgusting!' Things like that have made me never want her or anyone in my family to find out about it" (O'Neil 1984: 47–8).

5 Often, of course, these attempts are successful. In 1993 Bruce Bawer opened his paean to gay assimilationism, *A Place At The Table*, by recalling his observing a teenaged boy

surreptitiously reading a gay paper. Noting the sex-related photos and ads in the paper, Bawer was irked because "the narrow, sex-obsessed image of gay life that they presented bore little resemblance to my life or to the lives of my gay friends," and he wished that he could tap the youth on the shoulder and say, "Don't think those pictures of leathermen and cross-dressers and nipple clamps are what gay life is all about" (p. 20). Typical of knee-jerk stereotype decriers, it seems not to have occurred to Bawer that the boy might have been looking for precisely such images when he picked up the paper.

6   Reflecting on the "misreading" of gay-themed films by straight critics, gay writer Richard Goldstein noted, "We don't live in the same world. I know their society but they still don't know mine" (quoted in Russo 1987: 316). This is a common experience of ethnic, racial and sexual minorities.

7   Bronski cites the example of men's fashions, since the 1950s. Beginning with the 1950s "gay look" of sneakers and chinos and continuing through the adoption of blue jeans as a gay style, "what eventually happened was that the straight world was drawn to the erotic and psychological freedom that these gay clothes represented and they, in time, became an accepted staple of US apparel. . . . Each of these [successive] looks started in urban gay male communities and were quickly taken up by the fashion industry and marketed as the 'new look' for the heterosexual male. Each 'look' is progressively more sexual and more open – the 'tough' Levi outside covers willingly suggestive sexual undergarments. These looks became commonplace to US culture: the Marlboro Man and the Calvin Klein underwear man – to choose the most obvious and mythical examples – peered out of almost every magazine and newspaper, down from billboards, out of televisions. American men were discovering that they were sexual and they were learning it from queers" (1991: 9).

8   Of course, given the general awareness of the sexual *marranos* scattered throughout Hollywood, gay audiences might well have imagined that they were being winked at from the closet.

9   Another television format that has proved hospitable to lesbian and gay people is the daytime talk show pioneered by Phil Donahue in the late 1970s. By the early 1990s there were numerous talk shows running every day on broadcast and cable channels in the US and elsewhere (for talk shows in the UK see Livingstone and Lundt 1994). One thing that all of these shows have in common is that they all schedule lesbian and gay guests and themes with great frequency, especially during the crucial sweeps months. The hosts and, increasingly, the studio audiences can be counted on to take a liberal view towards sexual minorities – they are especially fascinated with transgendered people of any sort – and to endorse a "live and let live" attitude towards homosexuality. By the 1980s it is safe to say that most Americans were more likely to encounter an openly lesbian or gay person on daytime TV talk shows than anywhere else in our public culture. One can easily imagine the benefits of permitting these people to speak for themselves, calmly explaining their perspective on sexuality and society (Gamson 1995). The talk shows have also reduced their reliance on "experts" brought on to "explain" lesbian and gay guests to the audience (or to themselves), and they are also less likely than in the past to feel the need to include a homophobe for "balance" whenever scheduling lesbian or gay guests.

10   "Like you, I am also having a difficult time in dealing with the fact that I'm gay. My parents are not as [freaked out] as your patents are – but they're not far from it. . . . Sometimes I wish that we could have been friends. . . . As for me, if things don't get better soon – I feel like things will never work out. I truly hate being gay. *I would rather be dead* than disappoint my parents, friends, by them finding out that I'm gay. All this hiding is very tiring. Take care. [signed] Confused" (emphasis in original).

11   Los Angeles radio producer Greg Gordon, recalling his experience as a teenager ("I thought I was the only one"), found a way to reach into the closets and countrysides

where gays are painfully isolated: gay radio. He started *This Way Out*, a weekly half-hour show of news and commentary that now airs on seventy radio stations in six countries. . . . Those who tune in are often older gays in rural areas or young people who feel they can't talk to their parents or teachers about being gay (Price 1993).

REFERENCES

Bawer, B. (1993) *A Place At The Table: The Gay Individual in American Society*, New York: Poseidon Press.

Bergstrom, J. and Doane, M.A. (1989) "The female spectator: context and directions," *Camera Obscura* 20/21: 5–27.

Bobo, J. (1989) "Response," in J. Bergstrom and M. A. Doane (eds.) "The female spectator: context and directions," *Camera Obscura* 20/21: 100–103.

Bronski, M. (1991) "How homophobia hurts the publishing industry," *Gay Community News*, July 21, pp. 8–9. To be reprinted as "Stolen Goods," in L. Gross and J. Woods (eds.) *The Columbia Reader on Lesbians and Gay Men in American Media and Society*, New York: Columbia University Press (in press).

Cory, D.W. (1951) *The Homosexual in America: A Subjective Approach*, New York: Greenberg.

D'Acci, J. (1994) *Defining Women: Television and the Case of "Cagney and Lacey,"* Chapel Hill, NC: University of North Carolina Press.

De Certeau, M. (1984) *The Practice of Everyday Life*, Berkeley, CA: University of California Press.

Doty, A. (1993) *Making Things Perfectly Queer: Interpreting Mass Culture*, Minneapolis, MN: University of Minnesota Press.

Dunlop, D. (1996) "San Francisco library opens gay center," *New York Times*, March 13.

Dyer, R. (ed.) (1977) *Gays and Film*, London: British Film Institute.

Dyer, R. (1979) *Stars*, London: British Film Institute.

Dyer, R. (1990) *Now You See It: Studies on Lesbian and Gay Film*, London: Routledge.

Dyer, R. (1992) *Only Entertainment*, New York: Routledge.

Dyer, R. (1993) *Matter of Images: Essays on Representation*, New York: Routledge.

Feuer, J. (1989) "Reading *Dynasty*: television and reception theory," *South Atlantic Quarterly* 88 (2): 443–59.

Gamson, J. (1995) "Do Ask, Do Tell," *The American Prospect*, November.

Gerbner, G., Gross, L., Morgan, M. and Signorielli, N. (1994) "Growing up with television: the cultivation perspective," in J. Bryant and D. Zillman (eds.) *Media Effects: Advances in Theory and Research*, Hillsdale, NJ: Lawrence Erlbaum Associates, pp. 17–42.

Gross, L. (1989) "Out of the mainstream: sexual minorities and the mass media," in E. Seiter *et al.* (eds.) *Remote Control: Television, Audiences and Cultural Power*, London: Routledge, pp. 130–49.

Gross, L. (1993) *Contested Closets: The Politics and Ethics of Outing*, Minneapolis, MN: University of Minnesota Press.

Gross, L. (1994) "You're the first person I've ever told I'm gay: letters to a fictional gay teen," paper to International Communication Association, Sydney, July.

Hall, S. (1992) "What is this 'Black' in Black popular culture?" in G. Dent (ed.) *Black Popular Culture*, Seattle: Bay Press, pp. 21–33.

Hands, T. (1995) "Doin' it our way: queer reception, television and lesbian audiences," unpublished Master's thesis, Philadelphia, PA: Annenburg School, University of Pennsylvania.

Horton, D. and Wohl, R. (1956) "Mass communication and para-social interaction: observation on intimacy at a distance," *Psychiatry* 19 (3): 188–211.

Jensen, J. (1992) "Fandom as pathology: the consequences of characterization," in L. Lewis (ed.) *The Adoring Audience: Fan Culture and Popular Media*, London: Routledge, pp. 9–29.

Katz, E. and Lazarsfeld, P. (1955) *Personal Influence: The Part Played by People in the Flow of Mass Communications*, New York: Free Press.

Kinder, M. (1989) "Response," in J. Bergstrom and M.A. Doane (eds.) "The female spectator: context and directions," *Camera Obscura* 20/21: 199–204.

LaValley, A. (1985) "The great escape," *American Film*, April, 29–34, 70–71.

Liebes, T. and Katz, E. (1990) *The Export of Meaning: Cross-Cultural Readings of "Dallas,"* New York: Oxford University Press.

Livingstone, S. and Lundt, P. (1994) *Talk on Television*, New York: Routledge.

Mallinger, M.S. (1993) "I'm not a homosexual, but I play one on TV," *Au Courant* (Philadelphia), March 22, 11 (19): 11–17.

Mulvey, L. (1975) "Visual pleasure and narrative cinema," *Screen* 16: 3.

Nardi, P. (1992) *Diversity on Prime-Time Television*, report of the Media Image Coalition of Minorities and Women, Los Angeles, CA: County Commission on Human Relations, January 30.

O'Neil, S. (1984) "The vote of mass media and other socialization agents in the identity formation of gay males," in S. Thomas (ed.) *Studies in Communication*, vol. 1, Norwood, NJ: Ablex, pp. 201–6.

Price, D. (1993) "Friendly voices: gay radio eases isolation," *Detroit News*, March 4.

Riggs, M. (1991) "Tongues re-tied?" *Current*, August 12, p. 17.

Russo, V. (1981/1987) *The Celluloid Closet: Homosexuality in the Movies*, New York: Harper & Row.

Silberman, S. (1994) "We're teen, we're queer, and we've got e-mail," *Wired*, December, pp. 1–3.

Sontag, S. (1969) "Notes on camp," in *Against Interpretation*, New York: Dell.

Southgate, M. (1994) "A funny thing happened on the way to prime time," *New York Times Magazine*, October 30, pp. 52–5.

Steiner, G. (1980) "The cleric of treason," *New Yorker*, December 8.

Turner, P. (1994) *Ceramic Uncles and Celluloid Mammies*, New York: Anchor Books.

Van Leer, D. (1995) *The Queening of America: Gay Culture in Straight Society*, New York: Routledge.

Walsh, J. (1994) "Logging on, coming out," *Advocate*, October 18, p. 6.

Weiss, A. (1992) *Vampires and Violets: Lesbians in Cinema*, New York: Penguin.

White, M. (1987) "Ideological analysis and television," in R. Allen (ed.) *Channels of Discourse*, Chapel Hill, NC: University of North Carolina Press, pp. 134–71.

6 Particularistic media and diasporic communications

Daniel Dayan

FRAGILE COMMUNITIES, PARTICULARISTIC MEDIA

There is a long tradition of communications studies that is concerned with the role of the media in creating new, usually wider and ultimately political communities. This essay is concerned with another role that can be imparted to the mass media: that of reconstructing or maintaining in existence already established but somehow fragile or imperiled communities – minority groups, immigrants, exiles, diasporas.

The media seem here to play a role that is both internally cohesive and secessive *vis-à-vis* society at large. They tend to be particularist or particularizing, eliciting a number of questions, such as, how do they fulfill their particularistic role? Is the process of community construction accompanied by a parallel process of mediatic innovation? Does this particularistic vocation entail a necessary rejection of universalistic values? Is it at odds with a normative view of the public sphere?

In reference to political sociology, and to the vast range of studies that link media, identity and territory, this presentation wishes to point to the differences between the goals of a study on particularistic media and those of the research traditions that have addressed the role of the media in the formation of communities. It also attempts to situate the performance of particularistic media in a historical context characterized by economic globalization, fear of cultural homogeneization, and the rise of movements that reject universalism. But, fundamentally, it focuses on three sorts of questions:

1 What is the particular type of knowledge mobilized in the construction of a group's identity? How do particularistic media contribute to the construction, mediation and adoption of this identity?
2 What are the problems raised by the development of media which are capable of connecting to each other different segments of diasporas?
3 Particularistic media may offer competing versions of a group's identity. In what circumstances can they stop being mere clusters of media, and lead to the emergence of micro public spheres?

THE CONTEXT OF GLOBALIZATION

Redefining the local

The vast literature currently developed on the interaction between local and globalizing processes sounds curiously familiar to media specialists. When geographers and economists deal with globalization, they re-enact debates that often took place long ago in communication research. These are the debates between hypodermic needle paradigms, theories of powerful effects, theories of limited effects, theories stressing media users and their gratifications, theories of reception and resistance. Such a parallelism is understandable. In both cases a problematic of effects, impacts or influences is linked to a topgraphy of centers and peripheries; and, in both cases, mass communication systems happen to be central actors.

Such a parallelism becomes manifest with the abandonment of the early conceptualizations of the global/local relationship. This relationship is no longer seen as simply one of homogeneization. The image of a dominating center and a dominated periphery is abandoned (Racine 1995). The local is not merely the site of an endorsement or rejection of initiatives taken elsewhere. The local is made not only of victims but also of actors. This autonomy of local processes is visible in the cultural sphere. In the manifesto that opens the first issue of the journal *Public Culture*, Arjun Appadurai and Carole Breckenridge stress that transnational flows are much less homogeneizing than hitherto believed. The local is no longer the end of the road, the final and lowly destination of messages emanating from a lofty center. The local has become cosmopolitan in its own way. Cosmopolitanism comes in different guises and forms. Diasporas of migrant workers develop their own in reference to the host cultures, to the traditions of their respective groups, to the reconstruction of such traditions by their elites. These elites are no longer exclusive relays towards the global and the masses are no longer confined to the local. They are themselves in motion: they are made of tourists, of television watchers, of *gastarbeiters* (Appadurai and Breckenridge 1988a).

As a result of this interpenetration, globalization should interest anthropologists as well as economists. Anthropologists cannot avoid noticing the territorial shadows projected by globalization; they have to account for the metamorphoses occurring at the local level.

Particularistic movements: resisting homogeneization or universality?

Central to this essay are some specific responses to globalization. These responses take the form of stressing particularism, of reconstructing endangered identities. Are such responses laudable or dangerous?

Identity processes in the late twentieth century are characterized by a powerful return of nationalist themes; by the hasty, almost incessant, emergence of new nations. Often expressed in the language of ethnicity, the politics of these new nations gives a bad name to particularist politics. However, particularism may perhaps adopt forms that are not doomed to become horrible. Should we automatically stigmatize the maintenance of diversity in the face of homogeneization? Are particularistic media involved in an active rejection of universality?

There is no doubt that the maintenance of diversity may involve a rejection of universalism. It may lead to the secessive model that Todd Gitlin condemns in his *Twilight of Common Dreams* (Gitlin, 1995). It may foster the decline of that universalist model of the nation state that Dominique Schnapper rightly describes as a product of enlightenment: a territory in which nationalism has been superseded through the legal principle of a community based on citizenship (Schnapper 1994). When people no longer believe in a progress-oriented history, particularism might open the road towards regressions, romantic infatuations, mass graves.

Yet particularistic motives are not doomed from the beginning. They can involve a rejection of universalism but not necessarily so. In fact the discourse of particularism is far from monolithic. The media that insure the continued survival of certain groups tend to offer these groups competing versions of their identity. Some are lethal. Some are not. There are many sorts of particularist rhetorics, and many ways of mediating the knowledge required for community construction. Constructing identities, maintaining identities, involves various processes. Processes of what sort?

IDENTITY AS PROCESS: PRODUCTION, CONFRONTATION, ADOPTION

Maintaining or producing identity?

Particularistic media complement the role of institutions in charge of the custody and transmission of filiation and memory. Described among others by Lucette Valensi (1992) or Nicole Lapierre (1989), such institutions include universities, museums, schools; they involve the intervention of various actors; they often enter in dialogue with social enterprises (in Victor Turner's sense) or with social movements. But in fragile communities the question of identity is no longer one of routine maintenance and such institutions are mostly absent. In such communities maintaining a group's identity requires complex strategies. Two sorts of problems must be addressed.

The problem of autonomy: what are we? who are we? who says so?

Problems of a first sort emerge in those situations in which the concerned community is a minority, submitted to the decisions of a majority, and surrounded by "generalist" media whose messages are conceived for that majority. In such contexts it is necessary to distinguish between those constructions of identity that are independent, autonomous; and those that are produced either within the majority, or under its influence. Take the example of a group dispersed on the territories of several nation states. Are the respective versions of that group's identity always independent of pressures exerted by these states?

Following a suggestion made by Elihu Katz, one could imagine a systematic description of identity-producing-discourses in intercultural contexts (Katz 1993). Such a description would delineate a number of discursive possibilities, by distinguishing between constructions that are (a) about, by or for (b) a minority or the majority. Among the numerous possibilities included in such a discursive matrix, some are doomed to confront each other, leading to potentially explosive situations. At the heart of the confrontation is the conflict between the heteronomy of a "What are you?" and the autonomous "Who are we?" (Leca, in Badie and Wolton 1996). But, as suggested by the same matrix, there are many nuanced positions between these two extremes.

Choosing amongst identity proposals: identities in contest

Problems of a second type have to do with choosing among proposed identities. As in any other society, different versions of the identity of the same group will be constructed. These versions will confront each other in the fora that Appadurai and Breckenridge equate with their notion of a public culture and whose existence often depends on that of particularistic media. Debates, contests and sometimes social dramas can be expected to erupt around issues of identity. But these debates (such as those that surrounded a number of films or photographic exhibits on minorities in various countries) represent only a first stage of reception. They do not tell us how identities are adopted, how they become internalized or altogether indistinguishable from those who have adopted them. In other terms the process of identity construction remains unsufficiently analyzed if one only describes what takes place in the public sphere; if the analysis only deals with the level of the offer. In order to find out about the internalization of identity one has to take a second step and move into the private sphere.

Adopting identity: from public sphere to private sphere

This second step aims at identifying those discourses that have actually served as bases for decision making; those images that helped individuals to make crucial decisions. Originally made at a personal level, individual choices end up acquiring historical dimensions. Take the example of a minority group to whom one of the identities proposed was that of a symbiotic fusion with the surrounding majority. It is relevant to the history of that group that so many of its members chose emigration, thus rejecting the symbiotic model in favor of other constructions. Such constructions do play an essential part in the life of individuals. They confer historical intelligibility, explain momentous decisions such as that of leaving a given country, of speaking a given language, of being called by a given name. They are the subject of intense debates between siblings, between parents and children, between husbands and wives. They provide some of the insights usually found in literary genres and, in particular, in the *Bildungsroman*. In the absence of works of fiction, oral histories will provide a privileged access to constructions of this type and to those situations where the intimate meets the historical.

MEDIA AND DIASPORAS

Dispersed groups

The study of particularistic media seems particularly relevant when media are instruments of survival for endangered cultures; when their presence insures the maintenance of links within geographically dispersed groups. Among a growing number of such groups, one can mention the Jewish, Armenian, Palestinian, Kurdish diasporas; Iranian exile groups in the US; North African migrant communities in continental Europe; Pakistani and Indian communities in Britain, and so on.

Though they do form small-scale communities locally – neighborhoods, street corners, or housing-project societies – such groups often do not share a common space. Typically they spread over the territories of many nation states and their members are exposed to an unusually vast range of potential identities. Of course a nationalistic perspective is not always absent from the identities elaborated by/for these groups. Indeed most of the communities that concern themselves with particularistic media also refer to some "national" center. But this center is not necessarily political. Often it is no more than a founding myth, enshrined in collective memory.

A central example

Though many groups will serve as points of reference or comparison the first stage of this essay will focus on a specific group: the Moroccan Jewish diaspora. This group manifests various interesting characteristics:

1　A wide range of dispersion, allowing comparison between groups located in France, Canada, the US, Spain, South America, Israel.
2　Situation on both sides of the north/south or western/non-western divide.
3　Existence of competing potential centers, one historical (Morocco); one political and religious (Israel); one cultural and linguistic (France).
4　Rapid sequence of identity reformulations throughout the last 100 years, leading to the possibility of recording histories from individuals who successively went through the colonization process, the end of colonial rule and then the creation of the state of Israel.
5　Emphasis on the maintenance of identity sometimes associated with, and often dissociated from, a national project.
6　Possibility for the researcher to enter the picture and propose a reflexive analysis of his own practice.

The range of interdiasporic media

It seems unproductive to limit the definition of diasporic communication to the range of organizations conventionally defined as "media." Thus, instead of exclusively dealing with radio, cinema, television or journalism, this essay deliberately tries to account for other – for example, smaller – "media," and to focus on the various practices, institutions and organizations (Abeles 1995) that link the different segments of diasporic ensembles to each other. Among such practices (pilgrimages, religious occasions, family rituals, etc.) many can be described as "traditional." Yet they are no longer really "traditional." They would be better described as "neo-traditional." They are not reminiscences of another age but contemporary reconstructions; conscious redemptions of folk cultures. They include:

1   Production and circulation of newsletters; of audio and video cassettes; of holy icons; of small media in general. (Specialized shops sell "ethnic" videos in the immigrant neighborhoods of most large European cities.)
2   Exchange of letters, photographs, telephone calls, and travelers. (This last point is particularly important. Diasporas mobilize huge amounts of back and forth traveling. Entailing the creation of specialized organizations or agencies, they are charter flight societies. The dominant form of travel is linked to "family tourism." But traveling also includes prospective tourism, preparing the ground for emigration, or a tourism of pilgrimage usually marking the end of the acculturation process and the moment of rediscovery, or reinvention, of neglected traditions.
3   Constitution of religious communities or cultural associations, regrouping individuals of similar origins, attracted by the style of worship or nature of interaction.
4   Creation of interdiasporic networks (and circulation of directives, sermons etc.) by religious or political organizations with specific agendas.

But, of course, diasporic communication also mobilizes the major mass media. It manifests itself through the community oriented genres made available on the programming schedules, that is, religious programs on television and ethnic radio programs. (Eliséo Véron's 1988 study of genres in reference to types of social discursivity would allow a nuanced description of the role adopted here by mainstream media.) It also manifests itself through the development of community media such as daily, weekly or monthly newspapers and through exclusive radio or television channels. (The proliferation of such media in the United States has recently been stressed by Todd Gitlin, 1995.) Far from excluding each other the various media mentioned here interact with each other. They enter all sorts of combinations. The texture of such combinations, their moving hierarchies, are quite relevant to the cultural analyst. Some of the potential outcomes of the clusters that they form will be examined in conclusion.

CONCLUSIONS

Four major questions emerge respectively from notions developed by Peter Dahlgren, Benedict Anderson, Michael Schudson and Arjun Appadurai. Each will be summarized, then followed by brief comments.

1 Is it possible for clusters of particularistic media to be transformed into embryonic public spheres, thus serving as paradoxical vehicles for universalistic values?
2 Is the maintenance of diasporic communities, a technical problem only? Can it really be distinguished from the construction of the community?
3 Can one fully address the question of identity formation by simply analyzing the ideological constructions offered in the public sphere?
4 Can one speak of a new object for ethnographies? Of the passage from descriptions centered on territory to descriptions focused on networks?

Dahlgren: media clusters or micro public spheres?

Many studies have already been devoted to particularistic media, including Hamid Naficy's essays on the Iranian diaspora in California and the making of an exile culture (Naficy 1993); Larry Gross's remarkable analysis of the gay press in the US (Gross 1993); Annabelle Sreberny-Mohammadi's description of the mobilization of small media in the context of the Iranian revolution (Sreberny-Mohammadi and Mohammadi 1994). Susan Herbst's remarks on the role played by the press in the emergence of a black public sphere in Chicago are particularly suggestive in terms of the connection that they make between particularistic media and the question of the public sphere (Herbst 1994). This connection should be further explored here.

We know that the transmission of identity constructions mobilizes a very wide range of media – "big" and "small," modern and traditional. The diversity of such media is matched by that of their audiences. Some media tend exclusively to be the media of a given group. Some are shared with the rest of the population. The coexistence of all of these media seems to involve more than a simple contiguity. Thus one may raise the question of the relationship between particularistic media and the surrounding national public sphere; that of the continuities between minority and majority media.

But the emergence of clusters of media addressing given communities may lead to specific consequences inside such communities. These media clusters are expected to play a role of differentiation. They are meant to be particularizing. Yet – this is one of the hypotheses guiding this essay – they might induce the constitution of what Peter Dahlgren would characterize as micro public spheres (Dahlgren 1994a). If so – and despite professed particularistic ambitions – one can hardly imagine how such micro public spheres would manage to remain sealed to the public sphere at large; how they would prevent issues and behavioral models from circulating back and forth. Sooner or later one can expect the smaller sphere to become infiltrated by the values and procedural models that prevail in the larger one. Sooner or later one can expect traditional groups to be exposed to practices that include free argumentation and open debate. Sooner or later a process of homogeneization might take place, affecting the internal organization of the community; leading to new sites of power, to new modes of legitimation, to new internal strategies.

Naficy was already pointing to an irony of this type when he showed that, far from exclusively protecting traditional life styles, the construction of exile cultures served as a rite of passage into, and an instrument of acculturation to, the host society. Particularistic media are not always instruments of a secession.

Anderson: diasporas imagined by whom?

The role of the media in constructing communities has been addressed in a number of influential studies including those by Walter Ong (1997), James Carey (1992), Elizabeth Eisenstein (1979), Benedict Anderson (1983), Philip Schlesinger (1991) and Pierre Sorlin (1992). In many cases such studies are historical. In practically every instance they explore the societal impact of technological innovation. Two of the crucial questions they ask are: what distinguishes a type of sociation called an audience – or a public – from other social groupings or communities (be they ideological, religious, cultural, national, etc.)? What is the nature of the processes that may turn audiences into communities, or communities into audiences?

The latter is, in particular, the question asked by Benedict Anderson, when he explores the formidable impact of the press (and printed literature), in terms of: (a) reorganizing as continuous geographic spaces what were formerly perceived as distinct; (b) offering a shared experience of time to groups that lived by different clocks; (c) homogenizing various dialects into standard languages. By reinforcing each other, such transformations lead to the emergence of national communities. National communities are not only "imagined communities" but also communities that often started as audiences.

In contrast to this literature, and to the work of Anderson, the question raised here is not that of the construction of new communities. This essay does not mean to describe the part played by the media in the contagious dynamics that lead to the delineation of constantly enlarged sociations. On the contrary, it focuses on media whose vocation is not globalizing but particularistic; media whose aim is not to create new identities but to prevent the death of existing ones.

Yet this particularistic vocation is studied in reference to diasporas and the very existence of diasporas calls for a question inspired by Anderson. Instead of being unproblematic – given, merely "factual" – a diaspora is always an intellectual construction tied to a given narrative. Like other types of communities, but more so than most, diasporas are incarnations of existing discourses, interpretants of such discourses, echoes or anticipations of historical projects. They are "imagined communities" *par excellence*, and they can be imagined in a number of possible, sometimes conflicting, ways. Thus their maintenance, far from being a technical problem, involves a constant activity of reinvention.

Schudson: the "resonance" of proposed identities

Another point that should be stressed, concerning this essay, is the decision not to examine processes of identity construction exclusively at the level of the offer. Instead, there is a strong focus on the reception, adoption or rejection of identity models.

Of course, an important aspect of the construction of identities takes place in the public sphere. But, in order to avoid a reductive approach to a complex phenomenon, one must also examine the ways in which identity constructions, once proposed in public, are received in the private realm. How do community members behave *vis-à-vis* the proposed constructions? Why do they adopt them or not and when? Some events call for momentous personal decisions. Are they also decisive turning points in identity formation?

Quite helpful in this context is Michael Schudson's delineation of the various dimensions involved in the "power" of cultural objects. Defining "cultural objects" in a manner general enough to permit the inclusion of extremely different texts or practices (e.g. poems, telegrams, biblical narratives, television shows), Schudson distinguishes between their reach, rhetorical force, institutional retention, and resolution on the one hand, and the difficult question of their "resonance" on the other (Schudson 1989). While most sociological studies on the construction of identities have tended to deal with Schudson's first four dimensions, this essay is also concerned with the fifth.

Appadurai: the changing site of ethnographies

Finally, in contrast to an ideal practice of ethnography, the communities whose study is proposed here are quite problematic. Their borders are unstable. Their territories are uncertain. They are constantly restructured in response to the presence of media.

Yet, the traditional loci of anthropological fieldwork are progressively disappearing. Culture can no longer be studied in small, stable societies; in societies with precise borders. It has to be described in the context of societies increasingly characterized by their heterogeneity, by their connection to world economies, by the exportation of their members (Appadurai and Breckenridge 1988b).

In such a context, diasporic groups are no longer unfrequent or exceptional. When the cultural identity of an increasing number of such groups tends to become dissociated from any direct territorial inscription, one can expect ethnographers to shift their attention away from their traditional objects (spatially circumscribed communities) and to start studying those communication devices that maintain dispersed groups alive by linking peripheries to centers and connecting presents to pasts.

In other terms, ethnography can no longer afford to ignore media research. On the contrary, studies of the media and the groups that use them might become a new ethnographic field. Beyond its normative dimension, the notion of a public sphere might then turn into a descriptive instrument.

NOTE

In addition to including texts directly mentioned in this essay, the following bibliography on maintaining indentities and constructing indentities has been updated with the help of friends and colleagues. For this help, and also for their comments and suggestions, I have many thanks to offer. To Jostein Gripsrud at Bergen University and to the participants of the Media and Knowledge seminar: Klaus Bruhn Jensen, John Corner, Suzanne de Cheveigné, John Ellis, Sonia Livingstone, Graham Murdock and Roger Silverstone. To Hilde Arntsen, Michael Bruun Andersen, Svennik Hoyer, Knut Lundby and Tore Slaatta who attended my own seminar at the University of Oslo. To Philip Schlesinger who, by inviting me to Stirling, gave me the chance of continuing our ongoing conversation and of trying out some of the ideas presented here on Stuart Hall, Renato Ortiz and Helge Ronning. To Tamar Liebes who organized a wonderful conference in Jerusalem. I am grateful for her comments and for those of James Carey, James Curran, Lena Jayyusi, Todd Gitlin and Larry Gross. Elihu Katz made no comments but he inspired this essay.

REFERENCES AND FURTHER READING

Abeles, M. (1995) "Pour une antropologie des institutions," *L'Homme* 135, July-September.
Anderson, B. (1983) *Imagined Communities: Reflections of the Origins and Spread of Nationalism*, London: Verso.
Appadurai, A. (1990) "Disjuncture and difference in the global cultural economy," in M. Featherstone (ed.) *Global Culture: Nationalism, Globalization, Modernity*, London: Sage.
Appadurai, A. (1993) "Patriotism and its futures," *Public Culture*, 5 (3).
Appadurai, A. (1996) *Modernity at Large: Cultural Dimensions of Globalization*, Minneapolis, MN: University of Minnesota Press.
Appadurai, A. and Breckenridge, C. (1988a) "Editors comments," *Public Culture* 1 (1).
Appadurai, A. and Breckenridge, C. (1988b) "Why public Culture?" *Public Culture* 1 (1).
Appadurai, A. and Breckenridge, C. (1992) "Museums are good to think: Heritage on view in India," in I. Karp and S. D. Lavine (eds.) *Museums and Communities: The Politics of Public Culture*, Washington, DC: Smithsonian Institute.
Badie, B. and Wolton, D. (1996) *Identité et Territoire*, a round table conference involving contributions by Jean Leca, Dominique Schnapper, Michel Foucher, Jean Robert Henry, Robert Toulemon and Oliver Dollfuss held in Paris by Centre National de la Recherche Scientifique and Institut National de l'Audiovisuel. To be published by CNRS in the *Hermes* series.
Brody, J. (1995) *Rue des Rosiers*, Paris: Autrement.
Carey, J. (1992) *Communication as Culture: Essays on Media and Society*, London: Routledge.
Cohen, R. (1995) "Rethinking Babylon: iconoclastic conceptions of the diasporic experience," *New Community* 21(1), January.
Dahlgren, P. (1994) "La sphére publique à l'age des nouveaux médias," in D. Dayan and I. Veyrat-Masson (eds.) *Espaces Publics en Images*, *Hermes* series, vols 13 and 14, Paris: CNRS Press.
Dahlgren, P. (1994b) *Media and the Public Sphere*, London: Sage.
Dayan, D. (1997) "L'importance du local," in Laidi, Z. (ed.) *Le Temps Mondial* (Debate with Edgar Morin, Guy Hermet, Zak Laidi, Bessarab Nicolescu and Paul Virilio), Paris: Editions Complexe.
Eisenstein, E. (1979) *The Printing Press as an Agent of Change*, New York: Cambridge University Press.
Gillespie, M. (1995) *Television Ethnicity and Cultural Change*, London: Routledge.
Gilroy, P. (1993) *The Black Atlantic: Modernity and Double Consciousness*, London and New York: Verso
Giraud, M. (1996) "Les populations Caraibéennes en Amérique du Nord et en Europe," Paris: *MSH Informations* 73.

Gitlin, T. (1995) *The Twilight of Common Dreams: Why America is Wracked by Culture Wars*, New York: Metropolitan/Henry Holt.

Gross, L. (1993) *Contested Closet: The Politics and Ethics of Outing*, Minneapolis and London: University of Minnesota Press.

Habermas, J. (1991) *The Structural Transformation of the Public Sphere* (trans. Thomas Burger), Cambridge, MA: MIT Press.

Halbwachs, M. (1968) *La Mémoire Collective* (3rd edn), Paris: Presses Universitaires de France.

Hall, S. (1988) "New ethnicities," in K. Mercer (ed.) *Black Film, British Cinema*, London: Institute for Contemporary Arts.

Hall, S. (1990) "Cultural identity and diaspora," in J. Rutherford (ed.) *Identity, Community, Culture, Difference*, London: Lawrence & Wishart.

Hall, S. (1993) "Rethinking ethnicities: three blind mice one black, one white, one hybrid," Inaugural lecture, new Ethnicities Unit, University of East London.

Hannerz, U. (1990) "Cosmopolitans and locals in world culture," in M. Featherstone (ed.) *Global Culture: Nationalism, Globalization, Modernity*, London: Sage.

Herbst, S. (1994) "Race, domination, mass media and public experience: Chicago 1934–1960," in *Politics at the Margin: Historical Studies of Public Experience Outside the Mainstream*, Cambridge: Cambridge University Press.

Katz, E. (1993) "By, for and about," personal communication to Serge Proulx and Daniel Dayan, Annenberg School for Communication, University of Pennsylvania, Philadelphia.

Lapierre, N. (1989) *Le Silence de la Mémoire*, Paris: Plon.

Laidi, Z. (1997) *Le Temps Mondial*, Paris: Complexe.

Morley, D. and Robins, K. (1995) *Spaces of Identity: Global Media, Electronic Landscapes and Cultural Boundaries*, London: Routledge.

Naficy, H. (1993) *The Making of an Exile Culture*, Minneapolis and London: University of Minnesota Press.

Ong, W. (1997) *The Presence of the Word*, Minneapolis, MN: University of Minnesota Press.

Racine, J. L. (1995) "Les territoires de la globalisation; réseaux forts et espaces flous. Decideurs et citoyens," Unpublished paper to Unesco MOST Program Conference, Paris.

Robins, K. (1989) "Re-imagined communities," *Cultural Studies* 3 (2).

Rushdie, S. (1991) *Imaginary Homelands*, London: Granta Books.

Schlesinger, P. (1991) "On national identity: cultural politics and the mediologists," in P. Schlesinger, *Media, State and Nation: Political Violence and Collective Identities*, London: Sage.

Schlesinger, P. (1992) "Europeanness: a new cultural battlefield?" *Innovation* 5 (1).

Schnapper, D. (1994) *La Communauté des Citoyens*, Paris: Gallimard.

Schudson, M. (1989) "How culture works: perspectives from Media Studies on the efficacy of symbols," *Theory and Society* 18.

Schudson, M. (1994) "Culture and the integration of national societies," *International Social Science Journal* 139, 46 (1), Blackwell/Unesco.

Sorlin, P. (1992) "Le mirage du public," *Revue d'Histoire Moderne et Contemporaine* 39, Paris.

Sreberny-Mohammadi, A. and Mohammadi, A. (1994) *Small Media, Big Revolution: Communication, Culture and the Iranian Revolution*, Minneapolis and London: University of Minnesota Press.

Valensi, L. (1992) *Fables de la Mémoire: La Bataille des Trois Rois*, Paris: Hachette.

Véron, E. (1988) "Presse écrite et théorie des discours sociaux: production, réception, regulation," in E. Véron, *La Presse: Produit, Production, Réception*, Paris: Didier-Erudition.

7 The dialogic community

"Soul talks" among early Israeli communal groups

Tamar Katriel

INTRODUCTION

This essay explores the nature, meaning and construction of the dialogic vision embedded in culturally focal, communicative events that took place among youthful groups of early Israeli pioneers in the 1920s.[1] Natively referred to as "soul talks" (*sichot nefesh*), these unique speech occasions have become mythologized in Israeli collective memory over the years. In these communes of early Jewish pioneers (which later evolved into *kibbutzim*, communal settlements), and to which a good part of Israeli "foundation mythology" has been attached, a collectivistic, *Gemeinschaft*-oriented ethos was dominant. It was reflected in a variety of communal practices which were marked by a high degree of sharing in work, food and clothing, and shared leisure pursuits, such as communal singing and dancing. However, in the context of the nocturnal "soul talks" that were held in the communal dining-room, self-disclosive, individual expression was designated as a symbolically potent vehicle for the cultivation of a spirit of shared community.

The following excerpts – taken from diaries, letters, autobiographical and fictional accounts – testify to the cultural and personal significance of "soul talks" in the young pioneers' life-experience (they were all in their late teens and early twenties). They also attest to the multiplicity of voices and attitudes that have informed the cultural conversation about them.

The first excerpt is part of an entry found in the communal diary *Kehiliatenu* (*Our Community*) that was compiled by a group of pioneers in Bitaniya Ilit in 1921 and was originally published in 1922. The group of youngsters in Bitaniya Ilit was formed in 1920 after a rather painful process of social selection from among a larger group of pioneers who had been potential candidates for joining it. The selection process was mandated by the limited work possibilities at the new site but was also colored by an elitist attitude and a stress on interpersonal compatibility among like-minded individuals who could contribute to each other's personal growth.

The group was stationed in a temporary camp overlooking the Sea of Galilee, in Bitaniya Ilit. Members were engaged in a tree planting project sponsored by the British Mandatory authorities while waiting for the land that they needed to establish their own settlement. The members of this group came from Eastern

Europe (mainly Galicia) and Central Europe and belonged to the *Hashomer Hatza'ir* (Young Guard) youth movement (Mintz 1995; Evens 1995). They were from middle-class Jewish families. Most of them were well-educated and attentive to the intellectual currents of the time. Thus, they intermingled a Jewish culture with the influences of German youth culture, especially the philosophy of youth propagated by the social circle of Sigfried Bernfeld, and with Martin Buber's philosophy of dialogue.

Even before the publication of their communal diary, the members of the Bitaniya Ilit group made a name for themselves owing to the special spiritual ethos that they cultivated, which found its quintessential expression in their "soul talks." The following testimonial excerpt represents a participant's highly positive attitude towards the "soul talks." It was written by one of the four young women who were part of the group of twenty-six pioneers, and it gives voice to the profound experience of human connection that some of the pioneers felt that the "soul talks" engendered. She describes the group's nocturnal gatherings in ecstatic, even erotic terms:

> And the nights we spent in the reading room – (Oh, how beautiful it was!), when we all participated in long talks, nights of seeking the way from one person to the other – this is how I call these nights of holiness [*leilot kodesh*]. Hours, long hours of confessions and listening. Some of us were blessed with the power of expression; others stuttered; many kept silent . . . and in moments of silence – utter silence [*dmama daka*] – it seemed to me that a ray of light [*zik*] springs out of every heart and the rays merge up high [*mizdavgim*, copulate] into one big flame that reaches into the heart of the sky; and it seemed to me that one large spirit is walking silently around the hall and leaving the stamp of a kiss [*chotam neshika*] on our foreheads. And the stamp left by our talks will forever light our foreheads: it will be the sign which will allow us to know each other to the end of our days. And I loved these nights more than any other night, our nights of sharing.
>
> (Shulamit, in Tsur 1988: 229–30)

A similarly enthusiastic account of the role of the "soul talks" in the group's life is found in a letter written by Meir Ya'ari, the group's charismatic leader at the time, and a leading figure in Israel's left-wing Mapam party for many years later. It was sent to youth movement members who were still in Europe, and was reprinted in the 1988 publication of *Kehiliatenu* as well. In this letter, he points out the sense of alienation that existed between the groups of *Hashomer Hatza'ir* pioneers (to which the Bitaniya Ilit group belonged) and the other, more pragmatic and less radical groups of pioneers who were trying to make their home in Palestine at the time. He attributed a great deal of the distinctiveness of the Bitaniya group to the spiritual sharing ("erotic sharing," in his terms) that found its expression in the ritual of the "soul talk." The "soul talks" as he describes them are the epitome of a unique world of human connectedness. They are also a context where inner difficulties and self-doubts were openly confessed. Ya'ari writes:

People around us view us as some kind of Free Masons, or "Free Love Association," or hallucinating youngsters. Some regard us as a danger, others as an exotic phenomenon. Interpretations pile up, while we are still so far from realizing our main ideas.

And to my point, where do people celebrate such a spiritual feast after a day's work as they do here? We are completely addicted to the infatuating flavor of the confession and the ritual of the talk. The boys may represent oppositional stances in this spiritual feast, but they are nevertheless so close to each other. Therefore one's breast fills up with pride. You feel that **we are really different**. Not you or that other person, but that small group that is neither formally regulated nor cohesive, yet shines with spirituality.

Sometimes our song flies up high and there are no hills that can send back its echo, as Bitaniya is higher than the surrounding mountains. Our song is not strong and artificial – it is not a forced cry. **It is different**. Sometimes a few concrete words are thrown in, and again there is silence, mountainous and profound. **Our silence – is different**. Sometimes a cloud throws its shadow on the Sea of Galilee. Our eyes unintentionally interlock and lose themselves in the shadow of the lake in a moment of evening grace. The wild, drunken mountain air invites people to denude themselves They cannot find their way. **Our communal spirit is different**.

And despite all of this, every one of our talks is a desperate scream of helplessness and self-recrimination. We cannot be self-indulgent or we'll be lost.

(Ya'ari, in Tsur 1988: 277; boldface in the original)

Contrary to these appreciative accounts of the "soul talks" as the centerpiece of the ethos of the "intimate group," other accounts gave voice to some members' reluctance to participate in these confessional exchanges, their mistrust of the spiritualized nature of these dialogic communities and a distaste for the coerciveness of the group pressure that these encounters involved. In a few months, Ya'ari, the charismatic group leader, would leave the group in a dramatic step of disengagement, forsaking the uniqueness of group spirit which he had so ardently described, partly because of internal opposition on the part of those members who did not become infatuated with the group's ongoing "spiritual feast." A major, early internal opponent of the "soul talks" was a member by the name of David Horowitz who later became a leading figure in Israel's financial establishment. What was a flaming of spiritual contact in the first excerpt, and a touch of spiritual grace in the second, becomes an experience of spiritual torture in the following autobiographical retrospective account of the period, where David Horowitz describes the "intimate group" experience in these terms:

Bitaniya resembled a secluded monastery of a religious sect, a sect with its own charismatic leader and set of symbols, with its ritual of public confession, the kind of confession that calls to mind the attempts of religious mystics to wrestle with God and the devil at one and the same time. . . . It was also the peak of disconnection from real life and its material difficulties, a kind of escapism into spiritual suffering which involves the test of an ongoing confrontation with *memento mori*, in the dense atmosphere of a Godless monasterial order, immersed in directionless search and longings . . .

Work began at sunrise. . . . After a short break for a poor meal at noon, labor continued till sunset. . . . But all this was considered only secondary to the real life. Everyone knew that in Bitaniya life begins in the evening, with the "[soul] talk" [*hasicha*], that public confession and lengthy and pain-filled dialogue about life, the individual, society and anything that goes beyond real, concrete, daily reality. It was a rather rich spiritual meal, but full of useless self-recriminations. . . . The talks were conducted in semi-darkness, in a dense and spiritually tense atmosphere, which bordered on lunacy. This mysticism, this state of mind, penetrated every corner of the group's life, leaving the individual not even one hidden corner for himself. Every person had to face constant social criticism and judgement by the group, to the point of spiritual cruelty.

(Horowitz 1970: 105–6)

The above excerpts represent just a few of the multiple voices attending the cultural project of self-fashioning and community-building undertaken by the group of young pioneers. They were, on the one hand, adamant about maintaining a small-scale group framework, yet they also sought to provide a social model for other Jewish groups around the country. Thus, while they attempted to maintain cohesive, intimate relations among themselves, they also disseminated the idea of the new kind of society that they envisioned to other parts of the country as well as to pioneering groups in Europe and North America.

In what follows, then, I reconstruct the idea of the "intimate group" as dialogically constituted through intense experiences of face-to-face communication. Then I explore the dissemination of this cultural project of intentional community-building through the forms of public communication that were available in Palestine in the 1920s. One of the most intriguing of these forms of dissemination – or broadcast medium, if you will – involved the publication of "collective diaries" (such as the aforementioned *Kehiliatenu*). These diaries gave first-hand expression to the experience of the "intimate group." In later years, the diaries and the story of their composition and compilation became incorporated into the Israeli nation-building mythology.

These communal diaries can be described as inscriptions that reflected, elaborated, complemented or served as mediated alternatives to the "soul talks" held orally by members of the "intimate group." Both at the time and in later years they became "cult books" and, like the "soul talks" themselves, they served as privileged sites for the articulation of the central cultural dialectic of "self" and "society" through enactments of confessional discourse (Naveh 1988). In both, the dominant form of discourse was a public performance of talk that was self-oriented and self-disclosive. "Soul talks," then, in their oral form as well as in their written counterpart, chart a unique image of individually focused yet communally oriented face-to-face or mediated communal encounters.

The data I have so far gathered allows me to delineate the nature of "soul talks" as communicative occasions in a preliminary fashion, and to point out some interesting junctures in their symbolic career in Israeli sociocultural history. The study thus addresses two issues. First, employing a research perspective that focuses on speaking as a cultural performance, and drawing on both literary and historical materials, it seeks to offer an interpretive reading of the structure and functions of "soul talks" as ideologically infused and culturally sanctioned speech occasions among some of the early pioneering groups in Palestine. Second, focusing on the subsequent partial re-enactments and re-textualizations of "soul talks," and the ethos to which they gave expression, it explores the symbolic construction and cultural force of images of dialogic engagements in the creation of mediated "imagined communities" of later generations of Israelis. This study thus moves from a consideration of a particular class of speech occasions as cultural performances (next section) to a consideration of the commemorative processes whereby such performances may become part of the collective memory and cultural politics of a particular group (last section).

"SOUL TALKS" AS COMMUNICATIVE EVENTS

The view that discursive practices, and especially ritualized communicative forms, play a central role in the ongoing construction and negotiation of social reality is a well-recognized feature of many contemporary approaches to the study of sociocultural life. The research program known as the "ethnography of speaking" (Gumperz and Hymes 1972; Hymes 1974; Bauman and Sherzer 1974; Saville-Troike 1982) has made a distinctive contribution to the understanding of the interplay of language use and social life in promoting the development of linguistically informed and anthropologically oriented frameworks for the study of culturally coded ways of speaking and occasions for talk. This perspective helps us to explore how they become conventionalized, ritualized and symbolically marked in given speech communities.

The present study is thus informed by recent directions in communication-oriented anthropological and historical research. It employs the speech-centered mode of historical anthropology proposed by Hymes (1974) who spoke of "socio-linguistic reconstruction." Bauman's (1983) study of the symbolism of speaking and silence among seventeenth century Quakers is an outstanding example of an anthropologist's attempt to study speech from a historical perspective. At the same time, historians interested in the social history of linguistic conduct as part of their larger enterprise have also begun to explore ways of speaking in their historical context. Peter Burke has cogently argued for a systematic application of sociolinguistic approaches, and particularly the ethnography of communication perspective, to the study of historical materials, and has summed up the potential value of this interdisciplinary scholarly enterprise as "the attempt to add a social dimension to the history of language and a historical dimension to the work of sociolinguists and ethnographers of speaking" (Burke 1993: 7).

As the testimonies cited in the first section indicate, the "soul talks" were communal conversations marked by a high degree of expressiveness, self-disclosure and social pathos. They involved an uninhibited sharing of self-doubts and internal conflicts as well as a great deal of mutual criticism and censure. They were recognized as a central feature of the life-experience of some of the early Jewish pioneering groups in Palestine, and served as a controversial model of communication for others. These pioneering groups were greatly influenced by a number of cultural strands: the ethos of the turn-of-the-century Russian revolutionary groups, the *narodniks*, who preached a return to land and nature, and the moral superiority of the peasantry and the working masses and their simple way of life. As mentioned earlier, they were also influenced by the spirit of the German youth culture, with its rejection of the ills of modernity and the decadence of an urbanized, atomized society dominated by the sign of *Geselschaft*. They also carried with them the spirit of their Jewish Hasidic roots (Fishman 1987). All of these various cultural strands and influences were drawn upon in their effort to create new cultural forms that sustain their utopian visions of the new society and the new Jewish person.

Indeed, these young pioneers regarded themselves as constituting "social laboratories" for the radical reconstruction of self and community in the context of the close-knit "intimate group." They proposed some sort of confederation of "intimate groups" as a social alternative to the formation of a more extended social grouping known as "*hakvutza hagdola*", or non-communal forms of social organization such as family-based settlements or towns. These "intimate groups" were largely modeled on the German youth culture notion of the "*bunde*," the small group of mutually invested and spiritually inclined individuals, as it was cultivated in such youth movements as the *Wandervogel* and its Jewish counterpart, the *Blau Weiss*. These cultural strands later also became central to the ethos of the *Hashomer Hatza'ir* youth movement in Europe and Palestine (Mintz 1995).

In fact, however, the group ethos epitomized in the "soul talks" was rejected by other segments of the pioneering movement, which foregrounded a rational organizational–economic ethos (Fishman 1987: 75). These groups criticized the inner-directedness and soul-searching of the "intimate groups" in the name of a more pragmatic, down-to-earth orientation. In both cases the solidarity they fostered was bred of mutual engagement in productive labor and political alliance, not a communion generated by the soul-baring movement of mutual confession (Mintz 1995).

Nevertheless, in these early years, the "soul talks" gained considerable symbolic potency and came to form a central, much publicized, feature of the life-experience of the groups of *Hashomer Hatza'ir* pioneers (and other pioneering groups influenced by them). They provided an alternative strand within the Israeli mainstream foundation mythology. Israeli major "origin myths" are grounded in notions of collective action and outwardly directed physical struggle (e.g. the action-oriented story of the settlement efforts subsumed under the symbolism of Tower and Stockade, Katriel and Shenhar 1990). In fact, I believe that the cultural conversation – whether celebratory or skeptical – that surrounds the ritualization of "soul talks" as utopia-driven models for the art of dialogue charts cultural themes that have subsequently emerged as central in Israeli ethos: most notably, the ideational tension between "words" and "deeds," the centrality of a sense of togetherness (natively referred to as *gibush*), and the discursive construction of the dialectic of "self" and "society" as an ongoing cultural project (Katriel 1986, 1991).

The culture-making efforts of the *Hashomer Hatza'ir* young pioneers were untypically but decisively oriented to the "words" end of the "words v. deeds" dialectic. They embraced the mainstream Zionist conscious (if partial) rejection of traditional Jewish religion and lifeways, and the elevation of physical, productive labor, which was epitomized in agricultural settlements as the material base for the new communities. At the same time, inspired by youth culture ideals, they made special efforts to chart new relational forms and possibilities among members of the "intimate group." They explored the viability of new, discursively sustained forms of social organization. Their story is thus a tale of agonized soul-searching and utopian strivings associated with the special spirit and turbulence of youth as it found its place within the larger nation-building project.

Studying their "soul talks" as culturally distinctive communicative occasions, which were precariously yet centrally set within the larger framework of communal life, provides an intriguing opportunity to explore the roles of speaking, silence and writing in a relatively well-documented sociocultural project. This project was designed to revitalize the face-to-face community in an ideologically saturated, anti-modernist social enclave. At the same time, such a study is necessarily constrained by the nature of the available documentation. In the absence of actual recordings of "soul talks," I need to rely for my interpretations on secondary documentation and interpretive elaborations, that is, first-hand and second-hand witness accounts found in diaries, autobiographies, and fictional treatments as well as secondary allusions found in a wider range of texts. As a result, my account is necessarily thin on direct ethnographic detail – I cannot provide more extended descriptions of situational features and communicative forms than participants in the events chose to remember and document. On the other hand, it is relatively rich in meta-communicative and interpretive material. The retrospective discussions of "soul talks" – in whatever form and context they appear – contain a great deal of self-probing and reflection on the nature and possibility of what Buber (and the young pioneers after him) called *hasicha kehavayata* (true dialogue). They therefore provide insight into their vision of the "ideal dialogue" and the impediments to its realization.

Thus, while I am often left wishing that I had more detailed descriptions of the actual unfolding of "soul talks" as situated speech events, so that they would be more malleable to analytic treatment – in terms of the Hymsian SPEAKING heuristic framework (Hymes 1974), for example – I must content myself with noting the paucity of first-hand descriptive data and the highly subjective and evaluative nature of the accounts that we have. These accounts highlight the experiential dimensions and existential meanings of the "soul talks" and the unique social world in which they were embedded. Whatever description I can sketch of the unfolding of "soul talks" as speech events needs to be extricated from the highly self-reflexive materials accessible to us today. The fact that so much secondary documentation exists today in the form of an ongoing cultural conversation about "soul talks" is in itself of great significance. It is a mark of cultural interest in this speech form. The shape that this cultural conversation has taken since pioneering days can teach us important lessons about the discursive construction of self, community and communicative ideology in Israeli culture.

So let us return to Bitaniya Ilit. Shortly before they left the high mountain spot where their encampment was located in order to establish their new settlement, the young pioneers began to inscribe some of their experiences and "soul talks" into a communal diary which was then edited by the author Nathan Bistritsky who had spent some time with them in their encampment. The communal diary was originally published in 1922 under the title of *Kehiliatenu*, and was disseminated to other pioneering groups in Palestine, Europe and even North America. Through the writing of the diary, the young pioneers sought to articulate their groupings for a distinctive communal "soul." Through its dissemination, they sought to enhance inter-group communication among themselves, among the groups of pioneers which were dispersed in various work-encampments around the country, and among the would-be pioneers who were still contemplating their move to the Land of Israel. The communal diary represented both an act of self-articulation and self-definition for internal group consumption and an outwardly directed gesture designed to promulgate the group's particular ethos and model of pioneering. It is probably because of the wide circulation of this communal diary (to which I will return) that the ethos associated with the "soul talks" as culturally focal speech events has become linked in Israeli cultural imagination with the saga of Bitaniya Ilit. Evidence of the spread of both the talks and the communal diary amongst other pioneering groups – as well as of their continued interest in the present – can be found, for example, in the recent publication of the communal diary of another such group, *Kvutzat Hasharon* (Opaz 1995).

Although "soul talks" were semi-institutionalized communal gatherings, and were recognized as part of the newly forming web of ritualized occasions that colored the early pioneers' experience, they retained an air of spontaneity and emergence as communicative events. The young pioneers perceived the "soul talks" and the "intimate group" as antithetical to larger social and political formations and institutions and the power relations that these entailed. To them, social institutions involved coercive forms of social integration which inevitably infringed upon the freedom and the spiritual growth of individuals. The following description by one of the foremost students of the early pioneers, Muki Tsur, summarizes this central point:

From the various descriptions of Bitaniya Ilit, we can say that the people of *Hashomer Hatza'ir* practiced in it for the first time an independent framework that combined ideological imaginativeness and connection to agricultural labor. They were very preoccupied with the question of the Free Society, Free

Love, the pathos of Love and Freedom. They abhorred the old social order. The place of institution was taken by the [soul] talk, which was a quasi-ritual of confession and prayer, which allowed the anxiety-filled inner world to find its expression. The talk revealed the enormous thirst for a life of togetherness, the exhilaration of the new life, and the unarticulated longings for the idyllic world of the youth movement, a world that became both unsettled and more mature as a result of the encounter with the realities of life in Palestine.

Indeed, the depth of these talks, and the tension that filled them had consequences in the area of social organization. In the spirit of Buber's and Landauer's teachings, they wanted to prove that their group does not require an organizational structure but the deepening of the connection, the encounter. One needs no institutions, only a dialogue, and the rules of society can be replaced by the desire for mutual recognition. But alongside the dream there was also great disorientation, lack of experience, longings for the parental home, and a sense of embarrassment that facilitated the rise of a strong leadership. Thus, the person who could give expression to their feelings, who had the power to chart a clear direction, gained authority.

(Tsur 1988: 5–6)

Responses to the social-communicative form of the "soul talk" varied greatly. Some group members felt empowered by this communal practice and partici- pated in it wholeheartedly, while others considered it a coercive form of discourse, a tool of social oppression, which some members of the "intimate group" promoted as part of the group's internal power politics. This range of responses finds its expression not only in the various entries included in *Kehiliatenu* but also in responses to it at the time of initial publication and in later years.

Indeed, the spiritualized community of newly arrived pioneers, who were stationed in Bitaniya Ilit, became highly controversial among other pioneering groups in Palestine from the very start. The responses to the stories circulating about them were marked by suspicion and consternation mixed with curiosity. They echoed both the fascination and the criticism voiced by such dissenting members of the group as David Horowitz, whose retrospective account is cited in the introductory section. The fear was that the spirit of this strange group of soul-searching pioneers, filled with a romantic vision, agonizing existential doubts and homo-erotic yearnings, would undermine the larger pioneering movement's pragmatic and realistic orientation; that the imaginary world of words and symbols which they spun together at the top of their isolated Galilean hill would take the place of the real world of fact-creating deeds, political alignments and family-based social groupings that the mainstream groups considered the building-blocks of the new Jewish society. A national convention held in 1920 in Haifa included pioneers who were graduates of the *Hashomer Hatza'ir* youth movement, as well as outsiders to it. The latter were bewildered by the discussions held in the movement's typical poetic language and ecstatic style. An extremely critical article published following this meeting claimed that the movement would not be able to fulfill the demands of a pioneering life as long as it sustained its spiritualized youth cult. The author's commentary focused on the baffling "soul talk" discussion format that the strange group of pioneers had employed:

"Discussed" – this is not the right word, young people don't discuss; youth does not weigh positions; the lyrical temperament of age 18–20 does not concern itself with issues. It ferments, it's like an Aeolian lute that sings of its own accord when the wind moves it. They talked in the way you talk in a small, intimate *kibbutz* during winter nights, in the attic of a dreamy friend – that's how they talked before the audience, in public.

(Cited in Tsur 1988: 265)

The "soul talk" idiom was held up to ridicule by depicting its use in this public context, but both the proponents and the detractors of the "soul talks" recognized their extraordinary power as enacted models for an idealized form of social exchange in the particular context of these early Israeli pioneering groups.

Given the foregoing depictions of "soul talks" by their participants, observers and students, what kind of analytic statement can we make about this model? "Soul talks" were, clearly, intentional gatherings in which the focal activity involved distinctive, normatively structured ways of speaking. The testimonial accounts cited earlier, and others like them, allow only for a partial analytic description of the texture of these encounters and the interactional norms regulating them, but one that can begin to illumine their nature as speech event types. I therefore turn to the ethnography of speaking framework, that is, the SPEAKING model proposed by Hymes (1974) as an acronym denoting various dimensions of context to be considered in the study of socially situated and bounded speech encounters, in an attempt to delineate the form and functions of "soul talks" and the communal ideologies that they enacted.[2]

The first contextual dimension that seems relevant to the characterization of "soul talks" concerns the physical setting and the psychological scene associated with them. As some of the foregoing citations suggest, an important feature of the enactment of these talks had to do with the isolated location of the setting in which the pioneering groups found themselves. This physical isolation had not only practical but also psychological implications as the sense of "togetherness" generated by the "soul talks" was a major source of solace given the condition of seclusion with which the group had to contend. The "soul talks," as noted, normally took place in the communal dining-room, which was turned into a center of social life and a reading room between meals, and was considered the official hub of community life.

Temporal dimensions of the setting and scene in which "soul talks" were enacted are also significant: these talks took place in the evenings after a long day's work, an afternoon rest and a communal supper, and often lasted late into the night. The night-time atmosphere – a sense of time out of time – clearly affected the level of intimacy and emotional intensity that characterized the talks. "Soul talks" were congregated at irregular intervals, and frequency of enactment was often associated in the communal diaries with a positive sense of community, even though the talks were often not outright celebrations of community but gave expression to self-doubts and interpersonal conflict. The very willingness and ability to hold the talks frequently, as a standard instrument of community life, were felt to be a sign of commitment to a meaningful group life.

Inscriptions in the communal diaries often reflect this attitude, as when the writing is described as a second-best to the open, oral talks that the group was unable to hold because of interpersonal tensions or lack of communal vitality. Other forms of group sharing, such as communal singing and dancing, as well as collective endeavors in the realm of work, though mentioned in the diaries, could not compensate for the scarcity of the "soul talks" at times when the unspoken listlessness of group members threatened the fabric of group life. Thus, while the temporal and spatial organization of "soul talks" was well regulated once enacted, the very question of when such enactments were deemed to be possible was left uncertain and was felt both to reflect and to affect the overall climate of communal feeling amongst group members.

Participation in these communal encounters was restricted to members of the "intimate group." Since membership in the Bitaniya Ilit group, as described earlier, was based on a process of selection – the leader chose one person, the two of them chose the third, and so on – a maximal degree of initial compatibility between group members was assured. A major distinctive feature of the communal social arrangement to which group members were committed involved a sharing in all aspects of their lives – work, leisure, possessions – not just in the verbal sharing of inner worlds in periodic encounters. Participant-roles in the "soul talks" were thus contingent on their roles as community members. This intense psychological sharing was dependent on other dimensions of a life of togetherness, but it also made it hard for participants to isolate the "peak experience" of the communal conversation from other life contexts. Thus, entries in the communal diary sometimes expressed the awkwardness that they felt at moving from the night-time, soul-baring talks to the sunlit workaday reality of the morning after, all with the same partners.

While all members of the "intimate group" were potential participants in the "soul talks," forms and degrees of participation varied among them. The most dominant participant in the talks was the group's self-appointed, charismatic leader who presided over the talks. He was frequently also the person who initiated the evening talk, but other members of the group could initiate it if there was an issue that they thought should be discussed or, more dramatically, if any one of them felt the pressing need to share his or her inner turmoils, doubts or joy with the others. The group was often summoned by sounding the bell that was placed at the entrance to the dining-room. The power of this summons was great, as the underlying assumption was that speaking which is empathetically received eases emotional pressures – in line with the "talking cure" advocated by the budding therapeutic culture of the times. People were expected to respond to the bell as to an urgent call even in the middle of the night. Both the summons and the "soul talk" that came in its wake were thus governed by a culturally compelling ethics of dialogue whose cornerstones are a sense of *presence* and mutual *recognition* between participants in an encounter, very much in the spirit of Buber's I–Thou relationships (e.g. Buber 1965). As noted, the *Hashomer Hatza'ir* pioneering groups had first-hand exposure to the teachings of Buber, and his call for the cultivation of I–Thou relationships which would go beyond the functional and interest related dimensions of social exchange were influential in their search for new forms of social relationships.[3]

Employing the language recently proposed by Gurevitch (1990) in his discussion of the "dialogic dimensions" of human exchange, the dialogic connection is grounded in "an ethical tension of regard for the Other. This regard is structured in dialogue as obligated gestures and attitudes the principle of which is *recognition*" (1990: 183; my emphasis). This sense of recognition is translated into a set of three obligations: the *obligation to speak*, the *obligation to listen* and the *obligation to respond*.

Clearly, these obligations, even if often left unarticulated, formed the normative backbone of "soul talks" as communal rituals, and regulated participants' expectations as to the kind of mutual engagement that these talks should entail. Thus, in the context of "soul talks," sharing one's inner world with others was not perceived just as an expressive possibility; it was a condition of the communal life that individuals committed themselves to upholding in joining the group. The norms governing the deployment of "soul talks" had to do with these general conditions of participation. More specifically, a central aspect of these talks was the confessional mode that they entailed.[4] The key (or tone) characterizing these confessional exchanges was one of emotional intensity, seriousness and utmost sincerity.

Indeed, although members of the pioneering group were evaluated by each other in terms of their contributions to the community as laborers or as daily companions, it was in terms of their potential for self-fashioning and communal participation through the medium of the "soul talks" that their social place within the group was determined. The obligation to speak, enacted in the form of dramatic self-disclosure in a group setting, employing a rhetoric of ecstasy and lamentation, thus became a token of satisfying social involvement. It also marked a road to social power. Those who felt too inhibited to share openly did not play the communal game as fully as they might, and remained at the margins of the group. They did, however, participate in its life in fulfilling the obligation to listen, which was felt powerfully enough to keep them awake late into the night after a long day's work, even to pull them out of deep sleep at the sound of the communal bell. The obligation to respond, of course, moved the self-disclosive outbursts into an openly dialogic frame.

Thus, although confessional discourse formed one of the basic genres of "soul talks" – along with discussion, argument and narration – it was talk that was intensely oriented toward specific others in their role as group members, directly soliciting their response – be it agreement or disagreement, support or censure. The kinds of topics that were raised in the "soul talks" can be gleaned from a reading of the communal diaries, where many of the entries are given as responses to issues which had come up in these oral talks.

Many of these topics had to do with aspects of community life as these were individually experienced and interpreted by particular persons. There was much discussion about attitudes and practices related to the stringent demands for physical labor. One person, for example, raised the question of whether work should be considered a necessity of life or a value in and of itself; another person expressed self-doubts as to his ability to participate in the physical demands of pioneering life; a woman protested against the gender-related division of labor, whereby women were allocated to service work; the question of whether a day of rest for all was desirable or feasible was raised in another entry.

Another central set of topics which triggered a great deal of discussion had to do with the place of eroticism, love and the formation of conjugal units (and eventually families) within the "intimate group." Confessional entries in the communal diaries relate tales of love found (and lost); there are painful expressions of loneliness and a longing for the possibility of genuine human contact – sometimes referred to as the ability to remove the hard shell (*klipa*) that stands in the way of the merging of souls.

There are entries which bring up the paucity of cultural life in the pioneers' encampment, attesting to the price that these young people paid in opting for a pioneering life, as in the case of a girl who tells of a trip to the city during which she happened to hear the sound of a piano, which stirred deep-seated yearnings associated with the many years that she had devoted to a musical life, a life she had chosen not to pursue.

The "soul talks" were also the platform where social relations within the group – and philosophical reflections concerning the proper shape that they should take – were brought up: personal grievances and vulnerabilities were aired, objectionable behavior was brought up for public consideration, and communal ideals were probed in relation to their everyday articulations. Whether the discussion related to the broader and public dimensions of group life, such as the relationship of the "intimate group" to the political landscape of the labor Zionist movement, or to the micro-dynamics of interpersonal relations within the group, it was always grounded in a deeply felt personal reality and colored by intense emotional tones. Personal sentiment was constantly shaped by, and checked against, idealized images of the pioneering life. The personal and the communal were merged not only in substance – through the genre of public self-disclosure – but also through the leveling effected by the employment of a pathos-filled, elevated stylistic code.

It is interesting to note the particular position of silence as a mode of communication in the social context of these pioneering groups. Like self-disclosive talk, silence was sometimes interpreted as an instrument of sharing and intimacy. Ya'ari's heartfelt statement (see p. 116), which claims that "Our silence – is different," points to the romantic view of silence as pregnant with meaning. While this view is reiterated from time to time, it is not universally espoused. Silence is also often presented as a failure of dialogue, and the communal diaries contain many references to silence in this sense. The dialectic of speaking and silence within the pioneers' attempts to create a life of dialogue was notable and distinctive enough to invite parody in Bistritsky's 1926 novel about Bitaniya, which contains the following biting account of a conversation between two pioneers:

> There's a meeting tonight, have you heard, Mishka? What's a meeting, Mishkale, do you know?
>
> A meeting is when one person doesn't talk, the other shuts up, and the third keeps silent. And then, with God's help, all forty people refrain from talking, shut up and keep silent. Now you know what a meeting is! And then suddenly someone gets up, mumbles three words into his respected nose, or into the ground – let the earth swallow him up! That's how they make speeches in Giv'at Aryeh [the fictional name for Bitaniya]. Then they keep silent a second time – the first, the second, the third, and all the forty of them. And then the first walks out, the second and the third, and all forty of them, as if in a funeral. This is a meeting! The intentional meeting with thirty-nine other persons is more suffocating to the soul than the silence in the yard.
>
> (Bistritsky 1978 [1926]: 63)

Another dimension of the use of silence relates to the aforementioned obligation to respond. While the obligation to speak seems to have been treated with caution – as is indicated by the many references made in the diaries to the withholding of one's voice in open discussion – the choice not to respond is held in great suspicion. The texts produced by and about the "intimate groups" of young pioneers abound with references to silence as a threat, as an ominous token of social refusal, or at least as a sign of the socially dysfunctional individual, who is unable to participate in open, communally oriented talk.

Thus, one of the most touching chapters in Bistritsky's "saga" of Bitaniya Ilit is the story of the fate of Marcus, a member of the group who had been a silently devoted childhood friend to Adel, one of the four girls in the male-dominated encampment, in whose company he had arrived from Vienna. When she paired up with Alexander Tsuri, the group's charismatic leader, and moved into a "family tent" with him, Marcus's accustomed silence, borne of characteristic reticence, became interpreted as a denial of response. He ignored Tsuri's repeated appeals to him to join them in their family tent as a third living partner and together form a new kind of "family." He kept his silence when Tsuri, guilt-ridden for having renounced his revolutionary principles and established the first bourgeois-style conjugal unit in the group, begged him to respond. His silence became so unbearable to Tsuri that, successfully dramatizing the agony inflicted on him by Marcus's refusal to respond, he managed to persuade the other group members at a communal "soul talk" to "expel" Marcus from Bitaniya Ilit. The social legitimacy given to Tsuri's complaint through the act of expulsion was grounded in the normative expectation that talk which is directly addressed to a person should be acknowledged in some manner. Silence in this case was an act of disconfirmation. Clearly, the normative power of the obligation to respond was in turn reinforced among group members by this social drama, but as for Marcus – he left in the middle of the night, without uttering one word.

In sum, "soul talks" were cultural sites in which the dialectic of self and community, inner-experience and social reality could be articulated and temporarily resolved. They were sites in which dialogic connection was both a goal and an accomplishment of social life. In these groups of early Jewish pioneers the essential uniqueness, complexity and richness of individual inner-experience was highly prized, the power of face-to-face spoken engagements was recognized, and the cultivation of communal sentiments and values was cherished.

Even though these communicative occasions were clearly culturally and historically situated, their general contours can be traced in other sociocultural contexts as well. Thus, confessional gatherings of the type charted in the study of "soul talks" were traced in relation to other ideological communities (e.g. Kanter 1972; Zablocki 1980), and it is quite clear that the "intimate groups" of early Israeli pioneers were part of a socialist–utopian wave that swept over Europe around the turn of the century. Perhaps the distinctiveness of the "soul talks" which I have considered in this section lies not so much in their initial enactment as social forms as in their further career as cultural symbols, to which I turn in the next section.

"SOUL TALKS" AS CULTURAL SYMBOLS

Israeli foundation mythology is replete with symbols of heroism and sacrifice, and it is within the context of this larger cultural web that "soul talks" as symbolically charged images of community-making find their place. The myth of Bitaniya Ilit as a foundational moment in settlement history underlines the world-creating power of dialogic exchanges rather than the pragmatic force of fact-creating deeds.[5]

The ambivalence surrounding the historical specter of the "soul talks" (as discussed earlier) was retained in later years. On the one hand, "soul talks" were depicted as discursive occasions in which an idealized spirit of *communitas*, marked by egalitarian social relations and self-disclosure, was enacted and routinized (Turner 1969). On the other hand, they were depicted as dramas of invasive group coercion, tyrannical attempts to blend together the individual and the collective, obliterating the boundaries between self and others by forceful fiat. Many depictions related to both aspects. The prominent, yet uncertain, symbolic position that "soul talks" came to occupy in Israeli cultural conversation repeatedly addresses this unresolved ambivalence.

The aforementioned collective diary, *Kehiliatenu*, marked the first step in the process of inscribing an idealized image of a "dialogic community" in Israeli collective memory. This process began shortly after the diary was compiled and edited by the writer Nathan Bistritsky who became a central cultural agent in promulgating its saga over the years. Notably, the collective diary, which was written and compiled in 1921, was published and disseminated to other pioneering groups in 1922. The temporal compression of the events – from the feverish experience of the "soul talks" and the "intimate group" model to the process of inscription for self-reference, to the broadcasting of these materials to a wide range of outsiders – may account for their immediacy and symbolic power. The communal diary was republished in 1972 and disseminated to all of the *kibbutzim* associated with the *Hashomer Hatza'ir* movement. It was again republished, on a commercial basis, by the Yad Ben-Zvi Institute for the study of Eretz Israel in 1988, with an introduction and commentaries by Muki Tsur, a prominent leader in the *kibbutz* movement, who serves as a major contemporary agent in the promulgation of the cultural memory of Bitaniya Ilit. In 1923 Meir Ya'ari, the aforementioned leader of the group, launched the open public controversy that surrounded Bitaniya Ilit by publishing an acrimonious article entitled "Uprooted Symbols" (*Smalim Tlushim*). In this article he attacked the spirit of Bitaniya Ilit, the very same spirit that he had helped to create.

Nathan Bistritsky's 1926 novel, based on the communal saga of Bitaniya Ilit as he had observed and experienced it in person, was entitled *Days and Nights* (*Yamim Veleilot*). This text, which included a detailed account of the pioneering project that produced the communal diary, was republished in 1940 in a censored version, and again in 1978 in a longer and revised version (Keshet 1995). The novel documents the events leading to, and accompanying, the compilation of *Kehiliatenu* as a quasi-sacralized communal text. In this account, the act of inscribing the communal spirit of the "intimate group" is presented in direct relationship to the enactment of "soul talks" as a social practice among the young pioneers. The invitation to inscribe their innermost thoughts on paper had a particularly liberating value for those individuals who felt it difficult to share their thoughts and feelings as fully as they desired in the face-to-face context of the "soul talk."

Both the diary and the novel about it were widely read upon their publication, and both provide rich materials for a socio-historical reconstruction of the phenomenology and texture of "soul talks" as part of the pioneers' lived experience. In 1980 Bistritsky published an autobiography entitled *The Hidden Myth* in which he provides an account of both the compilation of *Kehiliatenu* and the circumstances in which his novel *Days and Nights* was written. It is a text which is centrally about a text about a textualization. These various textualizations of the pioneers' lifeworld are at least partly responsible for the fact that the group's influence far exceeded the cultural impact that was warranted by its small size, and for the crystallization of the myth of Bitaniya Ilit, in later years.

Indeed, the saga of these groups and their "soul talks" has remained as an ever-present reminder of a largely unfulfilled, yet never-fading, cultural promise of an ultimate form of solidarity anchored in dialogue. As the years went by, with the increasing erosion of the early communal ideology and of pioneering values, "soul talks" became subject to nostalgic recreations and allusions on the one hand, and the topic of bitter cultural critique on the other. Whether invoked in the spirit of longing or of retrospective, self-critical reappraisal, "soul talks" were and remain "key symbols" in native-Israeli culture, charting imaginary scenarios in and through which the dialectic of self and community plays itself out in communicative action.

The following popularized version of the saga of Bitaniya Ilit, which is taken from a tour guide interpretation recorded in a pioneer settlement museum, is an example of the double-edged way in which it is routinely invoked. Note the narrator's shift from the use of past tense to historical present, and back, as well as the use of first person singular. These stylistic strategies serve both to personalize and to generalize the story of Bitaniya Ilit as well as to make it relevant to the present.

> Slowly, slowly people began to learn to be a *kibbutz*. People began to learn to live in a *kibbutz*. Because people didn't know. And, therefore, in Bitaniya Ilit, people come, idealists – urging equality to the very end, nothing to be left in private possession. That is, I'm not supposed to hide myself from my friends because that creates a sort of distance, and one should seek maximum closeness, sharing everything, and I shouldn't leave any private corner in my heart, one should expose everything that is in it. And that's what pushed some people to commit suicide.
>
> (Narrated by I.Z., Yi'fat Museum; recorded by Katriel, February 7, 1992)

Understanding the texture and role of "soul talks" in Israeli cultural conversation, therefore, is not only a way of recreating an aspect of the culture's basic world-view, rooted in some of its earliest experiential moments, but also a way of tracing the changes that this cultural experience has undergone over the years and the politics of culture implicated in this process.

Given the persistent move towards individualism that marks contemporary Israeli social experience, the cultural preoccupation with the webs of community that weave together individual lives is a notable phenomenon, even if this preoccupation finds its place increasingly in contexts of nostalgia. The nostalgic invocation of "soul talks" as conversational models is a telling gesture toward a half-forgotten dream of pure, unimpeded dialogue, whether it appears in historical accounts (in formal histories or in historical museum interpretation), in artistic reconstructions such as novels and plays, or in actual gatherings which seek to re-invoke the soul-searching spiritualism of the intimate groups.

A very well-known example of such a gathering was documented in a book, *Si'ach Lochamim* (*Soldiers' Discourse*), published shortly after the 1967 War, which contained a series of group conversations of young *kibbutz* members (Shapira 1967). Participants in these encounters shared their experiences as soldiers in the war, and candidly expressed their doubts, traumas and pain in a way which publicly undermined the heroic image of the Israeli soldier that was usually promulgated in other contexts. These conversations clearly followed the "soul talk" model, which provided in a supportive, therapeutic climate a culturally sanctioned discursive format for the expression of self-doubts and moral gropings in relation to the Israeli military ethos.

Muki Tsur, the editor of the 1988 annotated edition of *Kehiliatenu*, was also one of the editing team of *Si'ach Lochamim*. In a newspaper interview which he gave upon the publication of the 1988 edition of *Kehiliatenu* he was directly asked about his involvement in these two projects:

INTERVIEWER There is some continuity between this collection [*Kehiliatenu*] and *Si'ach Lochamim*. which you also edited after the Six Day War.

MUKI TSUR There is a connection: the very medium of conversation, and then written conversation. There is also a continuity in the self-questioning tone. It is certainly part of the story, in both collections.

(Bar'am 1988: 51)

The line of continuity between these two sets of inscribed conversations, set apart by almost fifty years, relates to the shared spirit of soul-searching enacted through self-disclosure within a group setting, and to the promise of a dialogic connection among participants in face-to-face encounters. *Si'ach Lochamim* had a record sale and is found in private libraries in many homes in Israel.

The cult-like atmosphere of group pressure attending the "soul-talks" was not discussed in relation to the 1967 *Si'ach Lochamim*. However, when the "soul talk" format was re-cast in the form of an extremely successful play entitled *The Night of the Twentieth*, the ethos of Bitaniya appeared in all its complexity, as a site simultaneously of communal utopia and of personal and interpersonal torture. The play was written by one of Israel's foremost playwrights, Yehoshua Sobol, and produced by Haifa Theater in 1976 and, again, by Habimah National Theater in 1990.

Thus, by the mid-1970s, the myth of Bitaniya had become generalized as one of the cornerstones of the pioneering mythology, with each commemorative gesture constituting a complex story of cultural celebration combined with cultural critique. The aforementioned article by Chaim Bar'am, which followed the republication of *Kehiliatenu* in 1988, and which was entitled "The Torments of *Hashomer Hatza'ir*," begins:

You have seen "The Night of the Twentieth", now you can read the original. The *Kehiliatenu* collection, written by the members of Bitaniya Ilit out of the social pressure cooker in which they were being cooked with Freud, Buber, Socialism, Eroticism, was published this month by Yad Ben-Zvi. Group dynamics in the spirit of *Hashomer Hatza'ir* when it was really young. Meir Ya'ari and David Horowitz were strengthened there, others broke down and went back to Mummy in Europe; one committed suicide.

(Bar'am 1988)

The double-edged attitude toward the dialogical possibilities intimated by the communal form of the "soul talk" was marked by both yearning and suspicion. It has continued to accompany the Phoenix-like reappearances of the "soul talk" format on the Israeli cultural scene. Each republication, reproduction or recreation of the mythology of the early pioneering "intimate groups" and their "soul talks" rekindled the debate associated with them, giving it subtle new inflections as the years went by.

Two recent re-invocations of the spirit of Bitaniya Ilit testify both to its potency and to its multi-vocality as a cultural symbol. In January 1993, the extremely popular weekly televised news magazine of Israel's public television broadcasting corporation, *Yoman Hashavu'a*, told the story of a group of 18-year-olds, members of the *Hano'ar Ha'oved* youth movement, who had recently formed one of six "urban" communes. The trigger for these new "intimate groups" was their members' exposure to Sobol's play *The Night of the Twentieth* which the youngsters had enacted as part of their drama activities, and had then decided to re-enact as part of their lives, "for real." They told the interviewer of struggles they were having with their parents, who considered their offsprings' dream of the ideal community to be an anachronism and tried to talk them out of it. The youngsters responded by consistently rejecting even their parents' attempts to offer some financial support, and reaffirmed their belief in the simple life and in the spirit of community. As in the days of Bitaniya Ilit, the response to these groups in their social environment was neither one of full endorsement nor one of outright rejection. While their dialogical–communal project was described with more than a tinge of amusement, their small size did not prevent them from drawing more than passing attention, and their cultural significance – in the spirit of the day – was signaled by prestigious TV coverage.

At the same time, a TV play entitled *The Loves of Bitaniya*, was written for Israeli public television by the playwright Moti Lerner and was first broadcast as part of the high-profile Day of Independence programming in 1994. In this play, the ethos of Bitaniya is harshly re-examined in light of present-day *kibbutz* reality, in which very few traces of the original pioneering values and dreams can be found. The setting of the play is the opening day of the fictive Bitaniya museum, and throughout the play's unfolding the very act of historical preservation is presented as the antithesis of everything that the ethos of Bitaniya strove to be or to bring about. The lifeless, depleted community of old-timers gather around the aging, still ruthless, once-charismatic leader of Bitaniya Ilit. The opening of the museum is represented as a sorry testimony to the communal dream that was never realized but is nevertheless museumized for future consumption.

The starry-eyed youngsters who ardently believe that their re-enactment of the "intimate group" will hold "forever," as one of them said, and the bitter indictment of the enormous gap between the communal dream and the reality it has bred, as it is artistically expressed in the language of contemporary drama, represent extreme, diametrically opposed attitudes to the pioneers' dream of a "dialogic community." The move away from a collectivist orientation in Israeli society has not completely eradicated the communal utopia that was relentlessly spun in the half-darkened dining-rooms of small pioneering communities strewn across Palestine in the 1920s and 1930s. The dream of communal blending, and the fear of losing oneself in the process, have combined to make "soul talks" the poignant speech occasions that they were, and to some extent still are.

The promise of a life of dialogue among members of "intimate groups," though clearly ensconced in the regions of myth and nostalgia, still reverberates in some corners of Israeli culture, at least as a sense of lost possibility. Over the years, as I have briefly demonstrated, it has been re-articulated and disseminated in the form of a range of cultural artifacts – layers of textualizations and dramatizations, and of public responses to them. Somewhat paradoxically, these nostalgic yet highly troubled imaginative recreations of an idealized image of a "dialogic community" constituted through distinctive moments of talk retain their place in the Israeli cultural conversation through the construction of mass-mediated "imagined communities" of contemporary readers, theater and museum goers and television viewers.

At the same time, of course, alternative notions of the "dialogic community" are being played out on the Israeli cultural scene. Some of these involve an attempt to refigure conceptions of both community and dialogue in a society that is increasingly urban, pluralistic and dominated by new forms of technology. The role of the electronic media in providing a nexus for these contemporary social experiences (and, perhaps, experiments) is of particular interest in this regard. Rather than recreating the intensity of communion inscribed in the image of the "intimate group," contemporary "media communities" are constructed by the much looser and less coordinated participation of unrelated individuals.

Examples of such mass-mediated attempts involve confessional and therapeutic call-in radio talk shows which have become a central feature of night-time programming in contemporary Israel. In these talk shows, as in the "soul talks" of yesteryear, public self-disclosure and confessional discourse serve as communicative centerpieces. Both "soul talks" and "talk shows" can be viewed as historically situated strategies for creating a shared sense of community through the production of "public intimacy." In fact, in contemporary parlance, the kind of confessional discourse that is heard on radio and television programs of this type is sometimes referred to in Hebrew as "soul talks." The ways in which these "media communities" utilize and transform the discursive possibilities charted by face-to-face communities such as the "intimate groups" of the "soulful" Israeli pioneers, whose memory is not yet allowed to rest in peace, seem to me to warrant further investigation.[6]

NOTES

1 A version of this essay was given as a Van Zelst Lecture at the School of Speech, Northwestern University in May 1996.
2 The SPEAKING acronym refers to the following dimensions of speech events: S for setting and scene; P for participants; E for ends (both individual intentions and communal functions); A for act sequence; K for key (tone); I for instrumentalities (message forms and message content); N for norms (of production and interpretation); G for genres.
3 The concern with an ethics of dialogue has recently become incorporated into social science research within a sociological–phenomenological framework by the Israeli sociologist, Zali Gurevitch (1990), who offers a contemporary discussion of the notion of "dialogue" as follows:

> I will contend that in dialogue, apart from taking from others and paying them back as in ordinary exchange, people also give their speech, their listening and their response, and thereby create and sustain a dialogical connection. . . . Dialogue is always the place of unrest. It is a social form of awakening the presence of the Self *vis-à-vis* an Other, of calling the Other and via the Other the Self into presence. It is a dialectic of immersion within the common on the one hand, and the mutual

calling for a sharp sense of presence on the other. In the act of making contacts individuals gear themselves toward a shared object or focus, but in facing together the same (intersubjective) thing, they must also face each other and relate to each other as Each Other. This awareness is also shared, partly in the form of ritualistic gestures . . . and partly as the genuine focus of consciousness seeking the person as ends rather than as means.

(Gurevitch 1990: 182)

I find Gurevitch's discussion appealing because of its normative focus, although I am aware that the phenomenon and discourse of "soul talks" should be related to the philosophy of dialogue of pioneering days. In future research I intend to explore this issue of the interplay between the early pioneers' own discursive constructions of a life of dialogue and the philosophical currents of their time. This essay, clearly, represents work in progress.

4 The central mode of self-disclosive talk in this context involves the mode of confession. Tom Farrell (personal communication) has developed an account of the conditions of felicitous confession. They are:

1 An explicit admission of wrong-doing is made.
2 The admission must be true.
3 The magnitude of the offense must be worth the effort of disclosure or witnessing.
4 There is remorse for the act or for its omission.
5 The confession is before the proper party – either the aggrieved party or the one empowered to forgive.

5 A prominent place-making myth is the narrative of "Tower and Stockade" (Katriel and Shenhar 1990), and there are the well-known Zionist myths of heroism such as, Tel-Hai and Masada (Zerubavel 1995; Ben-Yehuda 1995). See Katriel (1997) for the role of Israeli settlement museums as sites for the production of place-making myths.

6 This is actually part of a larger project entitled "Communication Patterns in the Production of Community: From 'Soul Talks' to 'Talk Shows' in Israeli Culture." The second part of this project, which is left for another essay, explores the role of "media communities" in contemporary Israeli life, focusing on confessionally oriented radio call-in shows and television talk shows. By juxtaposing these two very different cases – "soul talks" and "talk shows" – following as "thick" a description as possible of each one of them, I hope to address central issues related to the role of communication processes in the construction of communities, relationships and subjectivities, as well as in the history of sociological ideas in terms of which these issues have been theorized. Support for this research by the Basic Research Fund of the Israel Academy for Sciences and Humanities is gratefully acknowledged.

REFERENCES

Bar'am, C. (1988) "The torments of *Hashomer Hatza'ir, Kol Ha'ir,* June 24, p. 51.
Bauman, R. (1983) *Let Your Words Be Few: Symbolism of Speaking and Silence among Seventeenth-Century Quakers,* Cambridge: Cambridge University Press.
Bauman, R. and Sherzer, J. (eds.) (1974) *Explorations in the Ethnography of Speaking,* Cambridge: Cambridge University Press.
Ben-Yehuda, N. (1995) *The Masada Myth,* Madison, WI: University of Wisconsin Press.
Bistritsky, N. (1978 [1926]) *Days and Nights* Tel Aviv: Sifriyat Poalim (Hebrew).
Bistritsky, N. (1980) *The Hidden Myth,* Tel-Aviv: Yachdav (Hebrew).
Buber, M. (1965) *The Knowledge of Man,* New York: Harper & Row.
Burke, P. (1993) *The Art of Conversation,* Cambridge: Polity Press.
Evens, T.M.S. (1995) *Two Kinds of Rationality: Kibbutz Democracy and Generational Conflict,* Minneapolis, MN: University of Minnesota Press.

Fishman, A. (1987) "Religion and communal life in an evolutionary–functional perspective: the orthodox kibbutzim," *Comparative Studies in Society and History* 29 (4): 763–86.

Gumperz, J. and Hymes, D. (eds.) (1972) *Directions in Sociolinguistics: The Ethnography of Communication*, New York: Holt, Rinehart & Winston.

Gurevitch, Z. (1990) "The dialogic connection and the ethics of dialogue," *British Journal of Sociology* 41 (2): 181–96.

Horowitz, D. (1970) *My Yesterday*, Jerusalem: Schocken (Hebrew).

Hymes, D. (1974) *Foundations in Sociolinguistics*, Philadelphia, PA: University of Pennsylvania Press.

Kanter, R. (1972) *Commitment and Community: Communes and Utopias in Sociological Perspective*, Cambridge, MA: Harvard University Press.

Katriel, T. (1986) *Talking Straight "Dugri" Speech in Israeli Sabra Culture*, Cambridge: Cambridge University Press.

Katriel, T. (1991) *Communal Webs: Communication and Culture in Contemporary Israel*, Albany, NY: State University of New York Press.

Katriel, T. (1997) *Performing the Past: A Study of Israeli Settlement Museums*. NJ: Erlbaum.

Katriel, T. and Shenhar, A. (1990) "Tower and stockade: a study in Israeli settlement symbolism," *Quarterly Journal of Speech* 76 (4): 359–80.

Keshet, S. (1995) *Underground Soul: Ideological Literature – The Case of the Kibbutz Novel*, Tel Aviv: Hakibbutz Hameuchad (Hebrew).

Lerner, M. (1994) *Ahavot Bitaniya* [The Loves of Bitaniya]. TV play shown on Channel 1 of Israeli Public Television, April 14.

Mintz, M. (1995) *The Bonds of Youth: The Hashomer Movement 1911–1921*, Jerusalem: Zionist Library of the International Zionist Federation (Hebrew).

Naveh, H. (1988) *The Confession: A Study of Genre*, Tel Aviv: Papyrus (Hebrew).

Opaz, A. (ed.) (1995) *Sefer Hakvutza*, Jerusalem: Yad Ben-Zvi (Hebrew).

Saville-Troike, M. (1982) *The Ethnography of Communication: An Introduction*, Oxford: Blackwell.

Shapira, A. (ed.) (1967) *Si'ach Lochamim* [Soldiers' Discourse], Kibbutz Movement Publication.

Sobol, Y. (1990 [1976]) *Leil Haesrim* [The Night of the Twentieth], Or-Am Publishers. Produced by Haifa Theater in 1976 and again by Habima National Theatre in 1990, reproduced on national television (Hebrew).

Tsur, M. (ed.) (1988) *Kehiliatenu* (3rd edn), Jerusalem: Yad Ben-Zvi (Hebrew).

Turner, V. (1969) *The Ritual Process*, Itacha, NY: Cornell University Press.

Ya'ari, M. (1923) "Smalim Tlushim [Uprooted Symbols]." *Hedim* (Hebrew). Republished in E. Shadmi (ed.) *Mekorot* 1, Giv'at Haviva, March 1984, pp. 60–70.

Zablocki, B. (1980) *Alienation and Charisma: A Study of Contemporary American Communes*, London: Free Press.

Zerubavel, Y. (1995) *Recovered Roots: Collective Memory and the Making of Israeli National Tradition*, Chicago, IL: University of Chicago Press.

8 The dialectics of life, story, and afterlife[1]

Yoram Bilu

Postmodern anthropology is informed by a social reality in which the boundaries between the ethnographer and the informant are being systematically eroded: the "native" as an object of analysis may become an analyzing subject (Rosaldo 1989) and the "other" may appear as a critical reader of the ethnographic account (Clifford and Marcus 1986; Marcus and Fischer 1986). Under these circumstances, anthropologists have become more attentive to the reverberations of their fieldwork and particularly ethnographic writing in the lives and the social world of the people whom they study. The growing sensitivity to the effect of ethnographic accounts on the communities studied (and on other circles of readership beyond the relatively small professional group of colleagues and students) has recently given rise to two collections of insightful essays on the political and moral–ethical aspects of this subject matter (Blackman 1992a; Brettell 1993).

The essays in Brettell's edited volume, *When They Read What We Write*, discuss various dimensions of the complex relations between fieldwork, text and audience (when the natives talk back, when native scholars object and when the press intervenes). Blackman's (1992a) edited collection, which appeared as a special issue of the *Journal of Narrative and Life History*, was designated *The Afterlife of the Life History*. The articles subsumed under this title focus on the post-publication of what is written as life history.

> Afterlife makes the point that the life-history continues beyond the crystallization of the narrative into text to encompass audience response to the published work, reflections on its constructions as text, as well as its impact on the lives of its narrator and collector.
>
> (Blackman 1992b: 2)

Issues related to the afterlife of ethnographic accounts are particularly pertinent in Israel. On top of the fact that most Israeli anthropologists are studying their own society, the small size of the country, the relatively open avenues of communication and the wide exposure to the same few mass media agencies – all create problems of involvement with which anthropologists working in remote milieus are less bothered. I believe that the case I narratively present here – the post-publication vicissitudes of the life story of a legendary rabbi–healer who died in Morocco in the early 1950s – sheds light on some of these problems of involvement. Beyond the ethical problems of the "politics of the life story," amply discussed in Blackman's (1992a) collection, the case to be presented raises an intriguing epistemological question concerning the interplay between the ethnographic text and the reality that it is supposed to represent.

I first came across the name of Rabbi Ya'acov Wazana in 1975 when I was collecting data for my doctoral dissertation on Jewish Moroccan ethnopsychiatry in Israel. Focusing on two *moshavim* (smallholders' cooperative villages) of immigrants from southern Morocco near Jerusalem, I sought to study the traditional curing system through interviews with those inhabitants who turned to local rabbi–healers with all sorts of problems in living. The interviews were explicitly directed toward the current Israeli scene. But the informants often resorted to the Maghrebi chapters in their lives, basking in memories of an era in which the folk practices I was interested in were an integral part of the traditional ambiance. It was in this context of discussing episodes of illness and health-seeking behavior in Morocco that some informants invoked, with awe and astonishment, the name of Rabbi Ya'acov. "In all Morocco, there was no healer like Wazana," they would reiterate wistfully. "At times when physicians were practically non-existent, he was our only doctor."

Such admiring statements and the intriguing accounts of curing feats that usually followed them at once drew my attention to Wazana. But the urge to retrieve and explore his life story had to be weighed against three serious reservations. First, I soon found out that only a small number of the interviewees had known Wazana in Morocco. They all had come to Israel from the same circumscribed area in the Western High Atlas region, and this geographical boundedness accentuated Wazana's position as a provincial healer, a celebrity in a remote, peripheral place. His name was not known in the urban centers of the coastal zone where most of the Jewish population has been concentrated since the establishment of the French Protectorate. Why bother, then, with the life story of a peripheral figure who, in terms of popularity and renown, was far behind many more centrally located, urban healers?

Second, the first recollections of Wazana had already convinced me that he was a "deviant" type within the Jewish Moroccan curing system, given his antinomian personality and the audacious and extravagant manner in which he enacted the curing role. Hence Wazana's life story did not appear to be a good representation of the typical Jewish Moroccan rabbi–healer.

Third, in addition to his peripherality and atypicality, the fact that Wazana died in 1952 in Morocco, just before the massive wave of immigration to Israel eliminated the Jewish presence from most parts of the Maghreb, made him a mediated object of knowledge. His life could be examined only through texts elicited from people who knew him in other times and in other places rather than through straightforward facts of life history. In other words, these texts were constructed of historically situated memories replete with retrospective evaluations and interpretations and imbued with personal meanings to the narrators. This epistemological concern, although common to most forms of investigation which rely on narrative accounts, could be mitigated to some extent by replacing

Wazana, a shadowy figure from an elusive past, with a contemporary Jewish Moroccan rabbi–healer who could be addressed and studied directly.

That I remained engrossed with Wazana's figure despite these concerns attests to the compelling power of a dramatic life story. Yet beyond the immediacy and the emotional effect of a heroic–tragic narrative (to be unfolded presently), I felt that the selection of Wazana's life story as an object of study could also be defended on theoretical grounds. First, when seeking to portray a life as a totality in all of its complexity and uniqueness yet without the presumption that it should serve as an exemplary model or a typical representation of some collectivity, then the life story of a provincial figure is worth telling no less than that of a central, more popular one. Moreover, this idiographic justification seems altogether superfluous when the question of Wazana's atypicality is at stake, because it was precisely Wazana's deviant dimension that could bring to the fore and highlight core elements of the symbolic universe and the cultural setting of the Jewish Maghrebi communities. In the audacious, boundless manner in which he enacted the healer role, Wazana traveled to the edge of the social order. He went further than any other Jewish healer I have heard of in exploiting the potentialities of the idioms of his culture and in challenging and eventually defying its constraints. Dialectically, then, these idioms could be explored most lucidly through the intricacies of his admittedly exceptional biography.

The epistemological concern about Wazana as a mediated object of knowledge can become a virtue when the investigation is conducted from a constructivist rather than an essentialist perspective. It may appear presumptuous and naive to launch a fact-finding expedition in a time machine to expose Wazana's "authentic" figure in the name of historical positivism. It is no less unfounded to embark directly on the motivational bases of such a mediated figure in the name of psychological essentialism. But if the diverse layers of mediation that separate Wazana from the investigator – the dialogue between the informants and Wazana in the past (as fashioned and refashioned in memory), their ongoing dialogue with his image in the present, and the dialogue between the investigator and the informants – are deconstructed rather than ignored, then we can draw nearer to the complex, multivocal process in which a figure from an increasingly dim past is developed and mythologized. I espoused this multidialogic approach in dealing with Wazana's life story.

Before embarking on the repercussions or afterlife of Wazana's life story as promulgated in my work, which is the gist of this essay, a brief sketch of his biography and my analysis of it is in order. My engagement with Wazana, which now spans two decades, gave rise to three written accounts of his life. The short section on his life in my dissertation (Bilu 1978) was expanded into an article in Hebrew (Bilu 1986) and later in English (Bilu 1988), and then developed into a book in Hebrew (Bilu 1993). The following account was abstracted from the book.

Wazana was born at the turn of the century in a small village nestled near the highest peaks of the Atlas mountains. He spent most of his life in this mountainous area, and his reputation barely exceeded it. The genealogy of his family was laced with pious rabbis acknowledged as saintly figures (*tsaddiqim*), and this virtuous background was conducive to his assumption of the curing role. Most noted among these venerated forefathers was Wazana's great-grandfather, Rabbi Avraham el-Kebir ("the great"), the source of the family blessing, whose miraculous accomplishments made his tomb near the town of Ouarzazat a popular pilgrimage site.

Wazana's father, also called Avraham, a pious student of Jewish mysticism, was a worthy successor to the family legacy. His miracle-saturated death account (see Bilu 1988) clearly resonates with similar episodes in the genre of saint legends. Young Ya'acov, still a child and away from home when his father passed away, could not resign himself with the loss. In a desperate attempt to catch another glimpse of his father's face, he dug up his tomb and exposed his body. When his mother died thirty years later, again in his absence, Wazana exhumed her body, too, for a last farewell. I interpreted these religiously forbidden acts in the narrated profile of Wazana as conveying his unrelieved pain and longing for his parents as well as his boldness and temerity. More specifically, they reflected his tenacious ambition to stare at what should be invisible and to retrieve what by all means is irretrievable. This passion would become the leitmotif for Wazana's curing activities in the future.

What made Wazana so unique in the Jewish Moroccan curing system was his profound involvement with Muslim practices – to the extent of dangerously blurring his Jewish identity. His passion for Muslim esoteric knowledge stemmed from his desire to gain control over the *jnun* (demons), the major source of affliction in Moroccan ethnomedicine. To that end, he studied under Muslim sages and went so far as to absorb himself in Muslim prayers and to marry a she-demon. It should be noted that a human–demon marriage was an option in the traditional Maghrebi setting. But it was considered an extreme act, dwelling on the limits of social conventions, because of its exclusively binding character: the husband of a she-demon could not marry a human. Although Wazana's demonic spouse and the children he begot remained invisible to his associates, no one doubted their existence. His demonic and Muslim leanings, which could easily bring about ostracism in bigger Jewish communities, were somehow tolerated in those peripheral areas where demons were givens in the culturally constituted reality and Muslims lived in close coexistence with Jews. Both groups, it should be remembered, amply enjoyed Wazana's therapeutic services, which were based on these eccentric leanings.

Wazana had an impressive appearance. Strong, tall, and good-looking, with his spotless white *jellaba* (gown) and red *tarboosh* (headcover) typical of Muslims, he gave the impression that age had no effect on him. The audacity with which he pursued his role was mitigated by the air of carelessness and lack of arrogance that surrounded him. His cheerful, gargantuan character made him the center of any social gathering. On these occasions, he would resort to his conjuring tricks to bring forth, by sleight of hand, *arak* (an alcoholic beverage), mint tea or tobacco. His associates believed that in these frivolous tricks, too, he was helped by his demonic kin. In seeking to epitomize Wazana's peculiar character, one of them stated that "he [Wazana] feared nothing, he cared about nothing, and he lacked nothing."

As an indefatigable healer, fortified by impressive Muslim-based curing devices, Wazana treated all sorts of life problems, but he was particularly renowned for his ability to expose sorcerers and to identify thieves. Other healers were reluctant to cope with these malefactors because of the potentially dire consequences of a confrontation with the identified offender – believed to be someone from the victim's close social circle. But for Wazana, unheedful of social conventions and fervently determined to unravel what should normally remain hidden and unknown, such intricacies were of negligible importance. It was this deter-mination "to go all the way" in his therapeutic undertakings, coupled with his arrogant contempt of the social order, that brought on him a horrible, untimely death.

Wazana died in the summer of 1952 when he was in his early fifties. There is a consensus that his tragic demise was precipitated by a forbidden cure. He was called on to remedy the moribund daughter of a famous Muslim sheik who had fallen prey to the demons' wrath after she had killed their offspring in snake form. Haughtily ignoring the demonic admonitions not to treat her, Wazana succeeded in bringing the girl back to life. This therapeutic victory was Wazana's greatest achievement as a healer, but it proved short-lived as the demons hastened to take their revenge on their ally turned adversary. They attacked him vehemently, and Wazana underwent a rapid physical and mental deterioration. Confused and panic-stricken, he made desperate attempts to extricate himself from his fatal condition but to no avail. He sank into a twilight state and died in agony and pain. The Jews of the village found his body fetid and swollen, soaked in buckets of vomit and blood, and hastened to bury him in the local cemetery. The tenor of Wazana's death account, sharply contrasted with the death legends of his saintly ancestors, seals the saga of the family with a tragic hue which is indicative, perhaps, of the ambivalence harbored in the community toward his anomalous lifestyle.

Based on Wazana's reconstructed biography, presented here in a very schematic form, I analyzed on two levels Wazana's calling and particularly the prodigious healing energies attributed to him.

First, without denying the aforementioned epistemological concerns of studying a mediated object of knowledge, I nevertheless sought to explore Wazana's motivational structure. In doing this, I followed the informants who, although reluctant to articulate their impressions of Wazana within a psychological idiom, were quite intrigued by his strong attachment to his parents and by his inability to resign himself to their deaths. Without going into their detailed accounts here, I raised the possibility that his unrelieved grief and sense of loss were the generator underlying his inexhaustible healing energies. His unique style of work, characterized by temerity, audacity, perseverance and resourcefulness, might have been molded by his desperate yearning to cure his parents and to bring them back to life. In this respect, the resuscitation of the daughter of the sheik constituted the ultimate cure that symbolically compensated for the death of his parents. Wazana's own death seems to reflect, beyond the culturally ingrained notion of restoring the equilibrium between the human and the demonic worlds, the extinction of that inner source of vitality once the mission of his life was completed.

Given the mediated process in which Wazana's figure has been constructed, I proposed a second perspective for analysis which moved the limelight from the protagonist's psychic reality to the dialogic reality of his encounter with the Jews of the High Atlas (symbolically maintained up to this day through memories and dreams). In this cultural–symbolic analysis, the ambivalence that Wazana's position at the edge of the social order had elicited in his community was taken as a starting point. The crux of the argument was that Wazana's liminal position was deemed threateningly dangerous and therefore discommendable, but, at the same time, it presumably made him capable of unleashing endless amounts of healing energies.

The negative, condemning aspect of this ambivalence becomes all the more conspicuous when the respective death episodes of Wazana and his father (as well as other pious ancestors) are juxtaposed and compared. The comparison, too elaborate to be depicted here, puts Wazana in a very unflattering light. His death account, communicating impotence and incompleteness, appears as the mirror image of the idealized death episodes of his forefathers which, in keeping with the genre of saint legends, are replete with miraculous events and convey strength and complacent harmony. Thus a tacit but firm condemnation is launched at the profligate son who abused the powers of his ancestors by crossing and dissolving the boundaries that they were so anxious to maintain.

Along with this harsh cultural verdict, Wazana's unique marginality and disregard for social norms also made him a vital therapeutic resource for his community. Presumably his image as a great healer in the eyes of the Jews and Muslims was related to the fact that he integrated and personified in his figure a set of seemingly contrasting categories which normally are sharply differentiated. Viewed at once as human and demon-bound, Jew and Muslim, pure and profane, old and young, single and married, Wazana crossed and dissipated the major ontological, ethnic, social, religious and moral boundaries that constituted the grid of the social order in traditional Morocco. This categorization-defying mobility is dangerous and unrestrained but also potent and creative because in crossing the conceptual boundaries recognized by the culture, it releases energies and modes of actions that those locked in social casts and rigid structural positions are not able to recruit or pursue.

In residing at the edge of the social order, Wazana appears as a liminal figure (Turner 1974) or a symbolic type (Handelman 1985), capable of employing the fluidity and disorder that were his essence to restore order and wholeness, and to cure. It should be noted, in this vein, that the word *wazana* in Arabic means "to balance." In bridging oppositions in Maghrebi cosmology, Wazana balanced worlds as shamans often do (Myerhoff 1976). His death account lucidly demonstrates what might happen when the shamanic gift of maintaining order, harmony and equilibrium is abused.

Although I became engrossed with Wazana in the context of studying folk healing and ethnopsychiatry, his name kept accompanying me when my interest in the vicissitudes of the Maghrebi cultural traditions in Israel led me, in the early 1980s, to the related realm of the folk veneration of saints (see Bilu 1991). Because the significance of the vicissitudes of Wazana's afterlife is couched in the renaissance of saint worship in Israel, the essence and main features of this cultural complex should be explicated.

Saint veneration, a hallmark of Moroccan Islam, was also a major constituent of the Jewish collective identity in traditional Morocco. The Jewish saints (*k'doshim* or *tsaddiqim*) were depicted as charismatic and pious sages, erudite in *kabbalah* (Jewish mysticism), who possessed a special spiritual force from which their adherents could benefit. Unlike their Muslim counterparts, most Jewish Moroccan saints were acknowledged as *tsaddiqim* only posthumously. Therefore, their tombs, densely distributed all over the country, were the foci of their cults. The high point in the veneration of the saints was the collective pilgrimage to their tombs on their death anniversaries and the celebration (*hillulah*) there. In the case of the more popular saints, these pilgrimages involved thousands of followers in a formidable spectacle, several days long, which combined high spirituality and marked ecstasy with excessive self-indulgence (e.g. feasting on slaughtered cattle and consuming large quantities of *arak*). In addition to the *hillulah* day, supplicants frequented the sanctuaries of the saints throughout the year with a wide variety of human afflictions.

One did not have to go on collective or individual pilgrimages to enjoy the saints' bliss because their presence was also strongly felt in daily routine. People would utter their names and dream about them whenever facing a problem. At home, candles were lit and festive meals organized in honor of the saints, and male newborns were conferred with their names in gratitude (and also to ensure the help of the sublime namesake). As a major cultural idiom for articulating a wide range of experiences, the pervasive and enduring relations with the saint often took a symbiotic form spanning the entire life course of the devotee.

The sociocultural fabric of Moroccan Jewry was ruptured following the massive *aliyah* (immigration) to Israel in the 1950s and 1960s. The folk veneration of saints was particularly vulnerable because it was associated with physical loci – tombs, shrines and sanctuaries – which had been left behind. Indeed, the first harsh years after *aliyah* witnessed a rapid diminution and decentralization in the celebration of *hillulot* (plural of *hillulah*). But this attenuation process was stopped and reversed when the new immigrants gradually and painfully alleviated the cultural shock and the enormous economic difficulties that were their share after *aliyah*. Specifically, Moroccan Jews were able to resume their intimate bond with the saints by employing various compensatory substitutes for the deserted Maghrebi sanctuaries. They annexed and "Moroccanized" old (local Israeli) pilgrimage sites attributed to various biblical, talmudic and mystical luminaries, and established new centers around the tombs of charismatic contemporary rabbis.

My research on Maghrebi saint worship in Israel has focused on a third alternative, more daring and innovative than the former two, which was called for to restore the forsaken Maghrebi saints of childhood – not merely to compensate for their absence. This alternative involved the symbolic transfer of Jewish saints from Morocco to Israel and their reinstallation in the new country (Ben-Ari and Bilu 1987). It was based on the spontaneous initiative of simple devotees of Moroccan background, men and women alike, who erected a shrine for a Maghrebi *tsaddiq* in their homes following an inspiring dream series in which the saint urged them to do so. They usually promulgated these dreams as "announcements to the public," which they circulated among Moroccan-born Israelis. I designated these individual entrepreneurs "saint impresarios" to convey their relentless efforts to develop their shrines and increase their popularity. Much of my work with the saint impresarios centered on their personal narratives and life stories (e.g. Bilu 1990; Bilu and Hasan-Rokem 1989). As articulated by them, these accounts, which always ended with the appearance of the saint's apparition and an enduring liaison with him, are based on life events which pave the way for the transformative visitational dreams.

At this point, Wazana's position *vis-à-vis* the Maghrebi cult of the saints should be clarified. In traditional Morocco, the authority and renown of rabbi–healers were primarily based on "the virtue of the ancestors" (*zechut avot*), that is, the divine powers enveloped in the blessing of sainted figures in the family, which worthy descendants were capable of inheriting. As we already know, Wazana's prodigious family background, saturated with many sainted figures, constituted a propitious ground for healing. Yet with his antinomian character and deviant lifestyle, Wazana appears as a negative template of the conventional *tsaddiq*. As I attempted to show in my analysis, he was the family's black sheep, the profligate son who, to gain extraordinary therapeutic powers, went so far as to embrace Muslim practices and demonic affiliations. Jewish saints were hardly made of this subversive stuff. Indeed in Israel, Wazana's memory was cherished by a relatively small group of associates and grateful ex-patients. He did not enjoy the popularity of his forebears and definitely remained outside the Jewish–Maghrebi pantheon of saints.

THE ANTHROPOLOGIST, THE MEDIA AND THE AFTERLIFE

My book in Hebrew on Wazana appeared in March 1993. Although it was published in a small number of copies by an academic press, it received relatively high media coverage. I believe that the concatenation of events that ensued was triggered by this media exposure (the credit for which should go to Wazana's colorful and intriguing character) and particularly by two lengthy pieces that appeared simultaneously in the weekend supplements of the two leading Israeli daily newspapers. I found out that the book, no less than its protagonist, was mediated object of knowledge. But this time, the filters through which Wazana's figure was conveyed to the public were newspaper and television reports in which his exotic and magical aspects were all the more accentuated.

At the beginning of April 1993, a 35-year-old man named Yoseph from the town of Beer Sheva, an ex-barber who now worked as a clerk in a local religious institution, called me in my office at the Hebrew University. Claiming that his parents had known Wazana in Morocco he started to unfold, in a trembling voice burning with excitement, a series of dream encounters with the late rabbi–healer. Although it was impossible to rule out the possibility that some of the dreams had preceded the publication, it became evident at the outset that the book, and particularly the attention drawn to it by the media, precipitated Yoseph's decision to "go public" with the nightly messages from Rabbi Ya'acov. Needless to say, Yoseph's phone call engaged my attention instantly. I suggested a meeting in Beer Sheva so that I could record or write down verbatim Yoseph's dream accounts. He wholeheartedly agreed but said that to expediate matters, he would send me the written version of his nocturnal experiences with Wazana. One day later, a handwritten, six-page-long account of six dreams reached me through the department's fax machine. Only after I read the dream report did I start to realize the scope of Yoseph's vision and my expected role in it: as Wazana's biographer (or more akin to Yoseph's point of view, as his hagiographer), I was assigned the role of Yoseph's confidant and adviser in his attempts to promote and give publicity to the name of the legendary but relatively unknown healer in Israel.

In the introduction to the dream accounts, Yoseph praises the greatness of Rabbi Ya'acov and the holiness of his great forebears. Then he asks, "How did it turn out that precisely now, fifty-one years after the death of Rabbi Ya'acov Wazana [in fact, only forty-one years had passed since Wazana's death], it was decided to erect this holy site, which bears the name of these *tsaddiqim*?" In his answer, he highlights the miraculous cures that Wazana lavished on his family but then moves on to give credit to my work:

> Professor Yoram Bilu . . . [here my academic title and position, as presented on the back cover of the book, are specified] traveled through the whole country in his attempts to inquire about the greatness of Rabbi Ya'acov Wazana. And he found out that many were the people who had known Wazana and his miraculous achievements. This journey in the footsteps of Wazana he described in a book (titled) *The Life and Death of Rabbi Ya'acov Wazana*. And he certainly deserves a credit for his wonderful work and commitment.

In an unmistakable allusion to Joseph, the great biblical dreamer, the dream series was titled "The dreams of Yoseph." It represents a coherent narrative sequence in which the drama of the multiple encounters with Wazana picks up until its final resolve. In the first dream report, Wazana reveals himself to Yoseph and asks him to erect a site for him and his forefathers for celebrating their *hillulot*. The ensuing pattern of the reported nocturnal interactions between the dreamer and the healer is indistinguishable from that reported by the saint impresarios I have studied in describing their emergent alliance with their patron *tsaddiq*. Like them, Yoseph initially assumes an ambivalent if not a reluctant position, doubting his ability to pursue the calling imposed on him by Wazana. But the latter, like the saints in the dreams of the impresarios, gradually disarms him of his resistance by showering him with messages of encouragement and promises of help.

In the fifth dream, Yoseph finally makes a solemn vow to erect this site and to celebrate the *hillulot* of Wazana and his ancestors. To this acquiescence, Wazana responds with a warm embrace and a blessing. In the sixth and last dream, these affectionate gestures are transformed into specific instructions: Yoseph is sent to the municipality to mobilize the resources for the project. The pursuit of these instructions represents the afterlife of the dream sequence. Against all odds, Yoseph was assisted by various functionaries in the municipality to achieve his goal. Some of them explicitly stated that they did what they did against their better judgment, as if activated by an external power. As a result of their compliance, Yoseph finally got hold of a huge public shelter not far from his home. His account ends with "a passionate appeal to the public" to make contributions for remodeling the shelter and transforming it into a shrine. In subsequent phone calls, he tried to recruit me to that end as well, begging me to look in Israel and abroad for benefactors for the site.

I soon found out, however, that Yoseph was concerned with remodeling Wazana's figure no less than with remodeling the shelter. Our first meeting took place in Beer Sheva at the end of May 1993, just a few days after I had discussed Wazana in a literary program on Israeli television. Once again, Wazana's antinomian character was in the limelight, but this time, Yoseph could not disregard it. He was devastated by the idea that his idol, for whom he was seeking to establish a sacred site, was presented in the program as a deviant healer, partly Muslim and partly demonic. In his despair, he even suggested eliminating all the copies of the book from the bookstores and that we write a revised version together after gaining the proper rabbinical approval. He withdrew his suggestion only after I made it clear that it was precisely the subversive side of Wazana that made me write down his life story.

This was, in fact, our one and only confrontation. Still, Yoseph could not resign himself to the unorthodox aspects of Wazana and did all he could to decrease their salience. In his discourse, he was cautious not to mention Wazana's name without juxtaposing it with his pious forebears, thus seeking to envelop him, as it were, in their saintly aura. When Wazana's oddities nevertheless came to the fore, he was adamant about removing their sting by positive reframing. Thus he would often resort to mystical causes, presumably incomprehensible to ordinary people, in accounting for Wazana's alliance with the Muslims and the demons.

Yoseph's efforts to deprive Wazana of his uniqueness and to recast him in the mold of a stereotypical Jewish Moroccan saint added a measure of unrelieved tension to our relations. Nevertheless, the dialogue between us could be maintained because it was based on a certain degree of symmetry, reciprocity and interdependence. As a university professor keenly interested in the figure whom Yoseph sought to idolize, I could serve as a source of legitimation and respectability for him in his efforts to popularize the new site.

But Yoseph was no less important to my work because I was determined to document and study the intriguing "resurrection" of Rabbi Ya'acov Wazana that he initiated. To some extent, my professional career was dependent on Israelis of Moroccan background like Yoseph – folk-healers, traditional patients, saint impresarios and other devotees – whose knowledge, beliefs, visions and misery I promulgated into scholarly work. In the case of Wazana, the taken-for-granted contribution to my academic standing was augmented by narcissistic gratification. The idea that my book was conducive to Wazana's re-emergence in a saintly guise was so captivating that I was resolute about investigating exhaustively the cultural phenomenon that I had helped to create. In a curiously symmetrical way, each of us managed to overcome or contain the problems posed by the other side – for Yoseph, the deviant aspects of Wazana emphasized in my book; for me, Yoseph's attempt to replace these aspects with saintly ones – recognizing the potential contribution of the other to one's own goals.

The uneasy complicity between Yoseph and me had been tested already on my first visit to Beer Sheva. In fact, I scheduled the visit on the same day that I was supposed to discuss my book on Wazana with students at Ben-Gurion University in Beer Sheva. In doing this, I was well aware of the two levels of discourse, pertaining to different epistemological realms, that I juxtaposed, yet I was confident, and even took delight in the fact, that I could maneuver between the two readings of Wazana – as object of enshrinement and veneration and as object of skeptical inquiry. Unlike the protagonist of my book with his shamanic power of bridging between worlds, I sought to maintain the compartmentalization of the two realms, but Yoseph interfered with my plan. When I tried to take my leave after visiting the shelter turned shrine, he insisted that I should stay overnight in his place, and I had to tell him about my other commitment. He immediately stated his wish to join me and dismissed all my alarmed attempts to dissuade him from doing so. Even though I made it explicit to Yoseph that the students might be particularly interested in those antinomian aspects in Wazana's lifestyle that he sought to silence, I felt quite insecure when we entered together the lecture hall where the meeting took place.

Despite my apprehension, the evening was quite successful. Sitting quietly among the students, Yoseph followed attentively my introductory remarks and the lively discussion that ensued (in which, as I expected, the bizarre side of Wazana was a central topic). Toward the end of the meeting, one student raised the issue of relevance; is it possible that people living in Israel in the 1990s are still moved by Wazana? To answer the question, I invited Yoseph to the podium, on the spur of the moment, to tell his story. Delighted to have the arena for himself, Yoseph unfolded the sequence of events that led him to erect the shrine to the Wazana family. I was amazed by his articulate and poised performance, which left the audience speechless. For one enchanted moment, the two realms of discourse mingled after all.

Elated by the effect that he had on the students, Yoseph felt very grateful to me for giving him the opportunity to tell his story in a setting that he considered very prestigious. Much later, I was puzzled to find out that he had recorded the whole affair on a small tape recorder which he carried in his bag. I do not know how, if at all, he used the recorded material, but the measure he had taken further reduced the traditional gap between ethnographer and informant. The taken-for-granted prerogative of the researcher to isolate and objectify data extracted from the other, rendering it amenable for processing and analysis, was thus seized and employed by that other.

My turn to use a tape recorder (and a video camera) came several weeks later, in mid-July 1993, when Yoseph invited me to "the first *hillulah* of Rabbi Ya'acov Wazana in Israel, commemorating the forty-first anniversary of his death," at his home in Beer Sheva. Because some members of the Wazana family were also among the guests, I was a bit concerned about possible negative reactions to the book but, to my relief, no one mentioned the anomalous aspects of Wazana. Moreover, from the compliments they bestowed on me for promulgating the life story of their kin, I came to the conclusion that none of them had read the book. From my perspective, the high point of the modest, domestic *hillulah* was an ornate speech delivered by a local rabbi, a remote kin of Rabbi Ya'acov and one of the most respected descendants of the Wazana family, which was sealed as follows: "Rabbi Ya'acov Wazana has made many wonders in his lifetime and in the afterworld, but his greatest miracle was to make a distinguished professor at the Hebrew University write this book."

Yoseph also delivered a speech in which he elaborated on my association with Wazana. He deconstructed my name, Bilu, an acronym for a Biblical verse, *Beit Ya'acov Lechu Venelcha* ("House of Jacob, let us go"), as indicating my eagerness to go from house to house (of would-be informants) in pursuit of Rabbi Ya'acov.

Note that, in both speeches, the two realms of discourse on Wazana were combined again, but this time it was the traditionally privileged social science perspective (Wazana as an object of investigation) that was appropriated and accounted for by the mystical perspective (Wazana as sainted figure). Of course, the process did not end there because my ongoing attempts to document it constituted some form of reappropriation, which was reflected, among other things, in this very presentation. The video camera, in particular, gave me an edge over Yoseph. Operated by a doctoral student of mine, it enabled me, by "freezing" the events of the *hillulah*, to transform them into an objectified topic of study amenable to multiple analyses and deconstructions. In the subsequent months, however, Yoseph added a video camera to the increasingly advanced arsenal of tools that he has been using in his attempts to promote his venture. The extent of his organizational efforts and sophistication became evident to me in the next public event that he initiated for promoting the shrine, which took place in May 1994.

This time, the celebration took place in a synagogue in Beer Sheva. From the invitation, I learned that the new shrine was designated "The Glory of the Ancestors – The Wazana Dynasty." The gathering was depicted in the invitation as "an evening dedicated to the Torah" in which many religious functionaries and political figures, from the chief rabbi of Beer Sheva to two deputy mayors, were supposed to address the company. My name, too, appeared among the local dignitaries, I was surprised to find out that I was "a member of the presidential body of the Hebrew University" and, even more so, that I was nominated "a member of the presidential body of [the sanctuary of] The Glory of the Ancestors – The Wazana Dynasty." The symmetry between the two designations and particularly their juxtaposition, was a lucid demonstration of how deeply engulfed I had become in the "sacred discourse" about Wazana that Yoseph had cultivated. Aside from my name, my attention was also drawn to an enigmatic statement in the invitation announcing that "the sacred book of the saint Rabbi Ya'acov Wazana will be presented in the synagogue."

The evening was well organized. Food and beverages were distributed to the 150 congregants, and a local band played popular religious music. An articulate master of ceremonies presented the speakers, and a professional team of photographers with all sorts of cameras, including video, documented the affair, including the speech I was asked to deliver. Realizing the delicacy of the situation, I decided to circumvent the issue of Wazana's oddities in my address and to limit myself to the genealogy of the Wazana family and the way in which I had collected the material for the book, I was well aware that in so doing I was acquiescing to Yoseph's attempts to sanctify Wazana, but in the ceremonial atmosphere that prevailed I did not feel that I could act otherwise. I comforted myself that my temporary betrayal of the protagonist of my book was a necessary price for maintaining the privilege of studying a phenomenon which I had inadvertently helped to set in motion. Moreover, there was something exciting, though at times upsetting, too, in documenting the very process into which I was drawn as a key participant.

Listening to the other speeches, I could witness once again how my academic involvement with Wazana was mobilized in the service of mythologically rearranging his figure. Thus I was amazed to hear that my voyage in the footsteps of Wazana was conducted in the remote areas of the Atlas mountains, where I withstood many a predicament. This way, the voyage (and, by implication, the figure that propelled it) was made grander and more heroic. Another speaker informed the impressed audience that in seventeen (!) universities throughout the world research on the Wazana family was currently being conducted. A common thread in many of the speeches was that my engrossment with Wazana could not be incidental. Rather, it was mystically informed and ought to be taken as another indication of Wazana's great stature.

Yoseph, respectfully designated "Rabbi Yoseph" by the master of ceremonies, was the last of the speakers. After unfolding the concatenation of events that led him to erect the shrine, he came to the highlight of the evening. He related how, following clues that he received from Wazana in a recent dream message, he was able to secure, after an arduous odyssey, one of the healer's enigmatic books. To appreciate the excitement that this disclosure stirred in the audience, it should be noted that Wazana's ex-associates consistently referred to his old, handwritten books, replete with magical incantations and esoteric formulas, as a major source of his power. Most of them, however, also contended that Wazana's few possessions, including these precious books, had all mysteriously disappeared after his sudden death. Despite persistent rumors claiming that one or more of the books had found their way to Israel, no one admitted to having seen them.

Following the public auction of gigantic colorful candles designed to collect money for the shrine, an indispensable part of such celebrations, the book was presented by Yoseph to the congregants. As far as I could see, it was indeed a genuine book of medicine, handwritten in the distinctive Judeo-Maghrebi discursive writing. The unmistakably Jewish origin of the book was incongruent with the recurrent claim that Wazana was exclusively relying on Muslim traditions in his work, but the participants were not bothered with questions of authenticity. Bustling and swarming, they congregated around Yoseph trying to touch the book with their hands and to kiss it. It was clear that in their eyes, the book – a sort of metonymic extension of the great healer – was endowed with great therapeutic powers which could be absorbed through physical contact. Having anticipated this enthusiastic response, Yoseph circulated special forms among the congregants in which they were asked to write down the names of relatives and friends "to be blessed by the book of the saint." This initiative proved very lucrative, as indicated by the growing pile of envelopes filled with forms and money that appeared on the podium at the end of the evening.

The celebration in the synagogue was the last public event associated with the shrine that I attended, but the story of the afterlife of Wazana (or no less important, of his promulgated life story) is still being developed. Becoming more concerned about my reluctant yet growing participation in the authorship of this afterlife, I decided to distance myself a bit from the shrine and its builder. The time was ripe for some disengagement on both sides because Yoseph, having established for himself a name as a saint impresario and a healer (owing to the fast-spreading therapeutic appeal of Wazana's book), was less in need of respectable legitimators.

The discovery of the book adds an ironic twist and a sense of narrative closure to the story of Wazana's resurrection. The symmetry of the two realms of discourse between which I was precariously navigating had been extended to the domain of the text, heretofore the cherished prerogative of the researcher. I could not escape the egocentric notion that the book of healing attributed to Wazana was brought to the fore, among other things, as a counterweight to my own book. The ethnographic writing, an initial booster but also a potential obstacle to the sanctification of Wazana, has been replaced with a sacred text, more suited to the folk–religious idioms of the believers, which tangibly retains his healing power.

In the narrative of Wazana's afterlife, however, these two books appear complementary no less then antagonistic. The revival of Wazana as a sainted figure, which may have been precipitated by my book, gained momentum with the discovery of the book of healing attributed to him. With a committed agent actively and creatively seeking to publicize his name, a shrine to commemorate him and plead for his intercession, and a book that encapsulates his bliss, the transformation of Wazana from a peripheral and antinomian healer into a venerated *tsaddiq* seems to have come of age. As this essay lucidly show, I became inextricably involved in this process. What started as an attempt to document and present as reliably as possible a dynamic reality evolved into an intricate situation, epistemologically precarious, in which the ethnographic product became a building block in further constructing and enriching this reality. In this process, I have inadvertently become a popularizer and propagator of Wazana – an impresario of saint impresarios.

NOTE

1 This essay was first published under the title "Ethnography and hagiography: the dialectics of life, story, and afterlife," in R. Josselson (ed.) (1996) *Ethics and Process in the Narrative Study of Lives*, London: Sage, pp. 151–71.

REFERENCES

Ben-Ari, E. and Bilu, Y. (1987) "Saint sanctuaries in Israeli development towns: on a mechanism of urban transformation," *Urban Anthropology* 16: 243–72.

Bilu, Y. (1978) "Traditional Psychiatry in Israel," Unpublished doctoral dissertation, Hebrew University of Jerusalem.

Bilu, Y. (1986) "Life history as text" (in Hebrew), *Megamot* 29 (4): 349–71.

Bilu, Y. (1988) "Rabbi Ya'acov Wazana: A Jewish healer in the Atlas mountains," *Culture, Medicine and Psychiatry* 12 (1): 113–35.

Bilu, Y. (1990) "Jewish Moroccan 'saint impresarios' in Israel: A stage–developmental perspective," *Psychoanalytic Study of Society* 15: 247–70.

Bilu, Y. (1991) "Personal motivation and social meaning in the revival of hagiolatric traditions among Moroccan Jews in Israel," in Z. Sobel and B. Beit-Hallahmi (eds.) *Tradition, Innovation, Conflict*, Albany, NY: State University of New York Press, pp. 47–70.

Bilu, Y. (1993) *Without Bounds: The Life and Death of Rabbi Ya'acov Wazana* (in Hebrew), Jerusalem: Magnes.

Bilu, Y. and Hasan-Rokem, G. (1989) "Cinderella and the saint," *Psychoanalytic Study of Society* 14: 227–259.

Blackman, M. B. (ed.) (1992a) "The afterlife of the life history" [Special issue], *Journal of Narratives and Life Histories*, 2 (1).

Blackman, M. B. (1992b) "Introduction: the afterlife of the life history," *Journal of Narratives and Life Histories*, 2 (1): 1–9.

Brettell, C. B. (eds.) (1993) *When They Read What We Write: The Politics of Ethnography*, Westport, CT: Bergin & Garvey.

Clifford, J. and Marcus, G. (1986) *Writing Culture: The Poetics and Politics of Ethnography*, Berkeley, CA: University of California Press.

Handelman, D. (1985) "Charisma, liminality and symbolic types," in E. Cohen, M. Lissak and U. Almagor (eds.) *Comparative Social Dynamics*, Boulder, CO: Westerview, pp. 346–59.

Marcus, G. E. and Fischer, M. J. (1986) *Anthropology as Cultural Critique*, Chicago, IL: University of Chicago Press.

Myerhoff, B. G. (1976) "Balancing between worlds: the shaman's calling," *Parabola* 1 (1): 6–13.

Rosaldo, R. (1989) *Culture and Truth*, Boston, MA: Beacon.

Turner, V. W. (1974) *Dramas, Fields and Metaphors*, Ithaca, NY: Cornell University.

Part III

Media, public space and democracy

9 Broadcasting in the Third World

From national development to civil society

Daniel C. Hallin

"The world in the 1970s," wrote Katz and Wedell, opening their classic work, *Broadcasting in the Third World* (1977: v), "is witnessing an important stage in the transfer of the electronic media of radio and television from the industrial countries of Europe and North America to the developing countries of the Third World." In the 1990s, in the part of the world where I live, things look a little different. San Diego lies in the US–Mexican border region; my house is about fifteen miles from the imaginary line and the thick steel fence which tries with mixed success to keep the countries marked by it separate. When I scan my radio dial, about half of the stations are in Spanish. On television I can watch ABC, CBS, NBC and their numerous new competitors. Or I can tune in to Televisa, Mexico's near-monopoly television company, the largest single exporter of television programming in the world, and watch one of its three networks. Or I can tune in to Univision, the Spanish-language network based in the US and owned by Televisa.

Developments of this sort – the growth of transnational media conglomerates such as Televisa in certain countries of what we are accustomed to call the Third World, and the flow of Third World cultures to the north – have in recent years forced a rethinking of the classic literature on broadcasting in the Third World. What I would like to do in this essay is to look back on that classic literature, written in the 1960s and 1970s, and try to sketch out some of the major ways in which the central questions of the field have changed. I will focus primarily on three works, Lucian W. Pye's *Communications and Political Development* (1963), Herbert I. Schiller's *Mass Communications and American Empire* (1969, 1992) and Katz and Wedell (1977). These works are extremely different from one another, of course; but taken together they provide a good representation of the debates that define the "classical" era in the field. They interest me in part because they are ambitious works, claiming to put forward general frameworks for analyzing broadcasting in the "Third World." That ambition can certainly be criticized, and indeed is one of the things that makes these works appear dated: the idea that one can hop around the world, knowing little about any particular country, and make broad proclamations about what the media are or should be in "developing nations." Still, the ambition of these works is appealing in a way; it seems to me that there is relatively little work today on broadcasting in the Third World which makes any attempt at theoretical synthesis.

I will argue that there has been a dramatic change in the last twenty-five years in the way in which intellectual and political issues in the field are formulated. This inevitably raises the question of how we evaluate the work of the classical era: was it hopelessly naive, blind to issues that we now can see clearly, or is it simply that the world has changed, and an analysis that made perfect sense for its own time requires revision in changed circumstances? Both interpretations are probably partly correct. A concern with national integration – which as we shall see is the central goal that was identified for broadcasting in the classical period – is no doubt more appropriate five years after independence than thirty years later. And the assumption of a one-way flow of culture, central to the early cultural imperialist school, was obviously more plausible in an era when even the largest Third World countries relied heavily on programming imported from developed countries, particularly the US, than it is today, when domestic or regionally produced programming dominates in many countries. (In Brazil, the market share of US programming peaked in 1971 at 47 per cent, but declined to 29 per cent by 1983 [Straubhaar 1991]. In many smaller countries, of course, US programming still dominates – and not only in the Third World.)

At the same time, I do think that new intellectual and political currents have awakened us to plenty of blind spots in the first generation of research. Even when we do historical work on early broadcasting in the Third World we must in many ways break with the assumptions of the classical works. To understand the early history of Mexican broadcasting, for instance, either strictly in terms of US domination or in terms of national integration, understood as something politically unproblematic, makes little sense (Sinclair 1986, 1990; Hayes 1996; my own current research is on Mexican TV news, and I will often return to the example of Mexico). The three works discussed come out of neither an intellectual vacuum nor an ivory tower. All are politically engaged works, and each can be understood, with some simplification obviously, as reflecting the point of view of a certain type of political actor: the authors of the Pye volume (1963) tend to reflect the perspective of western policymakers, concerned to manage "national development" in the post-colonial (or neo-colonial) era; Katz and Wedell's work is based on interviews with broadcasting policymakers in the Third World, and tends to reflect their perspective, and Schiller is closely attuned to the views of radical intellectuals and national liberation movements of the 1960s and 1970s. Each work is in this sense both firmly rooted in the political and economic realities of its era, and deeply affected by the insights, illusions and interests of particular types of social actors.

DOES THE "THIRD WORLD" EXIST?

It should be said at the outset that the term "Third World" is problematic in the modern context. It was always vague, of course – a term of popular politics more than of social theory. There has always been some ambiguity, for example, about whether it applied to Latin America. Pye writes of "the new countries of Asia, Africa and the Middle East," Latin America presumably being excluded because

Latin countries achieved their independence in the 1830s; other accounts obviously include them. Today, of course, the "Second World" has disappeared, and with it the cold war battle for position that made the Third World a "policy problem," so perhaps the term will fall into disuse. The deeper conceptual problem is that the nations assigned to that category are so diverse; this has always been true, but it is no doubt especially so today, as continuing, uneven globalization of production differentiates the Newly Industrializing Countries from those that look more like the "emerging nations" of the 1960s. Any category that includes both Brazil, which has an export-oriented television industry and had an overall trade surplus of $16.1 billion in 1989, and Malawi, which as of 1992 did not have television broadcasting (Ziegler and Asante 1992), is clearly too general to carry us very far in social analysis.

This leads me to my first observation about what we can call the "seventies paradigm" in the study of broadcasting in the Third World. One thing I find striking in all of the works that I have chosen to emphasize here is the absence of a comparative dimension in their analysis. Their authors are not unaware that nations differ – they know this perfectly well – but it does not interest them conceptually. Their intellectual enterprise involves abstracting from these differences to focus on a set of common functions of the media in Third World countries, or, in Katz and Wedell, for instance, three stages of media development – transplantation, acculturation and globalization – which apply to all. This kind of abstraction is not necessarily without validity; Katz and Wedell's three stages may indeed be common to many countries. But it seems to me that there is a tremendous amount lost in abstracting the media from the concrete histories and institutions which a more comparative approach might illuminate.

SHARED ASSUMPTIONS: COMMUNICATION FOR NATIONAL DEVELOPMENT

Despite many dramatic intellectual and political differences, the three works that I have chosen to analyze here have a great deal in common. Most important, perhaps, is that they all assume that the basic purpose of broadcasting in the Third World is to promote "national development." This in turn involves a series of assumptions, two of which I will emphasize here. The first is that the media are or should be primarily public service rather than commercially oriented enterprises. Wilbur Schramm, for example, in his essay in the Pye volume, lists the use of communication "to help extend the effective market" as one of six essential functions. But most of his essay, and most of the rest of the volume, focuses on the use of broadcasting for political and educational purposes, and the function that Schramm singles out for the most attention is "to teach necessary skills." Katz and Wedell similarly tend to focus on such uses of broadcasting as "achieving literacy, birth control, higher agricultural yields, and so on" (1977: 26). Schiller places much greater emphasis on commercialization as a reality of broadcasting in the Third World, but his view of what broadcasting *should* be is in this respect very similar to those of Katz and Wedell and the developmentalists. It is refreshing to look back to a day when commercialization of broadcasting was not taken for granted, but of course the reality is in this regard more and more as Schiller predicted: educational use of broadcasting is increasingly relegated to the margins.

The second assumption here is that broadcasting should serve "the nation." "Highest among the hopes for the broadcast media in the new nations," write Katz and Wedell, "is the hope that they will contribute to national integration (p. 171)." Pye and company were similarly concerned with "national development," while for Schiller and others, who pushed in the 1970s for the New World Information and Communication Order, national sovereignty and the integrity of national cultures were the key rallying cries.

A dramatic paradigm shift has clearly taken place: in the 1990s nation-centered views of the world communication system are increasingly subject to question. In part, this is because broadcasting structures have in fact shifted from a predominantly national basis to a much more complex system in which regional, national and transnational broadcasting coexist (Sreberny-Mohammadi 1991; Maxwell 1995). In part it is because research on the nature of national identity has increasingly emphasized its constructed and contested character; today "national integration" or the "integrity of national culture" cannot be taken as self-evident goals in the way in which they once were. One interesting illustration of this shift in consciousness – which is a change not only in academic discourse but also in political and popular discourse more broadly – can be found in the attitude of the Zapatista rebels in Mexico toward the international media. Drifting partially away from the traditional nationalism of the Latin American left, they appeal to international public opinion against the imposition of a particular vision of national integration by the Mexican state, using the Internet to reach out to the world media (Halleck 1994) while simultaneously threatening to kill any reporter from Televisa who should enter territory under their control. This kind of alliance of local movements with global opinion against national power is increasingly common. It carries us into my next and most important point, which has to do with the role of media in democratic politics.

BROADCASTING, DEMOCRACY AND CIVIL SOCIETY

Probably the most dramatic gap between the literature of the 1960s and 1970s and the concerns of the 1990s has to do with democracy. None of the authors considered has much to say about democracy; and each tends to take for granted an essentially statist model of media organization which conflicts with increasing concern in most developing countries today to expand civil society and the public sphere. Wilbur Schramm, for example, lists the following six "essential functions" of communication in developing countries (Pye 1963: 38–42):

1 To contribute to the feeling of nation-ness.
2 To be the voice of national planning.
3 To help to teach the necessary skills.

4　To help to extend the effective market.
5　To prepare people to play their new parts.
6　To prepare the people to play their role as a nation among nations.

Under the second function, he mentions that communication should be "two-way," and that there must be "avenues for criticism of policies and practices." But he considers two-way communication important "to maintain a sense of nation-ness"; and the emphasis is clearly on the role of the media in the "mobilization of national effort" in the service of centrally determined goals. Pye briefly mentions the "political organization and expression of interests," which he sees as "part of the general problem of political consensus" (p. 11). But he believes that "the two most general and fundamental problems in political modernization are precisely those of changing attitudes and reducing the gap between ruling elites and less modernized masses" (p. 13). So it is not surprising that he too places most of his emphasis on the need for effective communication from the center outward: "Development . . . involves the increasingly effective penetration of the mass media system into all the separate communal dimensions of the nation" (p. 26). Daniel Lerner is the one exception in the Pye volume: he places significant emphasis on the need for "the governed [to] develop the habit of having opinions, and expressing them" (p. 343), though he has little to say about what kinds of institutional arrangements are necessary for this to be possible. Schramm, however, on the only page listed in the index under the heading "democratic development", writes:

> Indeed, it is probably wrong for us to expect a country which is trying to gather together its resources and mobilize its population for a great transitional effort to permit the same kind of free, competitive, sometimes confusing communication to which we have become accustomed in this country.
>
> (Schramm, in Pye 1963: 55)

Katz and Wedell's priorities are similar. They list three major goals of broadcasting, which they report, are derived from their interviews with broadcasting policy-makers: national integration (the highest goal), socioeconomic development and "cultural continuity and authenticity of self-expression" (1977: 191), the "self" being understood in national terms. Their list of problems faced by developing countries includes "instability of governments and their need for legitimation" (p. 171); lack of effective participation does not make the list.

Herbert Schiller is a little different. As Dan Schiller (1996) has recently pointed out, one cannot understand the cultural imperialism literature without keeping in mind that it found its inspiration in the national liberation movements of the 1960s. These movements had a vision of a mass media taken out of the control of existing elites and made to serve "the people," and of a process of cultural transformation from the bottom up, which would overcome the internalized domination of the "colonized man." Schiller quotes Frantz Fanon:

> The struggle in itself in its development and in its internal progression sends culture along different paths and traces out entirely new ones for it. The

struggle for freedom does not give back to the national culture its former values and shapes; this struggle which aims at a fundamentally different set of relations between men cannot leave intact either the form or the content of the people's culture.

(Fanon, cited in D. Schiller, 1996)

In this sense one could say that the radicals of the cultural imperialism school were quite centrally concerned with democracy. But the left in this era tended to see democracy as something which would be achieved ultimately by military victory on the part of national liberation movements, which were assumed to represent the popular will; and scholars of the cultural imperialist school, like the left more generally, did not reflect very deeply about how democratic politics might be organized. Often the left shared with the right an assumption that media must be under the centralized control of the state, and conceived of democracy in terms of the interests holding state power. The term "democracy" does not appear in the index to Herbert Schiller's *Mass Communications and American Empire* (1969, 1992). There is a brief reference in his *Communication and Cultural Domination* (1976) to "claims to participate in communication policy-making" on the part of political parties, professional organizations and the like (p. 70), but this is by no means a central theme. *Communication and Cultural Domination* also concludes, in an analysis of the Chilean coup of 1973, that "pluralism in communication conceals class domination" (p. 108) – a formulation which both embraces the Leninist disdain for "bourgeois democracy" and seems to accept rather too uncritically the claims of advocates of Latin America's commercial media that the communication system that they dominated was indeed adequately pluralistic. As Dan Schiller (in press) points out, when national liberation movements declined in the 1970s, the cultural imperialist school was reduced to "emphasizing an austere and apparently unbridgeable political economy of transnational capitalist domination."

Today democratization is central to the political agenda in much of the Third World, and central as well to debates over the role of the media. This is most obvious in Latin America. Every country in Latin America except Cuba has now moved toward some form of multi-party democracy, with many of the region's most important countries – Brazil, Argentina, Chile – throwing off military dictatorships in the 1980s. Neither state socialism nor insurrectionist models of social change have much appeal these days, and the two most important revolutionary movements of the 1980s, in Nicaragua and El Salvador, are now legal political parties which conceive their role in terms of democratic political change. A new discourse has emerged in progressive circles which centers around the need to strengthen civil society. Latin American societies, writes Jorge Castañeda,

evolved without developing most of the strong sectors of civil society that emerged in other countries with at least formally representative institutions. This is partially because almost throughout the hemisphere the state emerged before the nation was truly constituted as such. This led to an over-powerful state in relation to civil society. . . . Labor unions, political parties, the mass media, peasant cooperatives, are all institutions that, while not absent in Latin America in the past, lacked the strength they attained in Europe or North America.

(Castañeda 1994: 182–3)

Today many argue that an "explosion of civil society" is underway in Latin America. In the case of Mexico, the "explosion" is generally described as beginning in the 1970s, and accelerating with the Mexico city earthquake of 1985 (Monsiváis 1988). The state proved unable to respond effectively to that disaster, and neighborhood groups were organized to fill the void. Since 1985 "grassroots groups" independent of Mexico's clientelist system, which since the revolution has performed the function of mobilizing popular loyalty, have become increasingly central to political life. They have interacted with increasingly effective opposition parties to bring the old structure of power into question and to produce growing demands for democratization.

It is certainly open to question how much the new social movements have actually succeeded in transforming Latin American political processes. But their rise, along with the clearly very real move toward more pluralist electoral systems, have certainly created a new context for discussion of the political role of the media (e.g. Fox 1988). In many countries popular organizations have made democratization of the media an important focus of their demands. In Brazil, for example, broad political coalitions have been active since about 1983 (Salinas 1986). One technological change is worth mentioning in this connection: the development of small-format video has made it possible for popular organizations to produce their own television, and this has probably accelerated the conceptual shift away from an assumption that culture must emanate from the center outward (Sarti 1988).

In Mexico the alliance between Televisa and the ruling party has become a major subject both of public debate and of negotiation between the government and opposition parties. Televisa, which boasts a 90 per cent share of the television audience, is a privately owned company but, like most big business, it is closely allied with the state and ruling party, and essentially operates as a propaganda organ for the latter. (Mexico is a one-party-dominant regime; its ruling party, the PRI, has been in power for nearly seventy years, longer than any other in the world, and is essentially fused with the state.) In the 1988 presidential election, when a leftist opposition party closely related to the new social movements mounted a surprisingly powerful challenge to the ruling party, Televisa's news broadcasts almost totally shut out coverage of the opposition. In 1994, under pressure not only from the government, which had entered into agreements with opposition parties to even the electoral playing field, but also from intense public scrutiny, including citizen groups doing content analyses, Televisa for the first time began opening its news coverage to the opposition (Hallin 1995). The primary issue regarding Mexican broadcasting today is not national integration or economic development (which is affected much more by telecommunications policy) or cultural authenticity, but *access* – the right of an increasingly plural civil society to have its voice heard in the public sphere.

Other regions of the Third World have not moved so consistently toward pluralist political systems in recent years, but in Asia and Africa, as well, democratization seems increasingly central to the political agenda, and the language of civil society increasingly current. F. Mitchell Land (1995), for instance, in a study of the televising of popular music in the Côte d'Ivoire, writes:

> struggling democratization is allowing the voices of civil society to rise from the timid whimper of post-colonial autocratic rule to increasingly bolder shouts as a new private press takes to the streets. These changes confirm the dynamic nature of culture – a social process constantly in flux as individuals and groups create and recreate [it].
>
> (Land 1995: 439–40)

Greater emphasis on democratization is closely related to another conceptual change, a move away from the dichotomy of tradition and modernity and from the assumption that progressive change must come from the center. In the developmentalist tradition, the main barrier to development lies in the "parochial practices and sentiments" of the periphery. The urban elite is assumed to possess "modernity," and the function of communication is to "[reduce] the gap between the ruling elites and the less modernized masses" (Pye 1963: 13). Katz and Wedell, writing after the critiques of cultural imperialism, are considerably more sensitive to the concern that something of value in the periphery may be threatened by modernization, that the flow of culture outward from center to periphery might be problematic in certain ways; they understand the problem rather narrowly, however, in terms of "the continuity of ancient tradition" (1977: 192). The cultural imperialists, of course, look to the periphery as the source of social change. Yet in another way they seem surprisingly similar to the developmentalists. Both, for example, tend to define the Third World in terms of lack. Thus for Pye the Third World, and particularly its periphery, is characterized by "lack of specialized opinion leaders capable of sifting the messages of the mass media," and "must usually operate with incomplete or inaccurate images of modernity (1963: 29)," while for Herbert Schiller, global cultural industries find it easy to penetrate "poor and vulnerable societies" (1969/1992: 53), "weak societies" (1969/1992: 153). The image that emerges in much of the writing of this period is a bit like the photographs of pitiful starving babies used by relief agencies to market compassion in developed countries (Benthall 1993). One of the great paradoxes of Schiller's argument is that his characterization of Third World societies makes it hard to see how liberation movements emerge; underlying the argument, it seems to me, is a vanguardist conception of social change, which dominated much of the thinking of the left in that era, but which is now increasingly questioned.

Today we proceed from a very different proposition, that while Third World countries and "marginalized" peoples do indeed lack many things, they are every bit as much social actors as elites in the metropolis, with their own cultural resources, and often an important impact on world culture. Celeste Olaquiaga, for example, writes of "an unprecedented degree of reciprocal appropriation and mutual transformation whereby cultural change can no longer be a matter of simple vertical imposition or ransacking, but is rather an intricate horizontal movement of exchange" (1992: 76). (I was amused, on a recent trip to Paris and Berlin, to find a proliferation of "Tex–Mex" restaurants in both cities.) In contrast to the earlier cultural imperialism tradition, but following in that of cultural studies, much modern research focuses on cultural adaptation, appropriation and resistance from below (e.g. Martín-Barbero 1993; Vargas 1995); resistance comes to be seen as something not apocalyptic but quotidian, not centralized but pervasive. And in contrast to the developmentalist paradigm, the barriers to change come to be seen as much in the "modern" center as in the "traditional" periphery.

Certainly if we take the case of Mexico, few would argue today that the barrier to political and social change lies solely in the "backwardness" of the masses. In politics the primary problem is the *dinosaurios*, entrenched elites who dominate the ruling party in a close though sometimes uneasy alliance with the *tecnocratos*. The owners of most of Mexico's media – rich, metropolitan and "modern" though they may be – belong to the *dinosaurio* camp. And often peripheral groups – indigenous communities, for example, which organize themselves and become part of the "explosion of civil society" – begin to appear in another sense far more modern. In this context, to come back to our point of departure, the use of the media to promote "national integration and loyalty to the center" appears as essentially reactionary and antidemocratic.

Does this mean that we should abandon altogether the notion that "integration" is an important and potentially constructive role of the media? Elihu Katz has long had a passion for community in the Durkheimian sense, and much of his work on the media has been guided by this concern. I have argued elsewhere that I think this approach can be extremely problematic in its failure to address issues of plurality and power (Hallin and Mancini 1994). But certainly the capacity of the media to integrate communities can play an important role in social change. A recent *New York Times* article on the Voice of Palestine radio, newly established on the West Bank, quoted talk show host Daniela Karim Khalaf as saying, "During the occupation we were so far away from each other, people in Nablus didn't know what was happening in Ramallah. Now they know. There's a collective feeling" (Greenberg 1996). For the Palestinians, as for the "emerging nations" of the 1960s, the concern with creating a sense of collective identity is very legitimate.

It is important to recognize, as well, that democratization and integration are not opposites. Consider, for example, the role of television in the transition from authoritarianism to democracy in Brazil. This took place in 1985, when an opposition candidate, Tancredo Neves, defeated a candidate backed by the military, which had ruled Brazil since 1964. The day before his inauguration, Neves fell gravely ill, forcing the cancellation of the inaugural ceremony. The stage seemed set for the military to declare a constitutional crisis and to reassert its power. What followed instead was a popular mobilization in support of the new regime, lasting through the death of Neves, a little more than a month after his inauguration date, and the subsequent inauguration of the Vice-President, José Sarney; a mobilization facilitated, and indeed actively cultivated, by continuous television coverage by TV Globo, Brazil's great media conglomerate, which had switched its allegiance from the military regime (Guimarães and Amaral 1988). This was far from being a pure victory of democracy, to be sure: it was at the same time the consolidation of a new structure of power, in which TV Globo would play a central role. But this was clearly a media event, in the sense of Dayan and Katz (1992), which played a crucial role in consolidating a social consensus in support of the basic principle of democratic rule.

Two related qualifications are necessary here to the discussion of democracy and civil society. First, it is important not to speak of the state and civil society, or the state and the public sphere, as though they existed purely as antagonists, in a zero-sum relation to one another. As Schudson (1994), Curran (1991), Dahlgren (1995) and others have pointed out, the state often plays an extremely important role in supporting the development of the institutions of civil society and the public sphere. One of the basic problems with broadcasting in most of the Third World has been the absence of public service broadcasting (Waisbord 1995) and of effective public regulation of commercial broadcasting – or to put it another way, the absence of a democratic state sector, with rules of transparency and access, from the broadcasting field. Second, it is important not to create too much of a sacred aura around the notion of civil society, which has tended to happen as if it had become a banner for social movements. I would cite here the work of Agbaje (1993) on the media in Nigeria, which not only argues the importance of seeing African media as rooted in civil society, and not merely in the state, but also shows that civil society is often the origin of the most bitter political conflicts, and that a media which expresses the divisions of civil society can function to escalate those conflicts. Civil society is not some sort of social cure-all; and there are certainly times when national integration, or integration at other levels, might be quite desirable. Nevertheless, it seems clear to me that issues of access, voice, the representation of diverse social interests and the creation of dialogue among them, belong today at the forefront of the agenda for both media research and media politics.

BROADCASTING AND POWER

If we are to place democracy at the center of media research, it follows that we must focus simultaneously on power. Who has access to the media, what interests they serve, how they handle social plurality – all of these things are shaped by the structure of power; and if democratization is to take place, it will necessarily involve a transformation of that structure. The silence of the research of the 1960s and 1970s on questions of democracy in Third World communication was matched by an equal silence on questions of power. Although the Pye (1963) volume is entitled *Communications and Political Development*, it has curiously little to say, beyond a few generalities, about politics. Its focus is much more heavily on psychology. David C. McClelland's chapter on achievement motivation can, I think, be described as the key contribution; it more than any other expresses the view of "modernization" which guides the rest of the volume, the idea that modernization is a matter of replacing passive traditionalism with dynamic modern modes of thought. Any change in power which may occur is assumed to follow naturally from this basic transformation of mass psychology. Katz and Wedell have a few interesting observations that bear on the political role of the media. They note, for example, that broadcasting enables rulers to "address their people over the heads of their representative assemblies and their ministers and civil servants" (1977: 106). But here they stop, not moving on to ask how broadcasting affects political structure: does the development of broadcasting, for instance, inhibit the development of a party system, or of representative institutions? And as for issues of power and control over broadcasting, nothing is really said beyond the general observation that most Third World countries move toward "unitary control and the unjustified muzzling of thought and expression ... [which] is bound to defeat the objectives of national development in the medium term" (p. 106). Schiller is again different – and not so different. His work is of course centrally concerned with power, and this is its greatest strength: *Mass Communications and American Empire* (1969, 1992) is about who controls the media, and how the media affect the global distribution of political power. The problem is that the cultural imperialism paradigm of this era had such a simple view of the structure of power, that it found it unnecessary to study it in any detail. In *Mass Communications and American Empire*, all power lies in the hands of American corporations and the American state. In *Communication and Cultural Domination* (1976), local power structures are raised for consideration, but not analyzed in any depth.

Here we can see the importance of the lack of comparative dimension, the impulse to universalize, mentioned above. Each of these works abstracts from the particular societies, their histories, institutions and cultures, to focus on the grand narrative of "modernization" or "imperialism," or, in the case of Katz and Wedell (1977), a somewhat more modest, but equally decontextualized, narrative about the social functions of broadcasting. Thus when Katz and Wedell discuss the efforts of the Brazilian government to expand the broadcasting infrastructure in the 1960s, they do not find it relevant to mention that Brazil was at the time ruled by a military dictatorship, let alone to inquire what social conflicts led the military to seize power or how these conflicts affected broadcasting policy (de Lima 1988). I am not the first to point out the need for communication scholars to undertake serious concrete analysis of social structures in the Third World. By the end of the 1970s this point was already being made by the second generation of scholars in the cultural imperialism tradition (e.g. Fejes 1981). I think it is fair to say, however, that there remains a great deal to be done in this area.

WHERE TO GO FROM HERE: RECEPTION ANALYSIS AND POLITICAL ECONOMY

The most important methodological trend in recent research on broadcasting in the Third World is clearly the turn toward reception analysis. Katz, of course, took this direction in his work with Tamar Liebes on cultural readings of *Dallas* (Liebes and Katz 1990). In Latin America much of the most important recent theory, of Martín-Barbero (1993), for instance, or García-Canclini (1992), or Jorge González and others connected with the Mexican journal *Estudios Sobre las Culturas Contemporáneas*, revolves around the point of view of reception analysis; and a number of extremely interesting empirical studies have been done (e.g. Alfaro 1987; Vargas 1995). The point of view of reception analysis is clearly central to much of the rethinking reviewed above: it has discredited simplistic notions of a one-way flow of cultural influence from center to periphery, and, in its emphasis on members of the popular classes as active social agents, it has contributed to the move to emphasize democracy.

I do think, however, that an over-emphasis on reception analysis can obscure the analysis of power that was called for above. Certainly I am not convinced by Liebes and Katz's claim that their study refutes the theory of cultural imperialism. A number of critiques of that claim have been made (e.g. Schiller 1991; Tomlinson 1991; Schiller 1996). Liebes and Katz's argument relies, for one thing, on attributing to the media imperialism school the most simplistic "hypodermic needle" theory of media effects. It is true enough that one can find statements in the work of Schiller and others in the 1960s and early 1970s to support that attribution. But if one is going to test a theory, it makes sense to test the strongest, not the weakest version of it; and modern views of power certainly do not rely on the assumption that those subject to it are passive or mindless. Liebes and Katz's argument also makes static what is actually a dynamic, historical claim about the shaping of global culture. The claim of the cultural imperialists is that global cultural industries are pushing all human cultures toward the culture of consumer capitalism (or, as Tomlinson correctly clarifies, that they play a significant role in a cultural change in that direction which has many causes). The claim is not that cultural differences are already non-existent; the claim is that many different cultures are being moved in the same direction. To test this claim one would have to look at cultures over time; comparing cultures at a single moment in time does not provide relevant evidence.

Reception analysis can be extremely useful, but it is important to be clear about what kinds of questions it can answer and what kinds it can not. Let me return to the example of Mexican TV news. Surveys show that a very high percentage of the Mexican public considers Televisa's news broadcasts to be credible sources of information, despite their extreme partisanship. It would be most interesting to know, beyond these thin statistics on credibility, how ordinary people read these news broadcasts. It seems unlikely that all would read them similarly: Mexico is far too diverse for that. If indeed people read the news differently, would we conclude that all those who consider Televisa's monopoly and its alliance with the ruling party a barrier to democracy are misguided, that it really makes no difference whether different political parties, different social interests, have access to the news? This would seem a strange conclusion to draw from such research. Between the two kinds of questions, "Is a system of political communication democratic?" and "How do different audiences read the messages it produces?" there is some overlap, but one can hardly be reduced to the other. One way to think about the problem is this: reception analysis by itself is not capable of distinguishing between democratic and authoritarian systems. In both kinds of systems, presumably, audiences have their own readings. I assume that, if one had been able to do reception analysis in the Soviet Union, with its tremendous cultural diversity, one would have found something very similar to Liebes and Katz's finding. This would show us something about the limits of power; it would not prove that power was non-existent. Many of the Latin American researchers who have led the turn toward reception analysis are centrally interested in issues of power. Martín-Barbero, for example, invokes Gramsci as part of the intellectual inspiration for his work. However, his work never really gets back to power but always leaves it in the background, recognized as profoundly important, yet unanalyzed.

In order to address questions of power, it seems to me essential to return to questions of the production of media messages. This kind of research is curiously unfashionable today. For Liebes and Katz, "the study of television is the study of effect" (1990: 57). For Tomlinson (1991), there is little interest in studying the macrosociology of media institutions, since "No one really disputes the dominant presence of Western multinational, particularly American, media in the world." The postmodernist spirit that dominates so much contemporary work generally favors studying "marginal" groups – which is probably just fine with the likes of Rupert Murdoch and Emilio Azcárraga (Azcárraga is the owner of Televisa). But macrosociology remains crucially important. One has only to compare a Mexican and a Cuban television program to see how much difference the context of production makes: the former, for example, which is produced as a commercial product in a society in which only the wealthiest 15 per cent of the audience is of interest to advertisers, includes almost exclusively wealthy characters; the latter, produced in a non-commercial context, is largely about the everyday lives of ordinary people. Neither, for quite different reasons, contains criticism of the government or ruling party. In both societies, no doubt, audiences are active as decoders; but this is not the only story to be told.

The story of media institutions, moreover, hardly seems as easy to summarize as Tomlinson suggests. This is a period of tremendous dynamism in media industries, with older organizational structures breaking down in the face of globalization, and of technological and political change. The dominant presence of western media is hardly constant, either in degree or in form. As we have seen, major Latin American countries such as Mexico and Brazil have developed their own transnational media companies, a development which seems likely in all of the larger cultural–linguistic markets, including the Chinese and Arabic markets. Now these industries are beginning to form alliances with companies from the "developed" world for wider international operations. Rupert Murdoch's News Corporation and the American cable firm Telecommunications Inc., for instance, have recently formed a joint venture with Televisa and Brazil's TV Globo for a Latin-America-wide direct broadcast satellite service. And of course, again, there is another, equally important story to be told, about the relation of these industries to the social structure within each society. Without analysis of these structures, postmodern notions of horizontal exchange and active audience can become just as reductive, just as simplistic as much of the writing of the 1960s and 1970s may seem to us today.

REFERENCES

Agbaje, A. (1993) "Beyond the state: civil society and the Nigerian press under military rule," *Media, Culture and Society* 15: 455–72.

Alfaro, R. M. (1987) "La pugna por la hegemonía cultural en la radio peruana, *Diálogos* 18: 62–73.

Benthall, J. (1993) *Disasters, Relief and the Media*, London: I. B. Taurus.

Castañeda, J. G. (1994) *Utopia Unarmed: The Latin American Left After the Cold War*, New York: Vintage.

Curran, J. (1991) "Mass media and democracy: A reappraisal," in J. Curran and M. Gurevitch (eds.) *Mass Media and Society* (1st edn), London: Arnold.

Dahlgren, P. (1995) *Television and the Public Sphere: Citizenship, Democracy and the Media*, London: Sage.

Dayan, D. and Katz, E. (1992) *Media Events: The Live Broadcasting of History*, Cambridge, MA: Harvard University Press.

de Lima, V. (1988) "The state, television and political power in Brazil," *Critical Studies in Mass Communication* 5: 108–46.

Fejes, F. (1981) "Media imperialism: an assessment," *Media, Culture and Society*, 3: 281–9.

Fox, E. (ed.) (1988) *Media and Politics in Latin America: The Struggle for Democracy*, Newbury Park, CA: Sage.

García-Canclini, N. (1992) "Culture and power: the state of research," in P. Scannell, P. Schlesinger and C. Sparks (eds.) *Culture and Power: A Media, Culture and Society Reader*, London: Sage.

Greenberg, J. (1996) "Wake up Palestinians! Your turn at the airwaves," *New York Times*, February 20, A4.

Guimarães, C. and Amaral, R. (1988) "Brazilian television: a rapid conversion to the new order," in E. Fox (ed.) *Media and Politics in Latin America: The Struggle for Democracy*, Newbury Park, CA: Sage.

Halleck, D. (1994) "Zapatistas on-line,' *NACLA Report on the Americas* 27 (September/October): 30–32.

Hallin, D. C. (1995) "Dos instituciones, un camino: television and the state in the 1994 Mexican election," Paper presented at the annual meeting of the Latin American Studies Association, Washington, DC.

Hallin, D. C. and Mancini, P. (1994) "Summits and the constitution of an international public sphere: the Reagan–Gorbachev summits as televised media events," in D. C. Hallin (ed.) *We Keep America on Top of the World: Television Journalism and the Public Sphere*, London: Routledge.

Hayes, J. (1996) "'Touching the sentiments of everyone': nationalism and state broadcasting in thirties Mexico," *Communication Review* 1: 4.

Katz, E. and Wedell, G. (1977) *Broadcasting in the Third World: Promise and Performance*, Cambridge, MA: Harvard University Press.

Land, F. M. (1995) "Reggae, resistance and the state: television and popular music in the Côte d'Ivoire," *Critical Studies in Mass Communication* 12: 438–54.

Liebes, T. and Katz, E. (1990) *The Export of Meaning: Cross-Cultural Readings of "Dallas"*. New York: Oxford University Press.

Martín-Barbero, J. (1993) *Communication, Culture and Hegemony: From the Media to Mediations*, Newbury Park, CA: Sage.

Maxwell, R. (1995) *The Spectacle of Democracy: Spanish Television, Nationalism and Political Transition*, Minneapolis, MN: University of Minnesota Press.

Monsiváis, Carlos (1988) *Entrada libre: crónicas de una sociedad que se organiza*, Mexico City: Ediciones Era.

Olaquiaga, C. (1992) *Megalopolis: Contemporary Cultural Sensibilities*, Minneapolis, MN: University of Minnesota Press.

Pye, L. W. (ed.) (1963) *Communications and Political Development*, Princeton, NJ: Princeton University Press.

Salinas Bascur, R. (1986) "Latin American communication policies: new battles around the old issues," in J. Becker, G. Horan and L. Paldán (eds.) *Communication and Domination: Essays to Honor Herbert I. Schiller*, Norwood, NJ: Ablex.

Sarti, I. (1988) "Between memory and illusion: independent video in Brazil," in E. Fox (ed.) *Media and Politics in Latin America: The Struggle for Democracy*, Newbury Park, CA: Sage.

Schiller, Dan (1996) *Theorizing Communication: A Historical Reckoning*, New York: Oxford University Press.

Schiller, Herbert I. (1976) *Communication and Cultural Domination*, White Plains, NY: International Arts and Sciences Press.

Schiller, Herbert I. (1991) "Not yet the post-imperialist era," *Critical Studies in Mass Communication* 8: 13–28.

Schiller, Herbert I. (1992 [1969]) *Mass Communications and American Empire*, Boulder, CO: Westview.

Schudson, M. (1994) "The 'public sphere' and its problems: bringing the state (back) in," *Notre Dame Journal of Law, Ethics and Public Policy* 8: 529–46.

Sinclair, J. (1986) "Dependent development and broadcasting: the Mexican formula," *Media, Culture and Society* 8: 1.

Sinclair, J. (1990), "Neither West nor Third World: the Mexican television industry within the NWICO debate," *Media, Culture and Society* 12: 343–60.

Sreberny-Mohammadi, A. (1991) "The global and the local in international communications," in J. Curran and M. Gurevitch (eds.) *Mass Media and Society* (1st edn), London: Arnold.

Straubhaar, J. (1991) "Beyond media imperialism: asymmetrical interdependence and cultural proximity," *Critical Studies in Mass Communication* 8: 39–59.

Tomlinson, J. (1991) *Cultural Imperialism: A Critical Introduction*, Baltimore, MD: Johns Hopkins University Press.

Vargas, L. (1995) *Social Uses and Radio Practices: The Use of Participatory Radio by Ethnic Minorities in Mexico*, Boulder, CO: Westview.

Waisbord, S. (1995) "Leviathan dreams: state and broadcasting in South America," *Communication Review* 1: 201–26.

Ziegler, D. and Asante, M. K. (1992) *Thunder and Silence: The Mass Media in Africa*, Trenton, NJ: Africa World Press.

10 Public sphere or public sphericules?

Todd Gitlin

THE PUBLIC SPHERE AND ITS DISCONTENTS

"The public sphere": the phrase has ballooned into the God-term of democratic discourse theory. It represents the ideal: the unmoved mover and sacred sphere against which standard violations and deviations are to be measured. The notion of a sovereign public – both deliberative and rational – stands at the heart of the Enlightenment ideal of a democratic republic. If the State is to be the instrument of the public good, the public must first be sovereign and capable of ascertaining its good, so that the State may belong to the public and act accordingly. Toward this end, the public needs *access* to information about matters of public moment; it needs *rights* of political organization, speech and assembly; it needs *deliberation*. The public needs, in short, a way to take shape, to become itself. This is why the regular, freely circulating supply of information occupies a special place in the Enlightenment ideal of autonomous individuals engaged in the practice of self-government. At one end of the ideal stands the French Encyclopedia; at another, the newspapers and coffee houses celebrated by Jürgen Habermas (Habermas 1989).

Metaphors are powerful, as discourse analysts know. Let us attend to the metaphor of "the public sphere" itself. It is, first of all, singular: it is *the* sphere, not *a* sphere. The unity image is also pleasing. The rounded sphere displays a perfect symmetry. The sphere looks the same from each point on its surface. It permits no privileged vantage point. No direction is superior to any other direction. On the surface of the sphere, each point is equal – equidistant from the center or, if one likes, equally marginal. Roundness, fullness, ripeness: the image of the public sphere conveys the sense of a planet, a fruit, something complete. The sphere in its perfection is, of course, an abstraction that nature only approximates; even the earth is flattened at the poles. Yet the sphere remains a Platonic form, easily identifiable and august. All spheres may be mapped onto all other spheres.

The *public* sphere, in particular, represents the intersection of two traditions in political theory: the democratic and the republican. The democratic implies that decisions are made by and for the people. The republican implies that the political realm has a high standing, independent of personal interest, and that the society cultivates the citizenly virtues, valuing political life, duty and public-mindedness.

In the United States and to a lesser degree in other democracies, both democratic and republican life have weakened over the course of decades. The signs are many and unmistakable: a decline in voting participation; a decline in party participation; a decline in public confidence in public officials; a decline in the prestige of political careers; the movement for term limits; the growth of harsh public attacks directed at political figures, in the form of American talk radio viciousness and kindred satire. A cynic might say that it is no wonder that the public sphere has taken on a theoretical luster – the theory basks in the glory of contrast. Not surprisingly, critiques of the practices of the public sphere in the light of the ideal of the public sphere have become familiar in political and communication theory. Behind them looms the standard of Habermas's "ideal speech situation" – an Archimedean point for social criticism, because if democracy requires deliberation, then equal access to the terms of deliberation becomes central to the entry of persons into the social world of democracy.

Perhaps the most surprising turn in the life of the concept of the public sphere is the fact that critiques of the actually existing public sphere have worked their way into American public discourse as well. Since 1988, for example, reports of the shrinking sound bite during presidential campaigns have been well known (Adatto 1990). (Indeed, the very popularity of the term "sound bite" is a measure of the disrepute in which television's abbreviation practices are held.) Media self-analysis during American presidential campaigns has become a staple of campaign coverage – as is the case to a lesser degree in France as well. Each presidential campaign cycle brings more bitter condemnations from a variety of political quarters. Charges that the press is "liberal" (usually) or "conservative" (sometimes) are staples of talk shows. Research by Richard Ansolabehere and Shanto Iyengar (1995) on the anti-participation effects of campaign commercials, reported in their book *Going Negative*, was widely discussed on American television. James Fallows' book *Breaking the News* (1996), which criticizes the complacency and corruption of Washington journalism, especially television's pundits, and endorses the movement for "public journalism," inspired sharp denunciations on the editorial page of the *New York Times* (Raines 1996) and in the *New Yorker* (Remnick 1996). Journalistic defensiveness is coupled with journalistic disillusionment. One of America's most prestigious political correspondents, Paul Taylor of the *Washington Post* – the man who during the 1988 campaign asked Gary Hart at a press conference, "Have you ever committed adultery?" – quit political coverage altogether and in 1996 campaigned, with limited results, to convince the television networks to grant free time to political candidates (Taylor 1990).

It is perhaps the most conspicuous sign of orthodox media self-doubt that the guest of honor at the Washington press corps' televised annual self-satisfaction dinner of 1996 was radio talk show host Don Imus, whose scurrilous patter embarrassed the president and first lady as they sat aghast at the head table. As Walter Cronkite, Dan Rather, Newt Gingrich and other notables gaped in astonishment and feebly tried to laugh along, Imus made harsh cracks at their expense. Embarrassed, the inviters expressed shock, shock that Imus had behaved so badly. But on this occasion, Imus did precisely what he routinely does every morning – tell nasty jokes at the expense of public figures, drum up demagogic attacks on politicians, and, in fact, behave badly. (The subsequent media flap had the effect of convincing ten more radio stations to pick up Imus's morning show.) Imus already had enough of an audience to convince Bill Clinton to appear on his show during the 1992 campaign, and he has now become a routine stopping-off point for politicians of both parties. The point is that the bad boy is now a stock character in the public sphere, and that the media establishment thought it would be interesting to invite a bad boy into their tent in the first place. The tabloidization of established political media proceeds apace.

Meanwhile, political scientist Robert Putnam's account (in two articles from 1995 and 1996, respectively) of the decline of Tocquevillian voluntary associations in the United States has also been a media rage – another recognition of the dignity of the embattled public sphere. Putnam's discovery that membership in parent–teacher associations and sports leagues along with fraternal associations and political parties has been declining for two decades is taken to demonstrate the breakdown of the Tocquevillian chain linking associational life with public participation. President Clinton met with Professor Putnam, and ABC News featured an affirmative segment which was framed by his view of the decline of the public. This is a remarkable record for an article published in two obscure, more or less academic journals. Putnam's conclusion that television-watching is the decisive solvent of civic association has been strongly disputed by Michael Schudson (1996) and Theda Skocpol (1996), among others. Perhaps new-style associations (community organizations, self-help groups) are on the rise while old-line associations are waning. Television cannot be the only factor in the decline – slackening leisure time must be a factor; so is the decline of newspaper readership, itself predating television. Voting participation in the United States has been declining for a full century, with upticks in the 1930s and 1960s (Piven and Cloward 1988). But whatever the truth of the matter, Putnam has become an undoubted presence in American discourse. In a sense, the public sphere is agreed that the public sphere is in trouble.

FROM SPHERE TO SPHERICULES

The unitary public sphere is weak, riddled with anxiety and self-doubt, but distinct communities of information and participation are multiplying, robust and brimming with self-confidence. If "speech" is the nugget term of the past, the core around which theories of democratic society are built, "information" is the nugget term of the present. The anxiety attending the growth of centrifugal tendencies is not the anxiety of millennial doom but the thrill of the competitive chase.

Nothing has promoted the notion that we are living in "an information age" more than the spread of the computer, especially the personal computer. In the United States, beginning in the 1970s, computer technology made it easier to tally audience subgroups, to sell access to segmented targets and to organize specialized media. Demographic specifics heightened advertisers' interest in direct targeting of audience segments. Direct mailers cultivated zipcode targeting, so that upscale magazines did not need to bother themselves about impoverished readers. In the 1980s, cable television followed radio in developing targeted channels for targeted audiences – sports for men, music for the young and youngish, African–American and Spanish-language programs, and so on. Most general-interest magazines – *Life, Look, Collier's, Saturday Evening Post* – are defunct. Desktop publishing enables young people to publish " 'zines," personalized assemblages of gossip and fandom – the magazine based on the primacy of personal taste. Segmented magazines are spawned by the score, targeted by audience (African–American sports fans, Asian–American women) and interest group (skiing, the Internet).

In the 1990s, the Internet spins its web of information and images into a swelling number of households. Little enough is known, it must be said, about who uses the Internet and for what purposes. The dynamism of the industry leaves scholarship in the dust. But anecdotal evidence suggests that the boom is nowhere near its peak, that Europeans are catching up to Americans and that considerable numbers of university students are transfixed by the process, using the Internet for one or two hours a day. More or less random "browsing" and "surfing" are common uses, but specialized linkages also thrive. As newspapers lose readers, on-line magazines start up. There are affinity groups organized around existing magazines, around philosophers, around leisure-time pursuits and political causes. There are literary magazines, magazines for investors, an international magazine for Iranian exiles. The claim is made that these forms are in the process of creating a vital community, expediting the organization of social protest, popular lobbying, and so on. The claim is that by bringing quasi-public links into the private space of the home or the office, the ensemble of these relations – what the writer Howard Rheingold has called "virtual community" (1993) – enables people to move their concerns into public life with a vigor and intensity of unprecedented proportions.

It is true that there are now perhaps thousands of worldwide linkages among citizen groups which are organized by political affinity. Petitions circulate, sometimes internationally (as in the protest against French nuclear tests). There are link-ups for groups such as Amnesty International, PeaceNet, and the Rainforest Action Network, as well as for neo-Nazis and white supremacists. A Rush Limbaugh fan places a summary of the daily Limbaugh conversation on the Internet. There are global contacts of a more informal sort, including news from Bosnia and other republics of the former Yugoslavia – keeping up ties among cosmopolitans. There are electronic exchanges among readers of magazine articles (one can converse with the author) and listeners to radio talk (one can converse with other listeners). There are the faxes and electronic mail networks that linked dissident Chinese students with their opposite numbers in the US during the democracy movement of 1989. There are the huge databases which enable journalists and private citizens to conduct rapid research.

By bridging the physical gulf between nations, some of the new linkages may contribute to the growth of cosmopolitanism – the understanding that one lives in a globally interconnected world. To some degree, the new communication forms expedite the development of what some have called, perhaps too optimistically, an international civil society. These communication networks heighten a global ecological awareness just as, put to different uses, they expedite global flows of capital, finance, resources and merchandise. The same technologies that have given capital unparalleled mobility may also – to some degree – further movements that seek to limit the prerogatives of capital. But to what degree?

Of course, there is one problem which the new means of communication do not address and may even worsen: the existence of a two-tier society. To those who are information-rich (or information-glutted) shall more information be given. At present, a little over one-third of American homes have personal computers. Less than half of these have modems which enable them to enter the "cyberspace" of computer networks. In other words, roughly 17 per cent of Americans can get onto the computer "superhighway" from their homes (Sandberg 1997). Without doubt, this 17 per cent includes scholars who wish to collaborate across the oceans; journalists wishing to expedite their research; graduate students who wish to chat, or procrastinate, with like-minded specialists; activists in search of affinity groups. But, at the same time, the gulf deepens between the information-saturated and the information-shallow. Among the latter are the more than 30 per cent who do not subscribe to cable television. Technology, in other words, aggravates a certain class division – the division between the political class and the rest. The global – even national – village turns out to have two tiers.

Such segmentation casts doubt upon the feasibility of a unitary public sphere – even reduces the hope to a pale nostalgia. Despite Ross Perot's fantasies of electronic town meetings, with instantaneous links, technology to date has expedited centrifugal motion. In this process, technology reproduces – and facilitates – the dynamics of secession, exclusion and segmentation which are characteristic of the United States, Great Britain and to a certain extent other European countries during recent years. Media saturation and the marketing of youth culture institutionalize the cues for self-transformation into a veritable rebellion industry. Moreover, under the sign of multiculturalism, today's media, organized by targeted markets and consumption subcultures, capitalize on identity boundaries. As cable television has diversified programming schedules, so have ethnic marketing campaigns proliferated. A considerable distance has been traveled from the "You don't have to be Jewish to love Levy's" rye bread advertisements of the 1950s to Gatorade's "¡Lleno de Gusto!" in the 1990s. Half of the *Fortune* 1,000 companies today have ethnic marketing campaigns. Procter and Gamble puts 5 per cent of its massive advertising budget into ethnic-specific advertisements. AT&T advertises in twenty different languages (Gitlin 161). Today, it remains true that immigrants wish to assimilate, but the America into which they wish to assimilate is not the America of white bread. It is an America where the supermarket shelves groan beneath the varieties of bagels, sourdough, rye, seven-grain, and other mass-produced loaves. One belongs by being slightly different, though in a similar way.

Thus does the ideology of multiculturalism redefine commonality. In brief, one becomes "American" now by taking pluralism to be the form of American commonality. As Alejandro Portes and other sociologists put it, the prevailing form of assimilation today is "segmented assimilation" – assimilation with a difference (Portes 1996). The affirmation of the left side of the hyphen becomes a way of affirming the right side.

This sociological point bears on the problem of political theory with which we began. Does democracy require a *public* or *publics*? A public sphere or separate public sphericules? Does the proliferation of the latter, the comfort in which they can be cultivated, damage the prospect for the former? Does it not look as though the public sphere, in falling, has shattered into a scatter of globules, like mercury? The diffusion of interactive technology surely enriches the possibilities for a plurality of publics – for the development of distinct groups organized around affinity and interest. What is not clear is that the proliferation and lubrication of publics contributes to the creation of *a* public – an active democratic encounter of citizens who reach across their social and ideological differences to establish a common agenda of concern and to debate rival approaches.

If it be argued that a single public sphere is unnecessary as long as segments constitute their own deliberative assemblies, such an arrangement presumes a rough equivalence of resources for the purpose of assuring overall justice. It also presupposes that the society is not riven by deep-going fissures which are subject to being deepened and exacerbated in the absence of ongoing negotiation among members of different groups. In current conditions, as I have argued in *The Twilight of Common Dreams* (1995), I think that these assumptions are unwarranted – even foolhardy.

To put the matter crudely, then: I suspect that we continue to travel away from the public square, circling and circling in centrifugal motion.

REFERENCES

Adatto, K. (1990) "The incredible shrinking sound bite," *New Republic*, May 28, pp. 20–23.

Ansolabehere, S. and Iyengar, S. (1995) *Going Negative: How Political Advertisements Shrink and Polarize the Electorate*, New York: Free Press.

Fallows, J. (1996) *Breaking the News: How the Media Undermine American Democracy*, New York: Pantheon.

Gitlin, T. (1995) *The Twilight of Common Dreams: Why America is Wracked by Culture Wars*, New York: Metropolitan/Henry Holt.

Habermas, J. (1989 [1962]) *The Structural Transformation of the Public Sphere* (trans. Thomas Burger), Cambridge, MA: MIT Press.

Piven, F. and Cloward, R. (1988) *Why Americans Don't Vote*, New York: Pantheon.

Portes, A. (ed.) (1996) *The New Second Generation*, New York: Sage.

Putnam, R. (1995) "Bowling alone: America's declining social capital," *Journal of Democracy* 72 (1): 65–78.

Putnam, R. (1996) "The strange disappearance of civic America," *American Prospect*, Winter, pp. 34–48.

Raines, H. (1996) "The Fallows fallacy," *New York Times*, February 25, sect. 4, 14.

Remnick, D. (1996) "Scoop," *New Yorker*, January 29, pp. 38–42.

Rheingold H. (1993) *The Virtual Community: Homesteading on the Electronic Frontier*, Reading, MA: Addison-Wesley.

Sandberg, J. (1997) "PC makers' push into more homes may be faltering," *Wall Street Journal*, March 6, B6.

Schudson, M. (1996) "What if civic life didn't die?" *American Prospect*, March–April, pp. 17–20.

Skocpol, T. (1996) "Unraveling from above," *American Prospect*, March–April, pp. 20–25.

Taylor, P. (1990) *See How They Run: Electing the President in an Age of Mediocracy*, New York: Knopf.

11 Crisis of public communication: A reappraisal

James Curran

In 1996, Elihu Katz advanced a commanding thesis: changes in the communications order are weakening the foundations of liberal democracy. His argument is built on three apparently solid pillars. The first is that people are no longer connected to each other through the central meeting-ground of mass television, watching the same programs and participating in the same dialogue about the public direction of society. Instead, the public is being dispersed and fragmented by the multiplication of channels. "Television," according to Katz, "has all but ceased to function as a shared public space. Except for occasional media events, the nation no longer gathers together" (Katz 1996: 22).

Second, the eclipse of public service broadcasting has resulted in high rating programs supplanting civic communication.

> No less than in the United States, the governments of Europe – once proud of their public broadcasting systems – are bowing to the combined constraints of the new media technology, the new liberal mood, the economic and political burden of public broadcasting, and the seductions of multinational corporations.
>
> (Katz 1996: 22)

Consequently coverage of public affairs on television "is being minimized and ghettoized and overwhelmed by entertainment" (Katz 1996: 24).

Katz's third claim is more complex. In essence, it is that liberal democracy is practiced primarily in nation states, and depends upon national identification to sustain popular involvement in the democratic process. However, national identities are being weakened by a growing separation between the television system and the nation state. Viewers are increasingly picking programs on the basis of individual taste from a plethora of channels supplied by the global economy, rather than as before watching the same, nationally determined schedule of programs.

The logic of this position, as Katz (1996: 23) explicitly acknowledges, is to regret the passing of monopoly based on "only one channel of public television commanding attention from all and offering the gamut of views." This proposition is illustrated by a history of Israeli television in which Katz mourns the dethronement of a once invincible 9 p.m. newsmagazine program. When it was in its prime in the golden era before competition, to caricature his argument a little, Israeli society shared the same heartbeat and participated every evening in a virtual town meeting.

Katz's general thesis carries conviction because it draws on assumptions that are widely supported. That the expansion of television is causing the mass public to splinter, and the polity to fracture, is part of the current received wisdom, eloquently argued in the preceding chapter. Equally mainstream is the view that public service broadcasting is everywhere in trouble. A rightly celebrated global review concludes, for example, that "public service broadcasting faces not only the danger of slow assassination . . . but the threat of suicide" (Rowland and Tracey 1990: 8). Equally uncontentious is the view that media globalization is weakening national media and national cultural identities (Morley and Robins 1995). Katz is seemingly advancing a synoptic view based on the very latest and most authoritative sources.

ONE EXCEPTION?

Yet, none of the fashionable assumptions on which Katz draws is seemingly borne out by the experience of the United Kingdom. In the first place, the mass audience has not been fragmented by the multiplication of TV channels. Cable TV was introduced in Britain in its modern commercial form in 1984, and was followed shortly afterwards by the development of second generation satellite television. By 1996, these two delivery systems had generated more than fifty new TV channels; yet, they accounted for only 10 per cent of total TV viewing (see Table 11.1).

In other words, British people spend nine-tenths of their time in front of the TV set looking at just four TV channels. Two of these, BBC1 and ITV, occupy over two-thirds of all TV viewing, and nearly three-quarters of peak time viewing. The nation still gathers together in a central space constituted by mass television. And it still talks, laughs, agrees or quarrels primarily through two channels that have been in existence for over forty years.

Second, public service broadcasting has not been eclipsed in Britain. While it is weakened in certain respects, its structures are still standing and it is still overwhelmingly dominant. Its channels, as we have seen, are the most watched in

Table 11.1 Share of all television viewing

	BBC1	*BBC2*	*ITV*	*C4*	*Cable/ satellite*	*Public service channels*
	%	%	%	%	%	%
All hours	32	11	35	12	10	90
Peak time	34	10	39	8	8	92

Source: BBC Broadcasting Research (average of all four quarters in 1996). This does not include the new public service channel, Channel 5, launched in 1997, which has attracted a very small audience. All figures are rounded up to the nearest whole figure.

Britain. They are also still guided by a public service commitment to inform as well as to entertain: their news programs are screened during prime time, and their documentaries obtain peak as well as offpeak slots. It is, simply, not true to say in a British context that "current affairs is being minimized and ghettoized and overwhelmed by entertainment" (Katz 1996: 24).

Contrary to Katz's general argument, British television continues to be also a national medium. The Independent Television Commission requires each of the commercial terrestrial channels (ITV, Channel 4 and the new Channel 5) to "originate" 65 per cent of its programs, which is in all but name a domestic production quota. A similar convention operates within the BBC. It does not apply to cable or satellite TV which, in the case of BSkyB, also breaches the European Union "where possible" requirement that half of its programs come from member states. But since these channels account for such a relatively small amount of viewing, this loophole is not very significant. British TV continues to be largely British because a conscious decision has been taken to limit globalization through discreet protectionist regulation.

Nor is it the case that the ties between nation and television are being severed. Quite the contrary, television in Britain promotes unity through diversity, a sense of togetherness informed by an awareness of regional difference. The BBC and ITV, a network' of regionally based companies (despite recent mergers), have devolved centers of production located in different parts of the country, and draw upon different cultural traditions. But they transmit what are in effect national program services, with only limited regional opt-outs. Crucially, the potentially separatist nations of the United Kingdom – Scotland, Wales and Northern Ireland – watch programs which are mostly made elsewhere in Britain and are watched throughout the country. They do not have their own "national" TV systems in a developed sense, with the partial exception of Welsh-speaking Wales which has its own TV channel, SC4, with a tiny audience.

In short, almost everything that Katz says is happening in general is not happening in Britain.

OR MANY EXCEPTIONS?

The second basis for reservation is more general. What is true of Britain seems to be true, to a lesser or greater extent, of other countries, certainly in Europe.

In general, the multiplication of TV channels has not led to the fragmentation of the viewing public in the way that it is widely assumed to have done In Germany, for example, the principal four TV channels accounted in 1993 for 76 per cent of all TV viewing (Hickethier 1996: 115, Table 4.7). In Italy, 70 per cent of prime time viewing was spent in front of just four channels in 1994 (Sartori 1996: 157, Table 5.7).

In part, this pattern reflects in some countries the slow diffusion of new technology owing to constraints of availability, cost and existing consumer satisfaction. Some people seem reluctant to pay for additional TV channels when they can obtain what they like for "free." In Spain, for example, only 13 per cent of homes subscribe to cable or satellite pay-TV channels; in Italy, take-up is reportedly even lower; and in Britain, where the figure has been swollen by cheap telephony and Murdoch's purchase of live TV soccer rights, it is still only 23 per cent (Anon 1997a: 4, Table 1).

However, there would appear to be a more fundamental and enduring reason for the continuing market ascendancy of a small number of generalist TV channels. They have much larger revenues and economies of scale than their rivals which enable them to spend very much more on programs. Even in the United States, where there is a mature multi-channel TV system serving a highly pluralistic, diverse and localist society, its "three and half" national channels accounted in September 1996 to May 1997 for no less than 62 per cent of prime time TV viewing (Anon 1997b). The United States is where much of the alarmist commentary about new technology and the decline of societal communication originates. Yet, even its core-television system still provides a common meeting ground for much of American society.

Katz would seem, superficially, to be on stronger ground when he points to the problems of public service broadcasting, and the rise of entertainment. Throughout much of the world, public service broadcasting is under a combined commercial, political and ideological assault (Humphreys 1996; Sinha 1996; Achille and Miege 1994; Aldridge and Hewitt 1994; Avery 1993; Blumler 1992; Rowland and Tracey 1990). New private channels have come into being; new deregulatory regimes have been introduced; and new, hostile lobbies have been formed. In general, it is widely argued, public service broadcast regimes have suffered from loss of legitimacy, underfunding, declining audiences and a less clear sense of purpose.

But in fact the position of public service broadcasting is more varied, and also more unresolved, than Katz's general account allows. In some countries where public broadcasting is identified closely with the state, as in France and Turkey, it has been destabilized (Catalbas 1996, Kuhn 1995; Vedel and Bourdon 1993); in others, where it operates without significant political support as in the United States, it is marginalized (Hoynes 1994; Rowland 1993); and in yet others where it has bored people, as in the Netherlands, it is in deep trouble (McQuail 1992; Ang 1991). Yet, in the majority of European countries – from Portugal to Poland – public service broadcasting is still well entrenched.

One problem with establishing the true position is that there has developed a misleading convention of equating public broadcasters with public service broadcasting. Public broadcasters' loss of audiences is then cited as evidence of systemic crisis (Katz 1996; Achille and Miege 1994, among others). But, in fact, private broadcasters that are subject to effective public regulation are as much an integral part of the public service system, in the sense of serving welfare rather than purely market goals, as public broadcasters. The transfer of audience time between public and regulated private sectors should not be viewed necessarily as evidence of "decline."

Indeed, it may signify the very opposite. There is a strong argument that the transition from public monopoly to a regulated mixed economy in a number of countries – such as Germany, Britain, Denmark, Sweden and Norway – renewed the public service system by making it more responsive to the public without detracting from its fundamental purpose (Curran and Seaton 1997; Humphreys 1994; Sepstrup 1993; Syvertsen 1992; Hadenius 1992). In other words, public broadcasters' loss of audience was, in these countries, a symptom of systemic renewal rather than of crisis – or, at the very least, of a system that was better able to withstand attacks upon it. Katz's requiem for the passing of public service broadcasting is premature.

Because public service broadcasting is still dominant in western Europe, the majority of its large-audience TV channels still give due prominence to coverage of public affairs (Humphreys 1996; Weymouth and Lamizet 1996; De Bens *et al.* 1992; Ostergaard 1992). The exclusion of news and current affairs from peak time, mass channel viewing – and consequent disenfranchisement of the public – is still an American rather than European phenomenon.

TELEVISION AND GLOBALIZATION

Katz is also mistaken in thinking that television is being transformed into a global medium. Preben Sepstrup (1990) points out that statistics about international program flows, seemingly documenting American TV's global hegemony, ignore the majority of TV programs which are not traded on the international market. Content analysis of actual European TV schedules reveals a very different and more complex picture than one of simple American domination. Hollywood has made specific inroads into films and TV series on many channels; into weak TV economies such as Ireland; and into unregulated commercial TV channels. Nevertheless, many leading TV channels in Europe import less than one-third of their programs from *any* country, including the United States (Humphreys 1996; De Bens *et al.* 1992; Sepstrup 1990; Hirsch and Petersen 1992).

It may be objected that the trend is towards globalization. The cost of importing TV drama can be as little as one-tenth of filling the same time slot with an original production, creating an irresistible pressure for global market integration. Television, it may be reasoned, will follow in the global footsteps of the cinema, for much the same economic reasons.

This ignores the offsetting influences that support television as a national medium. Television's staple output includes nationally specific content – chat shows, quiz shows, game shows, sport and even news – which is both popular and, more important, relatively cheap to produce. Second, many people like the programs produced in their own country more than imported ones. Thus, a study of TV audience ratings in six European countries found that national TV fiction normally came top, with American programs coming at best second (Silj 1988). These national preferences, rooted in the linguistic and cultural divisions of Europe, have so far protected national TV industries from effective attack by transnational TV enterprises, whether relying on European or American programs (Collins 1992). Third, national consumer preferences are supported by political power. European national governments sustain through public finance national TV systems, and some have also adopted unilateral protectionist measures limiting the import of non-European programs. Potentially, the use of "safe havens" by satellite broadcasters, in order to evade national regulation, could be prevented with relative ease by coordinated action throughout the European state (Commission of the European Communities 1992).

Katz's judgement that the "tendency is towards globalization, such that everybody, everywhere, will be viewing *Dallas* or *Dynasty* or the Olympics at the same time" (Katz 1996: 26) ignores these countervailing influences. In fact, what seems to be happening in Europe is something rather different: a dual system is beginning to take shape in which mostly successful national public service TV systems coexist alongside unregulated pay-TV systems, heavily dependent on cheap, imported products. These latter operate within a global television market that is subdividing partly into language markets, supported by new centers of production, rather than solidifying into one homogeneous unity.

Katz's view of globalization is also based on a questionable understanding of media historical development. He sees this as a serial process in which the newspaper was the "first medium of national integration," until its integrative function was taken over first by radio and then by television. But now that television is going global, "there is nothing in sight to replace" it (Katz 1996: 33). This is the basis of his fear that national cohesion and political participation is "in jeopardy."

In fact, the historical relationship between nation, globalization and communications is vastly more complicated than this. The key shift towards media globalization occurred between 1914 and 1939, with the emergence of American film hegemony, the global advance of American music, and its dissemination through the new media of records and radio. The subsequent period has exhibited some globalizing tendencies in terms of media ownership, trade and consumption. But in historical terms, television's defeat of the cinema represented a dramatic shift toward the restabilization of national media systems. Even now, despite the recent acceleration of globalizing trends, the core mass media of TV, radio and press are still based on nationally originated material in most countries. Just as political economists such as Hirst and Thompson (1996) argue that the globalization of the economy is a complex, uneven and discontinuous process (with the world economy being in some important respects less integrated now than it was before World War I), so much the same is true of media globalization. National identity is not on the critical casualty list because its communications life support machine is about to be switched off.

But perhaps the single most important reservation to be advanced against Katz's overall thesis is the way in which general trends are portrayed as inevitable. Various arguments can be mobilized to support his vision of the future. But this is not the same as echoing Katz's apparent view of the immutable nature of the changes that are taking place. What the remainder of this essay will seek to do is to emphasize their ambiguity, their potential to develop in different directions, and the possibility of acting upon events in a positive way. This will be attempted by examining one particular broadcasting system in transition, and the wider context in which it operates.

BRITISH CASE STUDY: THE DECLINE OF AN IDEA

At first sight, Katz's view of the *underlying* fragility of public service broadcasting is borne out by the British experience. It appears vulnerable because some of the beliefs that have sustained it for two generations are being questioned or rejected outright. This erosion of its core justification will be illustrated by a brief look at the reports of successive British public enquiries into broadcasting. These received evidence from leading institutions and they provide a good insight into changing elite perceptions.

One key justification for public service broadcasting, expressed in every major public report into broadcasting between 1923 and 1986, was that airwave frequencies are a scarce national asset which need to be managed in the public interest. This argument was finally laid to rest in a 1992 government White Paper. "The original justification," it declared, "for public service broadcasting – that a small number of services should be used for the benefit of the public as a whole – no longer exists" owing to the emergence of cable and satellite television channels (National Heritage 1992: 15).

This justification was always an ideological judgment masquerading as a technical argument. It presupposed that a public agency would serve society better than a private agency in a situation where broadcast services had to be rationed. Underpinning this was a benign image of the state, and of bodies appointed by the state to serve the public. This was the second strut supporting public service broadcasting to buckle.

Early broadcasting reports assumed that public service broadcasting worked for the general good because the BBC had been established by the state for this purpose. The Corporation, they pointed out, was in the care of public trustees, representing the nation, and was directed toward the welfare of society rather than making money. It was bracketed with the civil service (Ullswater 1936: 18) and likened to universities (Beveridge 1951: 217). It was a branch of the public services.

However, belief in the neutrality and efficacy of public institutions weakened. By the 1970s, misgivings were expressed about broadcasting's connection to the state which were only stilled by making a dubious distinction between parliament (good) to which broadcasting should be accountable, and government (potentially bad) from which it should be protected (Annan 1977: 38). The distinction was dubious because the governing party in Britain usually controls both government and parliament. This casuistry gave way in the Thatcherite 1980s to liberal anti-statism. In the key broadcasting report of that period, broadcasting regulation was tacitly equated with "censorship," and setting broadcasting free from regulation was established as the long term objective of public policy (Peacock 1986: 126, 132). The state was no longer viewed as a source of legitimation: instead it was a source of contamination from which broadcasting should be rescued through free market policies.

The third and more elusive development weakening public service broad-casting was a gradual erosion of the social and cultural values sustaining the public service ideal. This ideal found its most eloquent expression in the Pilkington report (1962). The discarding of the assumptions of that report reveals the emergence of new perspectives which are sapping the foundations of public service broadcasting.

The Pilkington report was produced in the Indian summer of Victorian reformism, at the tail end of the liberal Conservative government headed by Harold Macmillan. The report hailed television as a great agency of moral and cultural improvement, a means by which people could gain knowledge of others, develop active leisure interests, extend their intellectual horizons, and grow and develop as human beings. Good broadcasting, in its view, connected to "the whole range of worthwhile, significant activity and experience" (Pilkington 1962: 9), not simply high culture. Implicitly informing this approach was a moral–cultural aesthetic in which good programs were thought to be ones that engaged viewers' and listeners' imagination, extended their understanding and strengthened their moral sensibility. To achieve this, broadcasting had to be staffed by people of talent and integrity, who respected rather than patronised their audience, and who worked in a creative environment that supported good broadcasting rather than merely what was most profitable.

The Annan report, published in 1977, was a transitional document. Its most significant feature was to define and defend public service broadcasting as a negotiated settlement between elite and popular cultural values. It saw public service broadcasting as a system that delivered both good programs and popular programs in a form that maximized choice.

> Some programmes should be made for the most exacting intellectual and aesthetic mountaineers who have scaled the cultural heights. . . . But the bulk of programmes should be provided for the majority of people who will never reach these pinnacles. As a group they have paid most towards the broadcasting services.
>
> (Annan 1977: 331)

Public service broadcasting was not so much about quality as diversity: catering for both cultural mountaineers and couch potatoes.

It reached this position by being paradoxically both more culturally elitist and more relativistic than its predecessor. The Annan report viewed cultural value as a single scale or continuum, topped by high culture, in contrast to the multi-centered regime of moral–cultural value advanced by the Pilkington Committee. Annan also acknowledged, in contrast to the evangelism of its predecessor, that there no longer existed a consensus about what constituted program quality. "The ideals of middle class culture, so felicitously expressed by Matthew Arnold a century ago, which had created a continuum of taste and opinion" had not, the report noted regretfully, weathered the 1960s (Annan 1977: 14). It felt itself to be championing traditional cultural values which were being widely repudiated.

Informing the shift represented by the Annan report was also a different mind-set. It tacitly viewed its precursor's belief in progress as faintly ridiculous (Annan 1977: 30). Where the 1962 Committee saw public service broadcasting as a way of making society better, its successor conceived of broadcasting primarily in terms of service delivery. Although the two reports were separated by only fifteen years, they belonged in some respects to different worlds. One harked back to the great social movements that had created the free education, library and health systems: the other looked forward to the performance indicators and bland mission statements of 1980's managerialism.

The Annan report opened the pass through which the ideologues of the right effortlessly marched. As soon as the notion of program quality was relativized, it invited an alternative system of valuation based on market preference. The next broadcasting report, published in 1986, argued that broadcasting should "maximise consumer appreciation" in a market system where "viewers and listeners are . . . the best judges of their own interest" (Peacock 1986: 149, 128). If public service broadcasting is to be a negotiated settlement, then that settlement should favor the people. Viewers should get what they want, as registered in what they choose to watch and pay for. Consequently, the market system should be phased in, and the public service system should be reduced over time to a supplementary role.

The defence of public service broadcasting as a guarantee of diversity also came under attack in the Peacock report. The defence was accepted only in the short term on the neo-liberal grounds that the broadcasting market was under-developed. But in the long term, it was argued, investment in new technology and the development of a direct consumer payment system would deliver far greater diversity than exists now. Certain sorts of demanding but unpopular programs might not get made in the market system, but these could be funded by the broadcasting equivalent of the Arts Council. Quality was thus viewed primarily as high culture, which could be delivered through targeted grants, not as a defining characteristic of the broadcasting system.

This right-wing report argued, in effect, that the market empowers the consumer in a more effective way than public bureaucracy. It was a forceful and intelligent presentation of the neo-liberal case. But what gave it added force was the way in which the public service alternative had been hollowed out and eviscerated. This had been reduced to an argument for planned diversity rather than a universalist notion of quality. It had also been redefined as service delivery to the consumer rather than serving the needs of society. The Peacock report won the argument – even in the eyes of critics (Collins 1993) – because the public service case was left with such low-scoring cards.

The passage of time has also revealed another weak joist supporting the intellectual edifice of public service broadcasting. A view of American television as being crassly uniform – summed up in the phrase "wall-to-wall *Dallas*" – has been a significant feature of successive British public reports into broadcasting (including in a qualified form even the Peacock report). But this view does not take adequate account of the expansion of program variety on American television that has resulted from the development of specialist cable TV channels. It is an anachronistic and simplistic image, rather like the cartoon cliché of the cigar-puffing, top-hatted capitalist. Such delusions as this have a way of breeding disillusion.

In short, some of the central ideas on which public service broadcasting is based in Britain – the requirements of rationing, the benign state, working for progress, securing quality, the awfulness of the Yank way of doing things – have lost some of their persuasive force.

CONTEXT OF CRISIS

Public service broadcasting is in trouble not simply because its intellectual rationale is under attack. Its problems are likely to worsen, it can be argued, because they are rooted in fundamental changes in British society.

In the first place, public service broadcasting is made vulnerable by the rightward shift of British politics. A right-wing Conservative party won four successive general elections, and monopolized power throughout the period 1979–97. It was defeated by a revisionist Labour party, only after it had moved further to the right than at any time in its history.

The rise of market liberalism was a key element of this rightward shift. Its central tenets are implicitly opposed to the continuation of public service broadcasting. Private agencies are more efficient, more responsive and leaner, in its view, than public bureaucracies. The market system is also morally preferable because it fosters freedom and self-reliance. In line with these precepts, a wide range of public services were privatized, marketized, deregulated or run down during the 1980s and 1990s (Jenkins 1996; Riddell 1991; Kavanagh 1987). In these circumstances, it was hardly surprising that public service broadcasting should also come under fire.

A subsidiary theme of new right thinking is that liberal corporatism (that is, a system of governance based on consultation and conciliation between large corporate groups) has enfeebled Britain. It has entrenched producer interests at the expense of the public, and given rise to shabby compromise in place of the principled politics needed to reverse the country's relative decline. Public service broadcasting was indicted by the right on both counts. It was criticised as a producer-dominated institution that presented its vested interests as the public interest (Thatcher 1993). And it was condemned as an instrument of the old liberal consensus that had failed Britain (Tebbit 1989). This attack was prominent during the height of the Thatcherite 1980s, and could be revived again.

A third theme of neo-liberalism is that high levels of tax are throttling individual initiative and enterprise and are leading to an excessive level of public spending which is crowding out private investment. This is a potentially devastating line of argument, since it could lead very easily to the conversion of the license fee into a voluntary subscription to the BBC (a backdoor form of privatization), and the sale of Channel 4 – both proposals that have growing support among the right.

Yet while the rise of neo-liberalism is clearly a threat to public service broadcasting, there is still considerable disagreement among contemporary historians about the causes and extent of the right-wing shift in Britain. One culturalist interpretation argues that the rise of the right was accompanied by a successful mobilization behind right-wing ideological themes, in the context of "new times" when society had become more pluralistic and social identities had come to be defined less by class and shaped more by individual subjectivity (Hall 1988; Hall and Jacques 1989). Among other things, this mobilization had drawn upon resentments against welfare bureaucracy, the rhetoric of market freedom and choice, and the desire to define oneself through consumption. By implication, "new times" favored an expanded television system based on market freedom and choice rather than a restrictive one inherited from the era of rationing and paternalism.

Another interpretation explains the rise of the right primarily in terms of structural changes in the economy which have caused, among other things, a contraction of the working class and a weakening of trade unions (Jessop *et al.* 1988; Hobsbawm 1981). This has threatened in turn, it is argued, the welfarist social settlement that was forged on the basis of relative parity between organized business and labor. This alternative explanation actually offers even less comfort for defenders of public service broadcasting. Public service broadcasting came into being in response to the politics of class compromise (Scannell and Cardiff 1991), and has evolved in a form that informally guarantees rights of access and representation to opposed groups. In other words, it can be viewed as being part of the social settlement that is being destabilized by a fundamental shift in the power relations of British society.

A third interpretation attributes the rise of the right mainly to failures of leadership and internal divisions within the centre–left (Gamble 1990, 1988; Curran 1990; Heath *et al.* 1987). It sees the rightward shift of the last two decades as a process affecting the political elite more than the country as whole. Yet, this too has potentially negative implications for the future of public service broadcasting. The BBC fits uneasily into new market thinking. It is the inspiration of the Morrisonian public corporation, an approach to public ownership which is condemned in principle as much by revisionists in 'New Labour' as by the new right.

Public service broadcasting has also been weakened by the cumulative cultural changes that have transformed British society during the last three decades. Their corrosive effects can be glimpsed by comparing the different environments in which successive broadcasting enquiries deliberated during this period. When the Pilkington committee met in the early 1960s, it was pressed on all sides to defend and uphold broadcasting standards. Pressure came from much of the political establishment, churches, universities, schools, numerous voluntary associations and even much of the press, which were to a lesser or greater extent critical of commercial broadcasting. For example, the *Daily Mail*'s television critic, Peter Black (1972), thought that ITV's early giveaway shows, in which a housewife could earn a pound by correctly distinguishing her right foot from her left one or win a refrigerator by whitewashing her husband in thirty seconds starting from NOW, were not great programs.

The Annan committee in the 1970s would not have been so sure, or rather would not have been so certain that its judgment was shared. The overwhelming burden of evidence that it received from critical sources was directed against the "elitism" of the "broadcasting duopoly." This attack came from both left and right, and was directed at a wide range of broadcasting output. It signified that public service broadcasting no longer embodied a cultural as well as a political consensus. By the 1980s, these discontents were given a clear, neo-liberal programmatic focus in the demand for market reform, and in the argument that the only fair way to judge the quality of a program was whether people watched it. It was an argument that the Peacock Committee, as we have seen, largely endorsed.

Collective agreement about what constituted good broadcasting became more difficult because British society became more pluralistic. Inter-generational conflicts intensified in the 1960s, and were expressed in contrasting definitions of good music, with, as Chapman (1992) argues, the BBC making the strategic mistake of championing the musical tastes of the middle aged and elderly against the young. Youth groups, with divergent sub-cultural aesthetics, grew in number and influence from the 1960s onwards (Thornton and Gelder 1996; Hebdige 1979). The rise of feminism and ethnic identities established new axes of cultural value, which asserted the worth of certain forms of despised popular culture (McRobbie 1994; Geraghty 1991). The continued growth of the market for cultural goods provided also a means of affirming different definitions of the popular as "good," and of giving expression to individual subjectivity (Hewison 1995). Underlying this growth of pluralism was the decline of the homogenizing influences of nation, locality and class.

The power dynamics shaping definitions of cultural value also changed. In the early 1960s, a social coalition led by the liberal professions still had a shared understanding of what constituted worthwhile culture, which was challenged only from the margins. However the status of the liberal professions declined, particularly during the 1980s, and their influence as cultural arbiters diminished. Working class cultural deference receded throughout the post-war boom, fueled by the liberation of growing affluence. But perhaps most important of all, the middle class expanded, lost social cohesion and ceased to constitute a unified source of cultural judgment.

The rise of cultural studies in the 1980s and 1990s was emblematic of this sub-division within an expanded middle class. Cultural studies was based primarily in polytechnics, now the new universities, at the margins of class privilege. It developed a perspective that was defiantly opposed to the literary norms of traditional university English departments. The new discipline taught almost as an orthodoxy that cultural judgments are not so much verdicts on quality as forms of self-definition and social legitimation, a way of expressing group membership and exclusion (Frow 1995; McGuigan 1992; Bourdieu 1984). This led to a stream of publications perceiving in popular TV programs valid pleasures, progressive protests, or simply the expression of social experience, cultural tradition and collective membership whose value needed to be championed against social condescension (as well as from those who patronise cultural studies lecturers as much as the working class) (Geraghty 1991; Ang 1989; Hobson 1982).

In the changed climate, cultural judgments which had once appeared self-evident were made to seem problematic. "The word 'quality,'" wrote John Keane (1991: 120), "has no objective basis, only a plurality of ultimately clashing, contradictory meanings amenable to public manipulation." Instead of being lauded as a system that defended broadcasting standards, these standards were themselves questioned.

> The history of its [broadcasting] development in Britain has undoubtedly been coloured by the patrician values of a middle-class intelligentsia, and a defence of public service broadcasting in terms of quality and standards tied to prescriptive and elitist conceptions of education and culture is no longer feasible.
>
> (Scannell 1990: 260)

The institutional politics of the media also changed. A key factor in the original establishment of public service broadcasting in Britain was the absence of an economic lobby pressing, as in the United States, for the development of commercial radio (Scannell and Cardiff 1991). During the conservative 1950s, the commercial lobby was reformist, targeting only television and pressing for commercial television in a public service mold (Sendall 1982). But, in the last two decades, there emerged a formidable lobby fundamentally opposed to public service broadcasting. Its leading figure is Rupert Murdoch who controls one-third of the British national press (O'Malley 1994; Murdoch 1989).

In addition, public service broadcasting became exposed to the growing challenge of new media. These threaten to gnaw away at its audience and, over time, may further weaken both its legitimacy and its revenue base. The writing is on the wall, and it spells out – in the view of some – the slow death of traditional public service broadcasting.

COUNTERVAILING TRENDS

The trouble with this contingent reasoning, entirely in keeping with the hand-wringing tradition of the international "broadcasting crisis" literature, is that it stumbles into one awkward obstruction: the fact that British public service broadcasting, so seemingly beset by crisis, has remained resilient for so long. Why, if the political and social trends of society are so inimical to public service broadcasting, is it still standing bruised but intact? What calls for explanation is not why public service broadcasting should have severe problems but why these have not proved fatal.

Public service broadcasting is a popular consumer service in Britain. It was one of the first in Europe to make a compromise with market values when it incorporated in 1955 a regulated market as a central feature of its organization. It was therefore in a strong position to fight back against the new generation of market-based, cable and satellite TV channels. It did so, moreover, from a position of economic privilege. Well funded by a tax on TV ownership and by a restricted license to charge advertising on terrestrial television, public service channels outspent their rivals. Yet, unlike them, they levied no consumer charge.

These collectivist arrangements are supported by British political culture. Even during the heyday of Thatcherite dominance in the 1980s, there continued to be majority support for collectivist policies funded by taxation across a wide area of activity, as well as backing for extensive state action in support of welfare goals (Crewe 1988; Jowell *et al.* 1987; Jowell and Alrey 1984). British public attitudes remained markedly less individualistic and more statist, in response to identical questions, than those in the United States (Davis 1986). While the new right made ideological inroads, it failed to transform public attitudes. Its cultural ascendancy was exaggerated by Britain's first-past-the-post electoral system, in which a minority of votes was translated into a majority of parliamentary seats.

Public service broadcasting is also respected in Britain because it is thought to be politically independent. While broadcasting authorities were partly nobbled by government during the 1980s, rank and file broadcasters fought a determined rearguard action to defend their autonomy (including an unprecedented strike at the BBC in protest against government censorship). Successive surveys show that public service TV is thought to provide a more trustworthy and credible source of news than the market-based press (Negrine 1989; Curran and Seaton 1997) .

Public support strengthened the hand of traditionalists within the Conservative party who saw the BBC as a symbol of community and national prestige. Along with others, they also perceived regulation and public funding to be necessary to prevent the reduction of programs to the lowest common denominator. As William Whitelaw, Thatcher's deputy prime minister, wrote revealingly in his memoirs: "I am always disturbed by talk of achieving higher standards in programmes at the same time as proposals are introduced leading to deregulation and financial competition because I do not believe that they are basically compatible" (Whitelaw 1989: 285). The same thinking informed the unanimous report of the all-party Commons Home Affairs Committee which considered broadcasting legislation in the late 1980s. Its starting point was that "the principles of public service broadcasting should be an integral part of the new broadcasting environment" in order to maintain "high quality programmes," a commitment which it believed to be incompatible with market freedom (House of Commons 1988: x–xi). This seemed to indicate that the majority of MPs with a specialist interest in broadcasting still subscribed to the cultural values and assumptions on which public service broadcasting was founded even if these were being questioned in academic books, newspapers, think-tank reports and media industry speeches.

The BBC defused right-wing criticism by performing an organizational cartwheel. It introduced an internal market for its services, outsourced some program production and made staff redundant. This generated a wave of protest which government critics found reassuring. The right eventually split between gradualists and fundamentalists over the pace of broadcasting reform, with in the end the fundamentalists being isolated within the government as well as in the country.

The institutions of public service broadcasting in Britain – the BBC, Channel 4, and the agencies regulating commercial broadcasting – all survived. Viewed from the vantage point of the late 1990s, they now look much more politically secure than they did in the 1980s. Thatcherism made a less enduring and transformative impact, in hindsight, than some interpretations at the time assumed. Labour adjusted to its shrinking class base by reconstituting the social basis of the progressive coalition in Britain, and went on to win a landslide election victory in 1997. While Labour regrouped partly on the basis of a right-wing agenda, this did not extend to broadcasting. One effect of right-wing attacks on public service broadcasting was to strengthen, in an almost tribal way, the centre–left's support for it.

A price was paid for survival. The BBC is a more centralized, less creative institution than it was, while ITV has become unduly commercialized (Curran and Seaton 1997). But there is now time to repair past damage, and to lay down deeper and more secure foundations for the future. A political breathing space has been given to public service broadcasting. What is needed now is hard thought about how this time can be turned to advantage, rather than yet more speculation that public service broadcasting is being carried away by the tidal wave of history.

RENEWAL OF AN IDEA

Renewal should begin with reworking the *idea* of public service broadcasting. "Public broadcasters have failed," according to Rowland and Tracey (1990: 20), "to articulate an intellectual argument for the continuing validity of public service values." In the opinion of the American scholar, Craig Calhoun, "The standard defenses of public service broadcasting are weak," although he is good enough to allow that there is a case for a minority public service broadcasting service of the sort with which the United States is blessed (Calhoun 1996: 224).

In fact, the case for public service broadcasting is not quite as deficient as these, and other commentators, have suggested. The first step is to seek to change the terms of reference of debate about broadcasting from the needs of the individual to those of society. Any discourse that is defined solely by individual consumer satisfaction is loaded heavily in favor of a liberal market agenda. Any discourse that thinks about the wider requirements of society is, by contrast, cued to the public service case. In addition, the emphasis of the public service argument needs to be shifted from culture to democracy. This is because it is much easier to draw upon shared assumptions about the requirements of the democratic system than about the cultural needs of society. This said, the cultural case cannot go by default and needs to be reformulated to meet the challenge of cultural postmodernism.

What follows is an attempt to introduce new arguments into the debate. But, first, this needs to be set in the context of still valid traditional arguments as well as of the current rethinking that is taking place. Particularly important, in this respect, is the recent work of neo-Keynsians who seek to make a case for public service broadcasting on the basis of a critique of the free market in broadcasting (Graham and Davies 1997, 1992; Collins and Murroni 1996; Congdon *et al.* 1992). They point out that broadcasting is a "public good" which can be shared without incurring additional costs. Whereas a bar of chocolate cannot be eaten more than once, a program can be watched by one household without subtracting from the consumption of another. Collective provision of broadcasting takes full advantage of this public good characteristic. In contrast, a pay-TV system exploits it for the benefit of the private operator, and excludes by price people who could receive programs at minimal extra cost.

In addition, all advertising-funded markets are imperfect. They operate through the sale of viewers' attention, producing a bias against quality and variety. The advertising system favors high ratings rather than highly rated programs. It also favors majority rather than minority programs because advertising is insensitive to intensities of demand (unlike, in principle, a direct consumer payments system where people can opt to pay more for what they especially like).

Some neo-Keynsians also confront the fashionable liberal argument that public service broadcasting is a transitional arrangement which can now be phased out, since new technology is generating increased competition. In fact new technology, Graham and Davies (1997) argue, is reinforcing the need for public control. It is giving rise to a communications industry which still has high fixed and low marginal costs. This means that dominant producers can continue to achieve low unit costs by reaching large audiences (achieving economies of scale), and by using a wide variety of different formats (exploiting economies of scope). "Thus, while one source of monopoly, spectrum scarcity, has gone, it has been replaced by another – the natural monopoly of economies of scale and scope" (Graham and Davies 1997: 1). More channels and outlets will be created, but it is likely that they will be controlled by fewer companies.

The neo-Keynsian tradition often refutes liberal argument within a liberal frame of reference. It tends to be a way of saying that the consumer is not best served by free market policies, owing to market failure, and is better served by public regulation. However, an alternative approach involves asserting that people are not only consumers in the market economy but also citizens within the democratic system (Murdock 1992). Citizens have rights, including the right to be adequately informed about matters relating to the public good. The basis of this right is that the people are sovereign in liberal democracies. If they are to be effective and responsible, they need to be adequately informed.

This need is best served by public service broadcasting because it gives due attention to public affairs, and is less dominated by drama and entertainment than market-based broadcasting generally is. While the market has sometimes generated dedicated news or information channels, these have tended to attract elite audiences and to increase the knowledge gap between elites and the general public. By contrast, public service broadcasting raises general levels of political awareness by including news and current affairs programs in prime time on popular, generalist channels. One system takes into account the informational needs of democracy: the other does not, and tends to disempower large sections of the electorate through lack of information.

Second, public service broadcasting produces, it is argued, a better, more rational democracy (Scannell 1992; Garnham 1986). It encourages the transfer of relevant specialist knowledge to the political domain, and promotes balanced, evidence-based and reciprocal debate directed towards the public good. This contrasts with the market-based system in the United States where the drive to sustain ratings has encouraged the tabloidization of news coverage, the blurring of information and entertainment, and the increasing domination of political analysis by brief, and rapidly shrinking, sound bites that make few demands on the audience (Hallin 1996, 1994).

Third, public service broadcasting is in a good position to exercise a critical oversight of the state and other powerful institutions because it is not compromised by unregulated, private interests. Its record in uncovering state abuses in relation to Northern Ireland during the 1980s, for example, compared favorably with that of the national press, much of which was blinded by its partisan support of the Conservative government (Curran 1996). However, more should be done to sharpen the critical edge of broadcasting by shielding it further from government.

Fourth, and as we shall see more problematically, broadcasting stages a collective conversation about common social processes. Through mass television, society communes with itself, forms and revises collective opinion, and influences the public direction of society. Through the broadcasting system as a whole (including minority channels), people also explore their own group self-interest and relate this to the wider public interest. Thus, broadcasting is not only about individuals within society coming together but also about different groups within it constituting themselves, advancing their interests and negotiating with others within the wider totality.

Public service broadcasting is, in principle, in a uniquely strong position to stage this collective dialogue because its program making organizations and regulatory agencies are owned by the community and are not tied to the corporate business sector. It can perform a disinterested service in ensuring that views and perspectives challenging as well as supporting established privilege are aired. It can also serve society by extending social participation in collective debate. In this way, conflicting interests and opinions can be taken into account in a way that is likely to promote equitable outcomes.

The thrust of the traditional case for public service broadcasting is that it fosters an informed, intelligent and independent democracy. The thrust of this fourth argument is that public service broadcasting promotes an *equitable* democracy. However, this is not an argument that is presented in the official literature of statutes, government white and green papers, and official broadcasting reports published since 1979. Indeed, still more strikingly, in none of these official documents is the facilitation of an open public dialogue or the extension of participation in collective discussion even recognised as being an official objective of the public service system. One key dimension of its public role and legitimation has been written out.

This myopia is inscribed in the categories that are used in the official canon. Thus, "access" is discussed primarily in terms of access to broadcast signals in outlying areas. It is about an entitlement to reception rather than expression, the right to watch and listen but not to be heard. Similarly, the notion of "diversity" is understood primarily in terms of delivery: it is about catering for different tastes and needs. It is also invoked mainly in relation to non-political programs, whereas the cardinal virtue required of public affairs coverage is "due impartiality." The limitations of the prevailing approach is summarized in a recent government White Paper: "Programme requirements are focused on securing qualitative objectives or ensuring the accurate and impartial reporting of views and opinions, *rather than securing plurality*" (National Heritage 1995: 17; emphasis added).

In short, the democratic case for public service broadcasting is not presented in full. The problem is also, as we shall see, that it is not realized fully in practice either.

RETHINKING "CULTURE"[1]

"Quality"

The argument thus far is that the democratic system needs certain sorts of programs – ones that inform; sustain rational debate; critically overview the state; and support a collective dialogue that empowers. Public service broadcasting is better able to deliver "quality" programs in these terms than market-based broadcasting.

But when people talk about program quality, they usually have in mind its cultural quality. Supporters of the public service system usually resort to two sorts of quality argument, both of which have been weakened by technological change. The first standard argument is that public service broadcasting delivers demanding programs of high quality, usually associated with high culture. The second is that the system delivers a planned diversity of program catering for the different minorities that make up the majority. To this, the neo-liberal retort is now simple. High culture "quality" programs can be supplied by a publicly funded, elite channel (as in the United States), and does not justify an entire broadcasting system. Second, a mature broadcasting market generates specialist and niche channels catering for minority demand, such as those that are mushrooming on cable and satellite TV.

A new and better case has to be made – and delivered – that different facets of cultural "quality" run through the entire output of broadcasting. One way to attempt this is to think of a "cultural system," in a way that is analogous to the democratic system, with requirements that need to be met if it is to function properly. These requirements are perhaps conservation, innovation, reproduction, diversity and social access. They are better met by a public service than a market system of broadcasting.

Thus, public service broadcasting helps to conserve the cultural system by transmitting to the next generation works of literature, music and art which were judged to be of outstanding value by past generations. It renews the part of the cultural system constituted by broadcasting by supporting innovation through the allocation of resources to original and experimental work. It fosters the diversity of the cultural system through internal cross-subsidies within public service organizations which are designed to sustain production for minorities (including, crucially, ones that are not viable in the marketplace). It helps the cultural system to reproduce itself by sustaining concentrations of craft skill, experience and talent, and by supporting creativity through the ceding of a high degree of autonomy to production teams. And it facilitates social access to the cultural system through low, collectively subscribed costs of admission, and through mixed program schedules that encourage viewers to try new experiences.

Thinking in these abstract terms runs counter both to the empirical temper of British intellectual life and to the currently fashionable climate of cultural relativism. But the fact that there is no longer a cultural-value consensus does not make unnecessary or impossible judgments about the cultural needs of society. Not making a judgment does not mean in reality avoiding one: it merely delegates the task to TV company executives, advertising agency buyers and other decision makers within a market system. This is doubly problematic since a view of the wider needs of society does not inform transactions of the marketplace; and for the reasons that have been cited earlier, broadcasting markets do not "give people what they want."

This said, the history of public service broadcasting both in Britain and elsewhere also points to the dangers of over-privileging a self-referencing system of cultural value in a form that is only answerable to a committee-based chain of accountability. There are also positive virtues in a regulated market as a feature of public accountability, though not necessarily for the entire public service system.

"Community"

Culture is an ambiguous word. It can also be defined anthropologically as a way of life, a meaning that calls for different broadcasting systems to be evaluated in terms of the values and social relations that they sustain.

Public service broadcasting upholds the values of community, whereas the pure market broadcasting approach elevates the values of possessive individualism. One is organized in a way that both reflects and fosters a culture of mutuality and responsibility to others; the other derives from a culture of the marketplace, defined by cash nexus and contract, and centers on the wants and needs of self.

Thus, a strong sense of community defines how public service broadcasting relates to its public. In Britain, the BBC and the commercial TV regulator have invested heavily and uneconomically in transmission facilities which are needed to ensure that small, isolated communities in hill-bound areas are not left out. Similarly, cable TV in Britain (unlike the US) is required by regulation to include low-income as well as high-income areas. A strong sense of community also affects what programs are made. The core broadcasting system is protected from the global market in order for it to reflect adequately the concerns, interests and cultural traditions of British society. Public service broadcasting also has guaranteed access to key sporting and other "reserved" national events which commemorate the shared life of a community and which ritually affirm its sense of continuity. And, perhaps most important of all, a strong sense of community has influenced how programs are made. Public service broadcasting has nurtured a progressive social realist tradition of TV drama which powerfully expresses the values of social solidarity (McKnight 1997; Brandt 1993, 1981). Popular TV soap opera in Britain also regularly features working class life, in contrast to the glamorized, upscale settings that dominate much of American domestic TV drama. One of the many things, for example, that impart "quality" to the BBC soap, *EastEnders*, is the way that it renders visible, and symbolically affirms the centrality of, people who are being marginalized or excluded by the economic system.

Another feature of public service broadcasting is that it promotes sympathetic understanding of "the other." At best, its programs empathize rather than demonize; offer explanatory contexts rather than identikits of good and evil; render explicable the alien and unfamiliar; and sometimes find room for complexity rather than stereotypical simplification. This is because its programs are less subordinated to market dictates, and are produced by people with more opportunity to express their predominantly humanistic values, than is the case in the US networks. The need for "simple, and simply motivated, stories full of conflict, endings resolved, uplift apparent, and each act . . . [ending] on a note of suspense sufficient to carry the viewer through the commercial break," which Gitlin (1994: 165–6) argues characterizes US network made-for-TV films, is the product of a different political economy.

Yet, there are also disbenefits that come with these positive public service values. One is that the identity of the national community can be unduly emphasized at the expense of class and other sectional loyalties which are necessary for collective self-defence. The other is that the dominant public service code of ethical liberalism can be blind to the structures that divide and set people against each other and can see in conflict merely a failure of communication rather than the need for change. The culture of social integration and mutuality which is promoted by public service broadcasting needs to be more leavened by a culture of difference. Not only in public affairs journalism but also in the full range of drama and entertainment there needs to be more expression of perspectives which are opposed to those that are dominant and consensual.

DEFENCE THROUGH REFORM

Public service broadcasting should be strengthened through rethinking its rationale. This in turn requires that the actual practice and organization of public service broadcasting should change. Reform is the best form of defence.

First priority should be given to putting more space between broadcasters and ministers. The system of government appointments to broadcasting authorities in Britain has become corrupted and debased. All of those appointed to chair the BBC, for example, during the Conservative ascendancy were known Conservative supporters. Indeed, the former longstanding chairman of the BBC,

Marmaduke Hussey, was the brother-in-law of a cabinet minister; his predecessor, Stuart Young, was the brother of one.

Broadcasting appointments should be removed from direct, unmediated patronage. An independent appointments committee, made up of nominees from representative organizations in the country and from the broadcasting industry, should publicly recommend appointees to the Heritage Minister. Their brief should be to select people of talent who are drawn from a cross-section of society to represent the public. They should guard against not only government but also establishment "packing": eight out of twelve BBC governors in 1992, for instance, went to just three universities – Oxford, Cambridge and London.

The BBC should also be protected from financial intimidation. When its income automatically increased, owing to the growth in ownership of radio, TV and then colour TV, it was financially independent. When this natural growth dried up, the BBC became economically vulnerable to pressure from government which alone has the power to authorize license fee increases. In order to restore the BBC's economic independence and to avoid debilitating cuts, the license fee should rise automatically in relation to the increase in unit labour costs in the private sector (Graham and Davies 1997).

The other cudgel used to intimidate the BBC is the periodic renewal of its charter. The lead-up to renewal has often been the time when the BBC has been most sensitive to government and establishment opinion (Briggs 1985). The BBC should be established by statute. After more than seventy years' distinguished service, it should no longer be considered a probationer on a temporary contract.

In short, public service broadcasting needs increased protection from ministers. It will then be in an even stronger position to hold government and politicians to account and to serve the wider needs of the democratic system.

PUBLIC REDEFINITION

The official objectives of public service broadcasting in Britain should be revised in order to foster a shift in its style of journalism. This is still profoundly influenced by a civil service/professional model which stresses the disinterested mediation of information, the imparting of knowledge and the impartial umpiring of differences of legitimated opinion. It is a mandarin-like conception in which the electorate, the rulers of democracy, are briefed by intelligent and responsible public servants rather than merely entertained by market spectacle.

This conception is embedded in the culture and history of public service broadcasting. Lord Reith, the founder of the BBC, told the American journalist Edward Murrow that his "man-on-the-street" reporting "will drag radio down to the level of Hyde Park Speaker's Corner" (Persico 1988: 112). The same image of demotic speech, of self-appointed speakers and vulgar crowd abuse, was invoked with patrician disdain by the Annan report when it attacked the notion of broadcasting as "a mass conversation" or "dialogue." This misguided idea, it warned, would reduce broadcasting to the level of "an aerial Hyde Park Corner" (Annan 1977: 24).

But what this disdain overlooks is that, whatever the intention, broadcasting does inevitably reproduce a form of public dialogue that influences public opinion. An over-great stress on legitimated forms of public knowledge and accredited speakers unduly restricts participation in this dialogue. Indeed, this is a constantly repeated refrain of much academic research which suggests that TV news and current affairs is often defined by elite assumptions and sources (Eldridge 1995; Philo 1995; McNair 1995, 1988).

Old ways of doing things are made still more problematic by the decline of political parties They have lost much of their active, mass memberships. They have ceased to command the same degree of partisan loyalty and personal influence as before. And they are no longer as representative of coherent social–ideological blocs in society as they once were. Yet, their dominance over news and current affairs programs has, if anything, increased owing to the growing professionalism of their public relations. This dominance has tended to crowd out unduly other representative organizations and constrain broadcasters' responses to wider social currents and trends in society.

Yet, there is a powerful reform movement within the broadcasting community which is intent upon extending social access and expanding the range of voices and views on air. This has been manifested in new phone-in programs, audience participant formats and access slots (Livingstone and Lunt 1994). It has penetrated the citadels of conventional broadcasting, giving rise to outstanding programs which have enabled marginalized groups to occupy the center of debate (Curran 1997). Above all, it has resulted in Channel 4 developing in ways that were not fully anticipated. Norman Tebbit, a close ally of Margaret Thatcher, told its bemused chief executive that "Parliament never meant" there to be "these programmes for homosexuals and such," and had conceived of minority interests as being "hobbies" such as golf, sailing and fishing (Isaacs 1989). The legislative remit of the channel was in fact ambiguous, calling for innovation and minority programmes (HMSO 1981, 1990). This was interpreted to mean extending the ideological and cultural range of the broadcasting system.

This reform movement should be given public recognition and legitimacy. The older tradition of objective and informative reporting should continue to be part of the remit of public service broadcasting since this is an important element of its wider democratic role. To the "due objectivity" obligation, however, should be added a "pluralism" requirement. Licensed broadcasters should have a public duty to give adequate expression to a diversity of perspectives and viewpoints, and to facilitate the participation of different groups in the collective dialogue of society. This should be entrenched in new broadcasting legislation, incorporated into the Constitution of the BBC, and should become a public service objective which both the Independent Television Commission and the Radio Authority uphold.

REINVENTING TRADITION

Channel 4 was established in 1982 and was an imaginative way of reinterpreting the public service tradition. But there have been no public service experiments since then. Channel 5, established in 1997, is a low-budget equivalent of ITV. All of the remaining new TV channels have been largely free of public service regulation and are defined by a market logic.

Yet, digitalization is creating a wonderful opportunity to extend the repertoire of public service broadcasting. Perhaps, the next step should be to create an entirely new type of minority channel, "Free TV," which would be independent of both the state and the market. That is to say, it would be publicly funded (perhaps, eventually, from a higher license fee for digital TV) in order for it to be free of commercial control. At the same time, it would also be free of any state regulation other than the law of the land. Its brief would be, simply, to make good programs and to explore the potential of television as a medium to do new things.

Behind this idea is, above all, a feeling that public service broadcasting has been depleted by the Thatcher era. Arguably, the great strength of the British public service model is that it has traditionally allowed greater autonomy to its staff than either the market-driven model of the United States or the representative-ridden models of continental European broadcasting. This much vaunted autonomy of the past had strongly mythical elements (Schlesinger 1978; Burns 1977; Kumar 1975), but at its best it encouraged innovative and creative program making with a high level of technical skill. Yet, staff autonomy has been greatly diminished by managerial changes in the BBC, designed to reduce costs and avoid the giving of offence, and by the increased marketization of ITV following the auctioning of its licenses. A new institution is needed which will recapture and embody in a strengthened form the distinctive feature of the British broadcasting model, and which will set new standards of aspiration and achievement for the system as a whole.

This new institution would be centered in Glasgow and Liverpool. It would be exposed to a significantly different social and political culture to that of other TV channels, which are to a lesser or great extent dominated by high commands located in London. The hope is that it would give airtime to perspectives and experiences that are different from the mainstream of broadcasting.

This would break new ground, yet be faithful to the way in which broadcasting has evolved in Britain. Its public service system is organized on the basis of organizational pluralism. It consists of a massive public corporation (BBC), a publicly owned independent publisher (Channel 4), and publicly regulated, regional and quasi-national networks (ITV and Channel 5). To this would be added a regulation-free showcase of broadcasting talent, less encumbered by market or state constraint than any broadcasting organization in the world.

RETROSPECT

Elihu Katz's reading of the situation may be premature now, at least in relation to Britain and much of Europe, but could yet turn out to be a correct reading of the runes for the future. In particular, if new technology causes TV "channels" to disappear, transforming the TV set into a megalithic video store, his analysis will look more plausible as a prediction. But this is only one scenario. An alternative, more probable one in the medium term is that video-on-demand will be merely one more add-on service, among others, which is built around the existing but evolving core television system.

Underlying much speculation about technological transformations of communications is a symmetrical assumption that what is inevitable is also desirable. Katz differs in seeing the neo-liberal broadcasting utopia as a dystopia, but does not dissent from the technological determinism that informs it. Yet, there is another way of responding, which is to consider how global markets can be better regulated through international cooperation, how new technology can be harnessed to the general good, and how what is worth preserving from the past is carried forward into the future.

Katz invokes an image of the past, as a way of dramatizing what has been lost. But his view of the national community coming together in a public space which is represented by monopoly or near monopoly TV channels leaves out one thing. Most of the people doing the talking in these communal meetings, certainly in Britain, were power holders or members of elite groups. It is only by opening up these virtual meetings to more voices will it be possible to strengthen public identification with the broadcasting system.

Yet if this essay takes issue with what Katz has argued on this particular occasion, it does so with respect. Katz's work exemplifies an arresting social democratic vision of communications and society. It stresses people's independence of thought, rooted in strong social ties; the cultural resources available to communities to withstand domination; and, in an almost idealized way, the power of media events to transcend division and unify society.[2] Katz has always been an involved academic, whose engagement, as it happens, includes setting up an enduring public service TV system.[3] Audacious though this claim may seem, the general tenor of this essay is perhaps more faithful to the Katz tradition – is more truly Katzian – than the latest essay that Elihu Katz (1996) himself has written.

NOTES

1 For interesting alternative approaches, see in particular Frow (1995), Connor (1992) and Mulgan (1990).
2 See Chapter 1.
3 Elihu Katz was Israel Television's first Director. For a positive assessment of the institution he founded, see Etzioni-Halevy (1987).

REFERENCES

Achille, Y. and Miege, B. (1994) "The limits to the adaptation strategies of European public service television," *Media, Culture and Society* 16 (10).

Aldridge, M. and Hewitt, N. (eds.) (1994) *Controlling Broadcasting*, Manchester: Manchester University Press.

Ang, I. (1989) *Watching "Dallas,"* London: Routledge.

Ang, I. (1991) *Desperately Seeking the Audience*, London: Routledge.

Annan (1977) *Report of the Committee on the Future of Broadcasting*, London: HMSO.

Anon (1997a) "Being digital – dilemmas for Europe's terrestrial broadcasters," *Context Analysis Report* (Informed Sources International), 1 (3).

Anon (1997b) "America's television networks: the dash for the off switch," *Economist*, June 7, pp. 88–9.

Avery, R. (ed.) (1993) *Public Service Broadcasting in a Multichannel Environment*, White Plains, NY: Longman.

Barnett, S. and Curry, A. (1994) *The Battle for the BBC*, London: Aurum.

Beveridge (1951) *Report of the Broadcasting Committee*, London: HMSO.

Black, P. (1972) *Mirror in the Corner*, London: Hutchinson.

Blumler, J. (ed.) (1992) *Television and the Public Interest*, London: Sage.

Bourdieu, P. (1984) "The aristocracy of culture," in R. Collins, J. Curran, N. Garnham, P. Scannell, P. Schlesinger and C. Sparks (eds.) *Media, Culture and Society: A Critical Reader*, London: Sage.

Brandt, G. (ed.) (1981) *Television Drama*, Cambridge: Cambridge University Press.

Brandt, G. (ed.) (1993) *British Drama in the 1980s*, Cambridge: Cambridge University Press.

Briggs, A. (1985) *The BBC: the First Fifty Years*, Oxford: Oxford University Press.

Burns, T. (1977) *The BBC: Public Institution and Private World*, London: Macmillan.

Calhoun, C. (1996) "Comment on John Keane: the death of the public sphere," in M. Andersen (ed.) *Media and Democracy*, Oslo: University of Oslo Press.

Catalbas, D. (1996) "The Crisis of Public Service Broadcasting: Turkish Television in the 1990s," PhD thesis, Goldsmiths College, University of London.

Chapman, R. (1992) *Selling the Sixties*, London: Routledge.

Collins, R. (1992) *Satellite Television in Western Europe* (revised edn), London: Libbey.

Collins, R. (1993) "Public service versus the market ten years on: reflections on critical theory and the debate about broadcasting policy in the UK," *Screen* 34 (3).

Collins, R. and Murroni, C. (1996) *New Media, New Policies*, Cambridge: Polity Press.

Commission of the European Communities (1992) *Pluralism and Media Concentration in the Internal Market*, Brussels, CEC Green Paper.

Congdon, T., Sturgess, B., National Economic Research Associates, Shew, W., Graham, A. and Davies, G. (1992) *Paying for Broadcasting*, London: Routledge.

Connor, S. (1992) *Theory and Cultural Value*, Oxford: Blackwell.

Crewe, I. (1988) "Has the electorate become Thatcherite?" in R. Skidelsky (ed.) *Thatcherism*, London: Chatto & Windus.

Curran, J. (1990) "The crisis of opposition: a reappraisal," in B. Pimlott, A. Wright and T. Fowler (eds.) *The Alternative*, London: W.H. Allen.

Curran, J. (1996) "Mass media and democracy revisited," in J. Curran and M. Gurevitch (eds.) *Mass Media and Society* (2nd edn), London: Arnold.

Curran, J. (1997) "Television journalism: theory and practice. The case of *Newsnight*," in P. Holland, *Television Handbook*, London: Routledge.

Curran, J. and Seaton, J. (1997) *Power Without Responsibility* (5th edn), London: Routledge.

Davis, J. (1986) "British and American attitudes: similarities and contrasts," in R. Jowell, S. Witherspoon and L. Brook (eds.) *British Social Attitudes: The 1986 Report*, Aldershot: Gower.

De Bens, E., Kelly, M. and Bakke, M. (1992) "Television Content: Dallasification of Culture?" in K. Slune and W. Truetzschler (eds.) *Dynamics of Media Politics*, London: Sage.

Eldridge, J. (ed.) (1995) *Glasgow Media Group Reader*, vol. 1, London: Routledge.

Etzioni-Halevy, E. (1987) *National Broadcasting Under Siege*, London: Macmillan.

Frow, J. (1995) *Cultural Studies and Cultural Value*, Oxford: Oxford University Press.

Gamble, A. (1988) *The Free Economy and Strong State*, London: Macmillan.

Gamble, A. (1990) "The Thatcher decade in perspective," in P. Dunleavy, A. Gamble and G. Peele (eds.) *Developments in British Politics*, vol. 3, London: Macmillan.

Garnham, N. (1986) "The media and the public sphere," in P. Golding, G. Murdock and P. Elliott (eds.) *Communicating Politics*, Leicester: Leicester University Press.

Geraghty, C. (1991) *Women and Soap Opera*, Cambridge: Polity Press.

Gitlin, T. (1994) *Inside Prime Time* (revised edn), London: Routledge.

Graham, A. and Davies, G. (1992) "The public funding of broadcasting," in T. Congdon, B. Sturgess, National Economic Research Associates, W. Shew, A. Graham, and G. Davies, *Paying for Broadcasting*, London: Routledge.

Graham, A. and Davies, G. (1997) *Broadcasting, Society and Policy in the Multimedia Age*, Luton: Libbey.

Hadenius, S. (1992) "Vulnerable values in a changing political and media system: the case of Sweden," in J. Blumler (ed.) *Television and the Public Interest*, London: Sage.

Hall, S. (1988) *The Hard Road to Renewal*, London: Verso.

Hall, S. and Jacques, M. (eds.) (1989) *New Times*, London: Lawrence & Wishart.

Hallin, D. (1994) *We Keep America on Top of the World: Television Journalism and the Public Sphere*, London: Routledge.

Hallin, D. (1996) "Commercialism and professionalism in the American news media," in J. Curran and N. Gurevitch (eds.) *Mass Media and Society* (2nd edn), London: Arnold.

Heath, A., Jowell, R. and Curtice, J. (1987) "Trendless fluctuation: a reply to Crewe," *Political Studies* 35.

Hebdige, D. (1979) *Subculture*, London: Routledge.

Hewison, R. (1995) *Culture and Consensus*, London: Methuen.

Hickethier, K. (1996) "The media in Germany," in T. Weymouth and B. Lamizet (eds.) *Markets and Myths*, London: Longman.

Hirsch, M. and Petersen, V. (1992) "Regulation of media at the European level," in K. Siune and W. Truetzschler (eds.) *Dynamics of Media Politics*, London: Sage.

Hirst, P. and Thompson, G. (1996) *Globalisation in Question*, Cambridge: Polity Press.

HMSO (1981) *Broadcasting Act*, London: HMSO.

HMSO (1990) *Broadcasting Act*, London: HMSO.

Hobsbawm, E. (1981) "The forward march of labour halted?" in M. Jacques and F. Mulhern (eds.) *The Forward March of Labour Halted?*, London: Verso.

Hobson, D. (1982) *Crossroads*, London: Methuen.

House of Commons (1988) *The Future of Broadcasting*, House of Commons Home Affairs Committee, London: HMSO.

Hoynes, W. (1994) *Public Television for Sale*, Boulder, CO: Westview.

Humphreys, P. (1994) *Media and Media Policy in Germany*, Oxford: Berg.

Humphreys, P. (1996) *Mass Media and Media Policy in Western Europe*, Manchester: Manchester University Press.

Isaacs, J. (1989) *Storm over 4*, London: Weidenfeld & Nicolson.

Jenkins, P. (1996) *Accountable to None*, Harmondsworth: Penguin.

Jessop, B., Bonnett, K., Bromley, S. and Ling, T. (1988) *Thatcherism*, Cambridge: Polity Press.

Jowell, R. and Airey, C. (eds.) (1984) *British Social Attitudes: The 1984 Report*, Aldershot: Gower.

Jowell, R., Witherspoon, S. and Brook, L. (eds.) (1987) *British Social Attitudes: The 1987 Report*, Aldershot: Gower.

Katz, E. (1996) "And deliver us from segmentation," *Annals of the American Academy of Political and Social Science* 546.

Kavanagh, D. (1987) *Thatcherism and British Politics*, Oxford: Oxford University Press.

Keane, J. (1991) *The Media and Democracy*, Cambridge: Polity Press.

Kuhn, R. (1995) *The Media in France*, London, Routledge.
Kumar, K. (1975) "Holding the middle ground: the BBC, the public, and the professional broadcaster," *Sociology* 9 (3).
Livingstone, S. and Lunt, P. (1994) *Talk on Television*, London: Routledge.
McGuigan, J. (1992) *Cultural Populism*, London: Routledge.
McKnight, G. (ed.) (1997) *Agent of Challenge and Defiance*, Trowbridge: Flick Books.
McNair, B. (1988) *Image of the Enemy*, London: Routledge.
McNair, B. (1995) *An Introduction to Political Communication*, London: Routledge.
McQuail, D. (1992) "The Netherlands: safeguarding freedom and diversity under multi-channel conditions," in J. Blumler (ed.) *Television and the Public Interest*, London: Sage.
McRobbie, A. (1994) *Postmodernism and Popular Culture*, London: Routledge.
Morley, D. and Robins, K. (1995) *Spaces of Identity*, London: Routledge.
Mulgan, G. (1990) "Television's holy grail: seven types of quality," in G. Mulgan (ed.) *The Question of Quality*, London: British Film Institute.
Murdoch, R. (1989) *Freedom in Broadcasting*, London: News International.
Murdock, G. (1992) "Citizens, consumers, and public culture," in M. Skovmand and K. Schroder (eds.) *Media Cultures*, London: Routledge.
National Heritage (1992) *The Future of the BBC*, London: HMSO.
National Heritage (1995) *Media Ownership*, London: HMSO.
Negrine, R. (1989) *Politics and the Mass Media in Britain*, (2nd edn), London: Routledge.
O'Malley, T. (1994) *Closedown?*, London: Pluto.
Ostergaard, B. (ed.) (1992) *The Media in Western Europe*, London: Sage.
Peacock (1986) *Report of the Committee on Financing the BBC*, London: HMSO.
Persico, J. (1988) *Edward R. Murrow*, New York: Dell.
Philo, G. (ed.) (1995) *Glasgow Media Group Reader*, vol. 2.
Pilkington (1962) *Report of the Committee on Broadcasting*, London: HMSO.
Riddell, P. (1991) *The Thatcher Era and its Legacy*, Oxford: Blackwell.
Rowland, Y. (1993) "Public service broadcasting in the United States: its mandate, institutions and conflicts," in R. Avery (ed.) *Public Service Broadcasting in a Multichannel Environment*, White Plains, NY: Longman.
Rowland, Y. and Tracey, M. (1990) "Worldwide challenges to public service broadcasting," *Journal of Communication* 40 (2).
Sartori, C. (1996) "The media in Italy," in T. Weymouth and B. Lamizet (eds.) *Markets and Myths*, London: Longman.
Scannell, P. (1990) "Public service: the history of a concept," in A. Goodwin and G. Whannel (eds.) *Understanding Television*, London: Routledge.
Scannell, P. (1992) "Public service broadcasting and modern public life," in P. Scannell, P. Schlesinger and C. Sparks (eds.) *Culture and Power*, London: Sage.
Scannell, P. and Cardiff, D. (1991) *Serving the Nation, 1922–39*, Oxford: Blackwell.
Schlesinger, P. (1978) *Putting "Reality" Together*, London: Constable.
Sendall, B. (1982) *Independent Television in Britain*, vol. 1, London: Macmillan.
Septrup, P. (1990) *Transnationalization of Television in Western Europe*, London: Libbey.
Sepstrup, P. (1993) "Scandinavian public service broadcasting: the case of Denmark," in R. Avery (ed.) *Public Service Broadcasting in a Multichannel Environment*, White Plains, NY: Longman.
Silj, A. (1988) *East of Dallas*, London: British Film Institute.
Sinha, N. (1996) "Liberalisation and the future of public service broadcasting in India," *Javnost* 3 (2).
Syvertsen, T. (1992) "Serving the public: public television in Norway in a new media age," *Media, Culture and Society* 14.
Tebbit, N. (1989) *Upwardly Mobile*, London: Futura.
Thatcher, M. (1995) *The Downing Street Years*, London: HarperCollins.
Thornton, S. and Gelder, K. (eds.) (1996) *The Subcultures Reader*, London: Routledge.
Ullswater (1936) *Report of the Broadcasting Committee*, London: HMSO

Vedel, T. and Bourdon, J. (1993) "French public broadcasting: from monopoly to marginalization," in R. Avery (ed.) *Public Service Broadcasting in a Multichannel Environment*, White Plains, NY: Longman.

Weymouth, T. and Lamizet, B. (eds.) (1996) *Markets and Myths*, London: Longman.

Whitelaw, W. (1989) *The Whitelaw Memoirs*, London: Aurum.

12 Public journalism and the search for democratic ideals

Theodore L. Glasser and Stephanie Craft

One imperfect measure of the growing influence of "public journalism" in newsrooms throughout the United States is the *New Yorker's* reluctant recognition of it. Twice in one year the magazine played host to writers whose views amounted to unambiguous disdain for public journalism and what it portends for the future of American journalism. One essay, in late 1996, found the "do-gooding" philosophy of public journalism to be "a fraud" and a "bad idea"; its "high-minded" claims added up to a "dishonest" and ultimately "anti-democratic" role for the press (Kelly 1996: 46). Earlier that year James Fallows, author of *Breaking the News: How the Media Undermine American Democracy* (1996), was taken to task for expressing sympathy for a "movement in the media" that seemed to be "especially popular among ink-free journalism professors"; public journalism "may sound like a neat idea at NYU," referring to New York University, where Jay Rosen runs his Project on Public Life and the Press, but "[w]hen journalists begin acting like waiters and taking orders from the public and pollsters, the results are not pretty" (Remnick 1996: 41–2).

With a tone calculated to condemn rather than critique the tenets of public journalism, these and other attacks seldom offer more than a crude caricature or a snide synopsis of what represents a genuinely innovative, if not altogether successful, effort to move journalists away from thinking about the claims of "separation" that have long defined the practice of American journalism and toward thinking about the claims of "connection" that might redefine and reinvigorate the role of the press in a democratic society. Indeed, Rosen (1994a) uses precisely these terms to establish a dividing line between traditional and public journalism: "Traditional journalism worries about getting the separations right. Public journalism is about trying to get the connections right" (p. 9).

The separations of concern to Rosen, mostly dualisms and dichotomies which are endorsed in practice and, when necessary, cited as principles of professional conduct, cover considerable ground in and beyond the newsroom. Rosen cites ten claims of separation, each in its own way a contribution to a larger corpus of claims having to do with standards of performance appropriate for judging the role and responsibility of the press:

1 Editorial functions are separated from the business side.

2   The news pages are separate from the opinion pages.
3   Facts are to be separated from values.
4   Those who "make the news" are separated from those who "cover the news."
5   Truth-telling must be separated from the consequences of truth-telling so that journalists can "tell it like it is."
6   The newspaper is separated from other institutions by its duty to report on them.
7   One day is separated from another because news is what is "new" today.
8   A good journalist separates reality from rhetoric.
9   One's professional identity must be separated from one's personal identity as a citizen.
10 How you "feel" about something is separate from how you report on it. (Or: the journalist's mind is separate from the journalist's soul.)

(Rosen 1994a: 8–9)

Taken together, these claims capture in broad outline form the familiar notion of an independent press which is committed to providing citizens with the accurate and unbiased information that they need to govern themselves properly. They convey the ideal of a "watchdog" press, a Fourth Estate, a private institution designed to keep its readers, viewers and listeners posted on matters of public concern. They vivify the image that journalists need to have of themselves if the news media, as Schudson (1995: 211) recently put it, are "to act *as if* they were instruments of popular education in a rich, vitalized democracy."

Public journalism rejects the assumption of a "rich, vitalized democracy" and thus rejects as well the role that the press plays in it. It instead presumes a democracy in decay and posits a role for the press that is based, empirically and normatively, on what journalism can do to enrich a public discourse which has long been in decline. We, too, question the vitality of modern American democracy, but we have questions as well about what this arguably new role for the press might entail and what view of democracy it implies. We begin, then, with a review of what public journalism claims for itself, at least in so far as those claims can be discerned from the various proposals and projects that are commonly associated with the terms "public" or "civic" journalism. We next focus on areas where public journalism's conception of the press and the press's commitment to self-governance appear to be most problematic. We conclude with a brief assessment of the prospects for a public purpose for a private press.

THE PRINCIPLES OF PUBLIC JOURNALISM

If there is no consensus on what to call it, most American journalists – and increasingly journalists elsewhere – have no difficulty recognizing the term public or civic journalism. It denotes a simple but controversial premise: the purpose of the press is to promote and indeed to improve, and not merely to report on or complain about, the quality of public or civic life.

Whether it is being celebrated or criticized, there is little disagreement about what, basically, public journalism expects from the press. To recycle a description we have used elsewhere (Glasser and Craft 1996), public journalism expects the press to recognize its role in fostering public participation and public debate. It expects the press to embrace a kind of "good news," to invoke the title of a new and relevant study of news and community (Christians *et al.* 1993), which is not to say that it condones a witless boosterism which uncritically accepts – or mindlessly supports – the status quo. The good news of interest to public journalism conveys optimism about the future and confidence in "our" ability to get there. Public journalism thus strikes a hopeful tone; it stands as a corrective to a language of despair and discontent.

The origins of public journalism

Described by its proponents as a "grassroots reform movement" (Charity 1995: 1), which is intended to "recall journalism to its deepest mission of public service" (Rosen 1995a: 16), public journalism emerged in the late 1980s and early 1990s in response to what was taken to be a widening gap between citizens and government and a "general disgust with and withdrawal from public life" (Merritt 1995: 6). It also emerged in response to journalism itself, namely the dismal performance of the press in its coverage of the 1988 US presidential campaign.

Not only was the 1988 election depicted as a race, a contest, but to an unprecedented degree journalists insisted on giving readers, viewers and listeners an "insider's view" of politics – what Gitlin (1990: 19) described as a fascinating but mostly irrelevant tour "backstage, behind the horse race, into the paddock, the stables, the clubhouse, and the bookie joints." Didion (1988) made much the same point with her reference to "insider baseball," a game described mostly for the benefit of the players. What was being covered as the 1988 campaign, she observed, was not "the democratic process" to which citizens had access but a process so specialized and limited that only its own professionals – politicians, policy experts, journalists, pollsters, pundits – could be reasonably described as its participants (cf. Rosen 1991; Carey 1995). News of the campaign, in short, focused overwhelmingly on strategy rather than substance, a *schema*, as Jamieson (1993) puts it, which invited voters to ask not "Who is better able to serve as president?" but "Who is going to win?":

> In the strategy schema, candidates are seen as performers, reporters as theatrical critics, the audience as spectators. The goal of the performer is to "win" the votes of the electorate, projected throughout the performance in polls. The polls determine whether the candidate will be cast as a front-runner or underdog, whether the candidate will be described as achieving goals or "trying" to achieve them, and how the candidate's staged and unstaged activities will be interpreted. In the strategy schema, candidates do not address problems with solutions, but "issues" with "strategies." The language of the strategy schema is that of sports and war. The vocabulary lets reporters, candidates, and the public ask "Who is winning, and how?" The posture invited of the electorate by this schema is cynical and detached.
>
> (Jamieson 1993: 38)

No blue-ribbon panel formed to assess the 1988 election campaign and the news media's coverage of it; nothing like the Hutchins Commission of the mid-1940s,[1] that is, put forth a call for reform in a language sure to alienate the very journalists expected to lead the reformation. Rather, public journalism spread from working papers and workshops to proposals and projects; there was no grand plan, no manifesto, which probably contributed in untold ways to the favorable reception it received in dozens of newsrooms in the early 1990s. If Rosen took the lead in facilitating discussions about public journalism, he always made it a point to keep the discussions open-ended, which usually meant framing them as opportunities to contribute to a work in progress. When, for example, he spoke to a gathering of journalists and academics at the American Press Institute in Reston, Virginia, in 1994, Rosen began by disclaiming any canonical conception of public journalism: "The most important thing that anyone can say about public journalism I will say right now: we're still inventing it. And because we're still inventing it, we don't really know what 'it' is. We've come to Reston to find out."[2]

The genesis of public journalism coincided with, though only occasionally cited, a new and growing body of literature on the problems of modern democracy (e.g. Habermas 1989; Calhoun 1992; Putnam 1993), much of it focused on the collapse of a vibrant and accessible "public sphere," to use the term that Habermas popularized in 1989 with the publication in English of a post-doctoral dissertation he had written in German in 1962. This literature included a series of works focused on the American democratic experience (e.g. Barber 1984; Fraser 1992; Putnam 1995; Sandel 1996), many of them trying to explain, as one of the more provocative titles puts it, *Why Americans Hate Politics* (Dionne 1991); it included as well several critiques dealing specifically, if not always exclusively, with communication and journalism (e.g. Entman 1989; Carey 1987, 1995; Dahlgren and Sparks 1991; Keane 1991; Peters and Cmiel 1991; Christians *et al.* 1993; Fallows 1996). While these and other works neither explain nor account for the phenomenon of public journalism, they arguably added to the urgency of public journalism's call for reform and affirmed the legitimacy of public journalism's contention that little had been gained over the years by what Schudson (1995: 211) fairly terms the "platitudinous thinking about democracy that is the coin of the realm in and around journalism."

A journalism of conversation

Public journalism calls for a shift from a "journalism of information" to a "journalism of conversation," to use Carey's (1987) useful distinction. The public needs to be informed, of course, but it also needs to be engaged in the day's news in ways that invite discussion and debate. And engaging the public – rather than merely informing it – requires a different approach to journalism and different routines for journalists.

The approach is different in two important ways. First, public journalism expects the press to participate in, and not remain detached from, efforts to improve the quality of public discourse. Second, public journalism calls on the press to broaden its conception of politics by understanding democracy as a way of life and not merely as a form of government.

Public journalism rejects, emphatically and categorically, any interpretation of "objectivity" or "objective reporting" which holds that newsrooms must stand detached from, and disinterested in, the affairs of the community. If public journalism stops short of equating "doing journalism" with "doing politics," it none the less "places the journalist within the political community as a responsible member with a full stake in public life"; public journalism, Rosen (1994c) explains,

> does not deny the important differences between journalists and other actors, including political leaders, interest groups, and citizens themselves. What is denied is any essential difference between the standards and practices that make responsible journalism and the habits and expectations that make for a well-functioning public realm, a productive dialogue, a politics we can all respect. In a word, public journalists want public life to work. In order to make it work they are willing to declare an end to their neutrality on certain questions – for example: whether people participate, whether a genuine debate takes place when needed, whether a community comes to grips with its problems, whether politics earns the attention it claims.
>
> (Rosen 1994c: 11)

What public journalism also denies, however, is that its rejection of objectivity amounts to an endorsement of the kind of partisan advocacy that the press abandoned long ago. Public journalism's "golden rule," as Charity (1995: 144–6) describes it, positions the press as a champion of democratic means but not democratic ends: "*Journalism should advocate democracy without advocating particular solutions.*" Merritt (1995: 116) reaches essentially the same conclusion when he argues that public journalism needs to retain "neutrality on specifics" while at the same time "moving far enough beyond detachment to care about whether resolution occurs." What this usually adds up to is a commitment from the press to provide or otherwise facilitate more and better opportunities for public debate and discussion, presumably regardless of what is being debated and discussed.

Public journalism's concern for the quality of public discourse widens and to some extent clarifies journalism's view of politics by recognizing citizens as a source of political wisdom. This optimistic view of the electorate invites the press to expand the scope of political coverage beyond politicians and the issues that they regard as salient. More than that, it encourages journalists to appreciate the press as an agency not only *of* but also *for* communication, a medium through which citizens can inform themselves *and* through which they can discover their common values and shared interests. Public journalism therefore invites the community at large, reporters and readers alike, to consider, as Dewey (1927), Carey (1987, 1995) and countless others have urged, that "what we mean by democracy depends on the forms of communication by which we conduct politics" (Carey 1995: 379).

New forms of communication relocate not only politics but also the journalist, as Rosen (1995b) illustrates with reference to a journalist at New York *Newsday*, Jim Dwyer, who wrote a column, "In the Subways," based on his experiences riding the subways and enduring – and at times enjoying – what tens of thousands of New Yorkers endure and occasionally enjoy each day. Unlike reporters for, say, the *New York Times*, whose approach to stories about the subways usually begins and ends with interviews with officials at the Transit Authority, which has jurisdiction over the subway system, Dwyer's stories ordinarily begin with his experiences of riding the subways. The significance of the difference, Rosen points out, is that Dwyer's "immediate, flesh and blood connection to citizens" established his authority as a representative of – or surrogate for – his readers and their interests; Dwyer may end up interviewing officials at the Transit Authority, but by then "with some earned authority of his own," which, Rosen believes, addresses what public journalism needs to address when it encourages new routines for reporters: "Power without authority is the quickest way to arouse public resentment" (Rosen 1995b: 5–6).

Good journalism, good business

One of public journalism's most controversial claims rests on the supposition that good journalism, which is to say *public* journalism, will attract more and better readers and thereby enhance a newspaper's standing in the marketplace. In 1989, in an appeal to editors published in the *Bulletin of the American Society of Newspaper Editors*, Rosen more or less introduced the idea of public journalism by calling for an appreciation of the connection between a newspaper's vitality and the vitality of public life. It was an appeal aimed at beleaguered editors who worried about declining readership and who worried even more about the market-driven solutions being proposed by publishers and vice-presidents whose training in business, not journalism, was taken to mean that management could not always be counted on to safeguard traditional newsroom values.[3]

Cautiously but apparently convincingly, Rosen advanced the proposition that "a healthy public sphere is, in some respects, in the circulation interests of newspapers" (1991: 273). The chief executive officer of the Knight–Ridder newspaper chain, James Batten, an early and eager supporter of public journalism, agreed; in a lecture in 1990 Batten cited a Knight–Ridder study of 16,300 readers which found empirical support for Rosen's claim about the importance and relevance of improving the quality of a community's shared civic culture: "People who say they feel a real sense of connection to the places they live" are almost twice as likely to be regular readers of newspapers. Efforts to "enhance these feelings of connectedness," Batten concluded, may "produce at least part of the readership and circulation growth American newspapers are pushing for" (quoted in Rosen 1991: 273).

Batten and others thus understand public journalism as an "added value," to use the phrase Rosen (1994a) applies to public journalism's principal product – "connectivity." Any product or service, Charity (1995: 155, 158) explains, relies on its added value to position itself in the marketplace: "Over the long run, people will pay for a good or service only if it gives them something they wouldn't otherwise have gotten cheaper or better elsewhere." Most forms of journalism, according to Charity, offer little in the way of added value; the *news* media are barely distinguishable from other media. Public journalism, however, *adds value* to newspapers by helping readers to engage each other in an ongoing conversation; public journalism, therefore, "makes economic sense" (Charity 1995: 155).

Merritt (1994), too, wants to find a way to reconcile public journalism with the realities of free enterprise. But unlike Rosen and Charity, who view public journalism as a financially viable alternative to conventional journalism, Merritt prefers to frame public journalism as an adjunct to whatever role that the press needs to play to survive in the marketplace:

> The two roles – reviving public life while dealing with the realities of the popular marketplace – coexist in public journalism because they need not be mutually exclusive. Beyond the journalist's core responsibility to support public life, everything else that might go into a newspaper is optional and subject to no meaningful test beyond the informational and entertainment desires of readers. Provided that the core concerns are zealously guarded, what harm can come from knowing, and picking from, the reader's wish list for the balance of the newspaper, no matter how serendipitous or inconsequential it may seem?
>
> (Merritt 1994: 25–6)

A commitment to public journalism, Merritt argues, does not necessarily require a commitment of resources: "A change in culture, in attitude, in purpose carries no direct cost" (quoted in Rosen 1994b: 377).

THE PROBLEMS OF PUBLIC JOURNALISM

Public journalism's enthusiasm for democracy and democratic participation masks important differences between different forms of democracy and by implication different roles for the press. It is never quite clear whether the press is being called on to support "a republican *common* dialogue," to use Baker's (1994: 6) language, "or, alternatively, a diversity of groups each with its own concerns and dialogue." Fraser (1992: 122) raises similar questions (though, like Baker, not with reference to public journalism) when she reminds us that "welfare state mass democracies" of the kind that exist today in the United States and elsewhere operate within "stratified societies" where the "basic institutional framework generates unequal social groups in structural relations of dominance and subordination." Under these conditions, Fraser argues, it makes little sense to assume the existence of "a single, over-arching public sphere."

As public journalism begins to shift its focus from "special projects to sustainable routines" (Rosen 1995b: 2), problems persist with regard to not only the meaning of democratic participation but also what constitutes press reform. New routines, as important as they may be, may not be enough if, as Eliasoph (1988: 315) found in her recent study of a radio newsroom, "economic and organizational factors help determine news content more than the routines."

Public journalism and the quest for public opinion

If public journalism prefers to define itself as a "journalism of conversation," to return to Carey's (1987) framework, its view of public opinion – and certainly its use of public opinion polls – fits comfortably within the tradition of a "journalism of information." Notwithstanding the claim, implied throughout the literature on public journalism, that the quality of public opinion will improve as the quality of the conditions for public discourse improve, assessments of the value or worth of public opinion almost always give way to measurements of its amount.

Measuring public opinion through polls of one kind or another, one of several journalistic conventions from which public journalism seems unable to free itself, tends to reify public opinion in ways which are contrary to public journalism's familiar premise that debate and discussion need to be distinctively *public* and that the press has a special responsibility to secure their "publicness."[4] The use of polls generally weakens the opportunities for truly public discourse in three related ways:

1 They deny the publicness of public opinion by confusing the opinions of individuals with the opinions of publics.
2 They fail to distinguish between informed and rational opinion and mere expressions of preference and prejudice.
3 They obscure the news media's responsibility for setting an agenda for public debate and discussion.

First, by operationally defining public opinion as a compilation of individual opinion, pollsters and their polls in effect disclaim any requirement for individuals to stake a *public* claim for their opinions and the reasons for them. By focusing on the individual and on individual opinion, polls accentuate the "privateness" of opinion and neglect the importance of collective processes of deliberation which are aimed at reaching a publicly accepted consensus: individuals are effectively isolated from the very feature that makes public opinion distinctively public (Salmon and Glasser 1995: 449–50). Moreover, polls themselves, whatever they may be measuring, can foster a sense of alienation and dislocation by "forcing" responses and in a language that may be unfamiliar, inappropriate or even offensive to individual respondents. As Herbst (1993) found in her study of a politically diverse group of Chicago citizens, activists and non-activists alike, polls not only fail to capture public opinion but may well serve to inhibit it:

> Polls are believed to suppress critical thinking, and to dictate the questions a society asks itself as well as the possible range of answers. The people I spoke with seemed to understand just how polling restricts debate on their *own* issues of concern.
>
> (Herbst 1993: 450)

Second, polls produce opinions even in the absence of any sound basis for them. To be sure, polls *seduce* opinion, which is what Pollock (1976) means when he observes that much of what passes for "public opinion" are crude and unsupported stereotypes for which the individual respondent, questioned anonymously, is seldom held accountable:

> The contradiction between the compulsion to have an opinion and the incapacity to form an opinion leads many people to accept stereotypes which relieve them of the thankless task of forming their own opinions and yet enable them to enjoy the prestige of being in touch with things.
>
> (Pollock 1976: 229)

Third, as we have argued elsewhere (Glasser and Craft 1996: 130–2), the use of polls contributes to public journalism's view of public opinion as the source, rather than the consequence, of newsroom agendas. While Rosen expects the press to play a leadership role in the community, others are at best ambivalent about the press's agenda-setting role. Merritt (1995: 80), for example, categorically denies it: public journalism "isn't about newspapers setting a public agenda." Charity (1995: 24), in turn, refers to the *public's* agenda and how the press might "hear" it. No one seems eager to press the issue: Does public opinion exist prior to – and thus independent of – the press, presumably waiting to be discovered by politicians, journalists and their respective pollsters? Or, to take the counterpoised view (and to resort to an unfair dichotomy), does the press bring publics and their opinions into existence by stimulating discussion on issues of common concern? When Rosen (1994c: 15) calls on newspapers to have a "vision of the community as a better place to live," is he asking merely for an answer to an empirical question or for the press to own up to a role which it always plays but seldom acknowledges?

The press and public discourse: dialogue or deliberation?

Because public journalism emerged without a clearly articulated political philosophy, considerable confusion persists about what, precisely, democracy means and what counts as democratic participation. If democracy comes in many forms (Held 1987), public journalism seems unsure about which version it wants to embrace and which democratic norms it therefore wants to endorse. Nowhere is this uncertainty and confusion more apparent than in public journalism's grand but vague commitment to improving the quality of public discourse.

Public discourse means a little of everything in the literature on public journalism. It means creating the conditions for dialogue and discussion among citizens; it thus calls on the press – along with others in the community – to bring citizens together in the form of reading groups, roundtable discussions, salons, and so on. It also means "re-representing" these discussions for the benefit of citizens unable to participate in them; it thus expects the press to report on public gatherings with the same commitment and enthusiasm that it brings to its coverage of, say, city council meetings or sessions of the state legislature. It means, finally, using the press itself as a forum for debate; it thus requires journalists to establish criteria for selecting sources and to find ways to engage them in a serious and civil discussion on the day's issues. In his chapter on public journalism's responsibility for "public judgment," Charity (1995: 101–24) illustrates – and happily promotes – all of these approaches to public discourse.

By defining public discourse broadly and indiscriminately, public journalism evades one of its most important choices: deciding how democracy will work. If it is clear what forms of democracy public journalism rejects – an "administrative" democracy of the kind Walter Lippmann (1965) favored, for example[5] – it is less clear what form(s) it accepts. Indeed, the ideals of dialogue and deliberation point to very different models of democracy and envisage very different roles for the press. Dialogue implies standards of discourse associated with *speech*; it presumes an oral tradition grounded in interpersonal relations. Deliberation, in contrast, denotes a process, which may or may not be dialogic, through which reasoned judgments might be formed. Opportunities for dialogue may be all that is needed to create the conditions for deliberation, but it does not follow, as Thompson (1995) persuasively argues, that opportunities for deliberation require the conditions for dialogue; it is not the case, therefore, that a deliberative democracy begins where a direct, participatory democracy begins, namely with an open and unfettered dialogue:

> it is important to stress that a *deliberative* conception of democracy is not necessarily a dialogic conception. The formation of reasoned judgements does not require individuals to participate in dialogue with others. There are no good grounds for assuming that the process of reading a book or watching a television programme is, by itself, less conducive to deliberation than engaging in face-to-face conversation with others. On the contrary, by providing individuals with forms of knowledge and information to which they would not otherwise have access, mediated quasi-interaction can stimulate deliberation just as much as, if not more than, face-to-face interaction in a shared locale. This is not to say that all forms of mediated communication will, in practice, stimulate deliberation – doubtless that would be untrue. But it is to say that we should free ourselves from the idea that the process of deliberation, and the formation of reasoned judgement, bears a privileged relation to the dialogical form of symbolic exchange.
>
> (Thompson 1995: 256)

Except perhaps in the smallest of communities, and excluding the unproven potential for truly democratic participation in cyberspace, "direct" democracy has been difficult to achieve and even more difficult to sustain over time. The problem is largely, though not entirely, one of scale: Where do we find, or how do we create, democratic associations which are small enough to accommodate full participation among members? How can the press and other agencies of communication facilitate the proliferation of these smaller civil associations and at the same time promote a larger network of regional, state, national, and even international assemblies which work across spatially delimited locales (Held 1995: 237; cf. Barber 1984: 245–51)? Accordingly, the challenge for the press in a direct, participatory democracy rests on journalism's commitment not only to local associations and local dialogue but also to preserving the identity and integrity of these local associations as their discussions feed into successively larger discussions.

A deliberative democracy poses a different set of challenges for the press. While deliberation does not formally require journalists to accommodate an unrestricted dialogue among citizens, it does require that the day's news be written in a way that invites each citizen's considered judgment. At a minimum this means framing topics as issues rather than as events and then soliciting debate and commentary without regard for the speaker's power or privilege in society (Gouldner 1976: 98–9). What is important in a deliberative democracy is not that everyone gets to speak, to paraphrase Alexander Meiklejohn (1965), but that everything worth saying gets said; what needs protection, it follows, is not *individual* expression but the *content* of expression (see Norris 1976; Glasser 1991).

The political economy of public journalism

Public journalism remains conspicuously quiet on questions of press ownership and control. It also steers clear of related issues concerning the apparent contradiction between the interests of advertisers whose products and services appeal to a certain mix of readers and the interests of a press committed to empowering a broad spectrum of readers. These larger concerns may have seemed irrelevant at a time when public journalism presented itself as an occasional project, but they are likely to become important points of contention if, as Rosen hopes, public journalism becomes a bona fide movement "in the classic tradition of public-spirited reform" (Rosen 1995a: 16).

Rosen's confidence in public journalism as a bridge between a newsroom's commitment to public service and a publisher's commitment to profit, a belief now shared by several publishers and at least two newspaper chains, creates a considerable gap between public journalism and the conventional wisdom of press critics who have long complained about the constant and often debilitating tension between the newsroom and the boardroom – the peculiar agony, as one commentator puts it, of a "godless corporation run for profit" and a "community institution operated for the public good" (Bagdikian 1972: 8). While Rosen (1994: 16) acknowledges, for example, the difference between "consumers" of interest to advertisers and "citizens" of interest to public journalism, he and other proponents of public journalism fail to respond to the dilemma that public journalism faces when these interests come in conflict and threaten the presumed "synergy" between what the newsroom wants and what the marketplace demands.

Because most newspapers sell individual copies at a price well below cost and make up the difference – and sustain profits – through revenues generated by advertising, advertisers are ordinarily cast in the role of consumer of consequence. Put a little differently, the principal purchase in journalism, especially journalism on "free" television or radio, is made by advertisers, not readers or viewers or listeners; and what is being purchased is what advertisers want most: a demographically attractive audience. The implications for content are clear: by providing a substantial press *subsidy*, to use Baker's term (1994: 66), advertisers create a strong incentive in the newsroom to shape content to appeal to the "right" audience (Baker 1994: 66; see also Owen 1975; Bagdikian 1994).

Even if a robust public life brings more readers to the newspaper, it is unlikely that advertisers will want to subsidize content for these readers *unless* they are sufficiently affluent and in other ways appropriate for the goods and services being advertised. What advertisers will not subsidize is content aimed at readers unable or unwilling to consume what advertisers want consumed. Indirectly, then, advertisers subsidize a particular *class* of reader, which has implications for a newspaper's circulation as well as its content. In one of the few studies aimed at understanding the relationship between advertising, circulation and content, Blankenburg (1982) documents subtle efforts to skew circulation in favor of readers of interest to advertisers; this in turn justifies the newspaper's focus on – and exclusion of – certain types of content: "circulation policy," Blankenburg explains, "is a form of editorial policy, and withheld circulation is akin to suppressed information" (p. 398). Blankenburg's conclusion anticipates what may become one of public journalism's chief concerns: "The trouble with expelled subscribers, whether they meet marketing standards or not, is that they are citizens" (p. 398).

One way in which public journalism has been able to alleviate pressure from advertisers is to look elsewhere for a subsidy. Several foundations now support, directly or indirectly, public journalism and its projects. But philanthropic support, as welcome as it may be, calls into question the claims of both Rosen and Merritt, cited earlier, about the economics of public journalism. What can be said of a newspaper's commitment to public journalism when, to take but one illustration, the St Paul *Pioneer Press* solicits and receives a $61,000 grant from the Pew Charitable Trusts while its parent company, Knight–Ridder, posts a net income in 1995 in excess of $160 million?

A PUBLIC PURPOSE FOR A PRIVATE PRESS?

Public journalism lacks, by default or perhaps by design, a coherent public philosophy. Despite scores of articles and several books devoted to what it means in principle and in practice, the literature on public journalism offers little in the way of a sustained and systematic account of the role of the press in a democratic society. Virtually no literature exists, moreover, comparing public journalism with other plans to craft a public purpose for the press – models of public service media (cf. Keane 1991), for example, or the tradition of "development" journalism (cf. Shah 1996). Without a clear and compelling framework, separate and distinguishable from other frameworks, public journalism remains conceptually and intellectually dislocated.

Of course, public journalism's dislocation – its disarray as a normative theory of the press – probably accounts for some of its appeal among reporters and for much of its acceptance among newsroom managers. Rosen acted strategically and maybe even prudently in the early days of public journalism when he self-consciously abandoned his "theoretical framework":

> I used to be a media critic, and here's how I worked: I would observe what the press does, filter it through my theoretical framework – essentially, my dissertation – and then write about the results. You can discover a lot that way, but there's a problem. Journalists haven't read your dissertation; they don't have your framework. So whatever you discover is of little interest to them. After all, they have deadlines to meet. . . .
>
> I now employ a different method: I operate almost completely through the medium of conversation. My theoretical framework becomes whatever is needed in order to keep the conversation progressing. Public journalism is something journalists themselves must carry forward. What I think it should be doesn't matter as much as the version of it that I can share with reporters, editors, and news executives around the country.
>
> (Rosen 1995a: 23)

Now, however, Rosen worries about what will become of public journalism as it reaches "a critical point in its evolution":

> It has emerged from the birthing room with enough life to draw the attention of the profession – to get written up in trade journals, to get on the program at conferences, to get funded, to get named. But the period of attention-getting is over. We're on the radar screen and from now on when people turn their attention to public journalism they won't be asking: what's this? They'll be saying: what's there?
>
> (Rosen 1995b: 1)

The issue is not, obviously, whether public journalism can or will achieve a degree of academic respectability. The issue, rather, is whether public journalism will live up to its promise of reform by offering, clearly and convincingly, a truly fundamental "redefinition of journalism" (Merritt 1995: 5).

Public journalism faces any number of obstacles and challenges, but one key test of its resolve will be its relationship to market liberalism. Philanthropic support for public journalism only begs the question, because sooner or later foundations will move on to other projects. Will public journalism stake its future on the benevolence of a handful of publishers? Or, to cast the choice in its starkest terms, can public journalism muster the imagination to invite what Held (1995: 251–2) calls "democratic political intervention," which is to say intervention aimed at ensuring "the conditions for the pursuit of individual or collective projects with minimum risk of intrusion by coercive powers, whether these be economic, political or social?"

Intervention of the kind that Held describes underscores the importance of the distinction – and the difficulty of the choice – between systems of private exchange, focused appropriately on personal preference and individual freedom of choice, and public institutions designed to meet shared needs and common interests. Even in market-driven societies such as the United States, there is still considerable support for protecting libraries, museums, schools and the like from the vagaries of private exchange and the indeterminacy of market economies. What protection, if any, does public journalism need and deserve? Indeed, where along the private–public continuum does public journalism fall? Is it essentially a *private* enterprise which is fashioned ultimately by goodwill and a corporate conscience? Or does it live up to its name as a distinctly *public* endeavor the survival of which depends not on consumer choice but on the community's considered judgment?

NOTES

1 For a summary of the Commission's principal findings, mostly vilified and then ignored by the press, see Commission on Freedom of the Press (1947). For a worthwhile assessment of the Hutchins Commission and its work, see McIntyre (1987).
2 For a semi-autobiographical account of the development of public journalism and the Reston meeting, see Rosen (1994b).
3 For a useful study of the escalating tension between the newsroom and the boardroom, see Underwood (1993).
4 For an interesting exception, see Fishkin's (1991) "deliberative" poll.
5 Held (1987: 143–85) describes this form of democracy as "competitive elitist," a phrase intended to underscore the absence of widespread participation by ordinary citizens. For a useful critique of Lippmann's (1965) view of politics and democracy, see Carey (1995).

REFERENCES

Bagdikian, B. (1972) *The Effete Conspiracy*, New York: Harper & Row.
Bagdikian, B. (1994) *The Media Monopoly* (4th edn), Boston, MA: Beacon Press.
Baker, C. E. (1994) *Advertising and a Democratic Press*, Princeton, NJ: Princeton University Press.
Barber, B. (1984) *Strong Democracy: Participatory Politics for a New Age*, Berkeley, CA: University of California Press.
Blankenburg, W. B. (1982) "Newspaper ownership and control of circulation to increase profits," *Journalism Quarterly* 59 (3): 390–98.
Calhoun, C. (ed.) (1992) *Habermas and the Public Sphere*, Cambridge, MA: MIT Press.
Carey, J. W. (1987) "The press and public discourse," *Center Magazine* 20, March, pp. 4–16.
Carey, J. W. (1989) *Communication as Culture*, Boston, MA: Unwin Hyman. Reprinted in 1992 by Routledge.
Carey, J. W. (1995) "The press, public opinion, and public discourse," in T. L. Glasser and C. S. Salmon (eds.) *Public Opinion and the Communication of Consent*, New York: Guilford.
Charity, A. (1995) *Doing Public Journalism*, New York: Guilford.
Christians , C., Ferré , J. P. and Fackler , P. M. (1993) *Good News: Social Ethics and the Press*, New York: Oxford University Press.
Commission on Freedom of the Press (1947) *A Free and Responsible Press*, Chicago, IL: University of Chicago Press.
Dahlgren, P. and Sparks, C. (eds.) (1991) *Communication and Citizenship: Journalism and the Public Sphere in the New Media Age*, New York: Routledge.
Dewey, J. (1927) *The Public and Its Problems*, Chicago: Swallow Press.
Didion, J. (1988) "Insider baseball," *New York Review of Books*, October 19, pp. 19–21, 24–26, 28–30.

Dionne, E. J., jun. (1991) *Why Americans Hate Politics*, New York: Simon & Schuster.

Eliasoph, N. (1988) "Routines and the making of oppositional news," *Critical Studies in Mass Communication* 5 (4): 313–34.

Entman, R. (1989) *Democracy without Citizens*, New York: Oxford University Press.

Fallows, J. (1996) *Breaking the News: How the Media Undermine American Democracy*, New York: Pantheon.

Fishkin, J. S. (1991) *Democracy and Deliberation: New Directions for Democratic Reform*, New Haven, CT: Yale University Press.

Fraser, N. (1992) "Rethinking the public sphere: a contribution to the critique of actually existing democracy," in C. Calhoun (ed.) *Habermas and the Public Sphere*, Cambridge, MA: MIT Press.

Gitlin, T; (1990) "Blips, bites and savvy talk," *Dissent*, Winter, pp. 18–26.

Glasser, T. L. (1991) "Communication and the cultivation of citizenship," *Communication* 12 (4): 235–48.

Glasser, T. L. and Craft, S. (1996) "Public journalism and the prospects for press accountability," *Journal of Mass Media Ethics* 11 (3): 152–8.

Gouldner, A. W. (1976) *The Dialectic of Ideology and Technology*, New York: Seabury Press.

Habermas, J. (1989) *The Structural Transformation of the Public Sphere* (trans. Thomas Burger), Cambridge, MA: MIT Press.

Held, D. (1987) *Models of Democracy*, Stanford, CA: Stanford University Press.

Held, D. (1995) *Democracy and the Global Order*, Stanford, CA: Stanford University Press.

Herbst, S. (1993) "The meaning of public opinion: citizens' constructions of political reality," *Media, Culture and Society* 15: 437–54.

Jamieson, K. H. (1993) "The subversive effects of a focus on strategy in news coverage of presidential campaigns," in *1–800–President: The Report of the Twentieth Century Fund Task Force on Television and the Campaign of 1992*, New York: Twentieth Century Fund Press.

Keane, J. (1991) *The Media and Democracy*, Cambridge: Polity Press.

Kelly, M. (1996) "Media culpa," *New Yorker*, November 4, pp. 45–9.

Lippmann, W. (1965) *Public Opinion*, New York: Free Press.

McIntyre, J. (1987) "Repositioning a landmark: the Hutchins Commission and freedom of the press," *Critical Studies in Mass Communication* 4 (2): 136–60.

Meiklejohn, A. (1965) *Political Freedom: The Constitutional Power of the People*, New York: Oxford University Press.

Merritt, D. (1994) "Public journalism: what it means, how it works," in J. Rosen and D. Merritt (eds.), *Public Journalism: Theory and Practice*, Dayton, OH: Kettering Foundation.

Merritt, D. (1995) *Public Journalism and Public Life*, Hillsdale, NJ: Lawrence Erlbaum Associates.

Norris, S. E. (1976) "Being free to speak and speaking freely," in T. Honderich (ed.) *Social Ends and Political Means*, London: Routledge & Kegan Paul.

Owen, B. M. (1975) *Economics and Freedom of Expression*, Cambridge, MA: Ballinger.

Peters, J. D. and Cmiel, K. (1991) "Media ethics and the public sphere," *Communication* 12 (3): 197–215.

Pollock, F. (1976) "Empirical research into public opinion," in P. Connerton (ed.) *Critical Sociology*, New York: Penguin.

Putnam, R. D. (1993) *Making Democracy Work: Civic Traditions in Modern Italy*, Princeton, NJ: Princeton University Press.

Putnam, R. D. (1995) "Bowling alone: America's declining social capital," *Journal of Democracy* 6 (1): 65–78.

Remnick, D. (1996) "Scoop," *New Yorker*, January 29, pp. 38–42.

Rosen, J. (1989) "Newspapers' future depends on shaping trends in how people live," *Bulletin of the American Society of Newspaper Editors*, December, pp. 15–19.

Rosen, J. (1991) "Making journalism more public," *Communication* 12 (4): 267–84.

Rosen, J. (1994a) "Getting the connections right: what public journalism might be," paper presented to the *Project on Public Life and the Press*, First Summer Seminar, American Press Institute, Reston, VA, June 13.

Rosen, J. (1994b) "Making things more public: on the political responsibility of the media intellectual," *Critical Studies in Mass Communication* 11 (4): 363–88.

Rosen, J. (1994c) "Public journalism: first principles," in J. Rosen and D. Merritt (eds.) *Public Journalism: Theory and Practice*, Dayton, OH: Kettering Foundation.

Rosen, J. (1995a) "A scholar's perspective," in D. Merritt and J. Rosen (eds.) *Imagining Public Journalism: An Editor and Scholar Reflect on the Birth of an Idea*, Roy H. Howard Public Lecture, Indiana University, Bloomington, IN, April 13.

Rosen, J. (1995b) "Where is public journalism? The search for a new routine," paper presented to the *Project on Public Life and the Press*, Spring seminar, American Press Institute, Reston, VA, March 25.

Salmon, C. S. and Glasser, T. L. (1995) "The politics of polling and the limits of consent," in T. L. Glasser and C. S. Salmon (eds.) *Public Opinion and the Communication of Consent*, New York: Guilford.

Sandel, M. (1996) *Democracy's Discontents: America in Search of a Public Philosophy*, Cambridge, MA: Harvard University Press.

Schudson, M. (1995) *The Power of News*, Cambridge, MA: Harvard University Press.

Shah, H. (1996) "Modernization, marginalization, and emancipation: toward a normative model of journalism and national development," *Communication Theory* 6 (2): 143–66.

Thompson, J. B. (1995) *The Media and Modernity: A Social Theory of the Media*, Stanford, CA: Stanford University Press.

Underwood, D. (1993) *When MBAs Rule the Newsroom*, New York: Columbia University Press.

13 Promoting peace through the news media

Some initial lessons from the Oslo peace process[1]

Gadi Wolfsfeld

Why is there so much research about the role of the news media in political conflict and war and so little concerning the media and peace? Perhaps the role of the news media in peace processes is more subtle, while their importance in protests, terrorism and war is more obvious. Maybe it has something to do with the fact that there is so much more *news* about violence and conflict. Some might go one step further and suggest that there are simply not enough peace processes to study.

There are several studies which deal with related topics. There are studies which are concerned with the media as tools for foreign policy and diplomacy (Cohen 1986, 1987; Fromm *et al.* 1992; Henderson 1973; O'Heffernan, 1993; Serfaty 1991), several which relate to the problems that peace movements face in attempting to mobilize the news media (Glasgow University Media Group 1985; Gitlin 1980; Hackett 1991; Ryan 1991; Small 1987), and a few articles which deal with the role of the news media in disarmament and international cooperation (Bruck 1988; Dorman *et al.* 1988; Gamson and Stuart 1992). Yet, there is not one major study which has looked at the role of the news media in an ongoing peace process.

Even the most casual observer cannot fail to be impressed with the ability of the news media to serve an either constructive or destructive role in the promotion of peace. Just as the news media can serve to rally citizens "round the flag" in times of crisis and war (Hallin and Gitlin 1994), so the press can be an important tool with the onset of peace. The press, I would argue, can either reinforce or deflate images of the enemy, spread optimism or pessimism about the chances for peace, strengthen or weaken the public's willingness to make compromises, and increase or decrease the legitimacy of the ruling government. The goal of research in this area should be to explain how the role of the news media varies over time and circumstance.

The Israeli–Palestinian negotiations in the city of Oslo led, in August 1993, to one of the most important breakthroughs in the history of the Arab–Israeli conflict. Israel recognized the PLO as the legitimate representative of the Palestinian people and agreed to withdraw from Gaza and from Jericho, to set up a Palestinian authority for ruling these areas and to begin negotiations for several additional withdrawals within the West Bank. The PLO agreed to revoke those sections of their covenant that called for the destruction of Israel, to halt all terrorist activities against Israel and to work with Israel to prevent other groups from carrying out terrorist acts.

It was clear from the beginning that this agreement would be controversial. The PLO was considered by most Israelis to be one of their most vicious enemies, and Israel's refusal to negotiate with that organization had enjoyed a large degree of political consensus. While very few Israelis had any regrets about leaving Gaza, many were vehemently opposed to giving back any part of the West Bank. Judea and Samaria (the biblical names for this area) were considered integral parts of the Land of Israel and many Israelis had both military and religious reasons for opposing any territorial concessions. The question of whether to give back the territories in exchange for peace with the Arabs has been the most divisive issue facing the country for almost thirty years.

The news media were seen by the Rabin government as a crucial tool for mobilizing Israeli public opinion in favor of the peace process. Knowing that there would be a great deal of opposition to the agreement, it was essential that the government should succeed in persuading the public that the benefits of the accord far outweighed the dangers. The news media were the major source of information that people had about the process.

This essay is part of a larger research project which looks at the varying role of the news media in the Arab–Israeli peace process (Wolfsfeld 1997a, 1997b). The central source of data for this research comes from sixty in-depth interviews carried out with political leaders, leaders of protest movements, political and media advisors, political reporters and news editors. Leaders and advisors were interviewed from both the government and the opposition. The journalists came from a variety of news media and covered the peace process from a wide range of perspectives. The goal of these interviews was to understand better the ongoing struggle over media frames of the peace process.

I also conducted a content analysis of newspaper coverage which relates to a specific period during the peace process. The relative amounts of positive, negative and mixed stories about the peace process offer a rudimentary indicator of promotional success.

Studying the ongoing transactions between antagonists and journalists has provided some troubling lessons about the ability of leaders to promote peace through the news media. While there are also some more positive indications in this area, the findings suggest that there are at least three major ways in which the news media can serve as an obstacle to peace.

The first way in which the press can serve as an impediment to peace is related to the journalistic preference to focus on events rather than processes. Government policies, especially those that involve significant amounts of change, take a long time to implement. Journalists, however, are not in the business of waiting. They expect to see results immediately. Leaders who attempt to initiate significant amounts of change inevitably run into setbacks and problems. The event-centered orientation of journalists lead them to exaggerate the severity of such problems and to ignore more subtle developments which could, in time, prove more significant.

A second difficulty is that the news media focus on the unusual, the dramatic and the conflictual aspects of politics. Citizens are presented with an extremely pessimistic view of how the process is unfolding. When citizens learn only about the unusual – and usually negative – aspects of a particular subject or place, it is only natural for them to develop images and opinions based on this perspective. This propensity for drama over substance can be especially dangerous regarding news about peace. The need for drama provides important opportunities for extremists on both sides to receive more than their fair share of time and space. The quiet voices of compromise are drowned out by the shrill cries of nationalism.

A third and final problem is that the news media serve as an obstacle to successful negotiations. As every diplomat knows, negotiations can succeed only when they are held in private. Leaders and negotiators must constantly defend themselves against charges of "giving in" to the enemy. Leaks about concessions provide valuable ammunition for opposition forces in their attempts to discredit the government. Concessions, especially costly ones, are seen as failures. Both sides find themselves spending more time engaging in public posturing than in bridging the gaps that divide them.

All of these problems emerged in the Israeli news coverage of the Oslo peace process. While a good deal of the discussion will be devoted to detailing these difficulties, it is also important to place them in perspective by dealing with the other side of the coin. The Rabin and Peres governments also enjoyed important advantages in their attempts to promote peace and it is useful to begin by dealing with this perspective, before turning to more negative aspects of the issue.

THE PRIVILEGES OF POWER

At first glance, one is struck by the enormous advantages that governments should have when they are trying to utilize the news media as a tool for peace. Their high level of political status insures them a significant level of access and a considerable amount of legitimacy. The authorities also enjoy a high level of organization and resources which makes it easier for them to create media events and to employ a relatively large staff of professionals who are responsible for "handling" the press.

The Rabin and Peres governments certainly enjoyed these advantages. Four major offices were responsible for promoting the government's stand on the peace process: the Prime Minister's office, the Foreign Ministry, the Defense Ministry and the Government Press Office. Each of these offices employs full time, experienced staffs who are responsible for ongoing relations with the press. These offices become important sources of information for all of the journalists covering the peace process.

The breakthrough at Oslo was also a "big story" and in the early stages the government had exclusive control over information about what had happened. Journalists were extremely dependent on the government, and the opposition was caught by surprise. This provided leaders with a good deal of power in dictating media coverage. A number of the journalists interviewed complained about the very small circle of people who knew what was really happening. One political reporter, for example, was asked about whether he used any unofficial sources for the story:

> Very few. It's not part of my job definition to bring non-government sources. The situation in the present peace process is that there are very few non-governmental sources that know what's going on. There's no point wasting energy on them.

Rabin and Peres also enjoyed another important advantage in promoting the peace process to the news media: peace is an easy product to sell. Citizens, especially those who have lived through costly wars, yearn for peace and stability. The opposition finds itself in the unenviable position of "opposing" peace and this makes it easier to discredit them. The cultural resonance of peace also has an influence on journalists who generally support government efforts to end conflict. There can be little doubt that the majority of Israeli journalists supported the peace process. While questions of "bias" are impossible to prove, one is struck by the fact that almost every single interviewee agreed on this point. This includes both government sources and the journalists themselves who have an interest in denying such inclinations.

All of this helps to explain the tremendous enthusiasm within the press that marked the first month or so after the breakthrough at Oslo. There was a huge build-up by the media to the first ceremonies in Jerusalem and in Washington and the constant use of superlatives may have convinced some that the Arab–Israeli conflict was over. The dove and olive branch icons were everywhere and the enthusiastic coverage of the grand ceremonies contributed even more to the general sense of euphoria.

This euphoric period became known in many circles as the "peace festival." Government spokespeople all looked back on this period with nostalgia, as a time when the press was a willing partner in the promotion of peace. In the end, however, the sensational coverage may have produced as much damage as benefit. The realities of a peace process can never come close to meeting the expectations that such public celebrations create.

Journalists can remain government sycophants for only limited periods. The excitement ends and journalists move on to other aspects of the story, many of which are much less encouraging. This point can be illustrated by looking at the results of a content analysis carried out during the first eight months of newspaper coverage. This period starts with the initial news of the breakthrough in Oslo (August 27, 1993) and ends with the signing of the agreement in Cairo known as "Oslo A" or "Oslo 1" (May 5, 1994).[2]

The news stories were divided into a total of seventeen subject categories based on headlines. The categories were then classified into those considered "positive" news about the peace process, "negative" news and "mixed" news. The positive news categories included stories about progress in the peace process, negotiations, peace ceremonies (including preparations and the aftermath), economic benefits related to the agreement, non-economic benefits related to the agreement, international support for the agreement, new relations with Gulf states or other Muslim countries, and general optimistic statements in favor of the peace process. The negative news categories were: dangers associated with agreement, terrorism (including aftermath), standstill or difficulties in negotiations, parliamentary opposition to agreement, and extra-parliamentary opposition to agreement. The following categories were considered mixed news: mixed reports on the negotiations, reports about the negotiations with Syria, reports about the negotiations with Jordan, reports on the discussions in the Knesset, stories about how the government was dealing with terrorism, and news related to the Hebron massacre, in which Baruch Goldstein murdered 39 Palestinians.[3] The results are presented in Figure 13.1.

The comparison between the first month and the rest of the period is revealing. Positive news about the peace process went down dramatically, from 43 per cent of the articles to only 17 per cent. Negative news rose from 24 per cent to 36 per cent and mixed news rose from 33 per cent to 47 per cent. While many might find these results surprising, they probably *underestimate* the downturn in coverage. One reason is that the impact of stories and graphic pictures of terrorism is much greater than suggested by a simple count. Second, the mixed news includes stories about the Hebron massacre. This could easily have been coded as negative news about the peace process. However, because such news served to discredit the right wing opposition, it was decided to take the more conservative approach and consider it mixed.

In the long run, then, the Israeli press reported more negative news than positive. That is, after all, the nature of news. Journalists would argue that it was the peace process itself that went sour. Yet the long, difficult negotiations ended in the creation of a Palestinian authority, an unprecedented amount of communication and cooperation between the two peoples, an economic boom for

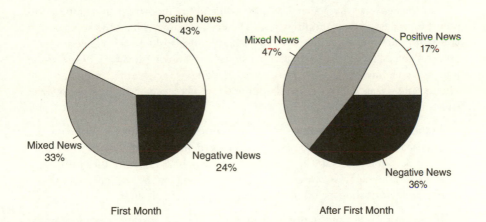

Positive News 43%
Mixed News 47%
Positive News 17%
Mixed News 33%
Negative News 24%
Negative News 36%

First Month   After First Month

Figure 13.1 Positive and negative news about the Palestinian peace process: changes over time
Source: Articles in *Yidiot* and *Ha'aretz* (sample days from August 27, 1993 to May 5, 1994)

the Israeli economy, new economic and diplomatic ties with many Arab and non-Arab states, a peace treaty with Jordan, and the creation of a negotiating framework for achieving a final settlement with the Palestinians. The question therefore, is why was there so much bad news about the peace process?

A FOCUS ON EVENTS RATHER THAN PROCESSES

It is helpful to look at the changing role of the news media in the peace process as a contest between two major antagonists for public attention. The Rabin and Peres governments were attempting to keep the public focused on the opportunities presented by the peace process, while the right wing opposition was seeking to demonstrate the dangers and the risks. Owing to the nature of journalism, a good deal of this competition centered on who could produce the most newsworthy "events."

As noted, the Rabin government initially had the upper hand in the creation of events, especially the signing ceremonies. The rest of the period however was marked mostly by the negotiations with the Palestinians that led to the two agreements (Oslo A and B). Such negotiations provide a perfect example of the difficulty that journalists have in reporting about an ongoing process. From a journalistic perspective, nothing is "happening." The closing of the gap between the two sides is gradual, hard to detect and, where possible, kept secret.

The comments of a central figure in the Israeli Foreign Ministry are helpful in this regard. His contacts with the Israeli and foreign news media extend over many years, and his job has become more difficult. The increasing speed of modern communications, he argued, has led to a gradual decrease in journalists' attention span. Their ability to collect so much information from so many sources makes it more difficult for any antagonist to keep public attention focused in one place.

Another reason why journalists have difficulties reporting on a long term political process is their emphasis on the here and now. The news media were constantly attempting to learn about whether the Oslo peace process was a "success" or a "failure," whether it was "over" or "moving forward." One of the journalists claimed that this short term thinking was part of a more general phenomenon where reporters and editors were increasingly attempting to write short, simple news stories.

> I think some of my colleagues – and this comes from the nature of the media, not because of their personalities – are far too definitive. That is why every time there is a terrorist attack, the peace process is over. And these are very respected people. It is caused, among other things, by the tendency within the media towards short headlines that leads to short conclusions.

Those who expect quick results from such negotiations are inevitably going to be disappointed. The need to provide daily reports about the negotiations serves only to exacerbate this problem: the constant repetition about lack of progress provides increasing evidence of deadlock. Policy makers take a long range view of such talks and understand that such setbacks are an inevitable stage of the process. The frustrations expressed by a television reporter are typical:

> The negotiations with the Palestinians and the Syrians go very, very slowly. Every phase is a story that goes on for long months and they are dealing with the smallest details of the smallest details and it goes on for days and days. It is not like every day they decide to go down from the Golan Heights. Look how little has happened since the Cairo agreement that dealt with "Gaza and Jericho First" till now [July 1995]. You could put all that into a few statements and that's it.

A peace process is not only long but also complicated. Negotiations were going on in a variety of locations and dealt with an enormous number of technical issues. The attempt to transfer authority for the Palestinian population involved long and difficult talks about such issues as taxes, customs, trade agreements, energy, water, industry, legal arrangements and security. None of these negotiations could easily be summarized in a sound bite.

Governments also face another difficulty in competing for public attention during such periods. The need to maintain secrecy makes it difficult for spokes-people to provide reporters with any real information. The political reporters who had been so important during the early stages of the process no longer had anything to report. When one stops feeding journalists, they find somewhere else to eat.

There were three major sources of opposition to the Oslo accords: the right wing and religious political parties in Israel, the extra-parliamentary movements, and the opposition forces among the Palestinians. While governments ordinarily find it much easier to produce events than do groups outside of power, the fierce resistance to the accords served to alter that equation. There were probably more than 100 groups active against the agreement and this provided a multitude of protest events to cover. While it is true that such events are organizationally expensive to produce, the variety of groups tended to distribute the burden and increase their level of novelty.

The most important competitor for public attention, however, was the Hamas movement. About 23 per cent of all of the stories about the peace process during the sample period were related to terrorism. A terrorist attack is not merely an event, it is a major event. The fact that terrorism increased during this period was seen by many as "proof" that the peace process had failed. While the peace ceremonies had been reported by the major newspapers in large blue letters, they were now being replaced by large red ones reporting on each new death. As one of Rabin's advisors put it: "there are simply much fewer blue headlines than red."[4]

The preference for events over processes was probably even more telling in reporting on what was happening within Palestinian society. A remarkably small 6 per cent of all of the articles dealt with what was happening among the Palestinians. The groundwork was being laid during this period for the creation of a semi-state. Hundreds of organizations and institutions were being created, tens of thousands of Palestinians were returning to their homeland, political parties and movements were being formed, and Palestinian society was adapting to the reality of independence and reconciliation with Israel.

Israelis, however, knew almost nothing of this. Of all the Israeli news media, only the newspaper *Ha'aretz* had a reporter living in Gaza. The rest depended on phone calls, short visits to the area, interviews with Palestinian political leaders, and reading the Palestinian press. Even then, of course, their primary concern was what Israel would have to give up and whether there would be more terrorist attacks. None of the major Israeli news media hired any Palestinian journalists or even any Israeli Arabs who might give them some insights into the Palestinian perspective about what was happening.

Yet, Israeli citizens who hoped to make a more intelligent evaluation about the chances for peace would want to know more about the many issues that were either ignored or slighted. They would want to know about the state of the Palestinian economy, about new buildings and industries that were being created, about the extent of support among the Palestinians for their new government and the peace process, about the state of human rights in the Palestinian authority, about the creation of a judicial system, and about the state of health, education and welfare. The majority of Israelis, who received their news from television and from the two more popular newspapers in Israel, would know very little about these subjects. While there can be little doubt that the media frames of Palestinians had improved after the breakthrough at Oslo, the focus on "events" left out an extremely important part of the picture.

THE NEED FOR DRAMA

The pessimistic view of the Oslo peace process can also be related to the well-known preference of the press for drama over substance. The increasingly fierce competition among the Israeli news media has led to an ever more populist format in which visuals, graphics, sensationalism and human interest stories play an increasingly central role in the production of news. Israelis found themselves riding an emotional roller coaster as they went from the grandeur and splendor of the peace ceremonies to the sickening sights of bodies being removed from blown up buses. If one were to judge the public mood solely based on news reports, Israelis were constantly moving between euphoria and despair.

The news media's reactions to terrorism can only be described as hysterical. Special editions of the major newspapers were created to allow the biggest possible headlines and pictures. Television and radio suspended all normal programming to broadcast continual coverage of the carnage, the fears and the grief. One of the most appalling instances was an issue put out by *Yediot Achronot* – the most popular newspaper in Israel – during the bus bombings of March 1996. The large red headline shouted: "A Country in Panic." It was accompanied by an icon of a screaming woman which was then used throughout the issue to flag all of the related news stories.

As noted, the advantage that terrorism stories have over those about peace talks cannot be fully appreciated if one limits oneself to a simple count of time and space. The emotional impact of these horror stories is bound to be far greater than dry reports about the give and take of negotiations. Even if one were to argue that the sensational coverage of the initial peace ceremonies should also be placed in this equation, the graphic stories of terrorism went on far after the last doves had been filmed.

Rabin and his advisors were especially angry about this coverage. One of his closest advisors had spent many years as a working journalist. He was asked about the changes that had occurred in terrorism coverage over the years:

> There's no similarities. When twenty-four soldiers were killed in a truck explosion in the Eilat port after an operation in Egypt . . . there was an ordinary headline in *Yediot Achronot*. Nothing like what we have today. There were two pictures, a list of the dead, and that was it. . . . I wrote once about an explosion in the central bus station in Tel Aviv. It was a story of one page long. People were killed. Today a bomb in the central bus station would be treated like the end of the world.

He went on to talk about the consequences of this type of coverage:

> It leads to anxiety, worry, and extremist views on all sides. Some say we should give back everything and others say kill all the Arabs. It also has an effect on what happens around here [the Prime Minister's office]. Voices get raised, the intensity of the problems goes up, people become agitated, and even here the opinions become more extreme.

The massive amount of terrorism coverage also served to increase the political standing of Hamas. Whereas Hamas was barely mentioned before the Oslo accords, within a short time the movement had become a major player. Here, then, was a second competition for public attention: between the Palestinian authority and the Islamic opposition. Using definitions of newsworthiness, Hamas was at least as powerful as the PLO. Yet, the results of surveys and the subsequent elections in the Palestinian authority demonstrated a relatively small amount of public support for Hamas. Editorial decisions to emphasize the importance of the Islamic opposition could lead many to conclude that the peace process was doomed to failure.

The media's emphasis on drama also gave an important advantage to the more radical voices in Israel. One of the surprising results of the content analysis was that protest movements received much more coverage than the right wing political parties in the Knesset. There were over three times as many articles about the movements as there were about the parliamentary opposition. As one editor put it: "if one group is talking and the other is doing, we're obviously going to cover the one that's doing something."

This tendency also gave a disproportionate amount of attention to the more extremist movements. Moderate groups had trouble competing with movements such as Kach, which favors expelling all Arabs from Israel and the occupied territories. The willingness of Kach to make extremist statements and to carry out more radical actions assured them easy access to the media, while conventional tactics were often ignored. Several protest group leaders admitted that they were under continual pressure to escalate their tactics in order to "make an impact."

One of the most important turning points in this process was the Hebron massacre. The content analysis reveals that Kach received about 13 per cent of all protest coverage before the massacre and 45 per cent after the incident. While none of this coverage could be considered favorable to Kach, it served to increase the public importance of the group.

One could argue that all of this should work to the benefit of the government. It was certainly easier to discredit the opposition when the news media was emphasizing the radical elements among them. On the other hand, an emphasis on the fact that the agreement had led to an increase in violence and terrorism might lead many to conclude that peace was impossible.

Many in Israel were also concerned about the level of internal conflict and violence in the country; some even talked about civil war. Leaders opposed to the peace process often claimed that Israel could only make peace with the Arabs when Israel had peace at home. This problem became especially acute in the summer and fall of 1995, immediately before and after the signing of Oslo B. The level of civil disobedience and violence reached an all time high, and Rabin was increasingly being called a traitor and a murderer at protest rallies. The Prime Minister was assassinated on November 4 of that year.

An intense debate emerged in Israel about whether or not the extensive publicity given to extremist groups might have been one of the factors leading to the murder. Incitement was considered one of the central explanations for the assassination and the press was seen as an important source for the dissemination of such beliefs. A few days after the assassination the Attorney General of Israel sent a stern letter to the Israeli news media warning them that they could be held criminally responsible if they continued to print and broadcast any materials that could be considered a form of incitement. The journalists argued that they should be applauded for exposing the extremists. Perhaps if others had paid as much attention to the "writing on the wall," they argued, the assassination could have been prevented.

It is not possible to come to any firm conclusions about this debate, but it is certainly worthy of further thought and study. The Israeli news media were not the major reason for the violence and the hatred that led to Rabin's assassination. There were many social and political reasons for what occurred. At the very least however, it can be said that the media's preference for drama and conflict was much more likely to inflame the atmosphere than to calm it.

All of these difficulties may be considered part of a general problem which might be called "representative deviance." Journalists are expected to report on the one plane that crashed, not on the hundreds of thousands that had no problems. Similarly, they are not expected to report on the thousands of Israeli–Palestinian joint patrols that proved successful, but rather on the one or two incidents where there were difficulties. But if news about planes is mostly about crashes and news about peace is mostly about failure, citizens are likely to assume that such deviations are the norm. News often generates fear, and such anxieties make it more difficult to get on the plane.

NEGOTIATING WITH THE PRESS

The third and final difficulty is that the media make negotiations more difficult. The experience gained during the Oslo negotiations is very revealing in this regard because there were several different sets of negotiations and the government applied a number of different models each time. The clear lesson that emerged from this system of trial and error is that less media leads to better talks.

The first set of talks between the Palestinians and the Israelis was held in Washington, when Prime Minister Shamir was still in power. These were very formal talks and the news media were always present. One of those who was closely involved in these negotiations describes the problems that emerged.

> The first year and a half of the negotiations the story was completely different. The media was a central concern for the other side, and up to a certain point also for us. Hanan Ashrawi and Bibi Netanyahu [then Assistant Foreign Minister] would have a press conference every day and blame each other, and at the same time nothing that was going on in the negotiating room was being kept out of the media, everything was getting out. But it could be that was part of the birth pangs of the negotiations.

These negotiations continued during the Rabin administration and eventually served as a convenient distraction so that the important negotiations could take place in Oslo.

There can be little doubt that an important reason for the success of the initial Oslo talks was that they were kept secret. These talks were extremely personal and informal, there were no leaks, and no need for public posturing. The Rabin government could present the agreement as a complete package, instead of having to defend each concession.

A comparison of these two sets of talks shows that the influence of the news media on peace negotiations is more complicated than some might think. The fact that negotiators are turning to the media, rather than dealing with each other, may be a *sign* that the talks are failing rather than a cause. The flow of influence, in other words, moves in both directions. The negotiators themselves have a certain amount of control over how much contact they want to have with the press. When the two sides are making progress they are less likely to turn to the news media, especially because they realize the damage such actions can cause.

Both sides must be committed to keeping the press out if it is going to work. This brings us to a second comparison: between the talks that led up to the Cairo agreement (Oslo A) and the talks that led to Oslo B. A person working in the Foreign Office was interviewed immediately after Oslo B had been signed.

> If you use the media too much, you end up simply exchanging declarations between the two sides. Take for example the Cairo agreement from last year

that was very exposed to the media. There were a tremendous number of announcements to the press, every meeting was a formal meeting in which the heads of the delegations made an announcement when they entered and when they left, and then there were leaks and press conferences. A great deal was taking place on the media stage. In hindsight everyone agreed that it wasn't effective. In this agreement, Oslo B, a different approach was adopted, through mutual agreement. Months and months of negotiations and none of the details were revealed, both sides played the game. And again both sides believe it was a much more effective way to work.

The media strategy adopted for the Jordanian talks was also successful. While the press knew about the times and places of the negotiations, they learned virtually nothing about their substance. Here too, however, it is important to remember that successful negotiations often lead to a successful media strategy. The talks with the Jordanians were extremely short, smooth and cordial. The lack of any serious conflicts between the two sides helped to foster cooperation in keeping the media out of the negotiations.

Why is it that the presence of the press makes it so difficult to negotiate? One reason is that the need to speak to the public conflicts with the need to make compromises. Concessions to the enemy are considered signs of weakness and failure, and the opposition is always ready and willing to seize such opportunities. The government is constantly attempting to convince the public that it made a "good" deal, meaning that it received much more than it gave up. Public declarations are often designed to demonstrate that leaders "remain firm," that they are "dedicated to protecting the country's vital interests." When each side is speaking to its own constituency, they have very little to say to each other. One of the Prime Minister's advisors put it this way:

> Any deal is better if you don't have to do it under the spotlight. Because the spotlight means "deadlines." Spotlights mean questions that you are not always eager to answer. Spotlights mean that the two sides will be much tougher about things than they would without those spotlights. It's much easier to do it secretly and quietly.

The escalation in rhetoric will often be magnified by the news media's emphasis on drama and conflict. The most insulting, inflammatory comments usually make the best headlines. Negotiators then waste valuable time in attempting to deny or explain what was quoted, or misquoted.

A second set of problems revolves around the issue of leaks. When governments lose control over the flow of information, it makes it more difficult to manage the negotiating process. Leaks about possible concessions bring about increasing public and private pressure on the government and this decreases its ability to maneuver. It raises the legitimacy of the opposition and lowers the legitimacy of the government.

Such leaks can also serve to undermine the government's bargaining position. One of Rabin's aides talked about this problem.

When people think that we're not doing enough, they leak things to the press. That position then becomes the starting line for negotiations, rather than the finish. Let's say that somebody thinks that we are not being just with the Palestinians. Not being good enough. He knows what we're going to offer Arafat. He can leak that Israel is going to offer Arafat this and that. For Arafat that's not the end of the line, it's the beginning. He says "OK, that's a suggestion, now let's start arguing."

Rabin often liked to tell the story of the first time that he was Prime Minister and was negotiating with Syria about how far to pull back Israeli troops after the Yom Kippur war. He sat with Kissinger all night and convinced him that the most that he could pull back was (say) 800 meters. Kissinger then insisted that Rabin give him a "fall back position" in case he could not get President Assad to agree. Kissinger returned to Damascus and spent many hours negotiating with Assad. Finally Assad turned to him and said: "Listen, I've already read *Ha'aretz* [Israeli elite paper] this morning; why don't you give me his "fall back position?"

The journalists who covered the peace process are quite aware of these problems, but are understandably unwilling to accept responsibility. A reporter's job is to get as much information as possible and to present it to the public. Democracy demands that governments operate openly and be subject to public criticism. In any case it is up to the government itself to maintain secrecy about the negotiations. While it is always easier to blame the press, any government who hopes to develop a successful media strategy must first take control over their own people.

There is, therefore an inherent conflict between the need to keep the pubic informed and the need to make progress in the negotiations. While the normative aspect of this issue is worth considering, it will have little bearing on what happens in the field. Governments will always prefer to keep things secret and the media will always attempt to learn as much as they can. The job of research is to better understand this competition and what happens when one side or the other comes out on top.

CONCLUSION

Many of the problems discussed go beyond questions about the influence of the press on a peace process. Whenever leaders attempt to carry out significant social or political change they are likely to face similar difficulties in dealing with the media. The emphasis on events rather than processes, the media's need to turn politics into melodrama, and the problems associated with operating under spotlights affect everything from welfare reform to significant changes in health policy. While communication scholars have been very adept at uncovering the power that governments have over the news media, very little thought has been given to the other side of the coin.

It would be a mistake, on the other hand, to attribute too much power to the news media in determining the final outcomes of political processes. Political success can usually be translated into media success. If the Rabin government had been more successful in preventing terrorism there would have been much less negative news about the peace process. If the negotiations with the Palestinians had been as cordial and cooperative as those held with the Jordanians, there would have been far fewer complaints about the media interfering.

The influence of the news media on a peace process can be thought of as a sort of wind that can either increase or decrease the time that it takes to reach one's destination. The strength and direction of that wind can be partially explained by the varying state of the political environment. The constant turbulence can also make the trip extremely unpleasant. If one has a sturdy enough plane, however, one rarely has to land simply because of a few gusts.

In May of 1996 Shimon Peres was defeated by Benyamin Netanyahu by less than 1 per cent of the total vote. Not surprisingly, the Oslo peace process was the central issue of the campaign. Peres was accused of conceding too much to the Palestinians and of failing to prevent terrorism. One can only speculate about whether a more sober coverage of the peace process could have convinced that small percentage to continue with Peres. One can only hope that the historical and political forces that have pushed the Israelis and the Palestinians toward reconciliation will prove powerful enough to overcome such obstacles.

NOTES

1 This chapter was first published in *The Harvard International Journal of Press/Politics*, 2:4 (Fall, 1997), pp. 52–70. © 1997 by the President and Fellows of Harvard College and the Massachusetts Institute of Technology.
2 The fifty days were selected at random and the analysis looked at all news articles about the peace process that appeared in the first three pages of two newspapers: *Yediot Achronot* and *Ha'aretz*. *Yediot* was selected because it is, by far, the most popular newspaper in Israel. While *Ha'aretz* has a smaller circulation than *Yediot*, it is considered the paper of choice for the elites in the country. A total of 577 articles were included in the analysis. Editorials and personal columns were excluded.
3 Two separate coders were trained and given a sample of 75 articles to test the reliability of the coding sheet. There was an 87 per cent rate of agreement between the two coders.
4 The longer the peace process went on the more difficult it became to get any blue headlines at all. Rabin and King Hussein held a large number of ceremonies to celebrate the peace treaty with Jordan. The Israeli press, however, soon grew tired of these publicity stunts and devoted less and less coverage to them. The Israeli television stations refused to provide live coverage of one of the last of these ceremonies, although not surprisingly one could watch them on Jordanian television.

REFERENCES

Bruck, P.A. (ed.) (1988) *A Proxy for Knowledge: The News Media as Agents in Arms Control and Verification*, Ottawa: Carleton International Proceedings.
Bruck, P.A. (1989) "Strategies for peace, strategies for news research," *Journal of Communication* 39: 108–29.
Cohen, R. (1986) *Media Diplomacy: The Foreign Office in the Mass Communications Age*, London: F. Cass.
Cohen, R. (1987) *Theatre of Power: The Art of Diplomatic Signalling*, London: Longman.

Dorman, W., Manoff, R. K. and Weeks, J. (1988) *American Press Coverage of US–Soviet Relations, the Soviet Union, Nuclear Weapons, Arms Control, and National Security: A Bibliography*, New York: Center for War, Peace and the News Media.

Fromm, J., Gart, M., Hughes, T. L., Rodman, P. and Tanzer, L. (1992) "The media impact on foreign policy," in H. Smith (ed.) *The Media and the Gulf War*, Washington, DC: Seven Locks Press.

Gamson, W. A. and Stuart, D. (1992) "Media discourse as a symbolic contest: the bomb in political cartoons," *Sociological Forum* 7: 55–86.

Gitlin, T. (1980) *The Whole World is Watching*, Berkeley, CA: University of California Press.

Glasgow University Media Group (1985) *War and Peace News*, Philadelphia, PA: Open University Press.

Hackett, R. (1991) *News and Dissent: The Press and Politics of Peace in Canada*, Norwood, NJ: Ablex.

Hallin, D. C. and Gitlin, T. (1994) "War, popular culture and television," in W. L. Bennett and D. L. Paletz (eds.) *Taken by Storm: The Media, Public Opinion, and US Foreign Policy in the Gulf War*, Chicago, IL: University of Chicago Press.

Henderson, G. (ed.) (1973) *Public Diplomacy and Political Change: Four Case Studies, Okinawa, Peru, Czechoslovakia, Guinea*, New York: Praeger.

O'Heffernan, P. (1993) "Mass media and US foreign policy: a mutual exploitation model of media influence in US foreign policy," in R. J. Spitzer (ed.) *Media and Public Policy*, Westport, CO: Praeger.

Ryan, C. (1991) *Prime Time Activism*, Boston, MA: South End Press.

Serfaty, S. (ed.) (1991) *The Mass Media and Foreign Policy*, NY: St Martin's Press.

Small, M. (1987) "Influencing the decision-makers: the Vietnam experience," *Journal of Peace Research* 24: 185–98.

Wolfsfeld, G. (1997a) *Media and Political Conflict: News from the Middle East*, Cambridge: Cambridge University Press.

Wolfsfeld, G. (1997b) "Fair weather friends: the role of the news media in the Arab–Israeli peace process," *Political Communication* 14: 29–48.

Part IV

Audience research:
past and future

14 Relationships between media and audiences

Prospects for audience reception studies

Sonia Livingstone

THE PROBLEMS AND POSSIBILITIES FOR AUDIENCE RESEARCH

This essay sets out to ask "what next?" for audience research.[1] "Audience reception analysis," "reception studies" or "audience ethnography" emerged and developed, with considerable success, from a convergence of hitherto opposed research traditions during the 1980s (Corner 1991; Livingstone 1998). Audience studies currently face a paradox in which many interesting papers, especially those reporting empirical observations, are being published, while simultaneously there exists a body of criticisms which have largely gone unanswered. This, then, seems an appropriate moment to consider the achievements, problems and future direction of audience reception studies.

In brief, I will argue that the construction of a research "canon" has generated this apparent paradox. The success of the canon has undoubtedly stimulated a range of interesting and innovative empirical studies. Yet it has also provided a legitimacy which permits researchers to bypass the criticisms by providing a template for audience research which does not require any more formalized theorization or research agenda. Thus, the critiques go unanswered partly because the field's failings can neither be set against its aims nor used to develop theory further. Yet by going beyond the canon, audience research can better address the critiques, thereby opening up audience studies to a more diverse set of questions which would move research toward a more explicit theory of audiences and hence toward more productive relations between audience studies and other domains of media and communications.

THE CONVERGENCE OF MULTIPLE RESEARCH TRADITIONS

Audience reception studies focus on the interpretative relation between audience and medium, where this relation is understood within a broadly ethnographic context. It would be inappropriate to identify any unitary origin for reception studies, and even dating their starting point depends on how one identifies the key precedents (Allor 1988; Jensen and Rosengren 1990). I would identify the following six trajectories toward reception studies which converged during the late 1970s as part of a broader movement toward interdisciplinarity in the social sciences. Each of these six routes may be characterized in brief by the advocacy of a central argument or core concept. One of these focused on the processes of producing and reproducing culture. Thus, when noting the beginning of "a new and exciting phase in so-called audience research," Hall (1980: 131) introduced the paired concepts of *encoding* and *decoding* to integrate text and audience studies. Hall welcomed the opportunity for cultural studies to examine empirically how "the degrees of 'understanding' and 'misunderstanding' in the communicative exchange . . . depend on the degrees of symmetry/asymmetry (relations of equivalence) established between the positions of the 'personifications,' encoder/producer and decoder/receiver" (1980: 131).

Simultaneously, researchers in a domain traditionally opposed to cultural studies, that of uses and gratifications, saw the new focus on audience interpretation as setting the scene for them "to build the bridge we have been hoping might arise between gratifications studies and cultural studies" (Katz 1979: 75). The rationale here was to account for the selective responses of audiences in the face of media excess, with the key concept being the *active audience*. Thus these researchers wanted to open up a broader conception of what audiences might do with texts, in order to allow for the ritual uses of communications as well as the transmission of media contents from producers to audiences (Carey 1975; Dayan and Katz 1992; see also Carey and Dayan, this volume).

A third route to reception studies drew upon moves within critical mass communications research to shift attention away from an exclusive focus on the ideological and institutional determinants of media texts toward including a role for a possibly active, but hitherto "disappearing," audience (Fejes 1984). This resulted in a focus on the *resistant audience*, as part of the questioning of such hegemonic theories as the dominant ideology thesis (Abercrombie *et al.* 1980), the cultural imperialism thesis (see Hallin, this volume) and the political economy approach (Murdock 1989). Some of the strongest and most contested claims for the autonomy of the active audience have been made in rebutting theories of media or cultural hegemony.

A fourth route depended on a broader dismantling of the then dominant structuralist approach to textual analysis (the "Screen Theory" tradition) as part of the move toward post-structuralism. This occurred both through the Birmingham School's approach to cultural studies and through the influence of German reception-aesthetics (e.g. Iser 1980) and American reader-response theory (Suleiman and Crosman 1980). Eco's (1979) theory of *the role of the reader* was crucial to the theorization of an integrated approach to text and reader. He proposed the "model reader" as an implicit set of assumptions detectable within the structure of a text which rendered the meaning of the text fundamentally open or unstable, depending on the actual interpretative contribution of "real readers." With this conception of the text and reader as mutually defining, literary or high culture theories were applied to the study of popular culture, asking specifically about the relation between model and actual audiences (Allen 1985; Seiter *et al.* 1989; Livingstone 1998).

Fifth, feminist approaches to popular culture allowed for the reconsideration of the often vilified (i.e. feminized) role of the popular culture audience within cultural theory. This challenged the mapping of good and bad, "masculine" and "feminine" genres (e.g. news versus soap opera) and cognitive and emotional responses onto high and low culture, and offered instead an alternative set of valuations which mapped primarily onto active and passive audiences, critical and normative readings and open and closed texts (Ang 1985; Radway 1984; Drotner 1992). The emphasis on the *marginalized audience*, then, provided a focus for arguments about re-evaluating or giving voice to those hitherto invisible to normative theory.

While the convergence of these five positions provided the major impetus behind reception studies during the 1980s, the recent "ethnographic turn," which shifts the focus away from the moment of textual interpretation and toward the contextualization of that moment, draws into the frame a sixth tradition. This involves the detailed analysis of the *culture of the everyday*, stressing the importance of "thick description" as providing a grounding for theory, together with an analysis of the ritual aspects of culture and communication (Carey 1975) and the practices by which meanings are re/produced in daily life (de Certeau 1984).

THE ACHIEVEMENTS OF AUDIENCE RECEPTION STUDIES

We are now in a position to assess the flurry of research activity which followed this convergence of traditions from the late 1970s through to the mid 1990s. For a time this seemed some of the most exciting and most interdisciplinary work in media and communications research, and, at a number of international conferences, reception studies were what people talked about. The excitement derived not only from the simultaneous convergence on (apparently) common arguments by very different theoretical traditions but also from the sense that such convergence might open the way to transcending the metatheoretical, epistemological and political differences on which these traditions rest. In other words, audience reception research provided a moment for cultural and media scholars to reconsider the enduring questions of the field – the relation between humanities and social scientific approaches, between macro and micro theories, between administrative and critical communications, and so forth (Jensen and Rosengren 1990; Carey 1975; Hall 1989; Livingstone 1998).

To open up a debate is easier than to resolve it, and disagreement remains over whether the hopes for a broader theoretical convergence across diverse traditions in media research has been as successful as the body of empirical audience reception studies that was generated in the attempt (Curran 1990). It is not even clear whether such convergence is possible or desirable at all (Ang 1990a; Grossberg 1994), but this is a longer debate than I have space to consider here. However, the body of empirical studies on audience reception has been influential, stimulating and informative. We may fairly conclude that the original agenda for audience research has been successful, although the arguments motivating this agenda need to be kept alive in case of a backlash against audience research. Such successes may be measured both intellectually and pragmatically.

Intellectually, all six traditions identified above have benefited significantly from their engagement with a convergent approach to audience reception studies, resulting in the generation of new and productive lines of research. While production, text and context analyses have frequently made implicit assumptions about the audience, only recently has it been realized that audiences may not fit these assumptions and that validity of many media theories depends on empirical audience research currently being or yet to be conducted. Thus, most importantly, reception studies have made *visible* an audience which has hitherto been devalued, marginalized and presumed about in policy and theory. As Allor (1988) comments, whichever social theory we draw upon, the concept of the audience represents a theoretical pivot around which oscillate key debates concerning individual and society, agency and structure, voluntarism and determinism.

In addition to this metatheoretical claim concerning the importance of investigating audiences empirically, reception studies have advanced media theory through a series of arguments which contrast sharply with previous approaches. Thus, media and communications research has moved on, irreversibly, from the assumption that media texts have fixed and given meanings to be identified by elite analysts, that media influence works through the linear transmission of meaning to a passive audience, that audiences are a homogenous, uncritical mass, or that high culture differs qualitatively in obvious and uncontentious ways from popular culture. Rather, it is established that audiences are plural in their decodings, that their cultural context matters, and that they often disagree with textual analyses. Researchers are sensitized to the ways in which the haphazard and contingent details of people's daily lives provide the context within which media are engaged with and responded to, and, moreover, to the argument that neglecting the "culture of everyday life" or the "politics of the living room" results in a gender bias which misrepresents the conditions of women's lives. Key earlier traditions are being rethought, particularly those of the problematic effects tradition (given the recognition of the active processes of text interpretation by audiences), and uses and gratifications theory (given the task of reconstructing a more social conception of audience "need" or pleasure). The supposed activity and resistance of the audience is widely cited as refuting theories of media hegemony or dominant ideology (Abercrombie *et al.* 1980; Hall 1989), and further critical empirical work on audiences is urged by social theorists (Thompson 1990).

Pragmatically, this new visibility of the audience has implications for diverse aspects of media research. Researchers working in a number of fields of media and cultural studies have now to include audience studies within their scope. Research proposals to examine media production or texts are increasingly likely to include an audience study. Reviewers for scholarly journals feel justified in questioning the validity of text or production studies which do not include the likely or actual role of the audience. The increased prominence of audience studies within media studies textbooks testifies to the established status of audience research. To take one recent example, in *Approaches to Media: A reader*, Boyd-Barrett (1995: 498) suggests that, "if obliged to define a single distinguishing feature of media study over the past fifteen years many scholars would focus on new approaches to audience or 'reception' analysis."

Yet, having established its success, and so secured a place in the textbooks (Corner 1995; Curran *et al.* 1996; Moores 1993; Morley 1992; Silverstone 1994), this new research field offers rather little idea of where to go next beyond generating more of the same. Certainly more empirical research on audiences is needed, but not without a clearer analytic framework to justify it than has yet been developed. I suggest that an agenda is partly lacking because much audience research was developed as a valuable polemic to reorient a problematic field. In other words, it looked backwards – to argue against, and define itself against, the various previously popular positions identified above – rather than forwards in its ambitions. Such a critical position was particularly adopted by cultural studies approaches to audiences, but also holds for uses and gratifications and effects research. However, such polemic forms of the argument may now become reified and unqualified, providing legitimation rather than justification for proceeding further.

THE CONSTRUCTION OF A RESEARCH CANON

Whether audience research is assessed intellectually or in terms of research practice, a related question arises. Intellectually, we may ask whether the six traditions hold together: are they sufficiently convergent in their approach to audiences that they can generate an emergent phenomenon, which we may term "audience theory," which contributes to media and communications research over and above the contributions of the diverse traditions that feed into it? More pragmatically, we may ask where such audience research is taking us and why, if it is so confident of its successes, has it been neglectful in rebutting its critics? While welcoming the fact that researchers have decided to include audiences where previously they were ignored, I suspect that such research is often envisaged with little idea of what might result, how it might be useful, or even, how to do it. What questions are being asked of focus group discussions or ethnographic interviews, and how exactly is audience research to be interfaced with other kinds of research?

I would identify the particular form of success, namely the construction of a research canon, as itself now posing a central problem for audience studies. By canon, I mean a small set of often-repeated examples of audience studies which are used both to justify the research enterprise – in which they have so far been successful – and, implicitly or explicitly, to direct it; this is more problematic in the absence of a clear set of guiding questions or arguments. It is probably not coincidental that some of the excitement has now worn off from empirical audience reception studies just as their success has resulted in entering the textbooks (Boyd-Barrett and Newbold 1995; Curran and Gurevitch 1991; Curran *et al.* 1996; Downing *et al.* 1990; McQuail 1994; Nightingale 1996; Price 1993). As a secondary-source or canonical account of the field emerges, a narrative is constructed which, as is typical of narratives, tells a story of progress toward enlightenment and does so via the construction of heroes and villains.

To simplify just a little, it would seem that while once upon a time audiences were studied by reductionist, quantitative positivists, this is no longer true, and that media and cultural studies now have their own exciting account of audiences (see, for example, the early chapters of Morley 1980, and Allen 1985), although Curran (1990) offers an alternative, revisionist, account. Such a narrativization of the field, while rhetorically powerful in raising the visibility of a research domain, is also proving restrictive for audience researchers, because the clash of diverse positions is being replaced by an institutionalized orthodoxy which frames and contains the new audience studies. The canon allows researchers to reproduce a successful research strategy without necessarily engaging with either the intellectual origins of the canon or the debates with, alternatives to or criticisms of the canon.

In addition to the problems of a canon *per se*, there are also the problems inherent in the construction of one particular canon over another. The research canon which has emerged in audience studies most typically centers on Morley's *Nationwide Audience* study (1980), Radway's *Reading the Romance* (1984) and Ang's *Watching "Dallas"* (1985), with some variants (see, for example, Lewis's (1991) discussion of "the new audience research," Silverstone's (1994) review of "recent audience research," Corner's (1991) overview of "new audience studies," and Boyd-Barratt and Newbold's (1995) and Nightingale's (1996) exemplar case studies). While this familiar litany of studies is undoubtedly important and influential and has played a vital role in the field's "successes" identified above, it is also parochial, not definitive, and so underplays the value of the actual diversity of audience reception studies currently being conducted.[2]

In addition to the identification of heroes and villains (the latter including that stereotyped outgroup of straw people – the hypodermic effects theorist, the social psychologist, the manipulative broadcaster, the elitist text analyst), the construction of a standard narrative inclines to tell, retrospectively, a linear intellectual history which tends to underplay certain theoretical influences. It is the route to audience reception via ideology critique (and as a rejection of the effects and uses and gratifications approaches) that is now most prominently retold, with the "new audience research" seen as stemming from the work of the Birmingham School and especially from the important, but not all important, encoding/decoding paper (see, for example, the accounts in Moores 1993, Price 1993, and Abercrombie 1996; see also the argument for "decentering Birmingham" in Wright 1996). Yet literary theory also, particularly through the reception-aesthetics of European scholars, provided an important theoretical input during the 1970s and 1980s. If this is neglected, the textuality of media products is more easily underestimated and the value of literary-type analyses as a complement to the more frequent discursive ones may be forgotten. Similarly, the feminist origins of audience research are being written out, with the danger that feminist audience studies become ghettoized rather than fully integrated with other approaches (Drotner 1992). Yet, for a number of researchers, it was the confrontation between feminist theory and "real" women that provided the primary focus, hence their concern with the soap opera and romance (Ang 1985; Hobson 1982; Radway 1984).

A single narrative makes it difficult to attend to the intellectual relations among feminism, reception theory and ideology theories, which remain in need of further elaboration. For example, audience research faces significant issues concerning the relations between marginal and dominant groups, between textual structures and audience understandings, between local knowledge and ideological processes, for all of which a diversity of theory is essential. While the limitations of the effects tradition provided another motivation for reception studies, how media research should now reframe the question of effects still requires attention (Livingstone 1996). It also seems that uses and gratifications research is proceeding separately from the reception tradition with which it had seemed momentarily to converge; the significance of psychological motivations for engaging with media remains neglected by culturalist approaches in comparison with their treatment of sociocultural factors. As the strength and excitement of the argument for theoretical convergence lay in its emphasis on the confrontation of multiple positions, rather than the avoidance or smoothing over of theoretical difference, the reduction of these through a canonical retelling of the field's history will neglect the richness from which new vitality can grow.

TOWARD A THEORY OF THE AUDIENCE

Both the canonization of and growing doubts concerning audience reception research may be explained by the observation that, for cultural studies particularly, audience reception served merely as a convenient arena within which to play out a series of critical theoretical problems regarding the relations among texts, ideology and social determinations, and so once these were resolved (or not), the field could be left alone once more. This may not be unproblematic for cultural studies either. As Press (1996: 2) notes, "we in cultural audience studies are at a crossroads . . . we are quickly reaching the limits of what have over the last twenty years become our comfortable and customary preoccupations." The interdisciplinary convergence which proved so productive for audience research has, Press suggests, proved problematic for cultural studies by detracting from the clear focus in which "audience" was a metaphor for critical, political actors; by implication, "audience" was never intended to be as all-encompassing as it subsequently became. Moreover, while cultural studies was mainly concerned with one of the research paths leading to reception studies, in making this popular it contributed to the neglect of other paths. Cultural studies neither set an agenda for audience reception studies nor addressed the critiques leveled at it, and nor did it set out to do so. Rather, the point of empirical research was to establish the possibility of a diversity of readings: this showed both how elite and popular readings differed, and how the divergences among audiences themselves could be located in terms of contextual categories in order to address arguments about hegemonic position and the possibilities of resistance.

Of course, differences were found: one of the costs of adopting an empirical approach is that, unlike the ideal theorizing of implied readers, empirical observations are always subject to variation. Unless interviewees are expected to speak in identical voices, observable differences are inevitable. The problem for audience research is to determine their significance – which differences reflect idiosyncratic factors and which merit explanation? Many of the key theoretical issues facing audience research concern the scale of these differences; for example, are audiences increasingly fragmented or homogeneous, are readings primarily normative or resistant, how far do actual viewing practices (e.g. zipping and zapping) undermine the textual and generic structuring of readings? Clearly it becomes important to relocate these findings of difference within a broader theoretical context.

Cobley (1994: 685) suggests that we need "a critical recapitulation of audience theory," while Jensen and Rosengren (1990) question the expectations of "theory" as well as of "audience." Questions about audience theory may be grouped into two categories. The first asks *how* to do audience research, or how it can be improved, to ensure that it adds up to something, whether or not we term this "audience theory." The second asks *why* we need a theory of audiences or, to put it differently, what a theory of audiences will contribute to research in media and communications more generally. My approach in the remainder of this essay will be to make a start on the former category of questions, with the aim that if we address the criticisms leveled at current audience research, a more formal account of the assumptions, findings and contribution of this research should result. Building on the existing strengths of audience research should also be productive for the broader field of media and communications, by generating an agenda which answers the "why" question as well as the "how." In other words, we need a theory which offers an agenda which in turn not only directs audience research but also ensures that the outcome of such research will serve to connect audience research with production/texts/context research as firmly as actual audiences are inevitably interrelated with actual production/texts/contexts (Livingstone, in press). Arguably, an agenda would not be needed if a productive diversity of research were evident. An agenda may seem too programmatic, even autocratic. Yet, while the diversity of research is potentially productive, the growing uncertainty over the aims of audience reception research suggests that a *laissez-faire* approach is no longer constructive.

A new research domain with high visibility inevitably, and rightly, attracts critical commentary. I have already suggested that the strength of support for the canon has resulted in relatively little attention being given to resolving the accumulating body of critique. Yet the active audience, negotiation of meaning, oppositional subcultures, resistance, even the notion of audience itself have all become subject to critique (Ang 1989; Schiller 1992; Seaman 1992; Seiter *et al.* 1989; Livingstone 1998). The nature of the criticisms can, however, be regarded constructively as pointing up the key claims and concerns of audience reception studies so that a response to critics is simultaneously a development of audience theory. We can summarize the kinds of critique levelled at reception studies as broadly concerning the following:

1 The claim for and limits of audience activity.
2 The power of texts to determine readings.
3 The problem of contextualization (or the tendency towards media-centerism).
4 Whether diversity in readings makes a "real" difference.
5 The validity of the concept of audience itself.
6 The relation between micro and macro levels of media theory.
7 Audience research methods and the politics of research.

Clearly these concerns encompass the core elements of audience theory.

BALANCING TEXTS AND READERS IN MUTUAL INTERACTION

One significant critique of the field has questioned the extent to which audiences are free to interpret texts in different ways. Where once the audience was thought in danger of disappearing (Fejes 1984), it is now the text which is in danger. Hence, Blumler *et al.* (1985) are concerned with excessive or "vulgar gratificationism," Fiske (1989) coined the much-attacked phrase of "semiotic democracy," Corner (1995) suggests that in much "active audience" research, the text tends to get lost altogether, and Ang (1994) questions the focus on divergences in interpretation in relation to the exclusion of observed commonalities.

In contradiction with this, there is also concern that the interactive emphasis of the text–reader metaphor tends to collapse back into a claim for textual determination, reducing back to a transmission model of communication (Carey 1975). The debate over the concepts of preferred and aberrant readings (Allor 1988; Ang 1994; Lewis 1991) provides a focus for this conceptual struggle, with Hall (1994) retaining a claim for a significant measure of textual determination against Lewis's suggestion that the preferred reading is simply what the majority of the audience supposes it to be.

Clearly the concept of the preferred reading was misnamed, being neither the audience's reading nor necessarily preferred by them. None the less the concept itself cannot be discarded without losing the interactionist focus on audiences *in relation to* texts (and to the motivations behind texts). Concepts such as the implied reader or model reader – the idealized concept of the reader as structured into the text, which encourages and legitimates certain actual readings over others – may be preferable. It is sometimes suggested that, as preferred readings or model readers can be identified only via analysis of actual audience responses, such concepts should be dropped in favor of reception analysis alone. But this is unconvincing, because such arguments tend not to be made either in relation to the interpretation of audience responses as texts themselves or to eliminate the conduct of textual analyses in domains other than audience analysis. If we can analyze texts and audiences, we can analyze the relation between them. As suggested earlier, Eco's (1979) attempt to specify in detail the mutual assumptions that link encoding and decoding is more helpful in this respect than the sketchy encoding/decoding model itself.

The contradiction between the first two critiques suggests that the balance between text and audience, while problematic, must remain central to audience theory. Why should such apparently simple balances and contextualizations prove difficult for audience reception and ethnographic research? I suggest that the establishment of a research canon tends to undermine the complexity that is central to the vitality of a field. We need to move beyond the canon to recognize, and to develop further, the *variety* of work that has been and will be conducted by audience researchers. Such variety is needed to remedy the present position of incomplete and unsystematic investigation. For example, why is there little or no research on male soap viewers, despite the popularity of arguments about gendered viewing of this genre? Why has there been an overly narrow focus on subsets of genres (soaps and news) when surely a survey of less well known work on other genres (e.g. sitcoms, game shows, access programs) would produce a richer understanding of the diversity or otherwise of viewers' engagement with broadcast media? Why is there so much on adult viewers but so little on children? Or on fans but not on the boredom of viewing? Or on television but not on other media? I could go on.

The question of audience freedoms (or social rather than textual determinations) can only be addressed through a greater diversity of research findings, and a greater cross-referencing of research findings, in order to come at the text–reader interface in systematically varied ways. However, further variety is unproductive unless research is also more integrative in orientation, addressing rather than underplaying the inconsistencies, trends and contradictions across research studies. For example, despite the sizeable body of work on the decoding of news (Cumberbatch *et al.* 1986; Gamson 1992; Graber 1988; Jordin and Brunt 1988; Lewis 1991; Morley 1980; Philo 1993), there has been little attempt to integrate these, address empirical contradictions, identify unfinished leads, and so forth. This is partly because findings are often cited illustratively rather than to ground theory, and each study appears to start again from the beginning. Yet there exist in the research literature many studies whose findings would be more useful if interpreted within a more integrated framework.

FROM CONTEXTUALIZATION TO COMPARATIVE ANALYSIS

Thus, the project of audience research depends on detailed empirical answers (the when and where and under what circumstances), perhaps with the guidance of a "cultural map" (Morley 1992: 118). Only then can it move beyond arguing over or, worse still, discovering whether audiences are sometimes active and at other times passive or whether they sometimes share experiences and at other times split into subgroups. However, by arguing for greater specificity, I do not mean simply greater contextualization, especially when this is seen not as resolving specific questions but as providing a blanket answer. Of course, the audience's engagement with media is complexly context-dependent.

Moreover, the methodological commitment to ethnographic approaches has proved invaluable to audience studies, because the particular determinants of the complex and situated process of meaning construction cannot be predicted a priori (and hence built into a research design), and consensual or divergent audience readings are often made accountable only when the researcher shares the location of the researched and so can identify the determinants at work.

However, recognizing the embeddedness of viewing practices in everyday life results in local contexts of text–reader interaction becoming highly salient. As audience research moves further into the analysis of local, particular contexts, shifting away from specifically media analysis into the general analysis of culture, consumption and everyday life, a new focus on consumption tends to take the place of reception.[3] Ironically the very advantage of reception studies – the interactive link between text, audience and context – is lost as a consequence of their success. Our questions become everyone else's questions, and our conclusions are inconclusive. Analyzing "the whole way of life" (Willis 1990) may be too grand an ambition for audience research, and placing the primary focus on context is inappropriate because audience research requires a contextualized account of something specific – the relation between people and media. While I do not mean to advocate the kind of media centerism which presumptuously overstates the importance of the media in everyday life, it does seem important to legitimate a space within which some researchers can ask media-centered questions as part of a broader multidisciplinary intellectual endeavor concerned with culture, social change and communicative relations. Such media-centered research may or may not find for the importance of the media in everyday life, although their complete irrelevance is unlikely. But it should offer a clearer analysis of the nature and scope of that importance by exploring how audience research links with the analysis of other social and cultural agencies and institutions (work, politics, family, education, etc.).

There are, then, dangers associated with advocating increased specificity of research studies, since audience research is already losing the wood for the trees. Nor is it clear that a "cultural map" would help us through the wood. As cultural geographers argue, a map is a cultural construct, created to benefit certain groups with certain interests. It is precisely this question of interests which is unclear. Rather, I suggest that the use of comparative analysis, rather than the accumulation of diverse detail, would provide a viable strategy. When arguing for cross-national comparative studies, Blumler *et al.* (1992: 3) claim that "only comparative research can overcome space- and time-bound limitations on the generalizability of our theories, assumptions, and propositions." "Overcoming" may be too strong and not even desirable, but an awareness of these limitations is necessary. Comparative studies of audience subgroupings, media genres, historical periods, and so forth would tighten up speculations and focus research. Pragmatically, a comparative focus draws on a greater variety of empirical research than has been in focus hitherto, and, though much of this already exists (see the example of television news research above), the rather restrictive canon has obscured this.

More importantly, it is the case that in principle all research is comparative, whether or not this is acknowledged explicitly. To offer an analysis is to make a series of claims about how what is found differs from (or resembles) what might have been expected for other times, places, genres or social groups. When such claims remain implicit, it is impossible to check them out or to discover their scope. For example, is it appropriate to assume that Radway's (1984) analysis of American women romance readers holds for women everywhere, or that Schlesinger *et al.*'s (1992) analysis of women viewing violence is not also applicable to men, or that Morley's (1980) analysis of the response to current affairs (in terms of trade union participation, traditional labor market positions, etc.) is as relevant to the post-Thatcher period as to the pre-Thatcher one? Claims to generality or specificity may not be made by the original authors, but they emerge none the less as these works are taken up by others to exemplify the resistant, or diverse, or unexpected nature of audience reception.

Comparative analysis of audience reception can be organized according to two linked categories, following the emphasis on the dynamic relation between audiences and media texts. First, audience interpretation is structured by textual factors. A variety of concepts may be used to understand this, whether textual openness/closure, preferred readings, generic conventions, naturalizing discourses, or subject positioning. Second, audience interpretation is structured by (psycho)social factors. These too may be variously understood as, for example, sociodemographic position, cultural capital, interpretive community, contextual discourses, sociocognitive resources, national identity, even psychodynamic forces. However these two facets of the text–reader relation are conceptualized, both textual and social determinations must also be understood in relation to textual and social spaces for openness, contradiction, agency, polysemy, ambiguity, and so forth. It is only from understanding this relation that we can understand the importance of social change, resistance and individuality, in the production and reproduction of meanings in everyday life. Clearly, this dualism reflects the broader structure–agency problem (cf. Moores' use of Giddens' structuration theory, 1993; see also Thompson 1994). Do social formations determine diverse readings or do such readings represent evidence of agency and the escape from determination (Ang 1994; Silverstone 1994)? It is inappropriate to argue simply that texts represent structured constraints while audiences find spaces within these to exercise agency, because this leads us down the path of hegemonic forces trying to manipulate free individuals. Rather both text and reader must be understood in terms of structural and agentic factors.

These comparative categories have, with a few exceptions, been regarded as contributing to an analysis of the contemporary. The textual or social determinants operating in the present are assumed to have a wider applicability than a historical or temporally sensitive perspective would support.[4] Research findings do not necessarily hold true across time, nor do they simplistically mark a break between now and "how things used to be." New media, and new forms and flows of information, raise new questions about the fragmentation of the hitherto mass audience, globalization of the hitherto national audience, interactivity for the hitherto passive audience, and so forth. But if we assume that a few canonical studies encapsulate the field, we divorce rather than locate research in its time and place, collapsing across differences rather than treating them as informative. In short, the comparative perspective should be extended to include a historical dimension to audience research.

SO WHAT? RETHINKING THE AUDIENCE

The significance of diverse interpretations has been much questioned in audience studies. This "so what?" question has mainly been raised in relation to the putative link between active audiences and political or ideological processes, since activity has tended to be understood as opposition, subversion or resistance. As has been variously pointed out (Gitlin 1990; Morgenstern 1992; Schiller 1992; Seaman 1992), one cannot claim that any kind of interpretative activity involves resistance, opposition or subversion, without having a clear test of whether a divergent reading is subversive or normative, of whether it originates primarily in the text or from the viewer, and without having shown how such supposed resistant decodings actually do make a difference politically.

This question of putative micropolitical impacts highlights the importance of adequately contextualizing the text–reader balance within a theory of social action, political participation and identity politics. Here audience research inter-faces – potentially at least – with other domains of social theory (Murdock 1989), requiring not only comparative analysis but also the integration of micro and macro level theory (Alexander *et al.* 1987). For example, an audience researcher may investigate the participation of listeners in a talk radio show in which the laity are constructed as the public. But it requires a comparison with face-to-face talk (i.e. lay talk in private), and with traditional media debate (i.e. expert talk in public) in order to understand fully the significance of radio talk. Moreover, such analysis needs a more macro framework which draws on theories of the public sphere and of political communication in order to consider how such shows relate to the democratic process (cf. Livingstone and Lunt 1994).

The "so what?" question (or, why do audience research?) has been addressed via a traditional and often implicit mapping of the audience onto the micro and the politically or culturally important onto the macro.[5] Consequently, to justify audience studies, researchers find themselves in the position of needing to show how the micro-level processes of audience reception are of importance for macro-level societal and cultural processes. This argument for the effect of micro on macro – for want of better terms – has been strongly advocated both by social psychologists (as part of the social constructionist position) and by cultural studies (via concepts of resistance and subversive reappropriation). As a result, researchers find themselves under pressure to produce findings which are startling to macro-level theorists (together with hard evidence for simplistically conceived causal links). Unfortunately it may not be – or at least has not in practice been – always the case that if we "actually looked at the audience," we would "be surprised" (indeed, the absence of surprises should also be an interesting finding).

In other words, a broader framework for audience research must extend beyond the issue of the politics of representation, of making visible and validating marginalized and resistant voices. While this has undoubtedly been an important motivation for critically oriented audience researchers, it cannot carry the whole weight of audience research (Livingstone, in press).

The implications of the active audience are further complicated by the apparent confusion between two positions, the *in principle* argument that audiences' constructive and interpretative practices represent a vital link in the societal circulation and reproduction of meanings and the *empirical* argument that audiences are in practice unpredictable, diverse or resistant. The first position argues that micro and macro levels of analysis (or, the micro-level lifeworld and the macro-level system, to use Habermas's terms) require an integrated theory of mediated communication. The second position argues that the empirical identification of resistance in decoding significantly challenges that analysis of power which maps power/ideology and powerlessness onto encoding and decoding respectively.[6] The empirical case for this may be weaker than the claim merits, yet a reversal of the mapping (i.e. simply attributing more power to the audience) is equally untenable.

Emphasizing the interaction between text and reader, combined with an integration of micro and macro levels of analysis, offers a response to the attack on the concept of the audience. In brief, this attack is critical of the tendency to adopt the broadcasters' concept of audience (i.e. that used for organizing, controlling and profiting from people in everyday contexts; Ang 1990b) and/or to adopt an overly homogeneous concept of the audience which stimulates artificial questions stemming from a reified object of inquiry (Allor 1988). While the charge of collusion with exploitative elites is too extreme, there is reasonable doubt over whether it is appropriate to conceptualize people first in their relation to the media (i.e. as an audience) and only then to formulate the research questions about their relation to the other ways in which people may be conceptualized – as a market, a public, consumers, a nation, a community. Yet each of these terms, when considered as an alternative to the audience, seems similarly problematic, because each term accesses different debates (about the economy, democracy, desire, identity, etc.). As an aside, I would suggest that if Ang's book had been entitled "Desperately seeking the public," presenting a critique of the public opinion industry, researchers would not have responded by rejecting the concept of the "public." Surely the concept of audience also can be separated from the industry which profits from it. The audience concept recognizes the historical emergence of audiencehood, the construction of people as spectators of social life, as recipients more than as producers of meaning. To pursue the analogy, I suggest that "Desperately seeking the market" would be unnecessary, because the market is by definition that measured at point of sale and so readily accessible. Hence, while the public precedes the industry which measures it and the market is constructed by the industry which measures it, the audience is somewhere in between. As a concept, it has the advantage of being primarily defined by neither political nor economic theory, but simply in relation to the media; how audiences then relate to publics or markets becomes an important but distinct question.

Thus, rather than asking what they are as individuals or a mass, or what they, as an artificial reification, are *really* like, research should conceptualize "audiences" as a relational or interactional construct, as a way of focusing on the diverse set of relationships between people and media forms.[7] Instead of asking what texts mean or what people do with texts, research should ask how texts are located and understood as part of, indeed as agents in, the practices of people's daily lives. Audience reception research is pulled in two contrary directions, since it must stay with the text, while simultaneously exploring the connections between text and context, where context is ever more broadly conceived. This cannot be an either/or choice, but remains a tension at the heart of the field which should be productive not destructive of understanding the connections among audiences, media and contexts.

The audience becomes, then, a shorthand way of pointing to ways in which people stand in relationship to each other, rather than a thing of which people may or may not be a member and whose peculiar ways must be discovered. One consequence would be that of replacing the emphasis on concepts which imply a struggle between media and audience (negotiation, influence, appropriation, resistance, effect) with those concerned with modes of connection relationship or communication (dialogic or monologic, direct or mediated communication, parasocial interaction; e.g. Thompson 1990). The task for audience research becomes that of charting the possibilities and problems for communication, or relations among people, in so far as these are undermined or facilitated, managed or reconstituted by the media. Research may then avoid the tendency to reassert the reduction of the audience back to the (social)psychological or micro-level of analysis. Rather, audiences (plural) can be conceived relationally as an analytic concept relevant to, and providing links across, relations among people and media at all levels from the macro economic/cultural to the individual/psychological. Similarly, "context" also must be understood vertically as well as horizontally, not simply as encompassing an ever wider spatial surround to the moment of viewing. And while changes in these relations between people and media may occur (or be conceived) primarily at one level of analysis, they will have implications for other levels.

In this essay I have argued that canonization of the field should be resisted. No unitary tradition and no one question can bear the weight of audience research – whether it is the issue of resistant voices or contextualized embedded audiences or divergent readings. Nor can we seek a grand model which integrates all variables in grand schemes as these always tend towards reductionism and functionalism. I have suggested comparative analysis as a valuable research strategy for the next phase of audience research. This would make use of (and generate more) diversity in empirical findings in order to address contradictions, to identify central tendencies, to specify limits for hitherto unbounded claims and to research empirically the comparisons often implied in the literature.

Such a comparative approach will cut across multiple levels of theorizing, because the specification of dimensions for comparison themselves tend to draw upon different levels of analysis. This should become an explicit feature of audience theory. By reconceptualizing the audience as a construct which addresses relations between people and media in context at a number of interlinked analytic levels, several problems may be resolved. Particularly, the weak connections between audience research and neighboring fields could be strengthened (see also Alexander and Jacobs, this volume, while the weaknesses within the field, which are generated by the reduction of audience research to the empirical demonstration of difference (even if such differences can be shown to be significant), may be addressed. Clearly, these two points are related. If the audience research agenda addresses a broader range of questions through multilevel comparative analysis, it will generate conclusions which are both specific to particular contexts and amenable to comparative analysis beyond those contexts. This in turn will represent research which is more directly valuable to fields including and beyond media theory.

NOTES

1 An earlier version of this essay was presented to the *46th International Communication Association Annual Conference*, Chicago, 1996. I am grateful to the many colleagues who have commented on the earlier versions of this essay.
2 Those included in the canon may not wish to be incorporated in this manner, and there is an irony in critical audience researchers themselves constituting something so conventional, and now conventionally deconstructed, as a canon.
3 We may paraphrase this as asking whether, for today's audience researchers, it matters *what* is on television, or whether researchers are interested only in where, how and why television is viewed? Similarly, one wonders why media content is considered important when media are analyzed as a cultural form (e.g. in production or text analyses) but somehow gets dropped when we consider the audience's response.
4 For example, the concerns of, say, Morley's (1980) *Nationwide* project may begin to appear dated as Britain becomes much less clearly stratified by social class as was traditionally the case and as the trade union movement is significantly weakened by the years of Thatcherism. This is not to argue for the removal of the project from the canon, since it tells us about audiences in the 1970s which may still hold true or which may contrast informatively with contemporary research. But for such an informative prospect, we need a lot more than three or four projects in the "canon."
5 The emphasis on contextualization may itself have been intended as a response to the "so what?" question, but also got lost in the micro level of daily routines.
6 There may be less ideological cases of "resistance" also, as in the market failure of certain products (e.g. the early history of the home computer), showing that perceptions and beliefs have an impact on production and economics.
7 Interestingly similar problems relating to the concept of 'the public' are avoided in the public sphere debate (Habermas, 1969) because the question is not what is the public and how does it think/act/respond, but rather, in what ways do people in their everyday activities constitute a public, what forms of communication are appropriate for a public sphere and what discursive or institutional threats does it face (Livingstone & Lunt, 1994)?

REFERENCES

Abercrombie, N. (1996) *Television and Society*, Cambridge: Polity Press.

Abercrombie, N., Hill, S. and Turner, B. (1980) *The Dominant Ideology Thesis*, London: Allen & Unwin.

Alexander, J. C., Giesen, B., Munch, R. and Smelser, N. J. (eds.) (1987) *The Micro–Macro Link*, Berkeley, CA: University of California Press.

Allen, R. C. (1985) *Speaking of Soap Operas*, Chapel Hill, NC: University of North Carolina Press.

Allor, M. (1988) "Relocating the site of the audience," *Critical Studies in Mass Communication* 5.

Ang, I. (1985) *Watching "Dallas": Soap Opera and the Melodramatic Imagination*, New York: Methuen.

Ang, I. (1989) "Wanted: audiences. On the politics of empirical audience studies," in E. Seiter, H. Borchers, G. Kreutzner and E. M. Warth (eds.) *Remote Control: Television Audiences and Cultural Power*, London: Routledge.

Ang, I. (1990a) "Culture and communication," *European Journal of Communication* 5 (2–3): 239–60.

Ang, I. (1990b) *Desperately Seeking the Audience*, London: Routledge.

Ang, I. (1994) "In the realm of uncertainty: the global village and capitalist post-modernity," in D. Mitchell and D. Crowley (eds.) *Communication Theory Today*, Cambridge: Polity Press.

Blumler, J. G., Gurevitch, M. and Katz, E. (1985) "Reaching out: a future for gratifications research," in K. E. Rosengren, L. A. Wenner and P. Palmgreen (eds.) *Media Gratifications Research: Current Perspectives*, Beverly Hills, CA: Sage.

Blumler, J. G., McLeod, J. M. and Rosengren, K. E. (1992) "An introduction to comparative communication research," In J. G. Blumler, J. M. McLeod and K. E. Rosengren (eds.) *Comparatively Speaking: Communication and Culture across Space and Time*, Newbury Park, CA: Sage.

Boyd-Barrett, O. and Newbold, C. (eds.) (1995) *Approaches to Media: A Reader*. London: Arnold.

Carey, J. W. (1975) "Communication and culture," *Communication Research* 2: 173–91.

Cobley, P. (1994) "Throwing out the baby: populism and active audience theory," *Media Culture and Society* 16: 677–87.

Corner, J. (1991) "Meaning, genre and context: the problematics of 'public knowledge' in the new audience studies," in J. Curran and M. Gurevitch (eds.) *Mass Media and Society* (1st edn), London: Methuen.

Corner, J. (1995) *Television Form and Public Address*, London: Arnold.

Cumberbatch, G., Brown, J., McGregor, R. and Morrison, D. (1986) "Television and the miners' strike," London: British Film Institute Broadcasting Research Unit.

Curran, J. (1990) "The new revisionism in mass communication research," *European Journal of Communication* 5 (2–3): 135–64.

Curran, J. and Gurevitch, M. (eds.) (1991) *Mass Media and Society* (1st edn), London: Arnold.

Curran, J., Morley, D. and Walkerdine, V. (eds.) (1996) *Cultural Studies and Communications*, London: Arnold.

Dayan, D. and Katz, E. (1992) *Media Events: The Live Broadcasting of History*, Cambridge, MA: Harvard University Press.

De Certeau, M. (1984) *The Practices of Everyday Life*, Los Angeles, CA: University of California Press.

Downing, J., Mohammadi, A. and Sreberny-Mohammadi, A. (1990) *Questioning the Media: A Critical Introduction*, London: Sage.

Drotner, K. (1992) "Modernity and media panics," in M. Skovmand and K. C. Schroder (eds.) *Media Cultures: Reappraising Transnational Media*, London: Routledge.

Eco, U. (1979) "Introduction: the role of the reader," in *The Role of the Reader: Explorations in the Semiotics of Texts*, Bloomington, IN: Indiana University Press.

Erni, J. (1989) "Where is the audience?" *Journal of Communication Enquiry* 13 (2): 30–42.

Fejes, F. (1984) "Critical mass communications research and media effects: the problem of the disappearing audience," *Media, Culture and Society* 6 (3): 219–32.

Fiske, J. (1989) "Moments of television: neither the text nor the audience," in E. Seiter, H. Borchers, G. Kreutner and E.-M. Warth (eds) *Remote Control: Television Audiences and Cultural Power*, London: Routledge.

Fiske, J. (1992) "Audiencing: a cultural studies approach to watching television," *Poetics* 21: 345–59.

Gamson, W. A (1992) *Talking Politics*, Cambridge: Cambridge University Press.

Giddens, A. (1984) *The Constitution of Society: Outline of the Theory of Structuration*, Cambridge: Polity Press.

Gitlin, T. (1990) "Who communicates what to whom, in what voice and why: about the study of mass communication," *Critical Studies in Mass Communication* 7 (2): 185–96.

Graber, D. A. (1988) *Processing the News: How People Tame the Information Tide* (2nd edn), New York: Longman.

Grossberg, L. (1994) "Can cultural studies find true happiness in communication?" in M. R. Levy and M. Gurevitch (eds) *Defining Media Studies: Reflections on the Future of the Field*, New York: Oxford University Press.

Hall, S. (1980) "Encoding/decoding," in S. Hall, D. Hobson, A. Lowe and P. Willis (eds) *Culture, Media, Language*, London: Hutchinson.

Hall, S. (1989) "Ideology and communication theory," in B. Dervin, L. Grossberg, B. O'Keefe and E. Wartella (eds) *Rethinking Communication: Paradigm Exemplars*, London: Sage.

Hall, S. (1994) "Reflections on the encoding/decoding model," in J. Cruz and J. Lewis (eds) *Viewing, Reading, Listening: Audiences and Cultural Reception*, Boulder, CO: Westview Press.

Hammersley, M. and Atkinson, P. (1983) *Ethnography: Principles in Practice*, London: Tavistock.

Hobson, D. (1982) *Crossroads: the Drama of a Soap Opera*, London: Methuen.

Hoijer, B. (1990) "Studying viewers' reception of television programmes: theoretical and methodological considerations," *European Journal of Communication* 5 (1): 29–56.

Iser, W. (1980) "Interaction between text and reader," in S. R. Suleirnan and I. Crosman (eds) *The Reader in the Text: Essays on Audience and Interpretation*, Princeton, NJ: Princeton University Press.

Jensen, K. B. and Jankowski, N. W. (eds) (1991) *A Handbook of Qualitative Methodologies for Mass Communication Research*, London: Routledge.

Jensen, K. J. and Rosengren, K. E. (1990) "Five traditions in search of the audience," *European Journal of Communication* 5 (2–3): 207–38.

Jordin, M. and Brunt, R. (1988) "Constituting the television audience: a problem of method," in P. Drummond and R. Paterson (eds) *Television and its Audience*, London: British Film Institutes.

Katz, E. (1979) "The uses of Becker, Blumler and Swanson," *Communication Research* 6 (1): 74–83.

Lang, K. and Lang, G. E. (1983) "The 'new' rhetoric of mass communication research: a longer view," *Journal of Communication* 33 (3).

Lewis, J. (1991) "The ideological octopus: an exploration of television and its audience," London: Routledge.

Liebes, T. and Katz, E. (1990) *The Export of Meaning: Cross-Cultural Readings of "Dallas"*, Oxford: Oxford University Press.

Livingstone, S. (1996) "On the continuing problem of media effects," in J. Curran and M. Gurevitch (eds) *Mass Media and Society* (2nd edn), London: Arnold.

Livingstone, S. M. (1998) *Making Sense of Television: The Psychology of Audience Interpretation.* London: Routledge.

Livingstone, S. M. and Lunt, P. K. (1994) *Talk on Television: The Critical Reception of Audience Discussion Programmes,* London: Routledge.

McQuail, D. (1994) *Mass Communication Theory,* London: Sage.

Moores, S. (1993) *Interpreting Audiences: The Ethnography of Media Consumption,* London: Sage.

Morgenstern, S. (1992) "The epistemic autonomy of mass media audiences," *Critical Studies in Mass Communications* 9: 293–310.

Morley, D. (1980) *The Nationwide Audience: Structure and Decoding,* London: British Film Institute.

Morley, D. (1992) *Television, Audiences and Cultural Studies,* London: Routledge.

Morrow, R. A. and Brown, D. D. (1994) *Critical Theory and Methodology,* Thousand Oaks, CA: Sage.

Murdock, G. (1989) "Cultural studies," *Critical Studies in Mass Communication* 6 (4): 436–40.

Nightingale, V. (1996) *Studying the Television Audience,* London: Routledge.

Philo, G. (1993) "Getting the message: audience research in the Glasgow University Media Group," in J. Eldridge (ed.) *Getting the Message: News, Truth and Power,* London: Routledge.

Press, A. (1996) "Comment on Livingstone and Trope/Pesach-Gaunt," Paper presented to the symposium, *The Media and The Public,* Jerusalem, May.

Price, S. (1993) *Media Studies,* London: Pitman.

Radway, J. (1984) *Reading the Romance: Women, Patriarchy and Popular Literature,* Chapel Hill, NC: University of North Carolina Press.

Schiller, H. I. (1992) *Mass Communication: An American Empire,* Boulder, CO: Westview Press.

Schlesinger, P., Dobash, R. E., Dobash, R. P. and Weaver, C. K. (1992) *Women Viewing Violence,* London: British Film Institute.

Seaman, W. (1992) "Active audience theory: pointless populism," *Media, Culture and Society* 14: 301–11.

Seiter, E., Borchers, H., Kreutzner, G. and Warth, E.-M. (1989) *Remote Control: Television Audiences and Cultural Power,* London: Routledge.

Silverstone, R. (1994) *Television and Everyday Life,* London: Routledge.

Suleiman, S. and Crosman, I. (eds) (1980). *The Reader in the Text,* Princeton, NJ: Princeton University Press.

Thompson, J. B. (1990) *Ideology and Modern Culture: Critical Social Theory in the Era of Mass Communication,* Cambridge: Polity Press.

Thompson, J. B. (1994) "Social theory and the media," in D. Crowley and D. Mitchell (eds) *Communication Theory Today,* Cambridge: Polity Press.

Willis, P. (1990) *Common Culture,* Buckingham: Open University Press.

Wright, H. (1996) "Decentering Birmingham," Plenary paper presented to *Crossroads in Cultural Studies: An International Conference,* Tampere, Finland, July.

Index